## A Revolutionary Chronology

### 1764

- **Sugar Act**—First law aimed at raising colonial money for the Crown.
- **Currency Act**—Prohibited colonies from issuing their own currency.
- First protests against "taxation without representation."
- Non-Importation boycott against British goods.

### 1765

- **Quartering Act**—Requires colonies to provide barracks and supplies for British troops.
- **Stamp Act**—First direct tax on the American colonies.
- Colonial protest becomes highly organized; Sons of Liberty created.
- Intimidated by colonial activists, royal stamp agents resign.
- The Stamp Act Congress is formed; passes a "Declaration of Rights and Grievances" to protest taxation without representation.
- Non-Importation boycott intensified.

### 1766

- Repeal of the Stamp Act; colonies end boycott.
- **Declaratory Act**—Affirms Parliament's right to make laws binding the American colonies.

### 1767

- **Townshend Acts**—Taxes levied on glass, lead, paint, paper, and tea.
- Non-Importation boycott resumed.
- John Dickinson published *Letters from a Farmer in Pennsylvania to the Inhabitants of the British Colonies*, asserting that Parliament had no right to tax the colonies.

### 1768

- *Massachusetts Circular Letter*—Samuel Adams's argument against taxation without representation is circulated, calling for unified resistance by all the colonies.
- Royal governor of Massachusetts dissolves the colonial legislature.
- British troops arrive in Boston.

### 1769

- Virginia House of Burgesses passes resolutions condemning Britain's actions against Massachusetts; asserts that only Virginia's governor and legislature may tax its citizens.
- Virginia legislature is ordered dissolved.

### 1770

- Townshend taxes repealed, except for the tax on tea.
- The colonies again stop the boycott.
- **"Battle" of Golden Hill**—Clash between citizens and British Troops in New York City.
- **March 5: Boston Massacre**—Violence breaks out between soldiers and a Boston mob; three Americans die, and two are fatally wounded.

### 1772

- **The *Gaspée* Affair**—Attack on a grounded British customs schooner near Providence, Rhode Island.
- Samuel Adams calls for a Boston town meeting to create committees of correspondence to communicate Boston's position to the other colonies; such committees spring up throughout the colonies.

### 1773

- **Tea Act**—Reduced taxes on imported British tea only, thereby giving British merchants an effective monopoly on tea, to the detriment of American merchants.
- **December 16: Boston Tea Party**—A group of Patriots disguised as Indians board tea ships in Boston harbor and dump the cargo.

### 1774

- **Coercive Acts**—In response to the Boston Tea Party, Parliament passes laws to punish Massachusetts: the Boston Port Bill closes Boston to trade; the Administration of Justice Act effectively makes Crown officials immune from prosecution; the Massachusetts Government Act puts the election of most government officials under Crown control; the Quartering Act broadens the Quartering Act (1765), allowing for the quartering of troops in occupied private dwellings.
- **September 5:** The First Continental Congress meets to organize resistance to British tyranny.

## alpha
books

- British troops began to fortify Boston, and seize ammunition belonging to Massachusetts.
- Massachusetts creates a Provincial Congress and a Committee of Safety.
- The Minutemen are organized.

## 1775

- **New England Restraining Act**—Bans trade between the New England colonies and any other nation besides Great Britain.
- **April 19: Battles of Lexington and Concord**
- **May 10: Second Continental Congress convenes in Philadelphia**—John Hancock elected president of Congress.
- **June 10:** Continental army created.
- **June 15:** George Washington named to command the Continental army.
- **June 17: Battle of Bunker Hill**
- **Olive Branch Petition**—Congress attempts reconciliation with George III; the king rejects the petition and declares the colonies in rebellion.
- Congress creates a navy and authorizes privateering.
- Congress initiates a search for foreign aid.
- Congress authorizes an attack on Canada, led by Richard Montgomery and Benedict Arnold. Montreal is briefly captured, and Quebec City is unsuccessfully besieged.

## 1776

- Thomas Paine published *Common Sense*, an eloquent, persuasive justification for revolution.
- The British evacuate Boston after an American siege, March.
- **July 4:** Congress declares Independence.
- **August 27: Battle of Long Island**
- Washington withdraws from Manhattan, October.
- Congress sends Silas Deane, Benjamin Franklin, and Arthur Lee to negotiate treaties of commerce and friendship with foreign nations.
- **October 28: Battle of White Plains**
- Washington retreats through New Jersey, crossing the Delaware River into Pennsylvania.

- **December 26: Battle of Trenton**—Washington crosses the Delaware into New Jersey to defeat the Hessians.

## 1777

- **January 3: Battle of Princeton**—Most of New Jersey is cleared of British forces.
- **June 14**—Congress authorizes a national flag.
- **September 11: Battle of Brandywine**—Washington defeated.
- **September 26:** British occupy Philadelphia.
- **October 4: Battle of Germantown**—Washington counterattacks—and loses.
- The Continental army encamps at Valley Forge, beginning a winter of near starvation.
- **Saratoga Campaign:** Battle of Freeman's Farm, September 19, and Bemis Heights, October 7; Burgoyne surrenders his army, October 17.
- **November 15:** Articles of Confederation adopted by Congress (ratified by the states, March 1, 1781).

## 1778

- **May 4:** Franco-American alliance ratified by Congress.
- John Paul Jones's victorious exploits at sea, April 1778–1780
- **June 28: Battle of Monmouth**—Tactically a draw, but a moral victory for the Americans.
- Joseph Brant leads Indian raids against the New York frontier, 1778–1781.

## 1779

- **June 21:** Spain joins the war against England.

## 1780

- **May 12:** British capture Charleston, South Carolina.
- Benedict Arnold turns traitor, May 1779-September 1780.

## 1781

- **October 17:** Siege of Yorktown ends with the surrender of Cornwallis.

## 1783

- **April 15:** After a year of negotiations, Congress ratifies the Treaty of Paris, formally ending the American Revolution.

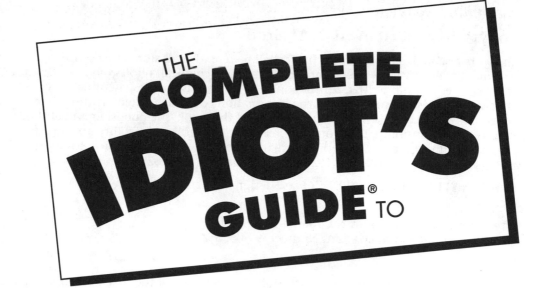

THE **COMPLETE IDIOT'S GUIDE**® TO

# The American Revolution

*by Alan Axelrod, Ph.D.*

**alpha books**

A Pearson Education Company

*For Anita, revolutionary wife*

## Copyright © 2000 by Alan Axelrod

THE COMPLETE IDIOT'S GUIDE TO and design are trademarks of Pearson Education, Inc.

International Standard Book Number: 0-02863379-2
Library of Congress Catalog Card Number: 99-067564

04   03   02          4   3   2

Interpretation of the printing code: the rightmost number of the first series of numbers is the year of the book's printing; the rightmost number of the second series of numbers is the number of the book's printing. For example, a printing code of 00-1 shows that the first printing occurred in 2000.

*Printed in the United States of America*

**Publisher**
*Marie Butler-Knight*

**Editorial Director**
*Gary M. Krebs*

**Product Manager**
*Phil Kitchel*

**Associate Managing Editor**
*Cari Shaw Fischer*

**Production Editor**
*Linda Seifert*

**Technical Editor**
*John Barrington*

**Copy Editor**
*Keith Cline*

**Cover Designers**
*Mike Freeland*
*Sandra Schroeder*

**Illustrator**
*Jody Schaeffer*

**Designers**
*Scott Cook and Amy Adams of DesignLab*

**Indexer**
*Brad Herriman*

**Layout/Proofreading**
*Angela Calvert*
*Svetlana Dominguez*
*Mary Hunt*
*Donna Martin*
*Michael J. Poor*
*Gloria Schurick*

# Contents at a Glance

# Contents

# Foreword

On the same day in 1995, Thomas Jefferson joined both the Republican and Democratic Parties. At a Republican Party fund-raiser, dubbed the Jefferson-Eisenhower Dinner, Speaker of the U.S. House of Representatives (and former history professor) Newt Gingrich spoke of Jefferson's Republican Party credentials. "This great Founding Father," Gingrich boasted, "knew the importance of limited government, the folly of 'entangling alliances,' and the need for equitable taxation." If alive today, he implied, Jefferson would be a Republican.

"No way," retorted Iowa's fiery New Deal Democrat, Sen. Tom Harkin. Speaking at the annual Democratic Party fund-raiser, the Jefferson-Jackson Day Dinner, Harkin hailed Jefferson as a "compassionate activist," dedicated to government interventionism on behalf of noble causes at home and abroad. "If alive today," Harkin said, "Jefferson would be a Democrat." Would the real Thomas Jefferson, please stand up?

Over 200 years after the American Revolution, myth and folklore have long replaced historical truth. To most Americans, the former is so much more enjoyable and convenient than the latter. Because of this fact, it is easy for today's political leaders to remake yesterday's political leaders. Sadly, our heritage is lost in the process, and ignorance reigns.

With *The Complete Idiot's Guide to the American Revolution,* Alan Axelrod spins a better tale than most Democratic and Republican spin-doctors. The truth, as they say, may or may not set you free, but it is always a good read in the hands of Alan Axelrod.

One of the benefits of the American Revolution, Benjamin Franklin once quipped, was the right to ignore it. Preaching a doctrine of self-reliance, tolerance, and moral commitment, the revolutionaries were dedicated to the "pursuit of happiness," but knew more about what they were against (British tyranny) than what they were for (democratic civil rights and liberties). This strange dichotomy is examined especially well, and the effort to resolve it is made obvious, courtesy of decent, no-nonsense, prose, all the way to the end of the book—and the beginning of the American experiment.

History ain't pretty. America eventually became the arrogant, imperial superpower like the British one it once despised. Even the real George Washington differed greatly from the legendary George Washington. But it's OK. There is no need to move into the cave. The country has lived up to the noble principles which brought it to Revolution, and Dr. Axelrod drives the facts home with a wicked good sense of humor, a liberal sprinkling of anecdotes, and damn good writing. Long Live the Revolution!

—**Tim Maga, Ph.D.,** is the Oglesby Professor of American Heritage (an "endowed chair" of U.S. diplomatic history) at Bradley University. Previously, he was a Foreign Affairs Coordinator for the U.S. House of Representatives Foreign Affairs Committee and a U.S. trade policy negotiator. He is the author of several books on U.S. diplomacy issues, including, most recently, *Hands Across the Sea?: U.S.-Japan Relations, 1961–1981* (1997), *The Perils of Power* (1995), and *The World of Jimmy Carter* (1994). In 1990 he was a finalist for the Pulitzer Prize in History for his work *John F. Kennedy and the New Pacific Community, 1961–1963*. Dr. Maga earned his Ph.D. from McGill University. When not writing the "Great History Book" or involved in a diplomatic mission abroad, he can be found teaching Shotokan Karate or forever tinkering with his 1965 Corvette.

# Introduction

Maybe it's those funny wigs the gentlemen wore, or their slightly comical tricorn hats, or their ornate and overly polite manner of speech and writing—but *something* about the eighteenth century makes it difficult for most of us to fire up our imaginations about the era. The Civil War seems more immediate to most of us, more real. Yet, as we know, 1863 is only four score and seven years later than 1776.

The fact is, the American Revolution is harder to understand than the Civil War. It was fought by far fewer people, but by more different kinds of people: Continental ("regular army") soldiers, militiamen (state and local volunteers), French regulars and volunteer officers from France, the German states, and Poland. It was fought by British redcoats ("regular army"), German mercenary troops ("Hessians"), Loyalist militia forces (the "Tories"), and Indians. It was fought by amateurs as well as by professionals, by frontier guerrilla fighters and by men and officers traditionally trained for combat on the wide-open battlefields of Europe. It was fought by people who believed passionately in their cause, as well as by others who were demoralized and discouraged, or who, for other economic or political reasons, were unwilling to give their all in battle.

Nor was there absolute unanimity on either side. Loyalists—Tories—people loyal to the government of King George III, formed a large minority of the American population. They wanted no part of independence from the mother country. In some places, Loyalists outnumbered "patriots," the people who favored independence and were willing to fight for it. Similarly, among the English, many people believed that the American colonies *should* be given greater freedom, perhaps extending to independence. Sentiments such as these were to be found even within the officer corps of the British army.

Different groups had different agendas. Indians fought on both sides (though most who did not remain neutral sided with the British), yet they fought first and foremost to further their own ends. As strategic allies, they were, therefore, undependable. Throughout the eight years of the war, the British employed German mercenary troops—popularly, though not always accurately, called Hessians—who were highly trained professional soldiers led by professional officers, but who consistently performed with poor success.

The Tories were perhaps the most problematic group of all. Their only fault was their loyalty to the legally constituted government of the American colonies. In return for this loyalty, the British Crown gave them little help and less support, and they were subject to persecution at the hands of their patriot neighbors, ranging from harassment, to seizure and destruction of property, to death. In retaliation, those Tories who took up arms typically practiced an especially brutal form of warfare, which was sometimes exploited by the Crown and sometimes shunned as a moral embarrassment to the British government. More than many historians care to admit, the Revolution was not just a war of independence, but also a civil war.

Finally, there was the nature of war itself more than 200 years ago. Eighteenth-century warfare was very different from "modern" warfare—the kind of combat ushered in by the Civil War, for example. Although Revolutionary-era armies made extensive use of artillery, high-explosive ammunition was unknown. Death was generally dealt man to man, one man at a time. The musket and the bayonet were the basic weapons of war, and combat was typically at close range. The most important tactics emphasized the speed and efficiency of fire rather than accuracy. Maneuvering, formation, drill, and discipline were very important, lending to many battles the air of ritual, as if combat were a minuet of relentless violence.

The operating range of eighteenth-century armies was severely limited, and transportation and communication were agonizingly slow. Many operations that began as the first steps in fulfillment of some grand strategy simply died of exhaustion or in acknowledgment of their impracticality. Disease among armies was always a more deadly foe than any politically ordained enemy. All these factors and more tend to distance us from a full understanding of the long, hard, painful labor that brought our nation to birth.

# How to Use This Book

*The Complete Idiot's Guide to the American Revolution* is an attempt to bring the reader closer to what is, after all, a remote time.

**Part 1, "Prelude to Independence,"** begins the book with an overview of the circumstances that produced the war and of the war itself: How Europe came to colonize the New World, with particular emphasis on how the British colonies came into being; how they related to the mother country, to each other, and to the New World colonies of other European powers; and the series of colonial wars that led up to the French and Indian War. The British government, partly in an effort to recoup treasure expended on the French and Indian War, sought to exploit its North American colonies, ultimately creating a set of policies that were economically, politically, and morally repugnant to most Americans.

**Part 2, "Heard 'Round the World,"** covers the beginning of the war, including Paul Revere's celebrated ride, the battles of Lexington and Concord, Bunker Hill, the siege of Boston, and other early battles. The section ends with the publication of Thomas Paine's epoch-making *Common Sense* and the issuance of the Declaration of Independence.

The rest of *The Complete Idiot's Guide to the American Revolution* is an account of the war, organized both chronologically and regionally.

**Part 3, "Times That Try Men's Souls,"** begins with the American loss of Long Island and New York, the retreat of Washington into Pennsylvania, and then his triumphant counterattacks at Trenton and Princeton. This section also covers the fall of Philadelphia to the British, a loss more than counterbalanced by the patriot victory over Burgoyne's army at Saratoga.

Part 4, "Winter of Discontent," starts with the loss of the important patriot forts on the Delaware River and the crisis of confidence in George Washington. From here, it goes on to narrate the ordeal of Valley Forge, then covers the role of the Indians in the Revolution, the southern theater of combat, and the infamous career of Benedict Arnold.

Part 5, "The World Turned Upside Down," takes the Revolution to its conclusion. The first chapter in this section deals with the war at sea, the second covers the fighting in the southern frontier—some of the most vicious and least understood combat of the war—and the siege of Cornwallis at Yorktown, Virginia, which, for all practical purposes, brought the war to an end. The last two chapters in this section address the difficult process of negotiating a full and just peace and assess the immediate as well as enduring effects of the Revolution.

## Extras

In addition to the main narrative and illustrations in *The Complete Idiot's Guide to the American Revolution*, you'll also find other types of useful information, including eyewitness accounts and important original quotations, important revolutionary sites open to the public, definitions of the key words of the era (with emphasis on military jargon), and anecdotes, biographical sketches, and fascinating "sidebar" facts. Look for these features:

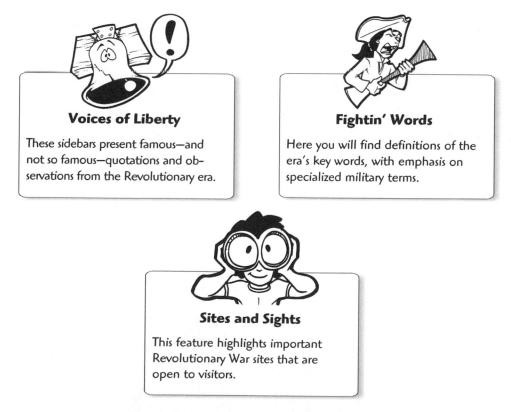

### Voices of Liberty

These sidebars present famous—and not so famous—quotations and observations from the Revolutionary era.

### Fightin' Words

Here you will find definitions of the era's key words, with emphasis on specialized military terms.

### Sites and Sights

This feature highlights important Revolutionary War sites that are open to visitors.

**We Hold These Truths**

This box provides fascinating anecdotes, biographies of key figures, and relevant historical documents.

# Special Thanks to the Technical Editor

*The Complete Idiot's Guide to the American Revolution* was reviewed by an expert who not only checked the historical accuracy of the text, but also provided valuable insight to help ensure that this book tells you everything you need to know about the American Revolution. We extend special thanks to John Barrington.

A native of New York City (b. 1959), John Barrington was educated in England, and received his undergraduate degree from Oxford University. He pursued his graduate studies at the College of William and Mary, in Williamsburg, Virginia, receiving his Ph.D. in 1997. Since 1993, he has been teaching full-time at liberal arts colleges: at Skidmore College, in Saratoga Springs, NY from 1993–1996, and at Furman University, in Greenville, South Carolina, from 1996 to the present. He is married, with no children. Apart from history, his interests include travel, hiking, gardening, and brewing beer.

# Part 1
# Prelude to Independence

*The immediate cause of the American Revolution is straightforward: The tyranny of taxation without representation. But the road that led to this issue and to the conditions that made the Revolution possible is longer and has many turnings. England enjoyed happy relations with its North American colonies when it left them alone, trading freely and profitably with them, but allowing them to govern themselves. Parliament had the right to tax the colonies, and certain taxes were even on the books, but the laws weren't enforced. The French and Indian War cost England a fortune to fight. King George III wanted the colonies to pay their share, and the era of salutary neglect ended, with new taxes, duties, and trade restrictions—and harsh laws to enforce them all.*

*This section looks at how the American colonies came into being, how they related to the mother country and to one another, how they fought the wars before the Revolution, and how the acts of a stubborn king prompted 13 separate colonies to unite first in protest, then in resistance, and finally in rebellion.*

# Chapter 1

# Why Did Washington Cross the Delaware?

## In This Chapter

➤ The American Revolution, as revolutions go

➤ The role of geography in creating the American Revolution

➤ Taxation without representation

➤ Problems of parliamentary representation for the colonies

➤ How acts of British oppression unwittingly forged a new nation

Americans are both the most idealistic and the most cynical people on the planet. We really do believe in things like the right to life, liberty, and the pursuit of happiness; we believe in justice and fair play; and we believe in the sanctity of basic human rights. Yet we are also quick to "debunk" great causes. Plenty of people sneer at the American Revolution as a group of wealthy colonial merchants and plantation owners who were tired of sharing their profits with British tax collectors.

Although it's true that the idealistic view of events doesn't always tell the whole truth, the cynical view isn't *automatically* more accurate. Parts 2 and 3 of this book deal in detail with the origins, causes, and beginning of the American Revolution, balancing economic with other motivations. This opening chapter is intended as a balanced overview of what the fighting was all about.

## You Call This Tyranny?

Consider two famous revolutions. The French Revolution (1787–99) had many causes, but chief among these were the following:

➤ The people of France were hungry, and the nation couldn't feed them.

➤ The French monarchy was indifferent to the condition of the people, and often harshly oppressive.

➤ The expanding well-to-do middle class was excluded from political power.

➤ The *philosophes*—the French political philosophers—provided a firm intellectual foundation for radical reform.

**Fightin' Words**

The **philosophes**—the "philosophers"—were the influential political philosophers of eighteenth-century France and included, among others, Descartes, Voltaire, Montesquieu, Diderot, and Rousseau.

Like the French Revolution, the Russian Revolution of 1917 resulted most directly from the desperate want of the people:

➤ The people of Russia were hungry, and the nation couldn't feed them.

➤ The *peasantry* and *proletariat*, excluded from all power for centuries, were finally ready to bring about change.

➤ The Russian monarchy was indifferent to the condition of the people and often harshly oppressive.

➤ Leaders such as Lenin and Trotsky gave the revolution political and intellectual direction.

**Fightin' Words**

The **peasantry** is the agricultural working class of a nation, whereas the proletariat is the industrial working class. Neither class has an ownership stake in the enterprise for which they labor.

We may think of the French Revolution and the Russian Revolution as classic revolutions, motivated by a popular instinct for survival. Conditions became so intolerable that change, by any means necessary, emerged as the only viable option, despite all the hardships and risks involved. Certainly these revolutions were complex, but their root causes were basic and easy to grasp. In a word, their cause was *desperation*. Not the American Revolution:

➤ Although life in the frontier regions was harsh, few Americans were hungry, let alone starving.

➤ Many of the policies of the monarchy were perceived as unjust, but King George III was not particularly oppressive in the treatment of his colonial subjects; indeed, the king's power was strictly limited by Britain's parliament and the traditions of common law.

➤ Most Americans retained ties of loyalty and affection to England and the Crown. They did not hate the king.

➤ The British government showed significant willingness to compromise and even yield on many colonial concerns.

In contrast to the conditions that caused the "classic" revolutions such as those in France and Russia, none of these things look like the ingredients for a violent revolt.

What caused the American Revolution, then?

## Mother Knows Best

As we will see in Parts 2 and 3, the road to revolution in America was long, beginning with a simple, inescapable fact of geography: America is very far from England, separated from it by a vast ocean. In the eighteenth century, when each ocean voyage was a dangerous and expensive undertaking, always uncertain, but at the very least guaranteed to take weeks, the Old World and the New were, quite literally, different worlds.

➤ Communication was difficult and slow.

➤ Government was difficult, both in terms of responding to the needs and wants of the people and in enforcing laws and policies.

➤ It became increasingly difficult for the mother country to identify with its distant subjects and for them to feel an affinity toward the mother country.

➤ In general, with the passage of time, geographic separation promoted a separate and unique identity for the colonies.

As discussed in Chapter 5, "All the King's Men," for many years the British government was content to accept the facts of geography and all that they created and implied. Happy to have in the American colonies a profitable source of raw materials to import and a ready market for manufactured goods to export, the Crown practiced a policy of "salutary neglect." Essentially, the colonies were left pretty much to govern themselves.

Then came the series of colonial wars, beginning in the late seventeenth century, that culminated in the eighteenth century with the French and Indian War. As discussed in Chapter 4, "Wilderness Wars," the colonial wars were extensions of greater conflicts involving the nations of Europe, but there were also local conflicts between French and English colonists and, quite often, between French-allied Indians and English colonists.

The colonists looked to the mother country for protection. This was provided—often inadequately and ineptly—and the effort produced two effects on the direction of British policy toward the colonies:

➤ There was an increased feeling of possessiveness toward the colonies. The Crown wanted a tighter grasp on that which it had fought to defend. There was a sense that the colonists now owed greater allegiance to the mother country.

➤ Faced with tremendous debt created by the war, King George III was no longer content to practice salutary neglect toward the colonies. He wanted them to help defray the cost of their defense.

These two changes in policy would quickly unknot the bonds of affection and loyalty that stretched so thinly across the Atlantic from England to America. Most immediately, however, in America, the French and Indian War created an impression of the mother country's general ineptitude and indifference:

➤ British military aid (many colonists felt) was stingy and inadequate; its commanders often ignored the realities of frontier warfare—and colonial militias bore the brunt.

➤ British military commanders treated colonial authorities with disrespect and even with contempt.

➤ British commanders answered to London, not to local authorities, and certainly not to the American people.

## You're Grounded

If the French and Indian War inserted a wedge between England and its colonies, an action King George took at the end of the war drove that wedge home. Although British victory in the French and Indian War ended French power in North America, the British Crown, having spent vast sums to fight the war, saw that it wasn't over. The conflicting interests of white settlers and Indians would inevitably erupt into conflict unless a buffer zone were created between the Indians and the colonists. Accordingly, on October 7, 1763, King George III issued a proclamation setting the lawful limit of western settlement as the Appalachian Mountains.

The Crown was at first pleased by the effect of the Proclamation of 1763. It brought to an eventual end the bloody coda to the French and Indian War known as Pontiac's Rebellion. However, even as it pacified the Indians, it enraged some settlers, who immediately defied the proclamation and pushed settlement across the forbidden mountains. Resentful Indians fiercely raided the trans-Appalachian frontier. When settlers appealed to royal authorities for aid, they were rebuffed, for the Crown had forbidden their settling in the West.

The Proclamation of 1763 deeply alienated only small groups within the colonial population that lived along the frontier region, often called the Piedmont, since much of it occupied the foothills of the Appalachians. The more settled coastal region, called the Tidewater, in

**Voices of Liberty**

"... it is just and reasonable and essential to our interest and the security of our colonies that the several nations or tribes of Indians with whom we are connected, and who live under our protection, should not be molested or disturbed...."

—King George III, Proclamation of 1763

the southern colonies was the focal point of revolutionary feeling and activity. The center of colonial government, the Tidewater increasingly found its traditional privileges of self-government challenged by the imperial authorities. As those challenges became increasingly serious, the leaders of Tidewater society steadily became more and more militant, leading the resistance movement that eventually culminated in the Declaration of Independence.

*George III, king of England, at about the time of the Revolution.*
(Image from the National Archives)

# Identity Crisis

During the years before the Revolution, thoughts of independence didn't come easily. For the most part, even the angriest frontier people clamored for reform of government at most, not independence.

## *God Made Us Englishmen*

Through most of the eighteenth century, the overwhelming majority of colonists thought of themselves not as Americans but as English men and women living in America. This fact argued strongly against revolution—one does not lightly betray one's heritage—yet it also provided some arguments in favor of revolution.

> ➤ The colonists identified themselves as English, yet felt that they were not accorded the full rights and privileges of English subjects.

> ➤ As the colonists saw it, if they were denied rights that their countrymen in Europe had enjoyed since King John signed the Magna Carta in 1215, they were the victims of tyranny.

# Pay, Pay, Pay

The most important cause of friction between the colonies and the mother country was Britain's introduction of new types of taxation in order to make the colonies share the costs of the debt left over from the Seven Years' War.

Passed in 1765, the Stamp Act required that every paper document, ranging from playing cards, to newspapers, to legal papers, bear a revenue stamp purchased from a royally appointed colonial stamp agent. As you'll read in Chapter 5, this was the most hated of a series of revenue laws enacted to make the colonies bear some of the cost of the late French and Indian War.

The economic impact of the various new taxes, duties, and regulations was bad enough in itself. Even worse, a Quartering Act was passed in 1765, requiring colonial governments to furnish barracks and provisions for royal troops—among whose functions was the enforcement of the new revenue laws. Additionally, to better enforce the unpopular revenue laws, more laws were passed, declaring that violations of the Stamp Act and other revenue laws would be tried in vice-admiralty courts, which answered directly to the Crown, not the local colonial courts, which owed their allegiance to the people of the colony. Not only did this usurp power from colonial government, it took away the Magna Carta right of trial by a jury of one's peers.

**Voices of Liberty**

"The Revolution was effected before the war commenced. The Revolution was in the minds and hearts of the people.... This radical change in the principles, opinions, sentiments, and affections of the people was the real American Revolution."

—John Adams, 1818

## Taxation Without Representation

The new taxes and the laws to enforce them caused outrage, of course, but it wasn't so much the taxes that were offensive—most colonists understood the necessity and inevitability of taxation—but the fact of "taxation without representation."

Among the limitations of the king's power in England's *parliamentary monarchy* was the principle that Parliament, not the king, levied taxes. This was crucially important, because the people were represented in Parliament and, therefore, the people determined what taxes could be justly levied.

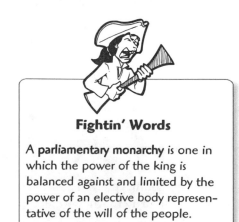

**Fightin' Words**

A **parliamentary monarchy** is one in which the power of the king is balanced against and limited by the power of an elective body representative of the will of the people.

As the colonists increasingly came to see it, taxation, without representation, was by definition tyranny. Some colonial leaders responded to this by simply lobbying Parliament for representation. Parliament lamely replied that it represented all English subjects, even those from the colonies, which were not accorded seats for representatives.

# Chapter 2

# In the Wake of Columbus

## In This Chapter

➤ Motives for New World exploration

➤ The voyages of Columbus

➤ Exploits and abuses of the conquistadors

➤ Early British exploration

➤ Roanoke and Jamestown

One way or another, most revolutions fail. They are either crushed, or, if they succeed in toppling the government, they produce an even worse regime, resulting in misery, oppression, and violent instability.

But the American Revolution achieved independence and installed a rational government closer to the ideal of democracy than any other in history. As we will see, the success of the American Revolution was largely the product of great good fortune: many extraordinary individuals—of the caliber of Sam Adams, George Washington, Ben Franklin, Thomas Jefferson—in one place and at one time.

But the Revolution's success can be explained in another way. Other major revolutions, such as in France and Russia, divided countries along sharp class and ideological lines. The two sides in the American Revolution did not represent different classes, nor did their beliefs represent opposite extremes. Both sides believed in individual liberties and constitutional government. When the conflict was over, the new state and federal governments created in the United States shared many features with the governments in the pre-revolutionary era. Most American Tories settled back into American society, because they shared so many beliefs with the patriots, enabling the talented Founding Fathers to create a stable and successful nation.

America's colonial status is key to understanding the nature and ultimate success of the American Revolution. But just what is a colony, and how did it come to be? This chapter is the first of three that answer these questions.

# Why Europe Needed a New World

Imagine the long timeline of European history. The expansiveness of classical Greek and Roman civilization, when great minds speculated freely on the nature of the entire universe, and the armies of empire ranged across the known world; followed by an era of contraction, the Dark Ages, civilization hunkered down behind the walls of towns and dreary castles, and the human mind reduced to the confines of orthodoxy and the status quo. Now, look as the Dark Ages brightened into the Renaissance, a time in which creativity and liberal thought were reborn. The castles and walled cities endured, but many people now ventured beyond them.

What drove this *Renaissance*, this "rebirth?" Perhaps it was something irrepressible in the human spirit, which might be muffled for a thousand years or more, but not forever. Ideas and discoveries, like seeds, took root, grew, and spread. In about 1450, the German printer Johannes Gutenberg developed movable type, enabling the relatively cheap mass production of books. From this point on, the progress of thought was almost unstoppable.

But there was another reason for the new restlessness of the European spirit. Europe was getting cramped. Renaissance Europeans wanted to get out into a bigger world. Whereas traditional European society had been divided into a tiny aristocracy and a vast peasantry, a new middle class of merchants now appeared on the scene. The survival and prosperity of the merchants depended on new and greater sources of import goods as well as markets for domestically produced goods. Supply and demand within Europe were limited.

In some areas, even the old, cushy aristocracy was feeling the pinch. Aristocrats were feeling particularly cramped in Spain and in England, which were dominated by a system of *primogeniture*, which meant that the first son in a family would inherit all titles and property upon the death of the father.

### Fightin' Words

The **Renaissance** (French for "rebirth") extended from the fourteenth through the sixteenth centuries, beginning in Italy and spreading throughout Europe. It was a general reawakening of humanistic learning.

### Fightin' Words

The word **primogeniture** is from the late Latin, meaning first ("primo") birth ("geniture"). It signifies the right of the firstborn child—almost always exclusively the *male* child—to inherit the whole of his family's wealth, titles, and privileges.

And then there were the lower classes, the peasantry. Prospects for them, as always, were the least promising of all. Put all this together, and it is clear that by the so-called High Renaissance—by the fifteenth century—Europe needed a *new* world.

# The Weaver's Son

When Europeans began to look for new opportunities outside the confines of Europe, they were searching in a world that they had long known was round. Ancient Greeks such as Pythagoras and Aristotle had said the earth was a sphere, and, in the third century B.C., Eratosthenes of Cyrene (ca. 276–195) put together his understanding of shadows, distance, and geometry to make an incredibly accurate measurement of the earth's circumference.

## We Hold These Truths

Eratosthenes calculated the earth's circumference as 23,990.4 miles and its diameter as 7,578.6 miles. These figures are amazingly close to what we know today as the earth's circumference, 24,887.64 miles, and its diameter, 7,926 miles. The distance from the Spanish coast to the Bahamas, via the route Columbus took, is about 3,900 miles.

Cristoforo Colombo was born to a weaver in Genoa in 1451. As a boy, he was not well-educated, but he always had an open, curious mind. As a youth, he took to the sea. In 1476, shipwrecked off Portugal, he went to Lisbon, then sailed as far as Ireland and England and even claimed to have sailed from England to Iceland, where, many believe, he heard stories of an ancient place called Vinland, far across the "Ocean Sea," discovered some 500 years earlier by the Norseman Leif Erikson.

After Columbus returned to Genoa in 1479, he began devouring shadowy accounts of westward voyages. He made the mistake of believing Marco Polo's calculation of the location of Japan (1,500 miles east of China) and Greek astronomer Ptolemy's (ca. A.D. 100–70) calculation of the circumference of the earth. Ptolemy grossly underestimated the girth of the globe and greatly inflated the size of the Eurasian land mass. As a result, the world seemed pretty small. And Columbus was further encouraged by the miscalculations of the Florentine cosmographer Paolo dal Pozzo Toscanelli. It seemed that Japan (which Columbus called Cipangu) was a 5,000-mile voyage *west* of Portugal, over an ocean containing numerous islands where a ship could land for supplies.

## Hard Sell

In 1484, Columbus secured an audience with King John II of Portugal, to persuade him to sponsor a voyage to Cipangu—Japan—an island in a region generally called the Indies, or India, a largely untapped opportunity for trade and, most important, a source of spices. Aromatic spices were *essential* to the preservation of food before refrigeration, and spice was as highly valued as gold. John understood the value of the spice trade, but correctly believed that the distance between Europe and Asia was closer to 10,000 miles. More importantly, the Portuguese were pioneering a route to Asia around the coast of Africa, and John did not want to divert resources from the Africa route to support Columbus' dream of sailing westward.

Columbus approached Don Luis de la Cerda, count of Medina Celi, who arranged an audience, on or about May 1, 1486, with Queen Isabella I of Castile. For six years, Columbus cooled his heels in the Spanish court of Isabella and her husband, Ferdinand II of Aragon. He used the time to make some influential friends, including a courtier named Luis de Santangel, who ultimately persuaded the monarchs to sponsor a voyage.

## Passage to India

Columbus set sail from Palos on August 3, 1492, in the belief that he was in passage to Cipangu. The voyage of the three small ships—the *Niña*, the *Pinta*, and Columbus's own flagship, the *Santa Maria*—extended far beyond what Columbus had promised his crews. Realizing he had seriously miscalculated transoceanic distances, Columbus began to keep two logbooks—one, for the benefit of the crew, containing fictitious computations of distances, and another, for his own records, consisting of accurate figures. The crews of all three ships verged on mutiny by the second week in October, just before the *Santa Maria*'s lookout sighted land on the 12th.

Columbus encountered the "New World" at a place the natives called Guanahani and Columbus named San Salvador. Most modern historians believe this first landfall was present-day Watling Island, although, in 1986, a group of scholars suggested that the true landfall was another Bahamian island, Samana Cay, 65 miles south of Watling. The voyagers were welcomed by friendly Arawak tribespeople. Because he believed he was in the Indies, Columbus called these people *Indians*, and he sailed on to Cuba, looking for the court of the Mongol emperor of China, with whom he hoped to negotiate trade in spices and gold.

He was, of course, nowhere near the Mongol emperor. Disappointed, he pushed on to Hispaniola (modern

**Sites and Sights**

If you are fortunate enough to vacation in the Bahamas, why not visit the lovely island of San Salvador? The Columbus Monument, at Long Bay, a white cross, erected on December 25, 1956, commemorates the landfall of Christopher Columbus on October 12, 1492. In the little town of Palmetto Grove, nearby, you'll find the New World Museum, which houses local pottery and artifacts from an original Arawak Indian settlement—the kinds of artifacts Columbus saw.

Santo Domingo), where, in a Christmas Day storm, the *Santa Maria* was wrecked near Cap-Haitien. Columbus deposited his crew safely onto the shore, left a garrison of 39 at the place he christened La Navidad, and, on January 16, 1493, returned to Spain in the *Niña*.

# Whose World Is It, Anyway?

The success of Columbus' voyage triggered a dispute between Spain and Portugal, whose king had turned thumbs down on the Great Navigator back in 1484. Despite having declined to back the voyage, the Portuguese crown now pressed claims to Columbus' discoveries.

The only question was who—Spain or Portugal—would get what. That one or both were entitled to own this "New World," already inhabited by Indians, was never in doubt.

Pope Alexander VI issued a pair of papal bulls (*Inter Caetera* and *Inter Caetera II*) in 1493, which divided the newly discovered and yet-to-be-discovered world between Spain and Portugal. The two nations formalized the papal decree with the Treaty of Tordesillas (June 7, 1494), which established a line of demarcation at 370 leagues west of the Cape Verde Islands. On one side of the line, all would be Spain's; on the other, all Portugal's.

## *Conquistadors*

In the wake of Columbus, the conquistadors—the "conquerors"— followed. During 1508–1509, Puerto Rico was subjugated by the conquistador Juan Ponce de Leon, who (according to partially credible legend) had come to the New World in search of a fabled Fountain of Youth. (What he found was death, pierced by an Indian's arrow in Florida.) Then Jamaica and Cuba fell to the Spaniards in 1510 and 1511.

The battle for Mexico was far more dramatic and consequential. Hernan Cortés, a minor nobleman with a yen for adventure, led an expedition in 1519 into the present-day region of Tabasco, defeating the Tabascan Indians on March 25. By September 5, he triumphed over the Tlascalas as well, enlisting them as allies in his campaign against their traditional enemies, the powerful Aztecs, who dominated Mexico. Not that the mighty Aztecs greeted him with hostility. On the contrary, the ambassadors of their emperor, Montezuma II, humbly welcomed Cortés, perhaps in the belief that he and his men were incarnations of their gods, or perhaps in the hope that these invaders could be bought off with a few gifts of gems and gold. Accepting the gold, Cortés remarked: "Send me some more of it, because I and my companions suffer from a disease of the heart that can be cured only with gold." On November 8, 1519, Montezuma II invited Cortés and his men into Tenochtitlan, today's Mexico City, as guests. Cortés soon repaid the Aztec Emperor's hospitality by holding Montezuma hostage in one of the city's palaces.

In fact, Cortés's only problem came from his own countryman, Panfilo de Narvaez, who was on his way to arrest Cortés for having overstepped his authority by conquering

**15**

**Fightin' Words**

*Noche Triste*, Spanish for sad night or night of sorrow, was the name the Spaniards gave to June 30, 1520, when they were (temporarily) driven out of the Aztec capital, Tenochtitlan.

Mexico. Cortés set out to intercept his rival, leaving Tenochtitlan in the hands of a subordinate, Pedro de Alvarado. Inexplicably, Alvarado unleashed a frenzy of brutal atrocities upon the Aztecs, which incited a general rebellion. After triumphing over Narvaez, Cortés returned to Tenochtitlan just in time to help his beleaguered men fight their way out of the city during the *Noche Triste* of June 30, 1520. On that "sad night," Montezuma II was killed. Aztec accounts say the Spanish murdered him, while Spanish records report that he was assassinated by his own people.

Ten months after his retreat from the capital, Cortés returned and laid siege to the city for three months. Starving and wracked by disease, the inhabitants gave up their city, and their empire, to the conquistadors on August 13, 1521.

## Borderlands

Cortés achieved what Columbus had sought in vain, access to unimaginable wealth, and a host of other conquistadors came to the New World hoping to repeat Cortés' success. Francisco Pizarro conquered the Incas of Peru in 1531, but was plagued by dissension among rival Spanish groups and by ongoing Inca resistance. Although he did find wealth nearly comparable to that of the Aztecs, he himself was assassinated on June 26, 1541, and the Spanish did not succeed in wiping out the last Inca resistance until 1572.

The exploits of Cortés and Pizarro inspired Spanish expeditions into the northern borderlands of the Aztecs—that is, the present United States. After all, Indians had told Columbus tales of frontier villages containing vast treasuries of gold. Alvar Nuñez Cabeza de Vaca, a member of a calamitous 1520 expedition led by Narvaez, wandered throughout the American Southwest for eight years, then brought back to Spain tales of the "Seven Cities of Cibola," villages rich in gold. Never mind that Cabeza de Vaca had not visited these Seven Cities personally. The rumors were quite sufficient, especially when augmented by the account of another conquistador, Marcos de Niza, who spoke of the treasures of the Hawikuh pueblo of the Zuni. Of course, Marcos de Niza had not actually *entered* Hawikuh—hostile Indians had prevented that—but the tale was good enough to send Francisco Vazquez de Coronado to the American Southwest and, in 1540, to Hawikuh in central New Mexico. Unlike Marcos de Niza, Coronado was able to subdue the pueblo and enter it. What he found there was very little. Certainly, there was no gold.

## The First American Revolutions

After Coronado's disappointment, Spain's interest in the American Southwest waned. Even when the English sea dog Sir Francis Drake landed on the central California coast in 1579, Spain was slow to respond, not launching another expedition north of the borderlands until 1598, when Don Juan de Oñate claimed for Spain all of "New Mexico," meaning a region that stretched from Texas to California.

Oñate colonized deep into Pueblo country, meeting resistance in no place except at Acoma, in western New Mexico. After the Indians killed 13 of the Spanish soldiers, Oñate retaliated by fighting their way into Acoma, killing most of the pueblo warriors, then taking captive 500 women, children, and non-combatant men. Of the latter, 80 over the age of 25 were condemned to the amputation of one foot and a period of 20 years' enslavement. (Did Oñate pause to consider the usefulness of 80 one-footed slaves?)

The brutality of colonizers such as Oñate was driven in large part by desperation. Under the Spanish imperial system, conquistadors financed operations with their own fortunes. When Oñate failed to turn up the gold he had hoped for, he used the Indians as slave labor, hoping to make a profit by large-scale farming.

Spanish authorities would not have accepted the use of the word *slave* in the foregoing description. Slavery was illegal in the Spanish empire; however, the Spanish Crown did grant loyal colonists a type of deed (called an *encomendar*) to specific tracts of land *along with* the right to use the Indians living on that land as laborers. Although the Indians had no choice in the matter, the Crown held that this was not slavery, because the colonist (the *encomendero*) was bound to pay the Indians wages, to look after their health and welfare, and to encourage their eternal salvation through conversion to Christianity. The latter feature of this *encomienda system* provided the impetus for extensive missionary work, which included the construction of chains of missions throughout the American Southwest well into the eighteenth century.

### Sites and Sights

Acoma Pueblo, in Valencia county, west-central New Mexico, (64 miles west of Albuquerque), is known as the Sky City. It is occupied by about 50 Indians, who live in terraced dwellings made of stone and adobe atop a sandstone butte 357 feet high. Phone 505–252–1139 to arrange for a guided tour of the pueblo.

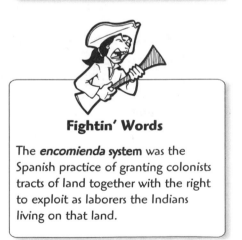

### Fightin' Words

The *encomienda system* was the Spanish practice of granting colonists tracts of land together with the right to exploit as laborers the Indians living on that land.

# The Brits Weigh In

Sir Francis Drake, who landed briefly in California in 1579, was not the first to sail to the New World under English auspices.

## King Henry's Sailor

In 1497, King Henry VII commissioned a Genoese seafarer, Giovanni Cabota, whom he called John Cabot, to find a new "Passage to India," a direct route to the spice-rich Indies.

Of all the European nations, England was farthest from the traditional trade routes with the East. If, however, the East could be reached by sailing *west*, English merchants would suddenly gain the edge in the worldwide spice market. Cabot sailed from Dursey Head, Ireland, in May 1497 and landed in Newfoundland on June 24. He explored probably as far south as Maine before he returned to England with the thrilling news that he had reached the northeast corner of Asia. Or so he thought. King Henry sent him off on a second voyage, with 200 men in five ships, all of whom disappeared at sea.

## Long Search for a Shortcut

Despite the claims of Columbus and John Cabot that they had reached Asia, it was becoming abundantly clear that the New World really was *new* and not part of Asia. It was indisputably a land mass separating the Atlantic and Pacific oceans and, therefore, separating Europe from Asia. The search for a passage through this body of land became even more urgent. From the sixteenth century and even into the twentieth, explorers probed the continent's waterways. The Frenchman Jacques Cartier, and the Englishmen Sir Francis Drake, Martin Frobisher, John Davis, Henry Hudson, Thomas Button, Robert Bylot, and William Baffin all searched in vain for a Northwest Passage.

# The Starving Time

One of the most ardent believers in the great New World shortcut was Sir Humphrey Gilbert, author of the 1566 *Discourse to Prove a Passage by the Northwest to Cathia* [China], to whom Queen Elizabeth I granted a charter to settle any lands not already claimed by Christians.

A supremely ambitious monarch, Elizabeth wanted her island nation to become the center of a great trading empire. With her blessing, Gilbert sailed to St. John's Bay, Newfoundland, in 1583 and claimed that territory for the queen. On the way back to England, however, Gilbert's overloaded ship sank with the loss of all hands. The royal charter passed to Gilbert's half brother, Sir Walter Raleigh, who, at 31, was the dashing favorite of Elizabeth.

## Phantom Colony at Roanoke

In 1584, Raleigh sent a small reconnaissance fleet to what would one day be called Croatan Sound in the Outer Banks of North Carolina. They returned with glowing reports of a land inhabited by "most gentle, loving, and faithful" Indians who lived "after the manner of the Golden Age." Raleigh named the new land Virginia, after his patroness, the "Virgin Queen," Elizabeth. Then, in 1585–86, he dispatched to Virginia Sir Richard Grenville with a small group of would-be settlers.

## We Hold These Truths

Raleigh never personally voyaged to Virginia, but, in 1595, he did lead an expedition to what is now Guyana, South America. Spanish documents as well as tales told by Indians persuaded him of the existence of Eldorado, a fabulous city of gold deep in the interior of the continent. Raleigh actually did find some modest gold mines, but he was unable to garner support for a colony in the region.

Sir Francis Drake found them a year later, starving and wanting passage back to England. Raleigh tried again in 1587, sending three ships with 117 men, women, and children to what is now called Roanoke Island, off the coast of North Carolina. Their leader, John White, planted them on a tract of swampy island, then returned to England to fetch the supplies Raleigh had promised, but failed, to send. (White could not have known that the supply ships had been delayed because of the attack of the Spanish Armada against England.)

When White returned in 1590, the settlers were nowhere to be found. There was the barest trace of a settlement—some rusted hardware and a name carved into a tree: CROATOAN. Croatoan was the name of a friendly group of Indians, living to the south. White was unable to go in search of the colonists among the Croatoans, however, because of the captain of the ship that had brought White to America was eager to sail to the West Indies to engage in piracy against the Spaniards. To this day, no one knows for sure what happened to the Roanoke settlers.

### Sites and Sights

Roanoke Island, part of North Carolina's Outer Banks, features *Lost Colony*, an outdoor drama about the ill-fated Roanoke colonists, regularly staged *except* from September to mid June. Call 1-800-488-5012. On the island, you might also visit the Elizabethan Gardens (919-473-3234) and the Fort Raleigh National Historic Site (919-473-5772), a reconstruction of what is conjectured to be the original fort.

## The Jamestown Venture

The disappearance of the Roanoke Colony did not end England's ambitions in the New World. At the opening of the seventeenth century, England was still militarily and commercially weak compared with Spain and Portugal. On the home front, as the medieval feudal system dissolved in the light of the Renaissance, England found itself with a displaced peasant class it could no longer feed, and a new merchant and artisan class in search of fresh markets. Although the English lacked the equivalent of the Spanish conquistador and had no zealous Catholic missionaries eager to convert natives, the nation needed a new world just as much as Spain did.

In 1606, then, two groups of merchants, the Virginia Company of London (sometimes abbreviated to the London Company) and the Plymouth Company, secured from King James I a charter to establish a colony in the territory of Raleigh's patent—which was held to encompass whatever portion of North America had not been claimed by Spain. The Virginia Company was granted a charter to colonize southern Virginia, while the Plymouth Company was given rights to "northern Virginia" (today's New England).

The Virginia Company moved swiftly to recruit a contingent of 144 settlers, including the families of moneyed gentlemen as well as poor people. The poor purchased their passage to America and the right of residence in the colony by binding themselves to serve the Virginia Company for a period of seven years, working the land and creating a settlement.

In December 1606, the small party of men, women, and children boarded the ships *Susan Constant*, *Discovery*, and *Goodspeed*. Thirty-nine died in the passage. On May 24, 1607, the remaining 105 arrived at the mouth of a river they named the James, and on its bank they scratched out the settlement of Jamestown.

It is called the first permanent English colony in the New World. But *permanence* proved to be a matter of degree. Jamestown was established in a malarial swamp in a season too late to plant crops. Not that the "gentlemen" of the venture—the wealthier folk who were not indentured servants—had any intention of engaging in manual labor so menial as digging in the earth. Within months, half the colony was either dead or had vanished into the woods, hoping to find charity among the local Indians. But the worst was yet to come. The year 1609 brought what the colonists called "the starving time." No crops. No forage. Desperate colonists resorted to acts of cannibalism and even looted the fresh graves of their own number as well as those of local Indians.

What saved Jamestown from going the way of the "lost colony" of Roanoke? One man. The Virginia Company had hired a soldier of fortune, Captain John Smith, to supervise the military defense of the colony. As colorful as he was resourceful (he had spent five years as a mercenary fighting against the Turks in Hungary and

### Fightin' Words

Most of the colonists obtained passage to the New World by signing a contract called an **indenture**, thereby becoming indentured servants—in effect, slaves for the seven-year term of the agreement. This was a very popular way to bring settlers to the fledgling colonies. The curious word indenture, which comes from a Latin root signifying tooth or bite marks, originated from the notches (indentations) made in the edges of medieval official documents to match up multiple copies.

Transylvania), Smith ingratiated himself with the local Indians, who were led by the powerful old chief Powhatan. From them he obtained enough corn and yams to keep the surviving colonists from starving. Then he set himself over the pathetic band as a benevolent despot, declaring that only those who worked would eat. By enforcing strict discipline, he saved the colony.

### We Hold These Truths

In December 1607, while foraging along the Chickahominy River, Smith was captured by some of Powhatan's braves. The story goes that Smith was saved from execution by Powhatan's 13-year-old daughter Pocahontas, who laid her head atop that of Smith as he was about to suffer the blow of a club. The story may well be true. In any case, it is one of the first popular legends of early America.

Although the "Powhatans" (the English named the numerous Indian villages after the single chief who controlled them) saved Jamestown, relations between the colonists and the Indians were chronically strained. Apparently in a bid to intimidate Chief Powhatan and his people into keeping the peace, Captain Samuel Argall kidnaped Powhatan's daughter Pocahontas in 1613 and took her to Jamestown and, later, to a new settlement, Henrico. Far from terrified by the experience, Pocahontas was fascinated by the English. She quickly learned their language and customs, effecting a rapid transition from hostage to ambassador. In 1614, with Powhatan's blessing, she married John Rolfe, a tobacco planter. This union brought peace for the next eight years, providing time for the Jamestown settlement to establish itself. (As for Pocahontas, Rolfe took her with him back to England, where she was an instant favorite of London society and the royal court. Sadly, however, she took ill and died, in England, on March 21, 1617, aged 22.)

The Jamestown settlement, having taken root, prospered. The indentured servants survived to satisfy their obligations, whereupon they were given control of their own land. They used their farms to plant tobacco, a crop brought by the English from the Spanish Caribbean. A great fondness for that weed soon developed in Europe, giving America its first export commodity, and the promise of growing rich from the cultivation of tobacco attracted more and more settlers. The English presence in the New World was thus established and secured.

As the population of Virginia grew, some form of local government became necessary, because England was too far away to make day-to-day decisions. In 1619, the Virginia

Company of London granted the wealthier, male settlers the right to elect representatives to an Assembly that would make laws for the colony. When the king later took over responsibility for the colony from the Virginia Company, the elected Assembly continued to function as the legislative body for Virginia. This Assembly, which expanded its powers and functions over time, became the model for colonial government throughout English America. In 1619 there was born in Jamestown the system of rights and liberties that later colonists would fight for in the American Revolution.

### The Least You Need to Know

➤ The Renaissance opened the European mind to exploration of new worlds.

➤ By the fifteenth century, opportunities had grown limited in Europe, so that social and economic conditions made the discovery of new worlds necessary and important.

➤ The first New World colonizers were the Spanish, who encountered sophisticated, densely populated Native-American empires in Mexico and Peru. The Spaniards therefore ended up ruling over a large Indian population.

➤ The English came later to the New World. Encountering much smaller, less sophisticated Indian groups, the English generally populated their colonies with migrants from Europe.

# Chapter 3

# The Colonial Way

---

**In This Chapter**

➤ Puritans, Separatists, and Pilgrims

➤ The Mayflower Compact: the first American "constitution"

➤ Founding the non-Puritan English colonies

➤ Slavery comes to America

➤ The French and Dutch colonies

---

The Spanish came to the New World to conquer, convert, and assimilate the natives. Spain's colonists created multi-ethnic societies in Central and South America, in which significant Native-American populations, communities, and cultural elements survived. The English, on the other hand, came to settle the land with white and later African populations, largely destroying or driving away the Native Americans. All English settlers sought economic opportunities that were lacking at home. Some Englishmen were also drawn to America by a variety of religious motivations.

This chapter explores the diverse motives of colonial Americans, who gradually reconciled their often intensely conflicting interests to create a new nation.

## A New Israel in the New World

When King Henry VIII ascended the throne of Britain, his kingdom was Catholic, its allegiance due to the pope in Rome. Then, in 1527, enamored of the saucy 20-year-old Anne Boleyn, Henry decided to do something about Catherine of Aragon, the dull, frail, and sickly wife who had repeatedly "failed" (as Henry saw it) to produce a male heir. Henry appealed to Pope Clement VII, asking that his marriage to Catherine be declared invalid, since she had been his late brother's widow when he married her. However, Pope Clement VII, having carefully reviewed Henry's case, decided that there was no legal or scriptural basis for Henry's request.

Henry responded with nothing less than a revolution. He separated the English church from Rome, declaring that the Church of England was, in effect, a spiritual department of state ultimately presided over by God's deputy on earth—namely himself, the king of England. Freed from Rome, Henry was free, in 1533, to wed Anne Boleyn.

## The Pilgrims' Progress

For Henry, the English protestant reformation was first and foremost a matter of marital convenience. Others, however, took the separation from Rome more spiritually. As early as the reign of Henry's daughter Elizabeth I, certain members of the Church of England began to feel that their church was still too Roman Catholic. A group of Anglican priests, most of them graduates of Cambridge University, began to advocate radical articles of religion, including

**Fightin' Words**

**Puritanism** was a movement within the Anglican Church, which advocated reforms in religious doctrine, discipline, and ceremony to distance Anglican practice as far as possible from that of the Roman Catholic Church.

**Separatists** shared Puritan beliefs about doctrine and ceremony, but believed that the Anglican Church was too corrupt to be reformed or purified. Separatists wished to create new churches that were completely independent of the Anglican Church.

➤ Personal spiritual experience—not mediated by a pope or even a priest, but a direct relationship between worshiper and God.

➤ Rigorously sincere moral conduct.

➤ Extremely austere and simple worship services, stripped of Roman pomp.

The mainstream Anglican church, these religious radicals declared, had failed in true reform. When James I ascended the throne in 1603, Puritan leaders clamored for more extensive reform, including the abolition of bishops. James refused, but *Puritanism*—as the new reform movement was called—grew in popularity, especially among common people, who resented the rich display of the traditional Anglican church.

## What Did the Mayflower Bring?

The Puritans who had left England before the first civil war were called, logically enough, *Separatists*. They were mostly impoverished farmers who had little to lose by leaving the mother country. The congregation led by William Brewster and the Reverend Richard Clifton left Scrooby, Nottinghamshire, for Amsterdam in 1608 and, the following year, moved to another Dutch town, Leyden, where they basked for a dozen years in Holland's religious freedom. Yet they were poorer than ever, and distressed that their children were growing up more Dutch than English. Despite the persecution they had suffered, these people were, first and last, English. At last, in 1617, they decided on a radical course of action. They would journey to America, which they thought of as the "New Israel," that is, a new land for God's chosen people.

Brewster was by no means an influential man, but he did know Sir Edwin Sandys, treasurer of the Virginia Company of London. Through him, he obtained patents authorizing the Scrooby congregation to settle in the northern part of the company's American territory. Somewhat less than half of the congregation boarded the *Speedwell*, bound for Southampton, England, where they were joined by a handful of Separatists from another congregation and others, non-Puritans whom the Separatists called "Strangers," who wanted to join the colonial venture. A total of 102 men, women, and children, fewer than half of them Separatists, embarked on the *Mayflower*, which left from the port of Plymouth on September 16, 1620.

The *Pilgrims*—as their first historian, William Bradford, later labeled them—sailed for 65 days before land was sighted on November 19.

They were supposed to establish their *plantation* near the mouth of the Hudson River, but Captain Christopher Jones, skipper of the *Mayflower*, claimed that rough seas off Nantucket forced them north to a landing at Cape Cod. Skeptical historians believe that it wasn't rough seas that sent Jones off course, but Pilgrim bribery. Cape Cod lay well beyond the northern limit of the Virginia Company's jurisdiction, and, by landing there, the Pilgrims were assured a high degree of independence from external authority. The *Mayflower* dropped anchor off present-day Provincetown, Massachusetts, on November 21.

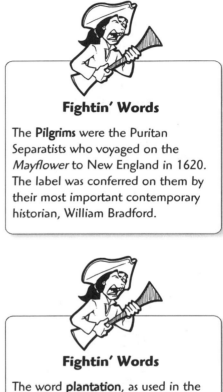

**Fightin' Words**

The **Pilgrims** were the Puritan Separatists who voyaged on the *Mayflower* to New England in 1620. The label was conferred on them by their most important contemporary historian, William Bradford.

**Fightin' Words**

The word **plantation**, as used in the seventeenth century, meant a newly established colony or settlement. Only later, by the end of the eighteenth century, did the word come to mean a large farming operation, especially in the South.

## Plymouth Rock and a Hard Place

After their long and perilous journey, the Pilgrims faced two immediate problems. First: What to do with the "Strangers," who were guided not by religious precept, but by a desire for commercial success. Second: Neither the Pilgrims nor the Strangers had been authorized by the British crown to settle in this region.

The Pilgrims had migrated in order to set up a society in which nobody but Separatists had freedom of worship. Having come this far, Pilgrim leaders were determined not to lose control of the colony, and they joined with a few of the Strangers who were sympathetic to Separatist ideas to sign the "Mayflower Compact," which allowed the Pilgrims to make all the colony's laws, no matter many Strangers might migrate to the region.

### Sites and Sights

Plymouth Rock is enclosed within a Grecian-style temple by the sea at Plymouth, Massachusetts, about 40 miles south of Boston. There are no contemporary mentions of the rock, but tradition says it was upon it that the first Pilgrim foot stepped. The town of Plymouth also features (much more interesting) a replica of the Mayflower and a reconstruction of "Plimoth Plantation." Call Plymouth's Visitor Center at 508-747-7525 or 1-800-USA-1620.

The Mayflower Compact concluded, the settlers looked for a promising spot to land and disembark. They found Plymouth Harbor, on the western side of Cape Cod Bay, and an advance party set foot on shore—supposedly on a rock now carved with the year 1620—on December 21. The rest of the settlers followed on December 26.

A promising spot? In truth, it would be difficult to think of a less congenial place and time for planting a colony. Winter was well under way, the stingy, flinty soil icy hard. Soon, people began to die. More than half of them would be gone before spring. Yet these settlers were made of sterner stuff than those who had struggled at Jamestown (see Chapter 2). In contrast to the Virginians, the New Englanders were neither moneyed gentlemen nor indentured servants. Over the next decade, accustomed to hard work and fiercely protective of their religious monopoly, the Pilgrims maintained their hold on Plymouth Colony by refusing to help, or even by attacking, other groups of settlers who tried to enter the area.

The colony's backers in England eventually lost interest in Plymouth and refused to invest any more money or effort in this intolerant religious enterprise. As a result, Plymouth Colony was largely a failure. Containing only 300 settlers in 1630, it was rapidly overwhelmed by the much larger migration of Puritans who began colonizing Massachusetts after 1629. Later, in 1691, Plymouth lost its separate identity and was absorbed into the colony of Massachusetts. Despite the important place that the Pilgrims hold in the American imagination today, in fact none of Plymouth's political or religious institutions had much influence on later American, or even on New England history. For the roots of New England's unique culture and society, it is necessary to look to the Massachusetts Bay Colony.

Under the influence of Anglican Archbishop William Laud, the government of James's successor, King Charles I, reacted with oppressive measures amounting to a campaign of persecution of the Puritans. Some 80,000 Puritans left England, settling in Ireland, the West Indies, and New England. Most Puritans, determined to reform the Anglican Church, remained in England, where they formed a powerful bloc within Parliament. Led by Oliver Cromwell, this group waged a bigger revolution than Henry ever dreamed of. The English Civil War of 1642–46 forced Charles to flee to Scotland, and in the course of a Second Civil War (1648–51), he was beheaded.

### We Hold These Truths

The Plymouth colonists received vital aid from neighboring Wampanoag Indians as they struggled to survive. Squanto (of the Pawtuxet branch of the Wampanoags) and Samoset (an Abnaki captive of the Wampanoags who spoke English) showed the Pilgrims how to plant and fertilize crops and improvise shelters. The Wampanoags aided the Plymouth colonists because they wanted these gun-wielding Englishmen to help them in their traditional wars with the neighboring Massachusetts tribe. The Wampanoag-Pilgrim Alliance, concluded at such meetings as the first Thanksgiving in 1621, led the Pilgrims to perpetrate a massacre of the Massachusetts Indians in 1623.

The 20,000 Puritans who migrated to New England originally came to the Massachusetts Bay Colony, which received a legal charter in 1629. With many more colonists, and with financial backing from a wealthy segment of English society, the Massachusetts colony was an immediate success. There was little hunger, and no major threat from the already-decimated Massachusetts Indians.

Governor John Winthrop established the colony's capital at Boston, then divided the surrounding countryside into townships, which became the basis of political and religious life for the colonists. Each town set up its own Puritan church, and the elders of each church decided which members of the town could be full members of the church. Adults not deemed spiritual enough were excluded from full membership, but they still had to attend services and pay taxes for the minister's salary! Adult males who were full church members could vote for the town government and to send representatives to the General Court, New England's first elected legislature. These institutions spread from Massachusetts to other colonies, including Plymouth, which began to model itself after its powerful northern neighbor in the 1630s.

## Many Mansions: Departures from the Puritan Path

According to the gospel of John, Jesus told his disciples, "In my Father's house are many mansions," but the Puritans hardly interpreted this as an invitation for each to worship God in his or her own way. Revolutionaries who had broken with a church that had prevented them from following their spiritual conscience, they themselves enforced a strict orthodoxy.

## Freedom in Rhode Island

As the Massachusetts settlers developed differences about the precise form of the Puritan church, discontented colonists moved out of the Massachusetts territory to found new colonies, where different groups or *sects* of Puritans could organize religion in their own way. Connecticut and New Hampshire were two colonies that grew from discontented settlers who left Massachusetts. The most radically different colony, however, was Rhode Island.

Within the framework of their orthodoxy, the Puritans never tired of disputing the fine points of their religion. One of the most brilliant was the Reverend Roger Williams (ca. 1603–83), who had immigrated from England to Boston in 1631. Offered the post of minister of the first Boston congregation, he declined because it had not formally separated from the Anglican Church. Williams left Boston for Salem, then moved on to Plymouth, and back to Salem again. Everywhere he went, he was dogged by criticism of his "strange opinions," including these revolutionary propositions:

➤ That lands chartered to Massachusetts and Plymouth actually belonged to the Indians.

➤ That a civil government had no authority to enforce religious laws.

➤ That religion itself rested, first and last, on profoundly individual conscience and perception, not on the word of the Bible nor on the authority of any priest.

At length, the Puritan fathers ordered Williams to change his views, and when he refused, he and his family were exiled from the colony by the Massachusetts General Court in October 1635. The unorthodox minister, together with a handful of followers, found refuge in January 1636 among the Indians on Naragansett Bay. At the head of that bay, Williams purchased from his protectors a modest tract, on which he founded a town he called Providence. It was the first settlement in Rhode Island.

**Voices of Liberty**

"[Coercion of conscience is] soul-rape."

—Roger Williams, 1644

For some 40 years, Williams governed Rhode Island, welcoming people of all religious persuasions. In 1644, during the English Civil War, he secured an official *patent* for the colony from the Puritan-controlled Parliament, which welcomed the addition of another non-royalist English settlement, even if its governor had strange ideas. Williams established in Rhode Island a genuinely representative government founded on the principle of religious freedom for all Protestant sects.

## Catholic Mary Land

The Puritans had hoped to create a "city on a hill," a holy and righteous place that would be a beacon to the world, broadcasting the one true religion. That Rhode Island flourished was dismaying. Even more repugnant was the colony called Mary Land.

In 1632, King Charles I of England, married to a French Catholic wife and eager to ease the persecution of Catholics in Protestant England, granted the Roman Catholic George Calvert, First Baron Baltimore, a charter to settle North American lands between the 40th parallel and the south bank of the Potomac. Although George Calvert died before the charter was executed, the papers passed to his son Cecil Calvert, Second Baron Baltimore. In November 1633, he led 200 Catholic colonists from England in *The Ark and the Dove*, which landed on March 24, 1634, on an island at the mouth of the Potomac they named Saint Clement, now called Blakistone Island.

From the Indians, the colonists bought Yaocomico, a village they renamed St. Mary's (it is present-day St. Mary's City), which served for the next 60 years as the capital of the Mary Land, or Maryland. Under Lord Baltimore's direction, in 1649, the Colonial Assembly passed the Act Concerning Religion. It was the first law in the American colonies that explicitly provided for freedom of worship. (That is, it provided for something approaching religious freedom, since it applied only to Christians.)

## Two Carolinas

After the English Civil War and the rule of the Puritans under Oliver Cromwell, the non-Puritan majority of Englishmen demanded the restoration of the monarchy under Charles II, the son of the king executed by the Puritans. Charles II was eager to expand England's empire in America, and in 1663 he granted a huge tract of land south of Virginia to eight of his political supporters. Called Carolina (from the Latin for "Charles"), the settlement of this colony did not get under way until 1670, with the founding of Charleston.

Carolina granted freedom of worship to all Protestants, and a variety of colonists migrated there: Some came from England, and many came from Barbados, an English colony in the Caribbean that had become overcrowded. A large number of French Protestants, persecuted in their own country, took refuge in Carolina, also. This mixed society at first made its money from trade with local Indians, mainly for Indian slaves and for deer hides. (The modern slang term "buck" for a dollar originates from the fact that buckskins were used as an early form of money.) Then around 1700, Carolinians near Charleston learned to grow rice, an extremely lucrative export, while, farther north, settlers imitated Virginia and began to grown tobacco. This large colony was governed as two separate parts almost from the beginning, and the two parts formally became the two separate colonies of North Carolina and South Carolina in 1719.

## Pennsylvania's Friendly Persuasion

How far, the New England Puritans lamented, would the New World—the New Israel—depart from the true path? They soon had an answer when members of another sect, also vigorously persecuted in England, arrived in the New World. Founded in the seventeenth century by the mystic George Fox, they called themselves the Society of Friends, but they were more familiarly called Quakers, a name derisively applied to them in 1650 by a judge whom Fox cautioned to "tremble at the word of the Lord."

The Friends believed in the "immediacy" of Christ's teachings; that is, true knowledge of God could not be mediated through scripture, ceremony, ritual, or clergy. Instead, it came to each person in the form of an "inward light."

While this sounds innocent enough to modern ears, as the Puritans saw it, Quakerism was dangerously subversive. The Quakers themselves believed in total non-violence and the equality of men and women and of all races. Respectful of all points of view, they were nonetheless viciously and vigorously persecuted in England. Some immigrated to America, settling in the Middle Atlantic region as well as North Carolina. An early community was established in tolerant Rhode Island.

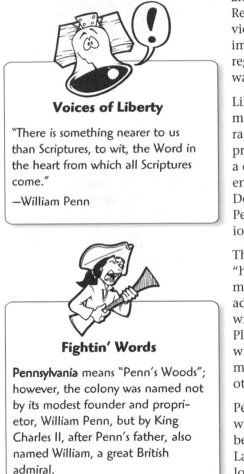

### Voices of Liberty

"There is something nearer to us than Scriptures, to wit, the Word in the heart from which all Scriptures come."

—William Penn

### Fightin' Words

**Pennsylvania** means "Penn's Woods"; however, the colony was named not by its modest founder and proprietor, William Penn, but by King Charles II, after Penn's father, also named William, a great British admiral.

Like the early Puritans, most Quakers were of modest means, but there were a few powerful people among their ranks. On March 14, 1681, William Penn, the son of a prominent British admiral, obtained from King Charles II a charter granting him proprietorship of the area now encompassed by Pennsylvania. The following year, Delaware was added to the charter, and that same year Penn founded the town of Philadelphia, a name fashioned from two Greek words signifying "brotherly love."

The name expressed Penn's intention of conducting a "holy experiment" in harmonious living. In contrast to most nations, which adopted warlike Latin mottoes to adorn their official seals, Penn designed a seal inscribed with the words "Mercy, Justice, Truth, Peace, Love, Plenty." He quickly concluded "a treaty of friendship" with the local Indians, and his colony enjoyed a greater measure of peace with the Native Americans than any other.

Penn proclaimed "The Great Law of Pennsylvania," which extended male suffrage to any who professed a belief in God and met property requirements. The Great Law almost completely abolished imprisonment for debt, long a blight on English society, and it restricted execution to only cases of treason or murder.

## Georgia: Prison and Utopia

All the colonies were expressions of what Thomas Jefferson, in the Declaration of Independence, would number as humanity's third inalienable right: the pursuit of happiness. The origin of the last British colony, Georgia, was yet more frankly utopian than the rest. James Edward Oglethorpe was an army general and a philanthropist visionary. In 1732, he organized 19 wealthy and progressive men into a corporation that secured a royal charter to colonize Georgia—named for King George II—as the southernmost of Britain's North American colonies.

Oglethorpe's aim was not only to provide a haven for all Protestant dissenters, but also a fresh start for debtors imprisoned in England and rehabilitation for those convicted of certain criminal offenses. The utopian aspects of the colony mattered less to King George II, who granted the royal charter, than the fact that it would serve as a buffer zone between the British colonies to the north and Spanish-held Florida.

A genuinely selfless man, Oglethorpe pledged himself and the other philanthropists to act as trustees of the colony without taking profits from the enterprise for a period of 21 years. He also instituted a series of utopian laws:

➤ The sale of rum was prohibited.

➤ Slavery was outlawed.

➤ Individual land holdings were limited to 500 acres in an effort to promote equality.

Unfortunately, Oglethorpe's utopian provisions were breached one after the other. Soon after the first farmers were installed on their tracts in 1733, the land restrictions were lifted. The reality was that Ogelthorpe's utopia had been co-opted from the start, for most of the original 100 colonists were financial speculators. Once the planters knocked down the 500-acre limit, slavery followed, and soon Georgia was no different from England's other southern colonies.

# Unwilling Immigrants: The Arrival of the Slaves

Of all Oglethorpe's disappointments with his colony, the introduction of slaves was the most profound. Disgusted with the enterprise, he returned to England. Like most enlightened men and women of his age, Oglethorpe believed slavery to be profoundly wrong. Yet the institution not only persisted, but expanded in the New World.

Slavery, of course, was not a New World invention. It is at least as old as civilization, but it became a significant commercial enterprise only after the New World colonies had been established. In 1562, the British seafarer John Hawkins began transporting slaves from Guinea, in western Africa, to the West Indies. Purchased from African chieftains, they were, at first, captives taken in raids or wars. Before long, however, the trade goods the chiefs received assumed so much importance, enhancing their prestige among their people, that tribes began to raid one another for the purpose of acquiring slaves to trade.

By the time Georgia was established in 1733, American slavery was already more than a century old. In 1619, only a dozen years after Jamestown had gotten its shaky start, Dutch traders imported African slaves at the behest of the Virginia tobacco farmers. There were no more than 20 in that first shipment, and, although they were slaves, they were not otherwise discriminated against. They were regarded as neither higher nor lower than the white indentured servants brought from England under work contracts. But as the plantations of Virginia, the Carolinas, and Georgia expanded, demand for slavery grew.

## We Hold These Truths

The earliest recorded mention of slavery is in the Babylonian Code of Hammurabi, about the twenty-first century B.C.: "If a slave says to his master, 'You are not my master,' the master shall cut off his ear."

It is estimated that between 8 and 15 million slaves were imported into America from the late 1500s to the early 1800s. About 6 million arrived during the eighteenth century.

Although the large-scale practice of slavery was limited to the South, the slave trade became an important part of the colonial economy, North and South. Slavery was a leg in the so-called *triangle trade*, in which ships leaving England with trade goods landed on the African west coast, traded the merchandise for slaves, then transported them (via a route called the "Middle Passage") to the West Indies or the mainland English colonies where they were exchanged for the very agricultural products—sugar, tobacco, and rice—slave labor had produced. The final leg of the triangle was back to England, laden with New World produce. New England ports soon became a regular stop for vessels about to return to Old England. The sugar and molasses acquired at Southern ports were purchased by Northern distillers of rum, an important New England export.

## Fightin' Words

In the **triangle trade**, ships with goods from England landed on the African west coast to trade for slaves, which were transported to the West Indies or the American colonies and traded for products of slave labor—sugar, tobacco, and rice—which were taken back to England.

Slaves were chosen for their health and strength, not so much because these qualities would make them good workers, but because such people would have the greatest chance of surviving the brutal voyage from Africa. Packed "spoon fashion" into the hull of the vessels, each slave was chained, fed minimally, and allowed no access to sunlight during a voyage that lasted from 21 to 90 days. At least 20 percent died en route.

# French Designs

At about the same time as the English were making their first tentative inroads into North America, the French began settling the continent. Religion was certainly part of the French motivation for settlement; "Black robes," Catholic missionaries, arrived in the wake of French explorers. These Catholic missionaries, who traveled hundreds, even thousands of miles into North America to convert the Indians, enabled the French to build alliances with many native tribes. Since far fewer Frenchmen than Englishmen migrated to North America, these native alliances were vital to the empire that France built in Canada and the Mississippi Valley.

Early French efforts to establish North American colonies were driven largely by Cardinal Richelieu (1585–1642), the power behind the throne of the weak-willed King Louis XIII. Richelieu's ambition was to make France the dominant power in Europe, and he saw in New World holdings an opportunity for the profits with which to finance that dominance.

## *Champlain, New World Booster*

Samuel de Champlain (ca.1570–1635), son of a naval captain, made a dozen voyages to North America, primarily in search of Indian tribes who would trade beaver and other furs for French textiles, metal goods, and brandy.

During a series of seven voyages between 1603 and 1616, Champlain mapped the Atlantic coast from the Bay of Fundy to Cape Cod, established settlements, and got the French fur trade off to a promising start. Of particular consequence were the alliances he concluded with the Algonquin and Huron tribes against the tribes of the powerful Iroquois League. These alliances made the French a strong threat to the English, who, unlike the French, made few Indian friends and many Indian enemies. Champlain planted the seeds of a series of French and Indian wars with the English, which culminated in *the* French and Indian War of 1754–63 (discussed in Chapter 4, "Wilderness Wars").

In 1608, Champlain founded Quebec; the following year, he sailed up from it via the St. Lawrence and the river later named after Louis XIII's powerful minister, Cardinal Richelieu, to a lake that would later be named after Champlain himself. On behalf of France's Algonquin allies, he fought the powerful Iroquois. Years later, in 1615, he traveled west, across the eastern end of Lake Ontario, and

**Fightin' Words**

The names Algonquin and Algonquian can be confusing. **Algonquin** applies to any of the various Native-American peoples who live or lived in the Ottawa River Valley of Quebec and Ontario, whereas Algonquian is the name of a family of Indian languages. Tribes related through dialects of this linguistic family are collectively referred to as **Algonquian**—not Algonquin. The other major Indian linguistic family in eastern North America is the **Iroquoian**.

helped the Huron Indians defeat the Oneidas and Onondagas—two tribes belonging to the Iroquois League.

Thus Champlain secured the entire St. Lawrence region for France. He understood that whoever commanded this region would dominate trade in the upper Northeast.

Champlain was every bit as crafty as Richelieu. He enthusiastically promoted Canada to the cardinal and the king, but he actively discouraged full-scale colonization. His objective was, with royal backing, to operate Quebec as his exclusive, personal trading post, and until 1628, New France (as it was optimistically named) had very few farmers.

Champlain's greed ultimately got the better of him, as he was forced to surrender Quebec to an Englishman, Sir David Kirke, after a brief Anglo-French War. Quebec was restored to French rule in 1632 (in return for payment of overdue installments on the dowry of the French-born queen of England's Charles I), but when Champlain died there on Christmas Day 1635, Quebec town was peopled by no more than 150 settlers.

## The Sun King's Ambitions

The son of the thirteenth Louis was born on September 5, 1638 and ascended the throne under the *regency* of Cardinal Mazarin when his father died in 1643. After Mazarin's death, in 1661, Louis XIV began to rule in his own right, and among the many matters to which he turned his attention was New France. He saw his nation's North American possessions not merely as a source of quick profit, but as the constituents of worldwide empire. Accordingly, he financed the passage of women to New France in an effort to entice the itinerant trappers there to settle down and raise families. As further inducement, the king offered a bounty for those who sired large families in New France. And if this carrot weren't sufficient, he brandished a stick as well, suggesting to the church that any man who abandoned farming without permission should be excommunicated.

Louis XIV was interested in settlement, not exploration, but Jean Baptiste Talon, his *intendant* (chief administrator) in Canada, defied royal policy by hiring a fur trader named Louis Joliet to investigate some things he had heard from the Indians. They were tales concerning a "father of all the rivers," the "Mesippi." Perhaps this would prove to be the elusive Northwest Passage to the Pacific.

**Fightin' Words**

A **regent** is a person or group who governs in place of a monarch who is absent, disabled, or too young to govern in his or her own right.

Accompanied by a feisty Jesuit priest named Jacques Marquette, Joliet found the Mississippi, which didn't prove to be a Northwest Passage, but did establish France's claim to a vast portion of what one day would be the United States. Wishing to placate the French monarch, Joliet gave the name Louisiana to the great territory, which encompassed (as the French saw it) all that lay between the Appalachian and Rocky mountains.

Louis was more than placated. Called the "Sun King" because of the magnificence of his opulent court and his even more opulent visions of empire, Louis XIV planned to create a vast agricultural kingdom in the New World—a suitable reflection of the glories of the Old. Yet, even to the end of the Sun King's long reign, New France remained nothing more but a few precarious outposts and settlements broadcast over vast spaces in Nova Scotia, along the St. Lawrence River, and in Louisiana.

# Dutch Treat

The first decade of the seventeenth century was most eventful for the New World. The English founded Jamestown in 1607, and the French established Quebec in 1608. The following year, an Englishman, Henry Hudson, sailed in the Dutch service up the river that now bears his name. Reaching the site of present-day Albany, he realized that, like all who had gone before him, he had failed to find the Northwest Passage. But his voyage did give the Netherlands a claim to the richest fur-bearing region of North America south of the St. Lawrence.

At first, only a few Dutch sea captains visited the region to trade for furs with the Indians, but, in 1621, the Dutch West India Company was founded, and it backed the establishment of New Netherland in 1623. In 1624, the company built a trading post at Fort Orange—present-day Albany—and, two years later, sent out Peter Minuit (ca. 1580–1638) to serve as first director-general of the new Dutch colony.

Minuit started by purchasing Manhattan Island from the Manhattan Indians, a band of the Delaware tribe, for trade goods valued in 1624 at 60 guilders. A nineteenth-century historian computed this as the equivalent of $24.

### We Hold These Truths

Almost certainly, the Manhattan Indians did not mean to sell the entire island of Manhattan to the Dutch for $24. Indian tribes did allow outsiders (other tribes, also Europeans) to use their land temporarily, in exchange for gifts. The closest modern equivalent to this transaction would therefore be a lease. The Dutch got a good bargain because they chose to regard a grant of temporary use of the land as a permanent purchase.

Minuit built a fort at the tip of the island and called it New Amsterdam. Soon, the Dutch established a profitable and peaceful trade with the Indians, at a time when, as we will see in the next chapter, the settlers of New England were fighting desperate and costly wars with their Native-American neighbors. It wasn't that the Dutch were friendlier than the English, but that they posed less of a threat to the Indians. The Dutch came to New Netherland not to acquire large tracts of land for farming, but to trade furs.

Only after the local beaver supply dwindled as a result of over-hunting did the Dutch begin to stake out farms. Once this happened, relations with the Indians deteriorated. In 1638, when Willem Kieft (1597–1647) took office as the colony's fifth governor, he imposed a heavy tax on the local Indians as payment for "defending" them against Mohawks. Actually, the Dutch still enjoyed trading relations with the Mohawks, whom Kieft, like the New York gangsters of the future, employed to terrorize the tribes he wanted to tax. Kieft's tax was nothing less than extortion—"protection money."

When the Raritan Indians, living near New Amsterdam, refused to pay the tax in 1641, then attacked an outlying Dutch colony, Kieft went to war with them. Two years later, he sent the Mohawks against the Wappingers, who lived along the Hudson River above Manhattan. They fled down to Pavonia (present-day Jersey City, New Jersey), just across the Hudson from Manhattan. Unaware that Kieft was an enemy, they appealed to him for aid. He responded by directing the Mohawks to Pavonia, then sent in Dutch troops to finish off the refugees. During the night of February 25–26, 1643, Dutch soldiers killed men, women, and children in what was later called the "Slaughter of the Innocents." The heads of 80 Indians were brought back to New Amsterdam, where soldiers and citizens used them as footballs. Thirty prisoners were publicly tortured to death.

The Pavonia Massacre turned 11 local tribes against the settlers of New Netherland and drove the panic-stricken colonists to the verge of rebellion. In 1645, the Dutch West India Company recalled Kieft to Holland and replaced him with Peter Stuyvesant, the crusty, peg-legged son of a Calvinist minister.

The new governor cracked down on colonists and Indians alike, taking special care to persecute the Quakers and the Lutherans, whom he thought likely to lead a full-scale colonial revolt, and taking care also to build a defensive wall on the northern edge of New Amsterdam along the east-west cow path that would later be named for it: Wall Street.

Ultimately, Stuyvesant's despotism merely hastened the decay of his authority. Relations between New Netherland and New England became increasingly strained as the colonies bitterly competed for Indian

**Voices of Liberty**

"... infants were torn from their mother's breasts, and hacked to pieces in the presence of the parents, and the pieces thrown into the fire and in the water, and other sucklings were bound to small boards, and then cut, struck, and pierced, and miserably massacred in a manner to move a heart of stone. Some were thrown into the river, and when the fathers and mothers endeavoured to save them, the soldiers would not let them come on land, but made both parents and children drown...."

—David Pietrsz de Vries, a Dutch colonist, describing the Pavonia Massacre loyalty and trade. The system of settlement imposed by the Dutch West India Company put New Netherland at a grave disadvantage. Whereas the English settled New England, Virginia, and the other southern colonies with a mix of wealthy planters and yeoman farmers, the Dutch were subject to the *patroon system*, by which land grants of approximately 16 miles along one side of the Hudson (and other navigable rivers) or about eight miles on both banks (and extending for unspecified distances away from the river) were made to absentee landlords who installed tenant farmers. This made New Netherland a colony mainly of tenants rather than property holders.

On September 8, 1664, a fleet of British warships sailed up the Hudson. The Dutch colonists, with little motive for patriotism, offered no resistance. Stuyvesant stumped angrily on his wooden leg, but had no choice other than surrender.

The British renamed both the colony and its chief town after the duke of York (the future King James II), Stuyvesant retired peacefully to his farm, the Bouwerie, and "New York" was added to the British colonial portfolio.

# The Bonds of Commerce

Well before the end of the 1600s, the British colonies dominated the eastern seaboard. Such dominance had not come easily and was not easy to maintain. Warfare with the French and their Indian allies was chronic. Frontier life was always hard, but in the coastal cities there was an increasing degree of sophistication, culture, and luxury, as the wealthier inhabitants strove to imitate the lifestyle of the English upper and middle classes.

By 1700, England's American colonists regarded themselves as free individuals, because they possessed certain liberties as subjects of the English Empire. Among the most important of these liberties was the right to trial by jury. Another cherished liberty was representative government. In every colony, adult males who met certain property requirements were able to elect legislative assemblies, which alone had the right to tax that colony's inhabitants. These, and other rights, made England's American colonists proud to be

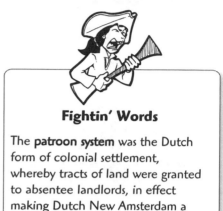

**Fightin' Words**

The **patroon system** was the Dutch form of colonial settlement, whereby tracts of land were granted to absentee landlords, in effect making Dutch New Amsterdam a colony of tenant farmers.

**Sites and Sights**

Stuyvesant's bucolic Bouwerie was, by the nineteenth century, a neighborhood of inexpensive dwellings and gaudy theaters, which became increasingly disreputable as the years passed. By the early twentieth century, the rural cow path traversing Stuyvesant's farm had become the Bowery, a dismal and dilapidated urban avenue of cheap bars frequented by derelicts. Today, though still gritty, the Bowery is a Lower East Side mecca for some of Manhattan's creative community, including a number of young artists.

### Fightin' Words

The **mercantile system** was a form of economic nationalism that called for strict governmental regulation of trade and commerce and held that the sole function of colonies was to enrich the mother country by furnishing raw materials, gold, and silver, as well as exclusive markets for goods produced by the mother country.

part of an Empire that, they believed, was the freest in the world. Certainly, no other European Empire in America granted these rights to its colonists.

One important type of legislation that was under the control of the English Parliament rather than of the colonial legislatures was trade regulation. The colonies existed under the *mercantile system*, a form of economic nationalism that not only advocated strict governmental regulation of trade and commerce, but held that colonies existed solely for the enrichment of the mother country. That is, the purpose of the colonies was to furnish England with gold, silver, raw materials, and markets. Although mercantilist policies were chiefly designed to enrich the mother country, mercantilist thinkers realized that rich colonies would mean a richer Great Britain. Mercantilist laws therefore sought to build up many aspects of the colonial economy, also, by protecting colonial trade and subsidizing some colonial products.

Mercantilism had both good and bad effects on the colonies. The main bad effect was that there were many items that the colonists could not directly ship to or from the continent of Europe. This restriction made some imports cost more, and restricted exports of tobacco, rice, and other colonial products. The advantage for the colonies, however, was that the mercantilist system enabled colonial merchants to trade inside the English Empire without having to face French, Dutch, or other competition. Seaports in the northern colonies, especially Boston, New York, and Philadelphia, profited immensely from this protected trade. In addition, the colonists enjoyed the protection of the British navy against pirates and other maritime raiders, without having to pay any taxes toward the navy's upkeep. Historians who have calculated the costs and benefits of mercantilism have concluded that the American colonies probably received more money than they lost from the system.

It is important to remember that Great Britain during the eighteenth century was the world's major industrial and financial power. Although the mercantilist system subordinated the colonies to the mother country, such subordination was not painful, since British manufactures were cheap and well made, and since British bankers were able to provide better credit than other European nations could. Trade and investment in British America during the colonial period laid the foundations of the capitalist system and of the later prosperity of the United States.

> ### The Least You Need to Know
>
> ➤ The settlers of New England were chiefly religious dissenters called Puritans.
>
> ➤ The New England Puritans were intolerant of other religions, a circumstance that helped lead to the founding of Rhode Island, Maryland (predominantly Catholic), and Pennsylvania (predominantly Quaker); Georgia was established less for religious than for utopian reasons.
>
> ➤ African slavery came to America in 1619, got off to a slow start, but, by the eighteenth century, was firmly established in the South.
>
> ➤ The Dutch and the French emerged as England's chief colonial rivals.

# Chapter 4

# Wilderness Wars

## In This Chapter

➤ King Philip's War: the "United Colonies" formed

➤ Causes of the French and Indian War

➤ George Washington's maiden battle

➤ The fall of Quebec

➤ The French and Indian War as a prelude to revolution

As we saw in Chapter 2, warfare between Europeans and Indians began almost immediately after Columbus landed in the Caribbean. Year after year, the Spanish accumulated a violent history with the Indians. The Dutch and Indians managed to live in peace for a time, but as increasing numbers of Dutch settlers turned from trade to farming, encroaching on Indian land, fighting finally broke out between New Netherland and its Native-American neighbors. In Virginia, the so-called Powhatan War erupted in March 1622 after the servants of a Jamestown planter killed a prominent Powhatan Indian as revenge for the murder of their master. With interruptions, the war lasted for 20 years.

The colonists of North America were well-schooled in the ways of wilderness warfare long before they decided to fight a war for independence. Here is the story of that long and bloody dress rehearsal for revolution.

# New England Bleeds

As violent as white-Indian relations were in the Middle Atlantic colonies and in the South during the 1600s, they were worse in New England.

The Pequot War was the result of competition for the fur trade and intertribal rivalries. The Pequots occupied a strategic location in the Connecticut River Valley, which was the best route in New England whereby northern furs could travel down to the sea. Whites in the colonies of Massachusetts, Plymouth, and Connecticut wanted to remove the Pequots, who charged high prices as middlemen in the fur trade. Meanwhile, the Narragansetts and Mohegans (a branch of the Pequots that had split off under separate leadership) wished to replace the Pequots as middlemen along the Connecticut River. All these groups looked for excuses to make war on the Pequots, and such excuses were not hard to find.

The actions of Massachusetts were aimed at economic domination of the Connecticut Valley, not at gaining a legal title to the area, which could only come from royal or parliamentary charter. Despite the massacre of the Pequots, the colony of Connecticut, not Massachusetts, ended up with legal title to the region.

**Fightin' Words**

**Client tribe** is a modern term describing the relationship of certain lesser Indian tribes to greater ones, a relationship similar to that between the eastern European "satellite" nations and the former Soviet Union.

John Stone was a thoroughly disreputable English sea captain, no better than a pirate, who had tried unsuccessfully to hijack a vessel in New Amsterdam, had brandished a knife before the governor of Plymouth Colony, and had been expelled from the Massachusetts Bay Colony for drunkenness and adultery. According to the Pequots, he was also a kidnapper, who had abducted several Indians. In 1634, however, to the English colonists, he appeared as a victim, barbarously wronged.

That year, as his ship lay at anchor in the mouth of the Connecticut River, Stone was killed. His murder was apparently the work of western Niantics, a *client tribe* of the much more powerful Pequots.

## Twilight of the Pequots

The Pequots had no interest in fighting a war over the murder of a man neither they nor (they thought) the English cared much about. They accepted responsibility for what members of their client tribe had done, and they concluded a treaty with the Massachusetts Bay Colony in which they promised to surrender the murderers, pay an exorbitant indemnity, relinquish rights to a vast tract of Connecticut land, and trade exclusively with the English instead of the Dutch.

An installment of the indemnity was paid, but the Pequots claimed that all of the murderers were dead (one at the hands of the Dutch, the others of smallpox), except for two who had escaped.

This satisfied Massachusetts Bay colonists for two years. Then, on June 16, 1636, Mohegan Indians warned the English that the Pequots, fearing that the colonists were about to take action, had decided on a preemptive strike. Colonial authorities summoned Pequot representatives to another conference, at Fort Saybrook, Connecticut, and new agreements were drawn up.

During this meeting, word arrived of the murder of yet another captain, John Oldham, off Block Island (today part of Rhode Island). Again, the Pequots played no part in the killing. This time, the crime was the work of Narragansetts—or, perhaps, a client tribe subject to them—and, like the Pequot chiefs, the Narragansett sachems were eager to avert war. They sent a force of 200 warriors to avenge the deaths on behalf of the colony.

But the Bay colonists were not satisfied. Capt. John Endecott was dispatched to Block Island with orders to seize the Indians' stores of *wampum*, slaughter all the men they could find, and capture the women and children for sale as slaves in the West Indies.

From sad experience, the Indians anticipated just such a vengeful move, and they fled Block Island. Arriving to find his prey had eluded him, the frustrated Endecott sailed on to Fort Saybrook, determined to punish the Pequots—even though everyone, including Endecott himself, knew they had nothing to do with the killing of Oldham.

"You come hither to raise these wasps about my ears," Fort Saybrook's commander, Lieutenant Lion Gardiner, protested to Endecott, "and then you will take wing and flee away."

Heedless, Endecott approached the Pequots who lived just beyond the fort.

"What cheer, Englishmen, what cheer, what do you come for?" a Pequot delegation greeted him.

When Endecott replied that he had come to make war, the Pequots suggested that they talk things over instead. No, Endecott blustered. It must be a fight. What's more, it must be an English-style fight, on an open field of battle, not an Indian-style fight, from behind trees and rocks. But the Pequots refused *any* fight and, instead, fled their villages. Endecott, his blood boiling, set fire to the deserted settlements.

### Fightin' Words

**Wampum** is the Anglicized version of the Algonquian word *wampompeag*. White settlers used the term to describe any kind of valuable item regarded as the equivalent of money, but, originally, the Indians applied it specifically to cylindrical seashells strung on strings or beaded into belts and used as money or as tokens of good faith; wampum belts were exchanged at treaty signings, for example.

### Voices of Liberty

"Since they sow the wind, they will reap the whirlwind...."
—Hosea 8:7

As a dutiful Christian, Capt. Endecott must have known well the verse from Hosea about the consequences of sowing the wind. For now the colonies reaped the whirl-wind, as the entire Connecticut Valley seemed to burst into flame. Enraged Pequots put to the torch one English settlement after another. The colonists responded against the Pequots in kind, and John Endecott had his war.

The very competitiveness of the New England colonies that made effective action against the Pequots nearly impossible. Not until the spring of 1637 were the poorly organized colonial forces able to recruit Indian allies—Narragansetts, Eastern Niantics, and Mohegans, all rivals of the Pequots—to aid in the fight. Under Captain John Mason, the colonial-Indian coalition attacked a village at Mystic, Connecticut, killing in 60 minutes perhaps 700 Pequots, mostly women, children, and old men.

**Voices of Liberty**

"Thus did the LORD scatter his Enemies with his strong Arm!"

—Captain John Mason, in his account of the Pequot War, 1637

The Mystic Massacre was so brutal that the Pequots never recovered from it. They lost their will to fight and were defeated in every encounter. Those who managed to escape death sought refuge among neighboring tribes. But those tribes, terrified by the colonists' display of savagery, turned the refugees away. The Pequots were trapped. On September 21, 1638, the survivors signed the devastating Treaty of Hartford. Pequot prisoners of war were apportioned as slaves among the Mohegans, Narragansetts, and Niantics. As if that weren't enough, the Pequots pledged that they would not inhabit their former country ever again, nor, the treaty stipulated, would they or anyone else ever again utter the name *Pequot*.

## The Costliest War in American History

To the Massachusetts Bay colonists, the Pequots had been pawns in the great colonial game they played against their Connecticut rivals. And, as pawns, they were *meant* to be sacrificed. But almost 40 years later, the next major Indian war seemed a lot less like a game.

King Philip's War began in a familiar way. On June 11, 1675, a Plymouth, Massachu-setts, farmer, seeing a Wampanoag Indian pilfering his cattle, summarily shot and killed him. The local Wampanoag chief, called Metacomet by the Indians and—sneeringly—King Philip by the English, sought justice from the local garrison. Predict-ably, King Philip was spurned. Just as predictably, the chief took justice into his own hands. Wampanoags killed the trigger-happy farmer, as well as his father and five other settlers. The war was on.

It was the culmination of deteriorating relations between the Wampanoags and the Plymouth colonists. Philip was the son of Massasoit, a Wampanoag chief who had been highly cordial to the New Englanders. When he came to power, however, Philip was anxious to check the colonists' insatiable hunger for land. As early as 1662, he began stirring up a rebellious spirit among the Narragansetts and the Nipmucks as well as his own Wampanoags. He encouraged cattle theft and other acts against the settlers.

## We Hold These Truths

Massasoit was born about 1590, near present Bristol, Rhode Island, and died in 1661. He was the grand sachem—in effect, the intertribal chief—of the Wampanoags of present Massachusetts and Rhode Island.

When the first English colonists arrived in New England, there began a pattern that would be repeated again and again throughout eastern North America. Massasoit rapidly befriended the Pilgrims, because he needed their help against his Wampanoag tribe's traditional rivals, the Massachusetts. Thus did the English get drawn into Indian politics at an early date. The friendship and alliance between the English colonists and the Wampanoags lasted until Massasoit's death.

His second son, Metacomet—called King Philip by the English—fearful of the colonists' insatiable land hunger, waged the costly King Philip's War (1675) against the colonists.

At first, King Philip's War consisted of a pattern of Indian raid and colonial reprisal, a string of murders and ambushes followed by mostly fruitless retaliation from the colonial militia forces. As in the Pequot War, the disorganized, highly competitive colonists proved incapable of unified action, and, as the raids spread throughout New England, the colonies suffered heavy losses during the first months of the war.

Late in 1675, however, the New England colonies finally joined forces—even referring to themselves as the United Colonies—to launch the single bloodiest battle of the war. In the Swamp Fight of December 18–19, 1675, Plymouth governor Josiah Winslow marched a thousand-man army through a snowstorm to the stronghold of the Narragansett sachem Canonochet (at present-day Kingston, Rhode Island), where they slaughtered 600 Indians, more than half of them women and children.

The massacre didn't end the war, however; it only escalated the violence. During the early months of 1676, Indians almost completely destroyed Lancaster, Massachusetts. Medfield, Massachusetts was wiped out next, as was Providence, Rhode Island. Sudbury, Massachusetts, was attacked, and many smaller settlements were hit, some of them annihilated.

But, if anything, the Indians were taking worse punishment. During July 27–30, 1676, some 180 Nipmuck warriors—all that remained of the tribe's fighting men—surrendered in Boston. A few days later, on August 1, troops under Benjamin Church captured King Philip's wife and son, and on August 12 they closed in on Philip himself, holed up in a swamp.

One vital reason why the colonists were not even more badly devastated by King Philip's War was that almost as many Indians sided with the New England colonists as fought against them. The Mohegans, the remnants of the Massachusetts tribe, and most importantly, the Iroquois, all joined with the United Colonies against traditional native rivals, the Wampanoags, Narragansetts, and Nipmucks.

In the end, it was a colonial-allied Indian who actually shot King Philip. The war ended with his death, but it had already been devastating for colonists and Indians alike. During 1675–76, half the region's towns were badly damaged and at least a dozen completely wiped out. The fragile colonial economy had been flattened. Trade in fur and fishing was halted by the war. Some 3,000 Wampanoags, Narragansetts, and Nipmucks died, and many more were captured and sold into slavery in the West Indies. Among the colonists, one in 16 men of military age had been killed, making King Philip's War, proportional to the population at the time, the costliest conflict in American history.

# The French and Indian *Wars*

As costly as King Philip's War was, it proved to the colonists the benefits of united action. Without such cooperation, they realized, New England might well have been totally devastated. And now the colonies were about to be drawn into something more than a local war. Beginning in the late sixteenth century, a series of conflicts, collectively called the French and Indian Wars, were the New World theater of larger wars that engulfed Europe. These French and Indian *Wars* would culminate, in the mid–eighteenth century, in *the* French and Indian *War*, the New World phase of the Seven Years' War, which many historians have described as the first "world" war.

## King William's War

The first of the French and Indian Wars was the American phase of the War of the League of Augsburg. It began this way.

England's King William III ascended the throne in 1689, after the Catholic James II, brother of Charles the II and son of the executed king, Charles I, had been ousted in a Protestant revolt. No sooner had he assumed power than William, on May 12, 1689, committed Britain to a Grand Alliance, joining the League of Augsburg and the Netherlands to oppose the French invasion of the Rhenish Palatinate. The result was an eight-year War of the League of Augsburg.

The struggle spread to America, as King William's War, between the French (with their allies, the Abnaki Indians of Maine) and the English, who secured a few allies among the tribes of the *Iroquois League*.

In Europe, the War of the League of Augsburg was fought by formally arrayed armies on open fields of battle. But in America, a new kind of warfare was born.

In 1689, Louis XIV dispatched Louis de Buade, comte de Frontenac to New France as the colony's governor. Frontenac had served in this capacity before (from 1672 to 1682), but he had ruled with such a stern hand that he was recalled to France at the earnest request of those he governed. The Sun King realized that a stern hand was precisely what the colonies now most needed, and the irascible 70-year-old Frontenac was prepared to deliver.

Frontenac's grand ambition was to invade New York. But as soon as he reached New France, he realized that he did not have the manpower for such an invasion. Indeed, he saw that he didn't have the military strength to face the British in anything like open battle. Nothing daunted, Frontenac decided to fight what he dubbed "a little war." It would not be a war of great strategic actions or grand battles, but a combat consisting of wily ambushes, stealthy murders, and outright terror—mostly carried out by those the British feared most: France's Indian allies. Given time, *la petite guerre* would wear down the British and secure victory for France.

King William's War presents a dreary chain of raids and counterraids. Decisive battles were few, but misery and mayhem were plentiful. A *guerrilla war*? It was more a succession of murders and massacres. At last, in September 1697, the Treaty of Ryswyck ended the War of the League of Augsburg in Europe. With this, King William's War in America was also officially brought to a conclusion.

Yet, although sheets of fine parchment with elaborate signatures and bright wax seals might carry much weight in European palaces, in the wilderness of the New World, such trappings meant almost nothing. The raids and counterraids continued sporadically.

**Fightin' Words**

The **Iroquois League** is an ancient confederation among the Mohawk, Oneida, Onondaga, Cayuga, and Seneca tribes. In 1722, the Tuscaroras, refugees from North Carolina, migrated and became the sixth member of the league. At the height of their power in the mid–seventeenth century, the Iroquois League occupied territory stretching from the Hudson Valley to Lake Ontario, and controlled much more territory and dominated tribes far to the west.

**Fightin' Words**

In French, "little war" is *la petite guerre*, a style of warfare that relies on surprise raids, enabling the French colonists to utilize their Indian allies, and to force the more numerous English colonists to tie down men and money in frontier defense.

# Queen Anne's War

Nor did Europe long remain at peace after the Treaty of Ryswyck. At the dawn of the eighteenth century, a new conflict arose among the European family of nations.

England, Holland, and Austria were uneasy about an alliance that had been struck between France and Spain after King Charles II of Spain, a Hapsburg, died in 1700, having named a Bourbon (that is, originally a Frenchman) as his successor.

**Sites and Sights**

St. Augustine is the oldest city in the United States. The most spectacular remnant of its early Spanish days is the 300-year-old Spanish fortress that is now the Castillo de San Marcos National Monument. For information on the Castillo, phone 904–829–6506; for information on St. Augustine, call the Visitor Information Center at 904–825–1000.

The French, of course, were all in favor of this arrangement, and they enthusiastically backed Charles's nominee, Philip of Anjou, the grandson of Louis XIV. England, Holland, and Austria wanted no Frenchman on the Spanish throne, and they championed the Bavarian Archduke Charles, second son of the Hapsburg emperor Leopold I. To enforce their choice, England, Holland, and Austria formed a fresh Grand Alliance in 1701. The following year, on May 4, 1702, the War of the Spanish Succession was declared between the Grand Alliance and France and Spain.

The European conflict was imported to America as Queen Anne's War, which got under way on September 10, 1702, when the South Carolina legislature authorized an expedition to seize the Spanish-held fort and town of Saint Augustine, Florida. A combined force of 500 colonists and Indians was unable to breach the fort's walls, so they contented themselves with setting St. Augustine to the torch.

The act brought the usual reprisals, in the form of counterraids from Spanish-allied Appalachee Indians. In response, South Carolina governor James Moore personally led a force of militiamen and Chickasaws in a murderous sweep of western Florida during July 1704. Seven villages and 13 Spanish missions (out of 14 in the area) were burned, and the hapless Appalachee were almost entirely annihilated as a tribe. Moore's expedition scorched a path into the bosom of French Louisiana. French colonial authorities scrambled to block the invasion, plying Choctaws, Cherokees, Creeks, and Chickasaws with trade goods and trinkets to win allies. The Chickasaws remained loyal to the English, the Cherokees declared neutrality, and the Creeks divided their allegiance between the English and the French.

But the powerful Choctaws eagerly joined the French, reasoning that it was preferable to share their country with relatively few French settlers than to relinquish it altogether in a massive invasion of Englishmen. The Choctaws effectively checked Moore's advance into Louisiana.

In the meantime, the French were having even more success in recruiting Indian allies far to the north. At the behest of New France, the Abnakis tore through the English settlements of Maine. Still farther north, in Nova Scotia, during July 1704, Benjamin Church, hero of King Philip's War (but now so aged that he had to be carried into battle on a litter), visited terror upon the French Acadian settlements of Minas and Beaubassin. Next month, the French and Indian forces retaliated by destroying the English settlement at Bonavista, Newfoundland.

The war ranged from Saint Augustine, Florida to St. Johns, Newfoundland (captured by the French just before Christmas 1708). Again, no titanic battles were fought between great armies, but, all along the coast and into the interior, people were murdered and settlements burned.

Through 1710, the war went badly for the British colonies. Desperate colonial authorities sent a delegation of loyal Mohawk chiefs to the court of Queen Anne in England. It was a brilliant public-relations move, designed to secure more royal aid for the war. The canny colonials left nothing to chance. They dressed the Indian ambassadors in "savage" attire—purchased from a London theatrical costumer.

Queen Anne was thrilled. She dispatched to the colonies a contingent of royal troops under Col. Francis Nicholson and a naval fleet commanded by Sir Francis Hobby. On October 16, 1710, the major Nova Scotia town of Port Royal fell to the British, followed by all of Acadia the next summer. An attempt to invade Quebec failed horribly, however, when the invasion fleet was shipwrecked at the mouth of the St. Lawrence, a loss of 1,600 men.

In 1712, a large overland invasion also faltered. By this time, however, Louis XIV was weary of war and burdened by the heavy debt his grand designs had accumulated. Moreover, the cause of the War of the Spanish Succession had become moot. The Grand Alliance's candidate for the Spanish throne, the Archduke Charles, had ascended to the Austrian throne in 1711. Since Britain and the Netherlands did not want to see Spain and Austria united, any more than Spain and France, the Grand Alliance lost its will to prosecute the war against Philip of Anjou. The Treaty of Utrecht, concluded on July 13, 1713, ended both the American and European wars. Hudson Bay and part of Acadia became English possessions, while the St. Lawrence islands fell to France. As for the Abnakis, they pledged allegiance to the British Crown, but nevertheless would continue to raid Maine for years to come.

## Wars Against the Tuscarora and Yemasee

Just as Queen Anne's War was cooling off, the Tuscarora Indians in North Carolina were becoming increasingly desperate. For years, they had been cheated and generally abused by colonial traders. Not only had they been swindled, but some of their number had been abducted and sold into the West Indies slave trade. The tribe wanted no war, so, in 1709, they petitioned the government of Pennsylvania for permission to migrate to that commonwealth. Pennsylvania authorities were willing to welcome the Tuscaroras, but the government of North Carolina refused to let them go. North Carolinians, after all, enjoyed the profit they made from the Tuscaroras.

In 1710, a Swiss entrepreneur, Baron Cristoph von Graffenried, established the settlement of New Bern at the junction of the Neuse and Trent rivers in North Carolina. The baron did not offer to purchase land from the Tuscaroras: With the blessing of North Carolina's surveyor general, he stole it, and started to drive the Indians off. The Tuscaroras could stand no more. On September 22, 1711, they attacked New Bern, killing 200 settlers, including 80 children. Von Graffenried was captured, but released. He negotiated a peace, but one of his colonists, William Brice, hungry for vengeance, captured a local chief of the Coree tribe (allied to the Tuscaroras) and roasted him alive. This outrage renewed the war, which was marked by great cruelty and widespread torture on both sides.

**Voices of Liberty**

"It is utterly impossible that the whites and Indians should ever live together and agree. The nature of things is against it, and the very difference between the two, that of colour, perceptible to our most ready sentinel, the sight, must always constitute them an inferior caste in our minds."

—William Gilmore Simms, in *The Yemassee* (1835), a novel about the Yemassee War

The colony of North Carolina called on South Carolina for help, and, in 1713, South Carolina's Col. James Moore contributed 33 militiamen and a thousand loyal Indians to join the troops of North Carolina. He led this combined force in a strike against all of the principal Tuscarora settlements. Hundreds of Tuscaroras perished, and some 400 were captured and sold into slavery to offset the costs of the campaign. A peace treaty was signed in 1715. Those Tuscaroras who managed to escape death or enslavement moved north to New York. In 1722, they were admitted into the Iroquois League as its "sixth nation."

But peace was a fleeting thing in the colonial southland. The very year of the defeat of the Tuscaroras, 1715, the Yemasees of South Carolina attacked their white neighbors for much the same reasons that had motivated the Tuscaroras: abuse, fraud, and enslavement. South Carolina governor Charles Craven enlisted the aid of Cherokees to hunt down the Yemasees to the point of tribal extinction.

# King George's War

The war named for England's George II began not with a murder or the seizure of land, but with the taking of an ear.

After Queen Anne's War, England and Spain concluded the *asiento*, a contract permitting the English to trade with the Spanish colonies in goods and slaves. When British traders almost immediately abused the privileges granted by the asiento, Spanish officials responded energetically. One British captain, Robert Jenkins, claimed that he had had an ear cut off during an interrogation by Spanish coast guards. Historians doubt his tale (he probably lost his ear in a barroom brawl), but his countrymen believed him, and in 1739 declared war on Spain, the "War of Jenkins' Ear." Within a year, the War of Jenkins's Ear had melted into a larger conflict. In Europe, it was called the War of the Austrian Succession (1740–48).

The death of the Holy Roman Emperor Charles VI in 1740 brought several challenges to the succession of his daughter Maria Theresa as monarch of the Hapsburg (Austrian) lands. Eager to lay claim to the Hapsburg territories, King Frederick the Great of Prussia invaded Silesia. France, Spain, Bavaria, and Saxony aligned themselves with Frederick's Prussia, while Britain came to the aid of Maria Theresa. As was true of the early European wars, combat spread to the colonies. Here, the fighting was called King George's War.

## We Hold These Truths

An account by a local historian concerning one Eunice Allen, a young resident of Fort Massachusetts at the western foot of Hoosac Mountain, paints a grisly picture of frontier combat during King George's War:

*A Mr. Eleazer Hawks was out hunting partridges on the hills, where the Indians lay .... He saw a partridge, and shot it. This alarmed the Indians, who supposed they were discovered. They immediately killed and scalped Mr. Hawks, and then proceeded to attack [others] .... [The father of Eunice Allen] was overpowered ... shot, and horribly mangled .... Miss Allen ... endeavoring to make her escape, ... was pursued by an Indian with an uplifted tomahawk and a gun .... The Indian overtook her, and buried his tomahawk in her head, and left her for dead .... [Later] an uncle came to her, discovered signs of life, and conveyed her home. Her wound was dressed by Dr. Thomas Williams, who took from it considerable quantities of brain.*

Eunice Allen recovered and lived into her 80s.

In the North, Massachusetts governor William Shirley commissioned Col. William Pepperell (1696–1759) of Maine to lead a New England militia force, supported by a Royal Navy squadron, against the heavily fortified French stronghold at Louisbourg on Cape Breton, Nova Scotia. The English laid siege to the fortress for 49 days during April–June 1745, finally forcing its surrender. While this was going on, however, the French and their Indian allies were busy raking the English settlements of northern New England and New York. This triggered combined English and Iroquois reprisals against French Canada during 1746–48.

In the South, Spain offered freedom to any slaves who could escape from South Carolina to Florida, sparking the Stono Rebellion of 1739, when about a hundred slaves killed their masters and tried to escape southward. South Carolina then organized a major expedition against Saint Augustine, led by Georgia's James Oglethorpe in 1740, but failed to take the Spanish fort there. Spain retaliated with an attempt to conquer Georgia and South Carolina in 1742, also a failure. Different Indian tribes raided British and Spanish settlements and each other, so that the frontier was an unstable and dangerous place throughout this war.

**Fightin' Words**

Many peace treaties specified a return to the *status quo ante bellum*—conditions as they were before the war. The Treaty of Aix-la-Chapelle restored the status quo ante bellum as far as territory was concerned, but one important loss to the British was that they had to give up the asiento, which they had forced Spain to grant in 1713.

By 1748, the war was over—and absolutely nothing had been officially settled. The Treaty of Aix-la-Chapelle ended the War of the Austrian Succession as well as King George's War, restoring (as the language of the treaty put it) the *status quo ante bellum*: the way things were before the war.

Nothing had *officially* changed, but, in fact, King George's War had served to crystallize the enmities and alliances among the French, the Indians, and the English. The colonies were primed for another war. They did not have long to wait, and this one would be far worse.

# The French and Indian War

On March 27, 1749, less than a year after signing the Treaty of Aix-la-Chapelle, King George II granted huge tracts of wilderness to a group of investors calling themselves the Ohio Company.

There was a royal catch, however. The grant stipulated that, within seven years, the Ohio Company had to plant a settlement of 100 families and build a fort for their protection. Spurred by this stipulation, the company aggressively promoted settlement, which promptly rekindled the hostility of the French and their Indian allies, who feared an English invasion.

## France and England Stake Their Claims

Rightly so. During 1749, British traders penetrated territories that had been the exclusive province of the French. In response, on June 26, 1749, Roland-Michel Galissonière, marquis de La Galissonière, governor of New France, sent Captain Pierre-Joseph Céleron de Blainville with 213 men to the Ohio country. By November 20, 1749, Céleron had made a round trip of 3,000 miles, burying at intervals lead plates inscribed with France's claim to sovereignty over the territory. He had, in fact, engraved into the soil the lines of battle.

In August 1749, La Galissoniére was replaced as governor by Jacques-Pierre de Jonquiére, marquis de La Jonquiére. The new governor realized that it would take more than buried lead plates to seize control of North America. He began to build forts.

While Jonquiére erected his outposts, an English trader named Christopher Gist negotiated a treaty, in 1752, at Logstown (Ambridge), Pennsylvania, between Virginia and the Ohio Company on the one hand and the Six Iroquois Nations, the Delawares, Shawnees, and Wyandots on the other. This agreement secured for Virginia and for the Ohio Company deeds to the vast Ohio lands—essentially, the area encompassed by today's Midwest east of the Mississippi River.

English authorities had little time to celebrate the treaty, however, because, during 1752, French-allied Indians drove the English out of the Ohio country, and Ange Duquesne de Menneville, marquis Duquesne, yet another new governor of New France, took up where Jonquiére had left off, building a chain of forts between Lake Erie and the Ohio River.

Duquesne nearly overplayed his hand. His construction was so aggressive that some Indians, now alarmed by French incursions, made overtures of alliance to the English. English colonial officials, however, responded contemptuously to these overtures. In doing so, Britain lost many opportunities to create key alliances.

## First in War: George Washington Fights

Just as British governors and administrators were alienating the Indians, Lord Halifax, in London, was pushing the British cabinet toward an outright declaration of war against France. His argument was that the French, by trading throughout the Ohio Valley, had invaded Virginia. The war fever spread from London back to Virginia. There, Governor Robert Dinwiddie commissioned a 21-year-old Virginia militia captain named George Washington to carry an ultimatum to the French "invaders." It was a simple message: *Leave voluntarily or be evicted by force.*

Washington set out from Williamsburg, Virginia's capital, on October 31, 1753 and delivered the ultimatum to the commandant of Fort LeBoeuf (modern-day Waterford, Pennsylvania) on December 12, 1753. The fort's commandant, a Captain Legardeur, 30 years older than the callow Washington, was polite but firm in his refusal to surrender the fort, and Governor Dinwiddie responded by ordering the erection of a British fort at the "forks of Ohio," the junction of the Ohio, Monongahela, and Allegheny rivers, the site of present-day Pittsburgh. Dinwiddie reasoned that whoever dominated the forks would thereby control the gateway to the Ohio country—the vast region beyond the Allegheny Mountains.

While Dinwiddie jousted with the French in the Ohio country, British authorities in Nova Scotia issued a demand to the Acadians there, the French-speaking Roman Catholic farmers and fishermen who freely intermarried with the Micmac and Abnaki Indians. They must swear loyalty to the British crown.

Pity the poor Acadians. Their misfortune was to live in the middle of the most abundant fishery in the world. All of Europe wanted control of these waters. If the British threatened the Acadians with expulsion from Nova Scotia, the French, in turn, menaced them with a promise to turn their Indian allies against any Acadian who took a loyalty oath to King George III.

While tensions mounted in Nova Scotia, they exploded at the forks of the Ohio. The French had hung back, watching construction of Dinwiddie's fort. Then they stopped watching and, in April 1754, attacked. The badly outnumbered British garrison surrendered on April 17. Rechristened Fort Duquesne, the new outpost was immediately occupied by French troops and Indian auxiliaries.

Dinwiddie was unaware of this when he sent Washington—now holding the rank of lieutenant colonel—with 150 men to reinforce the fort. Enroute, on May 28, Washington surprised a 33-man French reconnaissance party and traded fire with them. Ten Frenchmen were killed in this, the first real battle of the French and Indian War.

Washington now realized that the French would retaliate in force. The young commander sought aid from his Indian allies, but only managed to gather a mere 40 warriors. Too late to retreat, Washington erected a makeshift stockade at Great Meadows, Pennsylvania. He called it Fort Necessity.

On July 3, Maj. Coulon de Villiers, brother of one of the men Washington's detachment had killed, led a force of 900, including French soldiers, Delawares, Ottawas, Wyandots, Algonquins, Nipissings, Abnakis, and French-allied Iroquois, against Fort Necessity. By the next day—the 4th of July—half of the rude outpost's defenders had been killed. Feeling that honor had been sufficiently served, Washington surrendered. He and the other survivors were permitted to leave, save for two hostages, who were taken back to Fort Duquesne.

## We Hold These Truths

The Albany Congress was convened from June 19 to July 11, 1754 for the purpose of creating a defensive union of the British colonies in North America. Convened at the behest of the British Board of Trade, its main purpose was to reinforce the loyalty of the Iroquois League, which wavered between the French and the British. The Iroquois attended the congress and accepted gifts and various promises, but refused to commit themselves irrevocably to the British cause. Benjamin Franklin, delegate from Pennsylvania, presented a plan for colonial union. After much discussion, compromise, and dilution, the plan came to nothing. Although the Albany Congress foreshadows later colonial union, it was a failure.

Sent to evict the French from the Ohio country, Washington had to retreat, and it was the British who were evicted. As they had in other times of crisis, the British colonies made a stab at unity, convening a special congress at Albany, New York, from June 19 to July 10, 1754. The plan of union the congress produced pleased no one. And while the Albany congress dithered, the French and their many Indian allies, acting from their base at Fort Duquesne, raided throughout Pennsylvania, Maryland, and western Virginia.

## *"Who Would Have Thought It?"*

After much delay, in December 1754, the English Crown authorized Massachusetts governor William Shirley to reactivate two colonial regiments. These 2,000 men were joined by two of the worst regiments in the British regular army. When the French upped the ante by sending more troops as well, British forces were expanded to 10,000 men—all under the command of Gen. Edward Braddock, brave, blustering, and utterly without imagination or charisma.

On April 14, 1755, Braddock unveiled his plan of attack. Brig. Gen. Robert Monckton would campaign against Nova Scotia, while Braddock himself would capture Forts Duquesne and Niagara. Governor Shirley would strengthen and reinforce Fort Oswego and then proceed to Fort Niagara—in the unlikely event that Braddock were detained at Fort Duquesne. Another colonial commander, William Johnson, was assigned to take Fort Saint Frédéric at Crown Point, on Lake Champlain, just north of Ticonderoga, New York.

Monckton and a colonial commander, John Winslow, scored early successes in Nova Scotia, capturing important forts. But Braddock had a mighty struggle just getting his Fort Duquesne expedition under way. A typical regular-army commander, Braddock was contemptuous of Indian allies as well as the provincials, as colonial troops were called. He alienated both and secured little cooperation. Some colonial governors even refused to collect the war levies needed to finance the expedition.

### We Hold These Truths

Not too long ago, American schoolchildren read *Evangeline*, an epic poem published in 1849 by Henry Wadsworth Longfellow. It takes as its subject the separation of lovers during the French and Indian War. In July 1755, the Acadians of Nova Scotia, finally refusing to submit to the loyalty oath the victorious British demanded, were ordered deported by Governor Charles Lawrence. On October 13, 1,100 Acadians were sent into exile, and, over the succeeding months, many more followed, perhaps 7,000 in all. They resettled throughout the colonies, but especially in Louisiana, where, through a contraction of the word *Acadians*, they became *Cajuns*.

These 2,500 men were well-equipped, but could make little progress in the forested and mountainous terrain. If Braddock and Washington had been patient, they would almost certainly have forced the French to abandon Fort Duquesne, as Gen. Forbes, leading a similar, European-style regular army, did a few years later, in 1758. However, Braddock yielded to Washington's misguided advice to divide the force, leaving much of the heavy equipment behind. As a result, it was a smaller and less well-equipped army that advanced on the French stronghold.

### Voices of Liberty

"He was a bad man when he was alive; he looked upon us as dogs, and would never hear anything what was said to him. We often endeavoured to advise him of the danger he was in with his Soldiers; but he never appeared pleased with us and that was the reason that a great many of our Warriors left him and would not be under his Command."

—Scarouady, chief of the English-allied Oneidas, speaking of Gen. Braddock

Among those most impressed by Braddock's force were spies sent out from Fort Duquesne. They nearly persuaded the fort's commandant, Claude-Pierre Pécaudy de Contrecoeur, to give up without a fight, but a fiery young captain, Liénard de Beaujeu, talked him out of it. His advice? Take the offensive. Attack. All that was available were 72 French regulars, 146 Canadian militiamen, and 637 assorted Indians. But Contrecoeur and Beaujeu did have the element of surprise on their side, and, on the morning of July 9, 1755, they sallied forth.

The French and Indians fought from concealment. The British regulars, making no attempt to adapt tactics to the wilderness, tried to stand and fire. They were mowed down. Soon, they panicked. Troops fired wildly. Some shot at each other. Others simply huddled together, like sheep. Braddock worked furiously to rally and regroup. No fewer than five horses were shot from under him. Then he himself was felled. Mortally wounded, he watched the rest of the disaster unfold. Of 1,459 officers and men engaged in the Battle of the Wilderness, only 462 would return.

George Washington emerged unscathed, though he had had two horses shot from under him, and his coat had been pierced through by four bullets. Immediately after this battle, Washington gained a widespread reputation as a courageous and lucky warrior, whose skilled leadership in the midst of defeat had enabled him to lead hundreds of soldiers back to safety. Although in fact he was partly to blame for the disaster, Washington began, in 1755, to acquire the fame that would later place him at the head of the Continental army in the Revolutionary War.

As for Braddock, his dying words expressed only incomprehension: "Who would have thought it?"

Beyond the immediate loss of life, Braddock's defeat was disastrous because many more Indians now turned against the British, and, in the panic of battle, Braddock's private papers were left behind. The French now had his war plan and reinforced vulnerable positions accordingly. In the meantime, the frontier regions of Pennsylvania,

Maryland, and Virginia were convulsed by Indian raids. By June 1756, British settlers in Virginia had withdrawn 150 miles from the prewar frontier.

### We Hold These Truths

British colonists, especially those in outlying regions, hated and feared the Indians to such a degree that, on April 10, 1756, the colonial council of Pennsylvania initiated a "scalp bounty" on Delawares. Fifty dollars would be paid for the scalps of Delaware women and $130 for those of each man above 10 years of age. Just how officials were expected to determine sex and age, let alone tribe, based solely on the look of a scalp was never specified.

The French and Indian War had begun in North America. In 1756, it began to creep around world. Prussia invaded Saxony, then, in 1757, the Holy Roman Empire (in effect, Austria) declared war on Prussia, which responded by invading Bohemia. Bound by a web of alliances and secret agreements, the French, the British, the Spanish, and the Russians joined what would be known to history as the Seven Years' War. More than 30 major battles were fought in Europe, India, Cuba, the Philippines—and North America. As it became apparent that the French and Indian War was no mere provincial conflict, France sent one of its best young generals, Louis Joseph, marquis de Montcalm, to take charge of Canadian forces on May 11, 1756.

The officers of the British regular army, in the meantime, had never ceased arguing with provincial forces. British high command removed any number of skilled, committed, and capable colonial officers, replacing them with unimaginative regular army commanders, including the exceptionally dim-witted and cowardly Maj. Gen. Daniel Webb. He led his troops at a snail's pace to reinforce Fort Oswego, which occupied a strategic position in upstate New York. Montcalm easily took the fort on August 14, 1756, while Webb was still 100 miles distant. With Oswego gone, Lake Ontario fell to the French, and it was now impossible for the British to attack Fort Niagara. Even worse, the Iroquois, still officially neutral, smelled incompetence and inclined more sharply to the French victors.

## Pitt Turns the Tide

If 1756 was a disastrous year for the British, it ended on a more hopeful note when, in December 1757, William Pitt became British secretary of state for the southern department, a post that put him in charge of American colonial affairs. Pitt succeeded in making Britain the victor in the war for a number of reasons, the most important of which was his lack of restraint when it came to spending money. Great Britain put more men, guns, and ships into action under Pitt than ever before. Pitt found the money for his war effort by immense borrowing that brought short-term victory, but created long-term financial problems for the Empire. Pitt also took command away from inept, politically chosen officers, and gave it to those with genuine military skill, including many much-maligned "provincials." Now the tide gradually turned in Britain's favor.

## We Hold These Truths

The Brits had one more major disaster in store, even after Pitt took over. Daniel Webb abandoned Fort William Henry to the command of Lt. Col. George Monro and a skeleton garrison of 2,372 men, of whom more than half were incapacitated by smallpox. Commanding 7,626 men (including 1,600 Indian allies), Montcalm took the fort on August 9, 1757. Although Montcalm promised Monro safe conduct for his garrison, he simply stood by as his Indian auxiliaries massacred the English troops, beginning with those who languished in the smallpox hospital. (After scalping smallpox patients, the Indians acquired the disease themselves, creating a devastating tribal epidemic.)

In 1758 British forces, aided by some New England militia, took the vital French fort of Louisbourg on Cape Breton Island. With Louisbourg in British hands, the French could no longer send supply ships into the St. Lawrence River. Rapidly, the trade goods that helped sustain France's alliances with Indians in the interior of the continent began to become scarce and the natives, realizing the weakness of France, began to abandon the French cause. Brig. Gen. John Forbes, chosen by Pitt to command the third British attack in this war on Fort Duquesne, reaped the benefits of the British naval blockade of French North America. As Forbes and his well-equipped regular force advanced into the wilderness, there were, once again, many delays, and when the main force became bogged down in the mud not far from the fort, one of Forbes's subordinates, Col. Henry Bouquet, lost patience and, on September 11, ordered 800 of his Highlanders to charge the fort. Although the Highlanders retreated after one-third of their number were slain, losses among the Indian allies of the French were so heavy that most of them, already wavering in their loyalty because of the lack of French supplies, abandoned the cause. Even worse for the French, a treaty was concluded at Easton, Pennsylvania, in October 1758 between the French-allied Delaware and the English.

Not until November 24 did Forbes finally advance on Fort Duquesne. But, as he did, a distant explosion was heard. Rather than allow the English to capture the fort, the French had blown it up. The fort may have been gutted, but the gateway to the Ohio country was now in British hands.

As 1758 marked the turning of the tide in favor of the British, so 1759 spelled utter disaster for the French. On September 14, 1759, after a series of defeats elsewhere, the loss of Quebec brought an end to French power in North America. It was the most famous battle of the war, a contest between British general James Wolfe, a moody introvert who loved to quote by heart Thomas Gray's "Elegy Written in a Country Churchyard"—"The paths of glory lead but to the grave"—and the great Montcalm of France.

**Voices of Liberty**

"The Treaty of Easton has knocked the French on the head."

—Col. Henry Bouquet, 1758

During the summer of 1759, Wolfe made a number of unsuccessful attempts to storm the French position at Quebec, but it wasn't until September that Wolfe succeeded in breaching the lofty fortress town's defenses. The climactic battle, on September 14, was over in 15 minutes, leaving 200 French troops dead and another 1,200 wounded; the British lost 60 dead and 600 wounded. Among the fatalities were the two commanders, Montcalm and Wolfe—the latter surviving just long enough to learn that he had achieved his objective.

For all practical purposes, the outcome of the French and Indian War had been decided in September 1759 with the surrender of Quebec. Yet the fighting went on, mostly between the English and Indians, until February 10, 1763, when the Treaty of Paris officially ended both the French and Indian War and the Seven Years' War. The French ceded the entire St. Lawrence Valley to Great Britain, and they divided Louisiana between Spain (which received New Orleans and the territory west of the Mississippi River) and Great Britain (which gained the territory between the Appalachian Mountains and the Mississippi). As a result of these concessions, the French no longer possessed an empire in mainland North America. Spain recovered Cuba (in compensation territories it lost in Florida and in the Caribbean) and France retained the Caribbean islands of Guadeloupe, Martinique, and St. Lucia.

# The "Provincials" Learn a Lesson

The French and Indian War was a prelude to the coming American Revolution. For one thing, it created a massive British war debt, which was the reason for the taxes that the Crown would levy on the colonies during the next several years. Those taxes would generate the colonial outrage that culminated in their war for independence.

The French and Indian War made the British Empire the world's most powerful state. Victories in North America, the Caribbean, Europe, Africa, and India proved the power of Britain's armed forces on land and at sea. Pitt's leadership had largely erased the impression left by Braddock's disastrous defeat early in the war. In newspapers, sermons, and private letters, many colonists expressed a common thought: They were proud to be members of the world's strongest, most prosperous, and freest empire. Except in the frontier regions, few foresaw in 1763 that in just over a decade, the empire would be on the verge of dissolution.

## The Least You Need to Know

➤ Colonial American history, before the Revolution, was filled with frontier warfare.

➤ King Philip's War (1675–1676) was the most destructive colonial war prior to the French and Indian War; in proportion to the population of the colonies at the time, it stands as the costliest war ever fought on North American soil.

➤ The colonial wars leading up to the French and Indian War solidified French and Indian alliances against the English and their comparatively few Indian allies.

George III

# Chapter 5

# All the King's Men

## In This Chapter

➤ The chaotic government of George III

➤ The king tries to fence the frontier

➤ Taxation without representation

➤ The Stamp Act and the Stamp Act Congress

➤ Colonial response to the Townshend Acts

The British military and colonial administrators saw the French and Indian War as a victory and a vindication. Not only had the Crown won control of the bulk of the North American continent, it had proven its ability to defend and protect its Empire.

The colonists had seen two very different sides of the mother country during the French and Indian War. On the one hand, they had seen British officers and administrators who were incompetent at their jobs and arrogant in their dealings with Americans. On the other hand, late in the conflict, the colonists had witnessed some examples of inspiring political and military leadership by British political and military authorities. The latter impressions were more recent, and had left a stronger mark, so that at the start of the 1760s, except in the frontier regions, Americans' loyalty to Great Britain was at its height. But this loyalty was not passive. Participation in the successful war against France and Spain had boosted American self-confidence, and the colonists now felt they deserved to play a more assertive role within the British Empire. Initially, the Americans did not seek independence (in fact, they abhorred the idea of leaving the Empire), but only wanted to throw their weight on the side of those competent and heroic British leaders, like William Pitt, whose policies had won the war.

This chapter shows how colonial loyalty to Great Britain turned into revolutionary fervor.

# "A Clod of a Boy"

The first of the British kings named George was a German nobleman, the *elector* of Hanover, who was deemed heir to the British throne by virtue of his being the great-grandson of James I. He ascended the British throne in 1714, reigned for 13 years, never bothered to learn English, and never really bothered to govern, occupying himself instead with a succession of mistresses. His son, the second George, did learn English, which he spoke with a heavy German accent, but was eloquent enough to express how he felt about his subjects: "No English cook could dress a dinner, no English confectioner set out a dessert, no English player could act, no English coachman drive, no English jockey ride, nor were any English horses fit to be ridden or driven. No Englishman could enter a room and no English woman dress herself."

Nor did George II have much love for his firstborn son, Frederick Louis, the Prince of Wales, whom he called "the greatest beast in the whole world," adding, "I most heartily wish he were out of it." Frederick Louis married Princess Augusta of Saxe-Gotha, and to them, in 1738, was born George III, one of eight other offspring, none of whom was very promising.

### Fightin' Words

An **elector** was a German prince in the days when the disparate German states were part of the Holy Roman Empire. Electors were entitled to elect the Holy Roman Emperor.

### We Hold These Truths

Like other members of his family, George III was plagued by mental illness; however, his first incapacitating mental breakdown did not come until well after the American Revolution, in 1788. He recovered the following year, and managed to reign, despite episodes of insanity, until his violent breakdown in 1811. At this point, his son, the Prince of Wales (and future King George IV), was appointed regent and ruled as such until his father's death in 1820.

Many modern medical scholars believe that George's affliction was not psychological, but physical. It is believed that he suffered from porphyria, an inherited metabolic disorder in which an excess of porhyrins, purple-red pigments in the blood, poison the nervous system, producing agonizing pain, mania, paralysis, and delirium—all of which the king suffered.

Young George was 11 years old before he read his first word and has been variously described as lethargic, apathetic, and childish: According to historian J.H. Plumb, he was "a clod of a boy whom no one could teach." His mother repeatedly admonished him: "George, be a king!" George ended up becoming king sooner than expected, because his father, Frederick Louis, died prematurely, killed in 1751 when his windpipe was fatally fractured by an errant tennis ball.

Upon the death of his grandfather, 22-year-old George III was crowned on October 25, 1760. He meant to prove the lifelong contempt of his parents unjustified. He was determined to *be a king*.

### Voices of Liberty

"Had he been born in different circumstances, it is unlikely that he could have earned a living except as an unskilled laborer."

—J.H. Plumb, British historian, about George III

## Writs of Assistance

Among the first of George's kingly acts was to enforce a series of *Navigation Acts*, the first of which had been on the books since the mid–seventeenth century. These acts restricted some colonial trade to dealing exclusively with the mother country and, in all other cases, ensured that the mother country would be cut in for a fat share of the profits. The Navigation Acts regulated imports as well as exports, specifying that most goods had to be purchased from Great Britain alone and that many items—the so-called *enumerated articles*—could be exported only to Great Britain or other British colonies.

Enforcement of the Navigation Acts depended on local customs officials in American ports, who were sometimes ready to accept bribes or favor friends and neighbors when enforcing the acts. Before George III's reign, imperial officials were willing to ignore much of the corruption and laxity in the enforcement of the acts, as long as the bulk of imperial trade flowed within legal channels. This toleration of breaches in the acts provided a beneficial flexibility in the mercantilist system. Historians have labeled this tolerant attitude *salutary neglect*.

In 1760, however, George III suddenly began to enforce the Navigation Acts more strictly. He tapped a law that had been enacted (but little used) by George II in 1755, authorizing royal customs officers to issue *writs of assistance* to local

### Fightin' Words

The **Navigation Acts** were a series of British laws enacted during the seventeenth and eighteenth centuries regulating and restricting colonial commerce. The Navigation Acts included a list of **enumerated articles**, items that the colonies could export only to Great Britain or to other British colonies.

provincial officers, which forced them to cooperate in identifying contraband and arresting anyone evading the Navigation Acts. The writs also gave royal officials the right to search not only warehouses but private homes—at will and without court order.

### Fightin' Words

**Salutary neglect** describes the longtime policy of the British mother country toward its colonies. Until the reign of George III, import-export duties and restrictions on colonial commerce were not enforced. **Writs of assistance** were commands compelling provincial officers to cooperate with royal customs officials in curbing attempts to evade commerce regulations and import-export duties.

## Colonial Cash Cow

Embroiled in the closing years of the French and Indian War, the colonies had little choice other than to accept enforcement of the Navigation Acts. As George saw it, enforcement was critical to the British economy. The war in North America, together with the concurrent Seven Years' War in Europe and other parts of the far-flung British empire, was draining the English coffers.

Although the Treaty of Paris humiliated France and effectively neutralized Spain's New World power in 1763, George's England was groaning under massive debt. To make the colonies pay for the expense of defending them, particularly after the outbreak of Pontiac's Rebellion (discussed later), George decided to use the Navigation Acts. In the past, the acts had been used to regulate trade in the British Empire, to encourage certain economic activities and discourage others. British merchants had made money by trading with America, but the British government received no taxes under this system.

Now, George III decided to make the acts into taxation laws. The colonists had always accepted the mother country's right to *regulate* trade, because many colonists benefited from the regulations. Americans accepted trade regulations right up to the start of the Revolution. What made the colonists angry in the 1760s was the use of the Navigation Acts to raise *revenue* for the British government. George III was doing what no British monarch had done before: tax Americans, though they were not represented in Parliament.

Not everyone in George's cabinet agreed that vigorously milking the colonial cash cow was a good idea. William Pitt opposed the harshness of the king's new policies. In response, George engineered Pitt's ouster in 1761 and his replacement by Lord Bute. Parliament did not take kindly to the king's imposition of his handpicked minister, and forced Bute's resignation in 1763.

During this critical period, when both England and her colonies needed a strong, unified government, George and Parliament created political chaos. Prime Minister Bute was followed by Grenville, who was soon replaced by Rockingham, and then replaced by the return of Pitt (now the earl of Chatham), who almost immediately retired because of mental illness. George kept the prime minister's post vacant for some two years, pending Pitt's recovery. The prime minister returned to office briefly, then retired once again and became a member of the Opposition.

At last, in 1770, George found Lord North, a man who willingly submerged his own beliefs and opinions in obedience to the king. He would serve as prime minister for the next 12 years, earning enemies on both sides of the Atlantic.

# Pontiac Rebels and the King Draws a Line

We will hear much more from Lord North in Chapter 7, "Tea Parties and Sons of Liberty." Let's return now to 1763 and the end of the French and Indian War.

The papers signed in Paris meant little to Pontiac, war chief of the Ottawa Indians. He called a grand council of Ottawa and other tribes, including the Delaware, Seneca (and elements of other Iroquois tribes), and the Shawnee. Pontiac then persuaded the assembled war leaders to mount an attack on Detroit and many of the other western outposts the French had just surrendered to the English.

The violence of Pontiac's Rebellion was even more brutal than that of the just-concluded French and Indian War. Gen. Jeffrey Amherst responded to the massacre of settlers by ordering his troops to take no prisoners. All hostiles were to be killed.

### We Hold These Truths

Gen. Amherst authorized a form of biological warfare against Pontiac's warriors, directing one of his officers to attempt to infect the hostiles with smallpox. This plan was abandoned for fear of spreading the infection among the white settlements as well; but Simon Ecuyer, a Swiss mercenary temporarily acting as commander of the besieged Fort Pitt (the former French Fort Duquesne), called a peace conference with his Delaware attackers. As a token of esteem, he presented them with two blankets and a handkerchief. These had been provided by Capt. William Trent from the fort's smallpox hospital. "I hope they will have the desired effect," Trent remarked to Ecuyer.

They did. An epidemic decimated the Delaware tribe.

When news of Pontiac's Rebellion reached Britain, George III's government reversed Amherst's policy of destroying the Indians, and opted for the more practical policy of pacification. A royal proclamation was issued, forbidding whites from settling beyond the Appalachians. This "Proclamation Line" was not a permanent prohibition of western settlement, but a temporary measure designed to restore stability. Having fought a costly war to gain the trans-Appalachian region, the British were not going to abandon the idea of colonizing it. Individual frontiersmen, impatient even of temporary rules, defied the proclamation, crossed the mountains, and often seized land. This stirred up violence, which quickly spread throughout the frontier. The British decided that, in future, negotiated treaties would have to precede any settlement, and that there should be a clear demarcation of Indian and white territory. Sir William Johnson, a New Yorker married to an Iroquois woman of high rank, Mary Brant, was appointed chief negotiator. Knowledgeable of Indian culture, he managed to pacify one tribe after another, finally bringing Pontiac's Rebellion to an end in 1766. Almost immediately afterwards, he negotiated further treaties to open up limited sections of the trans-Appalachian west to settlers. From 1768 onward, new colonies were being projected for the west, and legal, orderly settlement began.

## We Hold These Truths

One of the most famous western pioneers of this period was Daniel Boone. Bankrolled by North Carolina entrepreneur Richard Henderson, Boone explored land Henderson planned to buy from the British government to set up a new colony called Transylvania in what is now Kentucky.

Boone was born in 1734 in southern Pennsylvania and, at age 19, moved with his family to Yadkin County on the North Carolina frontier. While serving under George Washington during General Braddock's disastrous campaign against Fort Duquesne (Chapter 4), Boone heard about Kentucky from a fellow volunteer. Toward the end of the French and Indian War, Boone traveled to Kentucky, where he often spent months alone, hunting deer and selling the skins. Later, believing that a fortune was to be made in opening up the territory to settlement, he began to lead groups of settlers into the land, placing them around the town he had founded, Boonesborough.

Colonists reacted in different ways to the new policy of western settlement. Wealthy Americans from coastal regions approved of the policy, and many prominent men (including Benjamin Franklin) bought western lands that they hoped they could sell later for a profit. Some frontiersmen approved, also, because the new policy brought security to the west, long ravaged by Indian raids. There were other frontier folk, however, who could not or did not want to pay for land. These men continued to seize lands illegally, often suffering from Indian counter-attacks as a result.

Pontiac's Rebellion added to Britain's costs of governing its empire. Large numbers of troops had to be garrisoned in forts spread throughout the region. Regular gifts and subsidies to the Indians were necessary to preserve peace. Lands could only be purchased from the natives by providing still more goods and cash. All these costs helped confirm George III's fatal decision to raise revenue from his American colonists. After all, he reasoned, the Americans would benefit more than anybody else from the pacification and settlement of the west.

# No Taxation Without Representation

During the premiership of Lord Grenville, with the endorsement of King George, the first of a series of colonial taxation acts, the Grenville Acts, were pushed through Parliament. These heavy import and export duties (which you'll read about next) outraged the colonists. To begin with, the colonies had been pounded by a business recession in the wake of the French and Indian War. But, economic hardships aside, it was not the tax that stung so much as being taxed without the benefit of Parliamentary representation.

This concept is a central cause of the Revolution. The colonists didn't enjoy paying taxes, but most were willing to pay their share of the costs of government—provided that they had a voice in that government. Representation was a basic English right, guaranteed in the Magna Carta in 1215. Indeed, no one on either side of the Atlantic would argue against this. They just interpreted it differently.

Only Parliament—not the king—could levy taxes. The colonists argued that they were not represented in Parliament, whereas the people of the mother country were. The Crown countered that members of Parliament did not represent the particular districts that elected them, but rather interest groups, such as doctors, lawyers, merchants, the landed gentry, and so on. In this sense, then, the colonists were given as much representation as anyone in the mother country. But the colonists persisted: This was not true representation. Members of Parliament were elected from the population of the mother country, not from the colonies.

In 1761, the distinguished Boston lawyer James Otis resigned from a lucrative position as the king's advocate general of the vice-admiralty court at Boston. His conscience would not allow him to argue on behalf of the writs of assistance, and, on February 24, 1761, he made a speech against the writs. John Adams heard it and took notes. Sixty years later, he wrote his recollection that "Otis was a flame of fire! ... He burned everything before him. American independence was then and there born."

Adams also remembered a ringing phrase of one of Otis's later speeches: "Taxation without representation is tyranny." It became the slogan that helped drive the Revolution.

*Engraving of Charles
Willson Peale's portrait of
John Adams.*
(Image from the National Archives)

## *The Sugar Act*

Stricter enforcement of old trade regulations was irritating, especially when harsh enforcement methods, such as the writs of assistance, were used. Yet the most important colonial protest arose against wholly new kinds of acts designed to raise revenue from the colonies. The first of those was the Sugar Act of 1764. It replaced an earlier measure, the Molasses Act of 1733, which had prohibited imports of molasses (from which New Englanders made rum) from the French and Dutch West Indies. Colonists forced to depend on molasses from the British West Indies had grumbled about the earlier act, but had not contested its legality, because it fell within Parliament's accepted power of regulating trade. The Sugar Act of 1764 was different, however. The purpose was to raise revenue for the British government. Although this act now legalized imports of molasses from the French and Dutch West Indies, it taxed these imports. Every time a colonist purchased non-British molasses to make rum, he would be paying taxes that no elected colonial representative had agreed to.

In addition to the tax on foreign molasses, the Sugar Act ordered that all cases involving breaches of the Sugar Act and of earlier Navigation Acts should be tried in vice-admiralty courts, which did not use juries. Parliament's intention in giving the vice-admiralty courts jurisdiction was to avoid having cases decided before juries, where sympathetic locals sometimes decided cases in favor of their neighbors. To colonists, the extension of the power of vice-admiralty courts was

### Fightin' Words

The **Non-Importation Agreement**, concluded in 1765 and revived at various later dates, was a colonial boycott of British imports in protest against attempts to tax the colonies.

one of the most sinister aspects of the Sugar Act. Trial by jury and taxation by elected representatives were among the most precious liberties of all Englishmen. The colonists felt that the Sugar Act was depriving them of their basic rights as members of the British Empire.

The first colonial protest in response to the Grenville Acts was peaceful. On May 24, 1764, a Boston town meeting proposed that the colonies unite in a *Non-Importation Agreement*, pledging to boycott a wide variety of English goods. By the end of the year, a number of colonies had joined the boycott.

## The Stamp Act

Parliament should have taken heed of the significance of this protest, for it was a *united* protest. The idea of taxing the colonies had been approved by Parliament back in 1724, but no action had been taken. Most likely, taxation would have been accepted readily back then. The colonies were too weak, too disunited to have mounted an effective protest. Now, in the 1760s, after the colonies had passed through the crucible of the post–French and Indian War, it was too late.

Instead of taking heed, however, Grenville ushered the Stamp Act through Parliament, which was put into force on March 22, 1765. The Stamp Act taxed all kinds of printed matter, including newspapers, legal documents, and even dice and playing cards. All such items required a government stamp, as proof that the tax on them had been paid.

The purpose of the Stamp Act was to help defray the cost of maintaining British soldiers in the colonies. But colonists had had their fill of British soldiery in the French and Indian War, and they resented the tax. Worse, any infringement of the new tax was to be tried in the vice-admiralty courts rather than by local magistrates.

Response to the Stamp Act was swift. In England, one Isaac Barré was among a handful of members of Parliament who opposed passage of the Stamp Act. In a speech, he referred to the colonists as "these sons of liberty." The phrase appealed to Sam Adams, a Boston brewer, bankrupt business-man, and brilliant political agitator, who orga-nized one of the first of many secret societies that sprung up in the colonies. Adams's group, like the others that would quickly follow, called itself the Sons of Liberty, and members made it their business to pressure the stamp agents. The Sons were effective at intimidation: All the stamp agents they approached resigned.

**Sites and Sights**

The seat of much revolutionary thought is preserved in Colonial Williamsburg, the first American theme park (opened in 1934) to use history for amusement. Among the meticulously restored buildings in this capital of colonial Virginia is the House of Burgesses, where Patrick Henry made the "If this be treason" speech as well as the more famous "Give me liberty or give me death" speech on the eve of the revolution. Call 1-800-447-8679 for Colonial Williamsburg visitor information.

Down in Virginia, passage of the Stamp Act motivated Patrick Henry, fiery and eloquent member of that colony's House of Burgesses (the legislative body), to introduce the seven resolutions that became known as the Virginia Resolves of 1765. The seventh of these was key, for it asserted that Virginia's colonial legislature had the sole right to tax Virginians, and to legislate on purely Virginian issues. Parliament, of course, still had the right to legislate on issues that concerned the Empire as a whole.

Henry combined his sophistication as a remarkably successful attorney with his frontier Virginia upbringing. Having been raised far from the Tidewater aristocracy, he shared the independence and revolutionary leanings of the typical frontiersman. Most of all, he was a brilliant orator. He pushed the Virginia Resolves through the House of Burgesses with a speech that closed most provocatively:

> *Caesar had his Brutus — Charles the first, his Cromwell — and George the third — may profit by their example …. If this be treason, make the most of it.*

The resolves were passed on May 30, 1765.

In the meantime, back up north, John Adams, who in contrast to Henry, was Harvard educated and married into a prosperous Massachusetts family, drafted a Stamp Act protest on behalf of his home town of Braintree, Massachusetts. Sent to the Massachusetts legislature, "Instructions to the Town of Braintree" became the model other towns followed in setting forth colonial objections to the Stamp Act. Documents such as this and the Virginia Resolves were communicated throughout the colonies. Local in origin, the protests quickly became continental in scope.

## Quartering Act

At the same time the Stamp Act was legislated, Parliament passed the Mutiny Act of 1765, which was aimed at improving discipline among British troops stationed all over the far-flung empire. The Mutiny Act included a provision for quartering troops in private houses. An outrage to the colonists, they at first simply evaded this provision of the act by pointing out that it did not *specifically* apply to Britain's overseas possessions. This legalistic dodge quickly moved Parliament to pass supplementary legislation, the Quartering Act, which did eliminate the provision requiring private homeowners to billet soldiers, but also required colonial authorities to furnish barracks and supplies for British troops. The next year, the act was extended to require the billeting of soldiers in taverns and inns at the expense of the colonists.

Once again, colonial legislatures resisted, this time refusing to allocate funds for the support of troops. In part, this refusal was financially motivated, but it was also a refusal to acknowledge Parliament's right to pass laws that forced colonists to pay taxes without the agreement of their legislatures.

## The Stamp Act Congress

Each protest brought the colonies another step closer to union. Then, James Otis, the orator Adams credited with having coined the taxation-without-representation-is-tyranny slogan, proposed a larger and more formal step: a meeting of the colonies in what came to be called the Stamp Act Congress.

It took place in New York City from October 7 through the 25th, 1765, and included delegates from South Carolina, Rhode Island, Connecticut, Pennsylvania, Maryland, New Jersey, Delaware, and New York. Virginia, New Hampshire, North Carolina, and Georgia declined to participate.

The Stamp Act Congress produced a 14-point Declaration of Rights and Grievances (probably drafted primarily by John Dickinson, a political leader and theorist from Delaware and Pennsylvania). The most important points made in the declaration were that

> ➤ Parliament had no right to tax the colonies.

> ➤ The Crown's vice-admiralty courts had no right of jurisdiction in the colonies.

In addition, the Stamp Act Congress endorsed the idea of non-importation, helping to extend the boycott to all colonies. The declaration was sent to the king and to the Houses of Lords and of Commons. It didn't fall on deaf ears. Many politicians in England didn't share King George's and Lord Grenville's mercantilist view of the colonies. In Parliament, a movement to repeal the Stamp Act was organized even before the act was scheduled to go into effect, and William Pitt heartily embraced the Declaration of Rights and Grievances. Other members of Parliament were being pressured by merchants among their constituents who complained that trade with the colonies had plummeted by 25 percent because of the Non-Importation Agreement boycott. In the meantime, most colonial governments refused to enforce the Stamp Act. Only in Georgia was the law actually put into effect and, even there, only to a limited degree.

A frustrated Grenville responded to talk of repeal at home and to defiance across the Atlantic by recommending that royal troops be used to enforce the Stamp Act. To this, Benjamin Franklin responded. The Boston-born Philadelphia printer and entrepreneur, who had served as a member of the Pennsylvania Assembly, was now postmaster general of the colonies and also an agent for Pennsylvania. Stationed in London, his job was to represent the business interests of the colony, and now his eminently reasonable voice was heard above that of the strident Grenville. Franklin argued that the colonies should not pay the Stamp Tax and, indeed, could not afford to pay it. Moreover, he warned, military intervention would likely provoke outright rebellion.

Franklin was most persuasive. On March 18, 1766, the Stamp Act was repealed, bringing great rejoicing in the colonies. The celebrations temporarily drowned out protest over a piece of legislation enacted on the very day of the repeal. The Declaratory Act declared Parliament's authority to make laws binding on the American colonies—"in all cases whatsoever." Parliament had acknowledged colonial rights, only to deny them again.

# Townshend Tries to Cash In

Charles Townshend was a British politician of the most cynical and opportunistic sort. He so reveled in his own reputation for changing direction with whatever political wind prevailed that he nicknamed *himself* "the weathercock." British historian Sir John Fortescue described him as "a man of great cleverness, great eloquence, and no principles."

In August 1766, Townshend accepted the post of chancellor of the exchequer (the British equivalent of secretary of the treasury) under Prime Minister William Pitt. When Pitt suffered a mental breakdown, Townshend took control of the cabinet and muscled through a series of acts named for him. The *Townshend Acts* included the following:

➤ The Townshend Revenue Act

➤ An act establishing a new system of customs commissioners

➤ An act suspending the New York Assembly

The Revenue Act imposed duties on lead, glass, paint, tea, and paper imported into the colonies, specifying that revenues generated would be used for military expenses in the colonies and to pay the salaries of royal colonial officials. The latter provision took away from colonial legislatures the power of the purse, as far as royal colonial officials were concerned. Now these administrators were effectively rendered independent of local government. They answered only to the Crown.

Among the worst royal officers were the customs commissioners Townshend un- leashed upon the colonies. Only secondarily interested in enforcing the new and existing duties imposed by the mother country, their main purpose was what historian O.M. Dickerson has called "customs racketeering." Typically, their scheme worked like this: Customs commissioners would, for a period of time, purposely refrain from enforcing the complex technicalities governing the duties. Then, without warning, they would suddenly crack down, seize all merchant vessels that were not in compliance with the hitherto unenforced regulations, and assess huge duties plus fines. Of all funds collected, a third went to the royal treasury, a third to the royal governor of the colony, and a third to the customs commissioner who had made the seizure. If the merchant could not pay, the ship and its cargo were sold at auction, with the proceeds divided the same way.

If Townshend had set out purposely to goad the colonies into rebellion, he couldn't have devised a better way than the Revenue Act and the customs commissioners.

### Fightin' Words

The **Townshend Acts** consisted of oppressive taxation and customs legislation sponsored by Britain's chancellor of the exchequer Charles Townshend in 1767. They provoked much colonial protest and resistance.

But he did even more. Attached to the Townshend Acts was a provision, put into effect on June 15, 1767, suspending the New York colonial assembly because it had refused to authorize funds mandated by the Quartering Act. The assembly would remain thus suspended until it complied with the Quartering Act.

The consequences of this suspension, which extended into 1770, are discussed in more detail in Chapter 6, "Regulators, Rioters, and a Massacre in Boston," but its immediate effect was to underscore the sense that the colonies were being subjected to out-and-out tyranny.

# Letters Forged in the Fires of Liberty

"Champagne Charlie," as Townshend's parliamentary colleagues called him, did not live to witness the effect of his Revenue Act. He contracted typhus, a terrible scourge of the era, and died the very year his legislation was enacted.

For their part, the colonies responded to the Townshend Acts by reviving non-importation, initiating a boycott of British goods so effective that the Townshend duties were repealed on April 12, 1770—except for the duty on tea.

## *Massachusetts Circular Letter*

In addition to non-importation, the Townshend Acts prompted the Massachusetts General Court not only to oppose the acts, but to inform the other colonies of just what it was doing—in effect, urging the other colonies to do the same. The *Massachusetts Circular Letter*, drafted by James Otis and Sons of Liberty founder Sam Adams, was approved on February 11, 1768. It published to the other 12 colonies the following revolutionary propositions:

➤ That the acts were "taxation without representation"

➤ That governors and judges must not be independent of colonial legislatures

➤ That Americans could never be represented in Parliament

This last point was particularly important. Whereas some earlier colonial leaders had complained about lack of Parliamentary representation, the more radical leaders now observed that such representation was impossible for a colony distant from the mother country.

There was more. The *Circular Letter* ended with a call for proposals of plans for concerted resistance. Chiefly because of this, the royal governor of Massachusetts dissolved the Massachusetts General Court on the grounds of sedition. But it was too late. New Hampshire, New Jersey, Connecticut, and Virginia announced their endorsement of the letter, and the Massachusetts House of Representatives voted overwhelmingly against rescinding it.

# *Farmer's Letters*

While the *Massachusetts Circular Letter* struck a blow for liberty, another "letter"—or set of letters—achieved wider circulation and explained the colonial situation on a more personal and passionate level.

John Dickinson's powerfully reasoned *Letters from a Farmer in Pennsylvania to Inhabitants of the British Colonies* appeared serially during 1767–68 in the *Pennsylvania Chronicle*, but were widely republished throughout the colonies and in Great Britain. Dickinson wrote not as an orator or statesman, but person to person, arguing that Parliament had no right to tax the colonies solely for revenue—although he conceded that it did have the authority to regulate trade. He also eloquently attacked the suspension of the New York Assembly as a grave blow to colonial liberty.

The compelling power of the *Farmer's Letters* lay in their combination of plainspoken conviction and the soundness of their constitutional argument. Dickinson didn't merely argue that taxation without representation was wrong, he made a case that it ran counter to British law: not only violating colonial rights, but the rights of all English people. In this, he not only helped create colonial unity, but crystallized substantial British support for more liberal treatment of the colonies. Even more, the *Letters* began to make the situation of England's colonies known to all the world. The cause of American liberty had taken its first step onto a global stage.

---

## The Least You Need to Know

➤ Under King George III and his ministers, a series of old import-export taxes were enforced and new ones created in an effort to raise revenue to defray the costs of the French and Indian War and the costs of the ongoing defense of the colonies.

➤ British taxes were not only a great financial burden to colonies still reeling from the economic disruptions brought by the French and Indian War, they were perceived as tyrannical because they were levied on people who were not represented in Parliament.

➤ George's ministers, especially Charles Townshend, levied taxes and enacted other oppressive legislation that not only alienated the colonies from the mother country, but gave them incentive to unite with one another.

➤ During the crisis created by the taxes and other legislation introduced by Grenville and Townshend, a core group of revolutionary leaders, orators, and theorists began to emerge from the colonies, including James Otis, John Dickinson, Patrick Henry, and Samuel Adams.

# Chapter 6

# Regulators, Rioters, and a Massacre in Boston

Assaulted though they were by new taxes and confronted with apparent tyranny, very few colonists in the 1760s contemplated outright independence from Great Britain. Americans thought of themselves as English men and women who happened to have a dispute with their government. The dispute was serious and often bitter but they *were* English, first and last.

As it was, colonial leaders did not resort to violent protest, but to political appeals, petitions, letters, and pamphlets. At least, that's how it was done at first. This chapter shows how words were turned into bloody deeds in a series of violent encounters that were a prelude to revolution.

## Falling Apart at the Frontier

Most schoolbook histories of the American Revolution paint the struggle as beginning with town meetings and then playing out in a series of battles fought between red-and blue-coated armies in or near those towns. While it is true that such meetings were important, and that certain key battles were, indeed, fought between formally consti-tuted armies, revolutionary violence began as a frontier affair and, once the war was in full swing, most of the fighting took place where it had during the French and Indian

War: in the wilderness. The combatants, more often than not, were irregularly constituted forces, not formal armies, and, typically, Indians fought on one side or both.

Frontiersmen were fighting different battles from those that engaged members of colonial legislatures and urban mobs. While coastal elites protested against parliamentary taxation of the colonies, settlers on the frontier protested against the hypocritical failure of the coastal regions to grant representation to the frontier. Other frontier issues were the lack of courts and disputed land titles. In several areas, especially Vermont, the Hudson Valley, and North and South Carolina, violent uprisings, directed against fellow Americans rather than Great Britain, broke out during the decade before the Declaration of Independence. These uprisings left behind bitterly polarized societies. When the Revolutionary War broke out, frontier folk took the opportunity to settle old scores against fellow colonists. Much of the frontier divided into groups that sometimes labeled themselves "patriots" or "loyalists," but that in fact had agendas entirely their own.

# The North Carolina "Regulators"

The frontiersman's most immediate dispute was not with King George III, but with the colonial governors and legislatures who clung to their coastal communities and refused to look very far west. Because frontier people felt they derived no benefit from the law, they began to take the law into their own hands.

About 1768, North Carolinian Herman Husbands organized a band of *Regulators*, a combination vigilante and revolutionary protest group. The North Carolina Regulators protested lack of representation in the provincial assembly, and they also railed against the embezzlement of public funds by officials of the crown. When their protests were ignored, they took action. On April 8, 1768, 70 Regulators rode into the settlement of Hillsboro, North Carolina, and freed a horse that had been seized from a local for nonpayment of taxes. They also shot up the house of Edmund Fanning, whom they perceived to be an agent of the eastern North Carolina elite.

**Fightin' Words**

**Regulators** were self-constituted, loosely organized frontier vigilantes and antigovernment protesters active in North and South Carolina chiefly during the 1760s.

Outraged, Fanning prevailed on Governor William Tryon to arrest Husbands and another Regulator leader, William Butler. This proved a mistake; for, suddenly, 700 Regulators materialized, and they were headed for the jail. Fanning prudently released his prisoners. The opponents and victims of the Regulators in the backcountry consequently sided with the British.

# A Bloody Act

In September 1768, Tryon led 1,400 troops against 3,700 Regulators. Although they enjoyed superior numbers, the Regulators saw that Tryon's men outgunned them, and they backed down.

But the troubles had only just begun. During the early days of 1771, Regulators seized Fanning, horsewhipped him, ran him out of Hillsboro, and then burned down his house. In response, the North Carolina assembly passed the "Bloody Act," which declared the Regulators guilty of treason and made them liable to execution.

## Crushed at Alamance

Come spring, and armed with the authority of the Bloody Act, Governor Tryon led a force in search of the Regulators. His plan was to link up with another body of troops, under General Hugh Waddell, at Hillsboro. Reaching this town, Tryon learned that Waddell's column, confronted by a large Regulator force at Salisbury, had halted. Tryon started toward Salisbury, and, on May 14, 1771, reached the Alamance River.

Five miles away, the Regulators were camped—some 2,000 of them, against Tryon's force of half that number. The governor had seen them back down once before. He knew that the Regulators had no real military leader, that they lacked artillery, and that some of their number were completely unarmed. He decided, therefore, to attack.

On May 16, Tryon deployed his men in two lines outside the encampment and demanded that the Regulators surrender. After arguing among themselves, the Regulators assumed defensive positions, and a battle opened. After about an hour's worth of sporadic shooting, the Regulators withdrew from the field. Each side had nine killed (some authorities report 20 Regulators dead) and many more wounded.

The next day, James Few, one the principal Regulators, was summarily executed. A dozen others identified as principals were taken back to Hillsboro, tried, and convicted of treason. Six were hanged on June 19; the other six, together with 6,500 settlers in the area, were compelled to swear their allegiance to the royal government.

Many of the Regulators left the region, migrating west of the Alleghenies. Both Tryon and Fanning also left the area, dispatched to new government posts in New York. The new royal governor, Josiah Martin, treated the remaining Regulators with much greater leniency, hoping in this way to secure their loyalty to the crown. Once the revolution broke out, however, the majority of Regulators fought on the side of the patriots.

Although there was no other pitched battle on the scale of Alamance in other colonies, there was violence a-plenty. In 1766 tenant farmers in the Hudson Valley, often migrants from Massachusetts, rebelled against their New Yorker landlords. In Vermont, a region claimed by both New Hampshire and New York, settlers with land titles granted by the former attacked those with titles granted by the latter. In South Carolina, a Regulator movement similar to that in North Carolina took the law into its own hands, sparking a contrary "Moderator" movement that tried to control Regulator excesses. During the Revolutionary War, these frontier regions again erupted in violence. Rival bands declared themselves for Great Britain or the United States, sometimes changing sides during the war, depending on which government would best serve their local interests.

# New Yorkers Fight the "Battle" of Golden Hill

If the frontier was turbulent as the 1760s ended and the 1770s began, so were two of the principal cities of the colonies. As discussed in Chapter 6, the New York Assembly had been dissolved because of its refusal to appropriate the funds required by the Quartering Act. The refusal came in 1766, and was accompanied by a great deal of tension between soldiers and citizens, which erupted into an armed clash on August 11, 1766.

### Fightin Words

Throughout the revolutionary period, Americans who supported the crown were called **loyalists** or **Tories** (the Tory party was England's conservative political party). Those who supported independence were called **rebels** by the British, but are known to history as **patriots**.

### Fightin' Words

A **liberty pole** was a tall pole erected as a symbol of defiance and rebellion. British colonial authorities would often tear down these symbols, which townspeople would then reerect. Liberty poles often served as the rallying points for anti–British protest and riots.

After the assembly repeatedly refused to support the Quartering Act, it was suspended on October 1, 1767. A new assembly was elected, but it, too, declined to cooperate. At last, in January 1769, a third assembly buckled to the crown's demands, voting £2000 for the quartering of royal troops.

By this time, opinion in New York was increasingly and irreconcilably polarized between *loyalists*, who supported the crown, and *patriots*, who demanded greater liberty. Alexander McDougall, a prosperous New York City merchant who led the New York chapter of the Sons of Liberty, published on December 16 a provocative broadside titled "To the Betrayed Inhabitants of the City and Colony of New York."

McDougall's broadside galvanized the outrage of New York patriots, inciting numerous clashes between citizens and soldiers after the New Year. At Golden Hill, patriots erected a *liberty pole,* which British soldiers unsuccessfully attempted to tear down on January 13, but succeeded on the 17th. Two days later, the Sons of Liberty responded with a flurry of additional broadsides, which provoked a riot at the site of the liberty pole.

Thirty or 40 redcoats were dispatched, bayonets to the fore, to disperse the rioters; the Sons of Liberty were armed with swords and clubs. A number of persons were severely wounded on both sides, but there were no fatalities. McDougall himself was arrested on February 8, charged with having written the first provocative broadside. Offered an opportunity to post bond, McDougall refused. He realized that his imprisonment made a powerful political statement, and he advertised himself as "at home" to those who would call on him in jail. Immediately, he was deluged with so many patriot visitors that callers were obliged to make appointments to see him.

On April 29, McDougall was arraigned, entered a plea of not guilty, and was at last released on bail. Although the case never came to trial because the state's witness died, McDougall was called before the assembly on December 13 and imprisoned for contempt until April 27, 1771.

# The *Liberty* Affair

People like Alexander McDougall were perpetual thorns in the British side. But McDougall was a New Yorker, and, therefore, something of an exception. Most New Yorkers were loyal to the crown. Boston was another matter altogether—a hotbed of rebellion. If New York City had one Alexander McDougall, Boston had scores of them.

By nature and inclination, John Hancock was no McDougall. Although both were prosperous merchants in their respective cities, Hancock was not a born leader. Even his business had been inherited from an uncle in 1764, and, although he joined the Sons of Liberty, he was not a likely candidate for rabble-rouser. But the arrogance of the royal government, in the person of its customs officials, pushed him over the edge.

## Sites and Sights

Golden Hill is the site of present-day John Street, a few blocks north of Wall Street, in Lower Manhattan. The "Battle" of Golden Hill was fought approximately where John Street now crosses William Street. Farther north, in Greenwich Village, colorful Macdougal Street and Macdougal Alley are named for rabble-rouser and, later, patriot general Alexander McDougall (despite the variation in spelling).

*Engraving of John Single-ton Copley's portrait of John Hancock.* (Image from the National Archives)

Like many men with money, John Hancock could afford to be contemptuous of those who deserved contempt. Among this group were the customs officials of Boston, and Hancock took every opportunity to annoy and embarrass them. For the British bureaucrats, Hancock's attitude was particularly galling because, no matter how contemptuous he became, he always obeyed the letter of law and was both meticulous and prompt in his payment of taxes and duties. So frustrated customs collectors began to bend the law themselves, in an effort to find something to prosecute Hancock for.

One day, two minor officers went below decks of Hancock's provocatively named sloop *Liberty*. The law clearly stated that they were not permitted below decks without permission, and John Hancock was not about to give such permission. Instead, he ordered the crew to eject them. (Most historians report that the inspectors were ejected, but Hancock biographer H.L. Allen writes that one official was sent home drunk, while the other was thrust into a cabin and the door nailed shut until the ship had been unloaded.) When the office of the customs collector complained to the attorney general of the colony concerning the disrespect shown his officers, that official ruled that Hancock had been within his rights. Once again, the customs collectors had been defeated by this most annoying of Boston merchants.

Then, on May 9, 1768, *Liberty* sailed into Boston with 25 pipes (some 3,150 gallons) of wine from Madeira. Hancock paid the required duty, unloaded the cargo, and took on a new cargo of tar and whale oil. Although the law specified that a ship's owner had to post bond for a new cargo before loading it, in practice, customs commissioners delayed the bond until the ship had cleared port. Hancock followed accepted practice rather than the letter of the law—a rare slip, which did not escape the notice of Joseph Harrison, the chief collector of customs. Moreover, Harrison believed the declared cargo was far below the ship's capacity, and he suspected (and hoped!) that Hancock was carrying more. He debated whether to seize the *Liberty*.

**Fightin' Words**

**Impressment** was the Royal Navy practice of kidnapping young men from merchant vessels (typically British or American ships) and from such sailor haunts as waterfront grog shops and pubs and "impressing" them into involuntary service as seamen on warships.

While Harrison pondered, two British warships, *Romney* and *St. Lawrence*, entered Boston Harbor. For the ordinary seaman, service in the Royal Navy was a grim fate. Captain William Bligh, whose name became synonymous with cruelty in *Mutiny on the Bounty*, was actually one of the Royal Navy's more enlightened and humane officers. Most were far worse. Little wonder, then, that the Royal Navy found few volunteers and relied instead on the practice of *impressment*, kidnapping young men (sometimes from other vessels, sometimes from waterfront grog shops) and "impressing" them into service.

The *Romney's* captain sent a press gang ashore. The gang entered a tavern and grabbed an American sailor named Furlong. But the waterfront crowd would have none of this. They hurled stones at the press gang, rushed them, and rescued Furlong. When the gang returned to the

*Romney* empty handed, the captain ordered the drums to beat to general quarters (preparation for battle). He trained his guns on the mob, but held his fire.

With the unerring bad timing of an inept bureaucrat, customs collector Harrison chose this very moment to seize Hancock's *Liberty*, adding insult to injury by using a boatload of armed sailors from the *Romney* to help him. The shore crowd saw what was happening, but was unable to move quickly enough to block the *Romney*'s longboat. *Liberty* was seized and towed alongside the British warship, under its looming guns.

Immediately, the patriot mob turned their rage on Harrison, his son, and another customs official, Benjamin Hallowell. The three were savagely beaten; the senior Harrison managed to get away, but his son was dragged by the hair through the wharfside streets, and Hallowell was left unconscious in a pool of his own blood. The mob then turned its fury on the homes of Harrison, Hallowell, and John Williams, inspector general of customs, breaking the windows of all. Other terror-stricken customs officials fled their offices and homes, seeking refuge aboard the *Romney* and then to the royal fortress known as Castle William.

Sam Adams and James Otis requested that the Massachusetts governor order the warship out of the harbor—lest a full-scale riot develop. Governor Francis Bernard replied that he would intervene to stop impressment—which he did successfully— and the customs officials offered to return Hancock's duties and those of others.

Having been thrust center stage in the drama of American liberty, John Hancock loftily declined the offer. No, he said, he preferred that the *Liberty* affair run its course through the courts. On March 1, 1769, in a rare prudent decision, the Crown simply dropped the case.

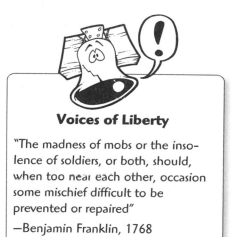

**Voices of Liberty**

"The madness of mobs or the insolence of soldiers, or both, should, when too near each other, occasion some mischief difficult to be prevented or repaired"

—Benjamin Franklin, 1768

## Unwelcome in Boston

As a result of the *Liberty* affair, the customs officials reported that Massachusetts was in a state of insurrection. The Crown reacted by dispatching two regiments of British infantry to Boston. They landed in October 1768.

*Lobsterbacks*, the Bostonians called the soldiers of the king. It was a term of utter contempt, a reference to the appearance of men whose loyalty was the product not of conviction but the lash. British soldiers were flogged for the slightest infraction, and a soldier's back typically bore the record of

**Fightin' Words**

**Lobsterback** was a mocking name colonists applied to British soldiers, whose backs often bore the scars of numerous floggings—the chief tool of discipline in the British army.

such punishment. As the Bostonians saw it, the British redcoats were not only the agents of tyranny, they were the beaten dogs of tyranny. And they would find no welcome, let alone quartering and feeding, in Boston.

# Taunts and Shots: The Boston Massacre

March 5, 1770 was gray, cold, and miserable in Boston, the ground snow covered. The hard life of a British soldier was particularly hard on days like these. The pay was meager to begin with, but even that wasn't all yours to keep. The cost of just about everything you needed, from the food you ate to the pipe clay required to keep uniform belts spotlessly white, was deducted from the tiny sums doled out by the paymaster. It was common, then, for British troops to seek outside work to occupy their off-duty hours and collect a little something to make ends meet. But times were tough for Boston civilians, too, and they did not take kindly to a lobsterback stealing scarce employment.

When an off-duty soldier sought work at Grey's Ropewalk—a wharfside establishment that made ship's ropes—a small riot broke out. The crowd continued to mill about the streets. At approximately 9:00 that night, what royal officials described as an "irresponsible mob of some 60 rioters" began to taunt sentry Hugh White, who was on guard outside the Customs House.

One young man, Edward Garrick, told White that his company commander was a cheat who had failed to pay his master for a wig. White called out for the accuser to step forward, and, when Garrick did, White struck him in the face with the butt of his musket. Another soldier chased the injured Garrick away at the point of a bayonet. The incident brought a bigger and bigger crowd. As more Bostonians arrived on the scene, a few citizens tried without success to calm the mob, which began to pelt White and other soldiers with icy snowballs. As for the soldiers, their commanding officers appeared, pleading with the crowd to be calm while they attempted to get control of their men. But their men were angry and not easily controlled.

"God damn your blood!" one enraged lobsterback screamed. "I'll make a lane through you all." Two officers tackled the man, and pushed him back into the guard barracks.

In the meantime, 40-year-old Captain Thomas Preston gathered seven soldiers to rescue Private White. When Preston arrived, he was approached by Henry Knox, proprietor of the popular London Book-Store and a future patriot general.

"For God's sake," Knox told Preston, "take care of your men. If they fire, they die!"

"I am sensible of it," came Preston's measured reply. Preston shouted an order to White to fall in with the detail of seven men he led. But when White tried to obey, the mob surged forward to prevent White's escape. Preston, unable to penetrate the mob with his troops, ordered them to form a defensive line where they stood. This served only to anger the mob further. They hurled ice balls as well as insults, daring "you sons of bitches to fire! You can't kill us all! Fire! Why don't you fire? You dare not fire!"

Preston hurriedly summoned Justice of the Peace James Murray and asked him to read the Riot Act, in the forlorn hope that a reminder of the severe penalties for rioting would sober the mob up. But they responded by hurling snowballs at Murray. Then a club sailed from out of the crowd and struck Private Hugh Montgomery, knocking him off his feet. Rising, he cocked his musket, and hurled the rioters' taunt back at the mob: "Damn you, fire!"

And Montgomery fired. Although the shot went wild, hitting no one, a merchant named Richard Palmes responded by striking out at Montgomery with the club he was carrying. Montgomery lunged back with his bayonet, and Palmes fled. The line that separates anger and violence had been crossed. Private Matthew Killroy leveled his musket at Edward Langford and Samuel Gray.

"God damn you, don't fire!" Gray called out. Killroy squeezed the trigger, a shot exploded, and Samuel Gray lay mortally wounded, a musket ball lodged in his brain. Just then, another musket sounded. Apparently it had been loaded with two balls, for Crispus Attucks, a 40-year-old runaway slave from the town of Framingham, took two rounds in the chest and died where he stood. The first man killed outright in the Boston Massacre, prelude to a war for liberty, was a black slave.

More shots rang out. Two more citizens were killed, and another fell with a wound that would prove mortal. After this: a dull silence, punctuated only by the sounds of the redcoats reloading. Then the crowd pressed forward again, and the soldiers, again, leveled their muskets.

But now Preston strode along the line of men, knocking each musket barrel skyward. "Don't fire!" he shouted.

Benjamin Burdick stepped out from the crowd and approached each of the British soldiers. "I want to see some face," he turned to Preston, "that I may swear to another day."

"Perhaps, sir, you may," Preston softly replied.

*The Boston Massacre as depicted by John Bufford. Unlike Paul Revere's more famous engraving, this one portrays the death of Crispus Attucks, the African American who may be regarded as the first fatality of the Revolution.*
(Image from the National Archives)

## We Hold These Truths

The name Crispus Attucks would have been unknown to history had he not fallen in the Boston Massacre of March 5, 1770. While most historians believe he was a black man, some argue that he was of mixed African and Natick Indian ancestry. Of his life, virtually nothing is known for certain. In the fall of 1750, a citizen of Framingham, Massachusetts advertised for the recovery of a runaway slave named Crispus, who is believed to have been Crispus Attucks. In the 20 years between his escape and his death, Attucks likely supported himself as a sailor aboard whaling ships.

The body of Crispus Attucks was carried to Boston's Faneuil Hall, where he was accorded the dignity of a martyr. The escaped slave lay in state there until March 8, when all five victims of the Boston Massacre were consigned to a common grave.

In 1888, a monument to Crispus Attucks was erected on Boston Common.

# Counsel for the Defense

A colonial court indicted Captain Preston and six of his men on charges of murder. The redcoats had every reason to believe that they would be delivered into the hands of the mob. The most prominent of Boston's Sons of Liberty, Sam Adams and the charismatic physician Dr. Joseph Warren, were doing their best to stir up and sustain the fury of Boston.

### Voices of Liberty

"Counsel ought to be the very last thing an accused person should want [lack] in a free country."

—John Adams, on volunteering to defend the British soldiers accused of the "Boston Massacre," 1771

Yet something remarkable happened. Two outstanding colonial attorneys, Josiah Quincy and John Adams—who would figure as one of the nation's most important founding fathers—volunteered to defend the accused. Mob rule, Adams believed, would be fatal to any people aspiring to be citizens of a free country. He was determined that the soldiers be accorded a fair trial.

The basis for the defense was that the men, threatened by a mob, had acted in self-defense. Adams and Quincy argued brilliantly, and it is a testament to the character of the people of Boston that the juries heard and heeded the lawyers' arguments with great impartiality. In the end, Preston and four of his men were acquitted. Two others were found guilty, not of murder, but of the lesser crime of manslaughter. They "pleaded benefit of clergy," an archaic plea in British law, which ensured that they would not suffer the death penalty. Instead, they were both discharged from military service with a brand on the thumb.

# The Master of Propaganda

Out of some 400 Bostonians present that March night, three were killed instantly and two subsequently died. To call this a "massacre" is an exaggeration, but Sam Adams was more than willing to exaggerate. He and Dr. Warren did their best to transform the riot into revolutionary propaganda. Indeed, some historians even believe that the Boston Massacre was no accident, but had been orchestrated by Adams.

Adams and Warren prevailed on the well-respected young Boston silversmith, Paul Revere, to make an engraving of the incident. It shows Preston, sword upraised, ordering his men to fire on the totally unarmed citizens of Boston. Pure fiction, of course, but many hundreds were hastily printed and distributed throughout the colonies.

Samuel Adams went on to prove himself a master of revolutionary propaganda, but his attempt to make the Boston Massacre a cause for immediate rebellion failed. Over time, the event would emerge as a milestone on the road to revolution, the first major incident that provoked widespread anti-British sentiment. Yet, in the short run, Adams's rabble-rousing was overshadowed by the outcome of the trials. For the most part, both sides felt that justice had been served.

Equally important, the Townshend Acts had been repealed in April 1770, and it looked as if colonists and mother country were starting to feel more kindly toward one another. This interval of good feeling would, however, prove to be nothing more than the proverbial calm before the storm.

---

### The Least You Need to Know

➤ The first prerevolutionary violence broke out on the North Carolina frontier when the "Regulators" rebelled against government dishonesty, inefficiency, and indifference.

➤ The Battle of Golden Hill, in New York City, was a riot in response to the suspension of the New York Assembly and the issue of quartering unwelcome British troops.

➤ The *Liberty* affair was a victory for John Hancock and the rights of colonial merchants, but it also prompted Britain to send troops to occupy the Boston garrison, a situation that led to the Boston Massacre.

➤ The "Boston Massacre" was a real—and tragic—event, but it was also a propaganda opportunity for Boston's Sons of Liberty.

➤ John Adams's and Josiah Quincy's able defense of the troops accused in the "Boston Massacre" scored an ethical and moral victory for the colonial cause.

# Chapter 7

---

# Tea Parties and Sons of Liberty

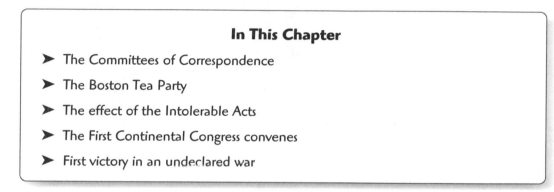

### In This Chapter

➤ The Committees of Correspondence

➤ The Boston Tea Party

➤ The effect of the Intolerable Acts

➤ The First Continental Congress convenes

➤ First victory in an undeclared war

The Boston Massacre did not have the effect Sam Adams and other radicals had hoped for. Not only did it fail to trigger an immediate rebellion, the subsequent trial and acquittal of the soldiers and officer involved actually calmed passions on both sides. Nevertheless, Adams and others kept the incident alive as a propaganda issue, and British authorities used it as an excuse to introduce into the colonies new restrictive measures. The revolutionary movement may have lost some momentum following the Boston Massacre trials, but events soon accelerated again.

This chapter shows how the Revolution assumed the form of an unstoppable juggernaut.

## Not-So-Secret Societies

Beginning in 1765, with passage of the Stamp Act, North American colonists began to organize—not to break off the connection with the mother country, but to protect what they believed to be the traditional liberties of subjects of the British Crown. The best-known and most effective colonial organization was the Sons of Liberty, which planned opposition to the Stamp Act in 1765. The organization began as a Boston group dubbed the Loyal Nine, and, as mentioned in Chapter 3, "The Colonial Way," they lifted their name from a speech by Isaac Barré, a liberal member of Parliament, who called the colonists "these sons of liberty."

Socially, the Sons of Liberty were a varied group. In January 1766, the Loyal Nine included a "distiller or merchant," a "brazier" (brass worker), a painter, a printer, a distiller, a merchant, and a jeweler. Samuel Adams, a member of the Loyal Nine and a founding member of the Sons of Liberty, was a brewer (but not a very good one; he ran his inherited brewery into bankruptcy), a political thinker, and a political activist. He served as a Boston tax collector from 1756 to 1765, but was so lenient that his supervisors found his collections £10,000 in arrears when he resigned the post after the Stamp Act was introduced in 1765. Collaborating with Adams in founding the Sons was Dr. Thomas Young, a radical, eccentric, self-taught physician.

*Sam Adams, patriot and master propagandist.* (Image from the National Archives)

## Rebels with a Cause

The Sons of Liberty came into being specifically to oppose the Stamp Act, and the Boston chapter served as the inspiration and model for chapters throughout the towns of the colonies. Soon, the Sons of Liberty were an effective network of colonial opposition to the Stamp Act.

Sam Adams and other revolutionary leaders understood that the key to opposition of the Stamp Act was unity. Adams used the Sons of Liberty to stage mass meetings, with the ultimate intention of transforming the entire "body of the people" into one great

Sons of Liberty organization. But the New York Sons of Liberty, not Adams and the Boston Sons of Liberty, made the first truly effective stride toward the elusive goal of colonial unity, becoming the unofficial hub of intercolonial communication. This network was formally dissolved after the repeal, but the revolutionary ties were never really unbound. Members still remained politically active, and they corresponded with one another on a regular basis.

In addition to coordinating protest and other action throughout the colonies, the Sons of Liberty were determined to maintain protest fervor while taking care that the revolutionary passion did not erupt into mere mob violence. Adams and others believed that mayhem and property destruction would alienate support. A key mission of the Sons of Liberty was to maintain public order.

### We Hold These Truths

Although the Sons of Liberty officially disbanded following repeal of the Stamp Act, the phrase "Sons of Liberty" continued to be applied to all radical or revolutionary colonial organizations. After the revolution, the Sons of Tamina was formed in New York City. Named after an Indian chief the organization called its "patron saint," the Sons of Tamina served as the model for the Tammany Society, which controlled New York City's infamously corrupt nineteenth-century political machine, Tammany Hall. Later in the 1800s, the Sons of Liberty name was appropriated by a number of singularly intolerant, anti-immigrant, and (usually) anti–African-American social organizations, such as the Sons and Daughters of Liberty, founded in Philadelphia in 1877.

## A Reign of Tar and Feathers

Although the Sons of Liberty worked to control mob violence, the organization also functioned as an instrument of coercion. Along with organizing opposition to the Stamp Act, the Sons intimidated into immediate resignation all the officials responsible for administering the Stamp Act in the colonies.

A favorite technique of intimidation was to resort to tar and feathers. A brutal and humiliating punishment, tarring and feathering was recorded in England as a routine judicial punishment as early as the twelfth century. Molten pitch or tar was poured on the victim, who was then covered in feathers. If he were particularly unlucky, tarred and feathered as he was, the victim might also be ridden out of town on a rail. Rails were logs split and hewn so that one surface of the log was a sharp-edged triangle. The victim was made to straddle this sharp edge, and the rail was hoisted on the shoulders of several men, who roughly jostled the mounted victim. Injury was typically severe, certainly painful, and often fatal. The Sons of Liberty singled out collectors of taxes and other Crown officials for such treatment.

# The *Gaspée* Burns

Assuming protest, political, police, military, and terrorist roles, the Sons of Liberty became a kind of shadow government in the colonies, at least until the repeal of the Stamp Act. The Boston Massacre threatened to bring back the Sons of Liberty in full force, but that furor soon subsided. Then came the *Gaspée* affair.

Narragansett Bay, off Rhode Island, offered an array of coves and inlets that made it a perfect haven for smugglers, who didn't bother to protest Crown duties and taxes, but merely evaded them. In June 1772, the Royal Navy dispatched the schooner *Gaspée*, Lt. William Dudingston, commanding, to put an end to the smugglers' activity there. Dudingston not only severely cut into Rhode Island smuggling, he managed to do so with such arrogance that he added the insult of his haughty insolence to the injury of loss of trade.

Rhode Island governor Joseph Wanton's threat to arrest Dudingston sparked a conflict with the fleet admiral. While the governor and the admiral exchanged heated letters, Dudingston and the *Gaspée* continued to go about their business. On June 9, Dudingston gave chase to a smuggler—only to run aground on a sandbar near Providence. Seeing the helpless condition of the despised vessel, Sheriff Abraham Whipple personally led a flotilla of small boats to surround the *Gaspée* that night.

Dudingston, already irritated beyond measure at having been grounded, called out to Whipple: "Who comes there?"

"I am the sheriff of the County of Kent, God damn you. I have a warrant to apprehend you, God damn you—so surrender, God damn you."

Dudingston refused, and the sheriff's men boarded the *Gaspée* by force. Dudingston aimed his sword at one of the boarders, who responded by shooting him in the groin. After surgeons stanched the skipper's wound, he and the rest of his crew were put off into boats. Whipple and his party then set the *Gaspée* aflame.

News of the *Gaspée* affair electrified the colonies. Colonists had captured and destroyed a hated instrument of enforcement of a hated tax.

# Sam Adams Brews a Revolution

The Crown made a half-hearted attempt to bring Whipple and the other perpetrators to justice. Officials threatened to transport them to London for trial on charges of piracy. Catching wind of this, Sam Adams organized the first Committee of Correspondence—really, a fully revived Sons of Liberty and often called by that name—to disseminate information and coordinate action.

In the end, the Crown declined to prosecute, claiming an insufficiency of evidence. In truth, it was clear that officials did not want to stir up colonial passions. But stirred they were—and, thanks to Adams, these passions were coordinated up and down the coast. The stage was set for the next bold act of protest.

## Anyone for Tea?

By 1773, most of the Crown's odious taxes on import commodities had been repealed, but King George kept a tax on tea primarily because he believed that "there must always be one tax" in order to preserve Parliament's right to tax the colonies. In principle, this might have disturbed many colonists; but, in fact, the tax was easily evaded. Colonial consumers bought smuggled tea from Dutch sources.

If anything, then, King George's tea tax was harder on the financially ailing East India Company than on the colonials. The chief reason for Parliament's decision to help the East India Company was that the company, in return for its monopoly, paid for all the expenses of the civil and military government of British India. If the company went bankrupt, one of the most important parts of Britain's Empire would be in difficulties. The Tea Act was aimed at helping India, rather than hurting the colonists. As happened more than once after the Seven Years' War, attempts to help one part of the unwieldy British Empire alienated another part. Crucial to helping the East India Company was boosting sales of tea.

Lord North proposed a swift expedient. The East India Company paid two taxes, one when it landed tea in Britain, whether for sale or transshipment elsewhere, and another tax when it landed a shipment in America. By means of the Tea Act (May 10, 1773), Lord North forgave the first tax and retained the lesser three-penny-a-pound duty due on landing in America. This would price East India tea cheaper than the smuggled tea, and the notoriously thrifty colonists would surely buy it. End of story.

Not quite. Instead of simply buying off American consumers, as he had thought would be the case, Lord North's Tea Act divided the American merchant community. In order to make the tea as cheap as possible for consumers, the Tea Act allowed the East India Company to sell its tea directly to American merchants, bypassing the British middle men. Americans who possessed connections with the East India Company would benefit from these contracts, and their competitors would lose out. These contracts to sell East India Company tea were potentially so lucrative that, if the tea were ever allowed to go on sale, many wealthy and influential members of the American merchant community would undoubtedly overlook their scruples about Parliamentary taxation and accept the tea. The powerful temptation offered to American merchants was what forced radicals in America to take drastic action against the landing of tea shipments. Traditionally viewed as alienating the American colonies, the Tea Act might also be seen as a clever way by which the British government might win influential support in the colonies.

Organized by the Sons of Liberty/Committees of Correspondence, colonial activists intimidated the consignees in Philadelphia, New York, and Charleston into resigning.

American captains and harbor pilots refused to handle the East India Company cargo. The tea ships were turned back to London from Philadelphia and New York. A ship was permitted to land in Charleston, but the tea was impounded in a warehouse, where it lay unsold until the Revolutionary government auctioned it off in 1776.

## The Party's On!

In Boston, as usual, something more dramatic happened. When three Tea Act ships landed at Boston Harbor, the Sons of Liberty prevented their being unloaded. For his part, Massachusetts governor Thomas Hutchinson refused to issue permits to allow the ships to leave the harbor and return to London.

It was a standoff. At a December 16, 1773 meeting of the Sons of Liberty, Sam Adams and other leaders sent Captain Francis Rotch to appeal to Hutchinson to grant the permit. While waiting for Rotch to return with the governor's reply, a crowd of some 7,000 accumulated at Boston's Old South Church. At 6:00 Rotch returned. The governor was adamant. The ships would not be permitted to leave unless the tea was unloaded.

Samuel Adams ascended the Old South pulpit. "This meeting can do nothing more to save the country," he declared, whereupon an ungodly imitation of a Mohawk war cry was raised outside. Three troops of colonists, 50 men each, faces painted to resemble Mohawks, began racing to Griffin's Wharf. They climbed into boats and rowed out to the three tea ships. With military precision, the three troops simultaneously boarded the ships.

Popular mythology portrays a wild scene of Indian-painted, war-whooping colonists hurling tea chests into the harbor. In fact, the operation was carried out quietly and without interference from the officers and crew of the vessels. Once the cargo had been jettisoned—342 tea chests valued at $90,000 in a time when the average laborer made less than a dollar a day—the "Indians" quietly climbed back into their boats and rowed ashore. It was a disciplined Sons of Liberty action, without disorder of any kind.

While the action excited and delighted radicals, it angered many more moderate colonists, especially outside New England, who saw the Tea Party as an act of vandalism that disgraced the American cause. Fortunately for Sam Adams and his comrades, George III and

### Voices of Liberty

"The flame is kindled, and like lightning it catches from soul to soul."

—Letter from Abigail Adams to husband John Adams, as the tea ships stood in Boston Harbor

### Sites and Sights

The Boston Tea Party Ship and Museum is moored to the Congress Street Bridge. For a $7 admission, you can explore *Beaver II*, a replica of the original *Beaver*, one of the three Boston Tea Party ships. Griffin's Wharf no longer exists; the replica is moored on the site of the house in which the Tea Party was planned. The ship and museum are closed from December through February.

Parliament overreacted to the Tea Party so dramatically, that they drove even these moderates back into alliance with the Sons of Liberty.

# The Intolerable Acts

Instantly, everyone seemed to realize that the Boston Tea Party would have profound consequences. John Adams wrote in his diary that its effects would be "so lasting, that I can't but consider it as an epocha in history."

In England, liberal voices rose in support of the Americans and called for the repeal of all taxes and coercive restraint of trade. But the more conservative voices were the loudest. Enraged, King George sputtered, "We must master them or totally leave them to themselves and treat them as aliens." It was as if the king himself—not some radical colonial leader—had declared a war for independence.

In Parliament, most thought that Massachusetts, long a hotbed of sedition, was in sore need of some harsh lessons. A series of Coercive Acts—dubbed by colonial activists the Intolerable Acts—was passed:

➤ The port of Boston was ordered closed.

➤ Massachusetts colonial government was curtailed. Although the colonial Assembly was not dissolved, the members of its upper chamber would be royal appointees from henceforth.

➤ Most local officials would now be appointed by the royal governor.

➤ Town meetings, the core of representative self-government, were restricted to a single annual meeting.

➤ The jurisdiction of colonial courts was greatly abridged. All capital cases would be tried in England or in another colony.

➤ The Quartering Act was extended, paving the way for British troops to be permanently quartered in Boston.

**Voices of Liberty**

"Leave the Americans as they anciently stood .... Let the memory of all actions in contradiction to that good old mode [of salutary neglect] be extinguished forever. Be content to bind America by laws of trade; you have always done it .... Do not burthen them with taxes; you were not used to do so from the beginning."

—Edmund Burke, speech before the House of Commons, after the Boston Tea Party

# The Martyrdom of Massachusetts

General Thomas Gage believed he knew America and Americans better than most other men did. Born in 1719 or 1720, Gage was the son of an irascible Irish peer and politician. He began his military career sometime between 1736 and 1740 as an ensign. Promoted to captain, he saw action in the brutal suppression of the Scottish uprising known as the Jacobite Rebellion of 1745–46, then campaigned in wars on the European continent during 1747–48.

Promoted to lieutenant colonel in March 1751, he came to America in the fall of 1754 and, the next year, marched with Gen. Edward Braddock in the disastrous Battle of the Wilderness to take Fort Duquesne during the French and Indian War (Chapter 4, "Wilderness Wars"). Gage acquitted himself bravely in the Battle of the Wilderness and served throughout the rest of the French and Indian War, becoming acting commander in chief of British forces in North America in 1762. The following year, the appointment was made permanent.

Gage, married to Margaret Kemble of New Jersey, struggled in vain to maintain order in the years following the French and Indian War. Late in 1772, he requested a leave of absence in England and sailed with his family in June 1773. Shortly after he arrived in London, he had an audience with George III. He told the king that the Americans "will be lions while we are lambs, but if we take the resolute part they will undoubtedly be very meek."

**Voices of Liberty**

"If you govern America at all, Sir, it must be by an army; but the Bill before us carries with it the force of that army; and I am of opinion they never will consent without force being used."

—Edmund Burke, debating the bill for regulating the government of Massachusetts, House of Commons, May 2, 1774

George liked what he heard, and, in April 1774, the king approved Gage's appointment as commander in chief of British forces in America *and* as royal governor of Massachusetts. On May 17, Gage arrived in Boston. The reception accorded him was as chilly as the cold rains of early spring. For weeks on end, Boston's church bells tolled as if for the dead. Citizens wore mourning badges.

Gage was having none of it. On June 1, he mercilessly implemented the most odious of the Intolerable Acts, the Port Act, shutting down Boston not only to overseas traffic but to seaborne shipments from other colonies as well. Still, Boston did not yield. To protest the removal of the capital from Boston to Salem, the General Assembly defiantly convened in that place as the Provincial Congress. Gage responded by dissolving the assembly, but delegates barred the doors against Gage's messenger. In the meantime, the exiled and outlawed Assembly voted a proposal to convene a Continental Congress, with delegates from all the colonies.

## The Quebec Act

Gage's harsh application of the king's policies did little to punish Massachusetts and much to create solidarity among colonies that were historically much more inclined to competition with one another.

Just when it was difficult to imagine how the crisis could be made worse, King George made it worse. On June 22, 1774, he signed into law the Quebec Act, by which the old borders of the Canadian province of Quebec were restored. Once again, as under French rule, they stretched down into the Ohio Valley and the Illinois country—the very West in which many Anglo-American colonists hoped to settle. Geographically, these borders made sense, since travel between the St. Lawrence, the Great Lakes, and the Ohio and Mississippi Rivers was much easier than travel across the Appalachian Mountains. The Quebec Act decreed that, in these areas, French would be spoken, French law would prevail, and the Roman Catholic Church would be officially recognized.

The changes brought about by the Quebec Act were Parliament's response to countless petitions from the French majority of the Province of Quebec and the Ohio country. In principle or in a different context, the Quebec Act would have been a wise and rational way of dealing with the many French-colonial nationals who still occupied the territories acquired by England during the French and Indian War. But, practically speaking, the timing of Quebec Act was bound to bring disaster. Many Anglo-American colonists now felt that the very Magna Carta, that ancient guarantee of the rule of English law, had been abrogated by the thoughtless royal tyrant. In addition, most American colonists were Protestants, and they retained an ancient, almost paranoid fear of the Roman Catholic Church, which they associated with tyranny and persecution. George III's and Parliament's support for such a Church convinced many Americans that British authorities had lost all affection for the traditional freedoms and common law of England.

The Quebec Act, like the Tea Act of 1773, represented the impossibility of reconciling all the diverse interests of Britain's huge, global empire: Attempts to satisfy one set of colonial subjects, whether in Canada or India, antagonized inhabitants of the 13 Anglo-American colonies.

## Rally 'Round

In the meantime, as Gage and King George drove wedge upon wedge between the mother country and its American subjects, the other colonies rallied round Massachusetts and Boston in solidarity. The Port Act, most odious of all the Intolerable Acts, had been intended to sever radical Boston from the rest of America. It had precisely the opposite effect.

There was no danger of blockaded Boston starving. The other New England colonies shipped foodstuffs into the city overland. From as far as low-country South Carolina came rice. Delaware sent cash. And—most astoundingly—Quebec sent down huge amounts of wheat.

# Call for a Congress—and a False Start

Fifty-six delegates from 12 colonies heeded the call of the Massachusetts Assembly for a Continental Congress. It convened at Carpenter's Hall, Philadelphia, on September 5, 1774, and it accomplished a great deal:

> ➤ It endorsed the Suffolk Resolves. A radical document drafted by Dr. Joseph Warren and adopted by a convention held in Suffolk County, Massachusetts, the resolves were rushed to the Continental Congress by Sons of Liberty courier Paul

Revere. The resolves deemed the Intolerable Acts unconstitutional, urged Massachusetts to form an independent government and withhold taxes from the Crown until the acts were repealed, advised citizens to arm themselves, and recommended a general boycott of English goods.

➤ By a single vote, it postponed consideration of "Galloway's Plan of Union," which proposed that the colonies remain subordinate to the Crown and Parliament, provided they were granted their own American legislature. Philadelphia lawyer Joseph Galloway's plan called for governance of all the colonies by a royally appointed president-general, who would enjoy veto power over acts of a Grand Council elected by the colonial assemblies. This American government would have broad authority in civil, commercial, and criminal affairs. Parliament would retain its ability to veto the Grand Council's legislation, in order to harmonize American and British law. This plan was strikingly similar to the Plan of Union drawn up by Benjamin Franklin, and passed by the Albany Congress back in 1754.

➤ The congress denounced the Intolerable Acts and the Quebec Act, as well as other repressive measures.

➤ It declared 13 acts of Parliament (passed since 1763) unconstitutional, and each of the delegates pledged their colony's support of economic sanctions against Britain until all the acts were repealed.

➤ In a set of 10 resolutions, the First Continental Congress enumerated the rights of colonists.

➤ The delegates signed a formal Continental Association, whose chief goal was to organize a renewed boycott of trade with Great Britain.

➤ The Congress prepared addresses of protest to the king.

➤ Congress published addresses to the people of Great Britain, Ireland, and Quebec, explaining American grievances, and inviting their fellow British subjects to join the Americans in taking action against tyranny.

# Overtures

In the meantime, Gen. Gage had been gathering and consolidating his troops. On September 1, 1774, a Boston-based detachment of his troops seized cannon and powder from arsenals in nearby Cambridge and Charles Town. The Salem-based Provincial Congress appropriated £15,627 to buy new military supplies and authorized John Hancock to head a Committee of Safety and call out the militia. The militia members were dubbed "minutemen," because these citizen-soldiers pledged themselves to be armed, assembled, and prepared for battle on a minute's notice.

On December 14, 1774, Paul Revere, the tireless rider who had carried the Suffolk Resolves to the Continental Congress in Philadelphia, now rode to warn the patriot general John Sullivan of Gage's plan to seize munitions stored at Fort William and Mary guarding Portsmouth Harbor, New Hampshire. Sullivan led a band of volunteers to the fort and so stunned the British guards that they surrendered without a fight. Sullivan carried off the guns and powder that had been stored at William and Mary. It might be counted the first patriot victory in a war that had yet to be declared.

## The Least You Need to Know

➤ The Sons of Liberty, organized to coordinate protest of the Stamp Act, formally endured only until the act was repealed in 1766; however, this organization created a highly effective and permanent intercolonial network of activists, radicals, and revolutionaries.

➤ The *Gaspée* affair inspired the colonies to come together through Committees of Correspondence.

➤ The Boston Tea Party was seen throughout the colonies as a momentous act of defiance; when it brought down harsh royal retribution, all the colonies rallied to the aid of Boston and Massachusetts.

➤ Passage of the Intolerable Acts and the Quebec Act prompted the colonies to convene the First Continental Congress, which laid the foundation for colonial unity and truly organized rebellion.

# Part 2
# *Heard 'Round the World*

*The opening moves of the American Revolution hold cherished places in our collective memory: the "midnight ride of Paul Revere," the minutemen, the "shot heard 'round the world" at Lexington and Concord, the exploits of Ethan Allen and his Green Mountain Boys, the gallant stand at the Battle of Bunker Hill.*

*This section narrates the stories behind these popular images—and goes on to relate the patriots' failed attempt to invade Canada and their successful effort to drive the redcoats out of Boston. We conclude with the documents that gave the newborn Revolution purpose, direction, and strength: Thomas Paine's* Common Sense *and The Declaration of Independence.*

# Chapter 8

# The Midnight Ride

After the Provincial Congress had appropriated funds to purchase military supplies, called for the organization of the minutemen, and set up a Committee of Safety, events began to unfold with a speed that befuddled Gen. Thomas Gage. Belatedly and impotently, he pronounced the acts of the Provincial Congress treasonable. But that body, having passed those acts, promptly dissolved itself and disappeared on December 10, 1774.

As the colonists were arming and organizing, Gage set about positioning, preparing, and quartering his troops. But he was continually harassed by colonial saboteurs, who sunk supply barges, burned the straw intended for the soldiers' beds, and wrecked provision wagons. Throughout New England, militiamen were drilling—and stealing munitions.

Was armed and open rebellion inevitable? Could there be a turning back? The answer would come quickly now.

# No Retreat

With acts of disorder and rebellion breaking out all over New England, Gen. Gage could hardly decide what fire to put out first. He knew that, whatever else had to be done, the theft of munitions must cease. So, at midnight of February 25, 1775, he sent Col. Alexander Leslie with the 240 men of the 64th Foot Regiment from Castle William, Boston Harbor, to Salem, Massachusetts, where, he had heard, the rebels were storing stolen cannon and munitions.

But Leslie did not know that, in advance of his march from Marblehead, where he and his troops landed, one John Pedrick rode to Salem to warn the people. Swiftly, the 19 cannon stored in town were moved, the drawbridge leading to the forge where the cannon were to be mated to carriages was drawn up, and patriot Col. Timothy Pickering assembled his 40 minutemen.

At the open bridge, the 240 redcoats confronted Pickering, his minutemen, and a crowd of Salem residents. Leslie demanded that Pickering lower the bridge. Pickering refused. Tensions rose, but before they could spill over into musket fire, a Salem clergyman brokered a compromise. He persuaded Pickering to lower the draw on condition that the soldiers march 30 rods into the town, see for themselves that there was nothing to hide, then march out again.

The redcoats discovered that, indeed, Salem harbored no arms. Marching back, the redcoats passed through a town called Northfields, where one Sarah Tarrant threw open the sash of her window and called down to the passing column: "Go home and tell your master he has sent you on a fool's errand and broken the peace of our Sabbath. What, do you think we were born in the woods, to be frightened by owls?"

### Fightin' Words

The **House of Burgesses** was the lower house of the colonial Assembly of Virginia.

Her words hit home, and an outraged lobsterback pointed his musket at her. "Fire," Sarah Tarrant called out, "if you have the courage—but I doubt it." It was a brief, homely, and defiant speech, that taunt of Sarah Tarrant, but, down in Virginia, about a month later, the rhetoric, equally defiant, was far grander.

Patrick Henry, a member of Virginia's *House of Burgesses* since 1765, had led his fellow legislators to meet at Raleigh Tavern on May 27, 1774, after John Murray Dunmore, the colony's royal governor, had dissolved the assembly. In one of its meetings-in-exile, on March 23, 1775, Henry rose to speak:

*There is no retreat but in submission and slavery! Our chains are forged. Their clanking may be heard on the plains of Boston! The war is inevitable—and let it come! I repeat it, sir, let it come!*

*It is in vain, sir, to extenuate the matter. Gentlemen may cry, "Peace! Peace!"—but there is no peace. The war is actually begun! The next gale that sweeps down from the north will bring to our ears the clash of resounding arms! Our brethren are already in the field! Why stand we here idle? What is it that gentlemen wish? What would they have? Is life so dear, or peace so sweet, as to be purchased at the price of chains and slavery? Forbid it, Almighty God! I know not what course others may take, but as for me, give me liberty or give me death!*

# A Silversmith of Charlestown

Were it not for the nineteenth-century American poet Henry Wadsworth Longfellow, the only people who know the name of Paul Revere would be collectors (and would-be collectors) of early American silverware. By the early 1770s, Revere was the best-known silversmith in Boston, turning out exquisite table articles of silver as well as gold, in addition to fashioning fine surgical instruments, spectacles, and even replacements for missing teeth. He also produced engravings, including his celebrated version of the Boston Massacre, mentioned in Chapter 6, "Regulators, Rioters and a Massacre in Boston." But, in 1863, Longfellow published his *Midnight Ride of Paul Revere*, which, until fairly recently, was dutifully memorized by generations of schoolchildren. Before long, this remarkable man became associated with a single, albeit dramatic action—a nocturnal ride to warn the citizens of Concord that the redcoats were coming.

### We Hold These Truths

Revere made a handsome living by his silver work, but, long after his death, when Longfellow's *Midnight Ride of Paul Revere* was published in 1863, the value of Revere silverware truly skyrocketed. Nineteenth-century financier J.P. Morgan offered Mrs. Marston Perry $100,000 (the equivalent today of at least $1,000,000) for a Revere punch bowl commemorating the Sons of Liberty. After 1863, folklore linked the unrelated facts that Revere made false teeth and that Washington wore dentures, concluding that Revere had made a set of false teeth for the Father of His Country. Pure folk fiction!

It is true that Paul Revere was not a great political thinker, orator, or military leader, and that he became universally known through the accident of having been the subject of Longfellow's poem. But his very obscurity makes him fascinating. The Paul Reveres of America in the late eighteenth century were responsible for the Revolution's success. They were not politicians or professional soldiers, just ordinary, extraordinary people who found themselves caught up in great movements in justice and liberty.

Born in 1735, Revere was the son of Apollos Rivoire, who came to America as a 13-year-old boy in 1715 or 1716, one of thousands of Huguenots (French Protestants) fleeing the deadly religious persecution they suffered at home. Rivoire was apprenticed to Boston silversmith John Coney and, in turn, his son Paul Revere became his father's apprentice. Young Paul was personable and popular, noteworthy for his inability to decline any dare. He served for two years with a provincial regiment against the French in the French and Indian War, then returned to Boston to ply his trade as a silversmith. He married Sara Orne, with whom he had eight children, five surviving infancy. After Sara died in childbirth, he married Rachel Walker, who also bore him eight children, of whom six survived infancy.

With a large family to feed, clothe, and shelter, it was a good thing that Revere excelled so handsomely at his trade. Yet he was not content merely to earn money. He became friendly with the political movers and shakers of Boston, Sam Adams, John Adams, John Hancock, James Otis, and Dr. Joseph Warren—the latter another of Boston's remarkable artisans (for, in those days, a medical doctor was considered more artisan than professional man). Warren trained with one of the best local physicians and advocated such advanced ideas as inoculation against smallpox, one of the eighteenth century's great scourges. During the deadly epidemic that swept Boston in 1763, Warren persuaded thousands to be inoculated. Of the 4,977 he treated, only 46 succumbed to the disease. Warren became a hero, which made him particularly influential when he became a Son of Liberty. By 1774, Dr. Warren was president of the outlawed Provincial Congress and chairman of the Committee of Public Safety.

With friends like the Adams cousins, Otis, Hancock, and Warren, Revere soon became deeply involved in the cause of liberty. In 1770, hoping to trigger rebellion, Sam Adams prevailed upon him to engrave the Boston Massacre propaganda piece (Chapter 6), and Revere also engraved many other political cartoons to further the cause. The Sons of Liberty also made extensive use of him as a courier (he carried the "Suffolk Resolves" from Boston to Philadelphia), and he was among the "Mohawks" who boarded the *Dartmouth*, one of the three tea ships of the Boston Tea Party.

## Paul Revere's First Warning

Thus, Revere was the obvious choice whenever a swift messenger was needed. As we saw in Chapter 6, Revere alerted Gen. Sullivan to the impending British seizure of supplies at Fort William and Mary. And on Sunday, April 16, Warren again sent Revere to warn John Hancock and Sam Adams that Gen. Gage was sending troops to arrest them.

In response to the petitions sent them by the First Continental Congress, King George and Parliament proposed the Plan of Reconciliation, whereby Parliament would refrain from taxing the colonies, if their assemblies would voluntarily contribute toward some of the costs of imperial defense. While wooing the majority of the colonies with this important concession, the British government continued to single out New England for punishment. The royal government stiffened New England's resistance by passing the outrageous Fishery Act, which restricted the trade of New England to Britain,

Ireland, and the West Indies, and banned them from fishing in Newfoundland's rich waters. After passage of this act, Massachusetts revived the Provincial Congress, which called on Warren and his Committee of Safety to transform the colony into an armed camp.

Mindful of what was happening, on April 12, Gen. Gage imposed martial law and issued a blanket indictment against the colonists, declaring all to be "in treason." Magnanimously, however, he offered full pardons to everyone—save the chief troublemakers, Adams and Hancock.

So, on the 16th, Revere undertook his first major mission of warning: riding to Lexington, Massachusetts, to tell the two revolutionaries that they must prepare to flee.

## Riders of the Night

His second mission followed hard on the heels of the first. In addition to his duties as rider, Revere supervised a ring of Boston citizen-spies. They had observed Gage's preparation of *grenadiers* and *light infantry* for an impending mission, and watched the British hard at work repairing whaleboats. Revere and his spies surmised that Gage was about to send the troops by boat from Boston to Cambridge, and then on to Concord.

When Revere returned to Boston from Lexington, he arranged the signal that would alert the Charlestown countryside to the movement of Gage's troops. He stationed his friend, John Pulling, in the steeple of the North Church. If the troops were seen marching out by land, a single lantern was to be shown from the steeple. If they were using those whaleboats to get across the Back Bay water, meaning they were embarking for an attack on the arms cache at Concord, Pulling was to show two lanterns. Longfellow would put it all in his poem: "one if by land, two if by sea."

During the day, on April 18, Gage dispatched mounted officers out along the Concord road to clear it of rebel couriers. That night, the sergeants were sent to awaken the sleeping light

### Fightin' Words

**Grenadiers** had been soldiers armed chiefly with grenades, explosives meant to be hurled. This required great strength, so grenadiers were typically the tallest, strongest, most able soldiers. By the eighteenth century, the grenade was not their weapon of choice, but the name stuck as a description of elite troops. The **light infantry** were the elite advance guard or shock troops of eighteenth-century armies. Lightly equipped, they were expected to move quickly and aggressively.

### Sites and Sights

Both the Paul Revere House and the Old North Church survive in Boston's picturesque North End. The oldest house in Boston, the Paul Revere House is located at 19 North Square and may be visited. Call 617–523–1676. Nearby, at 193 Salem Street, is the Old North Church, in whose steeple Revere's confederate John Pulling displayed the two-lantern signal on the night of April 18, 1775. The Old North is Boston's oldest church building; call 617–523–6676.

infantrymen and grenadiers—600 to 800 of Gage's best troops, indeed some of the best troops Europe had to offer. They quietly assembled on Boston Common and were put under command of the rotund and slow-witted Lt. Col. Francis Smith, assisted by Maj. John Pitcairn, Royal Marines.

At 10:30, the redcoats were ready to march. Two lanterns glowed in the North Church steeple; the British were bound for Concord, and Paul Revere and another Sons of Liberty courier, William Dawes, set out from Boston to alert the countryside. Dawes was assigned the longer land route to Concord, via Boston Neck to Cambridge and Menotomy (modern Arlington), and then west to Lexington and Concord. Revere took a shortcut by rowing himself over to Charlestown, and rode off by 11. His cry to the countryside was not "The British are coming! The British are coming!" but "The regulars are out!" And if he encountered a darkened window, he did not content himself with a shouted alarm, but threw pebbles against the glass.

*Early-twentieth-century depiction of the midnight ride of Paul Revere.* (Image from the National Archives)

Arriving at Lexington about midnight, Revere rode up to the home of Parson Jonas Clark, where John Hancock (the parson's cousin) and Sam Adams had taken refuge. William Munroe, of the patriot militia, was standing guard. A breathless Revere shouted to Munroe to open the door. "Please!" the guard cautioned. "Not so loud! The family has just retired and doesn't want any noise about the house."

"Noise!" Revere retorted. "You'll have noise enough before long. The regulars are out!"

At this, Munroe rushed into the house himself to rouse Hancock and Adams. "What a glorious morning this is!" Sam shouted. When Hancock shot him a puzzled glance, he added: "I mean for America."

For Revere himself, the "midnight ride" did not end in full glory. Dawes met up with him in Lexington about an hour after Revere's arrival. The two rode on together to Concord and were joined en route by Dr. Samuel Prescott, who had spent most of the evening courting his intended bride. Prescott joined the two riders in rousing the countryside. As Prescott and Dawes paused to wake a certain house, Revere rode on.

He was suddenly halted by a group of redcoats. "God damn you, stop!" one of them ordered. "If you go an inch farther you are a dead man."

Prescott and Dawes, approached by the soldiers, managed to escape, but Revere was detained. "Don't be afraid," the British officer said, nodding toward his men. "They will not hurt you."

If he was afraid, he didn't betray it. "You've missed your purpose," Revere sneered. The officer replied that they were merely looking for deserters.

"I know better," said Revere. "I know what you're after. You're too late. I've alarmed the country all the way up. I should have 500 men at Lexington soon."

The detachment's senior officer, a Maj. Mitchell, was sent for. Whereas the others had been courteous enough to Revere, Mitchell wasted no time. He cocked his pistol and put it against the silversmith's head, ordering him to tell the truth. Revere repeated his story: The entire countryside was prepared to fight. Mitchell ordered Revere to mount, and he gave the reins to one of his men to lead Revere off. But, after only a mile, he ordered his prisoner to dismount. Mitchell set him free; the damage, he realized, had already been done. The expedition against Concord had lost the element of surprise.

# War Begins

Revere made his way back to Clark's house, where, to his consternation, he found Adams and Hancock still debating what to do.

*Flee!* Revere told them, and he escorted the pair to a crossroads, from which they began the long ride to Philadelphia. It was now dawn of April 19, 1775.

## *Misjudgment Both Ways*

It seems that the British officers and soldiery had learned little enough from their experience of provincial warfare in the French and Indian War. Disregarding all that the Sons of Liberty had already accomplished, they looked upon the Yankees as nothing more than an undisciplined rabble. "Without rum they could neither fight nor say their prayers," one British officer scoffed.

**Voices of Liberty**

"I am satisfied that one active campaign, a smart action, and burning two or three of their towns, will set everything to rights."

—Maj. John Pitcairn, Royal Marines, April 1775, shortly before the battles of Lexington and Concord

When the colonists compared themselves to the British army, they saw two forces using two very different types of fighting technique. The British regulars were armed with muskets, weapons that were fairly inaccurate, but very easy to load. There was no point in fighting as an individual warrior with a musket: The chance that you could hit your target, however experienced you were, was slim indeed. Therefore the British trained their men to march in long lines, and to fire in unison. When a large number of muskets were fired in approximately the same direction at the same time, the inaccuracies of each weapon canceled each other out, creating a wall of fire that could decimate the opposing side. In contrast, the American colonists used rifles, weapons that were much more accurate, but even slower to load than the British muskets. Such weapons were ideal for hunting, but had limited uses in warfare: Riflemen could fire once, but would have to retreat to reload. Colonials armed with rifles might be able to harass a regular army, but they could not hope, without a miracle, to defeat the British. Yet confidence in God's support emboldened these descendants of the Puritans to attempt the impossible.

**Fightin' Words**

The **Brown Bess** was the standard-issue infantry firearm in the British army since the early eighteenth century. By the 1770s, it was 39 inches long, weighed 14 pounds, and fired a 0.75-inch, one-ounce bullet.

**Fightin' Words**

A **line of battle** was the standard eighteenth-century troop formation for most effective fire. Typically, it consisted of a line two or three men deep, so that one row could fire while the other reloaded.

## *Lexington*

"Two if by sea." In the dreary wee hours of April 19, the British regulars clambered out of the whaleboats that had taken them from Boston to Lechmere Point. They had to look forward to a cold, wet, early morning march of some 16 miles to Concord, loaded down with 60-pound packs, each toting the 14-pound musket, 39 inches tall, known as a Brown Bess. Until the order was given to "fix bayonets," the musket's 14-inch bayonet was carried in scabbard hung from the soldier's belt.

No sooner had they disembarked from the boats and begun their march than shots rang out and church bells tolled. The assault on Concord, the disheartened commanders realized, would be no surprise. Lt. Col. Smith and Maj. Pitcairn sent riders back to Boston to summon reinforcements. In the meantime, at Lexington, which lay squarely in the line of march between Boston and Concord, militia captain Jonas Parker formed up the ranks of the 70 or so citizen-soldiers he had been able to muster. They were assembled on Lexington's green, which fronted the Concord road.

The men might mock the British, and they could pity the miserable plight of the poor redcoat—but then they actually *saw* the approach of Maj. Pitcairn's advance guard, muskets shouldered, scarlet coats criss-crossed with gleaming white cartridge belts in the early-morning light. Now the brutal British drilling, so derided by the colonials, would pay off. Pitcairn ordered his men to form their *line of battle*. It was a standard formation, three men deep, calculated for efficiency of massed volley fire using the unbelievably cumbersome Brown Bess.

The British *Manual of Arms* listed 12 separate motions for loading, aiming, firing, and reloading the Brown Bess. The average soldier could get off two rounds a minute; a very good soldier, as many as five. The first volley fired was always the most effective, because the troops had had ample time to load their powder and the bullet carefully and to ensure that they were tamped down properly with the ramrod. In the heat of combat, however, once the 14-inch bayonet was fixed in place, shoving the ramrod down the barrel was a far clumsier operation. Many muskets misfired or failed to deliver the shot with maximum velocity.

Because loading, firing, and reloading was so ponderous, one row of men fired while the row or rows behind them stood at the ready. After the front row fired, it smartly retired behind the second (or third) row to reload. While it reloaded, the second row fired, and while they reloaded, the third row fired—by which time the original front row was back in front, reloaded, and ready to fire again. Soldiers loaded, rammed, cocked, primed the pan, and fired as each step was barked out by an officer. The operation was like the working of a machine, fire issued in a simultaneous, raking volley, one volley every 15 seconds. The effective range of muskets of the period was a mere 100 yards. The optimum range was 50. Ideally, your lines should *not* be the first to fire. It was more effective to close in until the enemy opened fire. You'd take your losses, then open up with your volleys, so close now that every shot, indifferently aimed as it may be, would find a mark.

The tactics of European battle were really very simple. The opposing troops would approach each other as two compact masses, each presenting a perfect target for the other. Whoever could fire, reload, and fire again at the fastest rate would lose the fewest troops and, therefore, would win. Such a mass now closed on Parker's little band, huddled on Lexington green.

Pitcairn called to the militia on the green: "Lay down your arms, you rebels, and disperse!"

"Stand your ground," Capt. Parker is said to have ordered. "Don't fire unless fired upon. But if they want to have a war, let it begin here!"

They were brave words, tailor-made for history—and probably written for him years later. Jonas Parker was a brave man, but not a foolish one. He did the kind of thing American forces would do many times in the course of the revolution. Called on to surrender, he neither surrendered nor offered hopeless battle against superior numbers. He just ordered his men to disband, telling them to take their weapons with them.

Pitcairn repeated his demand that they lay their weapons down. Then shots rang out. A redcoat was wounded slightly in the leg, and two balls grazed Pitcairn's horse.

Who had fired? The Americans or the British? No one knows. But the action was sufficient to elicit from a British officer the command, "Fire, by God, fire!" A volley was discharged into the American ranks, but Pitcairn ordered an immediate cease-fire.

"Form and surround them," he commanded.

Discipline, however, dissolved. The lobsterbacks had spent months pent up in Boston, the object of patriot taunts and insults. Instead of forming as ordered, they fired another volley. What rebels remained on the green returned fire, albeit in ragged fashion. Now the redcoats commenced a bayonet charge, which was enough to send the militiamen fleeing—all but Parker. Wounded in the first or second volley, he stood alone, reloaded, and was cut down dead by British bayonets before he could fire.

Eight militiamen, including Parker, lay dead on Lexington green. Ten more were wounded. A single British soldier was slightly hurt. So ended the Battle of Lexington, first battle in America's war for independence.

## And Concord

The British continued their march on Concord, but word of the engagement at Lexington reached that town well in advance. Militia companies poured into Concord from surrounding communities. No one knows just how many Americans were ultimately involved in the battle. Wild estimates have run as high as 20,000, but the most reliable computation is that, before day's end, 3,763 Americans had been engaged—although never more than half this number were involved at any one time. As fresh militia units arrived, exhausted men, their 40 or so rounds of ammunition spent, dropped out.

At the moment the British arrived, unopposed, in Concord, some 400 militiamen, more or less under the command of local resident Col. James Barrett, had assembled on a ridge overlooking the town. While the British commander, Lt. Col. Smith, dined at a local tavern with his staff officers (taking polite care to pay for all that was eaten and drunk), the grenadiers under his command began searching the town, house by house, for hidden munitions. They turned up less than they expected—just bullets, mostly— but then a number of gun carriages turned up, which they instantly put to the torch.

Seeing this, one of Col. Barrett's officers turned to him: "Will you let them burn the town down?" By way of reply, Barrett ordered the militia to march to the defense of Concord, cautioning them to hold fire unless fired upon. The captain of the British light infantry was stunned by the approach of the Americans. He ordered his men to form two ranks, the first rank to fire a volley, then run behind the second rank to reload while the second rank fired. It was the standard maneuver, drilled and drilled many times over. But something went wrong for the British that day. The Battle of Lexington had been easy. Here, at Concord, were many more men, men who really did look and move like soldiers. The familiar maneuver miscarried, the volleys at first falling short into the river before a few shots found their marks: Militia captain Isaac Davis fell dead, as did Abner Hosmer, the little drummer boy who had marched bravely at the head of the American column. "Fire, fellow soldier!" an American officer begged his men. "For God sake, fire!"

In his *Hymn Sung at the Completion of the Concord Monument, April 19, 1836,* the philosopher-poet Ralph Waldo Emerson called this, the first full American volley of the great Revolution, "the shot heard round the world." Three British regular soldiers died in the volley, and nine more lay wounded. The lobsterbacks retreated into the town, and Barrett's men cheered. Had they been more disciplined soldiers, the militiamen would have stopped cheering and pressed their advantage by pursuing the retreating British. But they did not. Instead, a lone "embattled farmer" ventured onto North Bridge, where the withdrawing British had left their dead and wounded, and, seeing one of the prone soldiers stir, buried an ax in his skull. This served to strike terror into the hearts of the light infantry who came marching back from searching Barrett's house. The Americans, they gasped, had *scalped* a soldier of the crown!

It was 10:00 in the morning. For now, the fighting had stopped. Col. Smith collected his wounded and prepared to leave Concord to return to Boston.

## Retreat to Boston

Back in Boston, at about 9 A.M., the sound of fifes and drums was heard. It was a tune the Americans recognized well. The words to it went like this:

> *Yankee Doodle went to town*
> *Riding on a pony.*
> *Stuck a feather in his cap*
> *And called it macaroni.*

Intended by the British to mock the Americans—a "macaroni" was a dandy, a pretentious fop who affected what he thought were sophisticated European manners and style—the rebels soon adopted the ditty as their own. But, just now, it marked time to the marching feet of some 1,400 redcoats, including 460 Royal Marines, drawing two 6-pound cannons, and led by 33-year-old Lord Hugh Percy. They marched over Boston Neck and through Roxbury, at first finding the countryside eerily still. Locals had removed the planks from the Charles River bridge, which delayed the column briefly, then they marched through Cambridge, which was deserted, silent.

The silence didn't last long. From every village and farm between Boston and Concord, militiamen poured, arraying themselves not in lines of battle, but crouching behind stone walls and trees and even in houses. The road to Concord became a bloody gantlet, as the Americans sniped at the marching British, picking them off one by one.

**Voices of Liberty**

"There was not a stone-wall or house, though before in appearance evacuated, from whence the Rebels did not fire upon us."

—Lord Percy to Thomas Gage, April 20, 1775

As Percy's harried column approached, Lt. Col. Smith commenced a retreat back toward Lexington. His light infantry mounted several successful counterattacks against poorly organized clumps of militia. Finding some in local houses, the British soldiers killed the men, then burned the houses. But the militia did not disperse. More and more men poured into the Concord area, taking up sniper positions on either side of the road, keeping up the merciless fire on Smith's retreating column. Trained and drilled and beaten so that they would learn to march, *then* form, *then* stand and fight, the British regulars were totally unprepared to be picked off by an unseen enemy before they had even reached the battlefield. Frightened, tired, and bewildered, the redcoats began to fall apart.

As he approached Lexington, Smith paused to re-form his ragged troops. It was appalling, really. These light infantrymen and grenadiers were the elite of the British army! And a handful of provincial rebels had routed *them*, forcing *them* to retreat! Smith dispatched Pitcairn to hold off any militiamen while he re-formed, but the Americans engulfed Pitcairn's marines, driving them in and forcing Smith to abandon any notion of re-forming. All he could do was resume the desperate retreat.

By this time, Smith's troops had been marching or fighting or running for some 20 hours. They entered Lexington little more than an exhausted rabble and could cheer but feebly as they were met in town by Percy's column of reinforcements, up from Boston. Percy trained his 6-pounders against the Americans, which kept them at bay for a time. But more militiamen were continually arriving. Had they been better led—indeed, had they been *led* at all—they might have annihilated Smith and Percy's 1,800 men. Coordinated action could have sealed off all avenues of escape from Lexington, and it would have been the French and Indian War's Battle of the Wilderness all over again.

But the so-called militia was, after all, a collection of "embattled farmers," not trained soldiers. Each man acted more or less on his own, and Percy and Smith were able to make good their retreat, leaving Lexington about three in the afternoon. The militiamen persisted in harassing the column, and the British retaliated, mainly by burning houses along the way or, when isolated patriots left themselves exposed and vulnerable, turning their wrath on them. The battle continued all the way back to Charlestown, where the British at last found refuge within range of the big guns of their warships.

Seventy-three redcoats were confirmed dead, and another 26, missing, were presumed dead. One hundred seventy-four British solders were wounded. On the American side, 49 had died, 5 were reported missing, and 41 lay wounded.

### Voices of Liberty

"Too much praise cannot be given to Lord Percy for his remarkable activity and conduct during the whole day. Lieutenant Col. Smith and Major Pitcairne did everything men could do, as did all the officers in general, and the men behaved with their usual intrepidity."

—Thomas Gage to Lord Barrington, British Secretary of War, April 22, 1775

## We Hold These Truths

*Hymn Sung at the Completion of the Concord Monument, April 19, 1836:*

*By the rude bridge that arched the flood*
    *Their flag to April's breeze unfurled,*
*Here once the embattled farmers stood,*
    *And fired the shot heard round the world.*
*The foe long since in silence slept;*
    *Alike the conqueror silent sleeps;*
*And Time the ruined bridge has wept*
    *Down the dark stream which seaward creeps.*
*On this green bank, by this soft stream,*
    *We set to-day a votive stone;*
*That memory may their deed redeem,*
    *When, like our sires, our sons are gone.*
*Spirit, that made those heroes dare*
    *To die, or leave their children free,*
*Bid Time and nature gently spare*
    *The shaft we raise to them and thee.*

—Ralph Waldo Emerson

# "Nothing Is Heard Now But the Trumpet and the Drum"

The American Revolution had begun. Almost a month later, when the Second Continental Congress convened in Philadelphia, the delegates found that armed rebellion against Great Britain had been initiated by local action, without Congress's agreement. Yet Congress had no choice, but to lead the fight. It mobilized 13,600 troops, and local militia throughout New England quickly assembled to march to Boston. The day after the battle, Smith's and Percy's troops had holed up in town, while New England's citizen-soldiers trooped into Cambridge with the aim of laying British-occupied Boston under siege, which you'll read about in Chapter 9, "Green Mountains and Bunker Hill," and Chapter 11, "The Battle for Boston."

A lady of Philadelphia, her name unknown to history, wrote a letter to a certain "Captain S____," a Boston-based British officer, whom she still regarded as her friend. In the wake of Lexington and Concord, she wrote, "All ranks of men amongst us are in arms. Nothing is heard now in our streets but the trumpet and the drum; and the universal cry is 'Americans, to arms!'" She continued:

> *We are making powder fast and do not want for ammunition. In short, we want for nothing but ships of war to defend us, which we could procure by making alliance: but such is our attachment to Great Britain that we sincerely wish for reconciliation …. The God of mercy will, I hope, open the eyes of our king that he may see, while in seeking our destruction, he will go near to complete his own.*

But the king's eyes would not be opened. "I am of the opinion," he wrote to the Earl of Sandwich on July 1, 1775, after receiving a much-sanitized report of the action at Lexington and Concord, "that when once these rebels have felt a smart blow, they will submit; and no situation can ever change my fixed resolution, either to bring the colonies to a due obedience to the legislature of the mother country or to cast them off!"

---

### The Least You Need to Know

➤ The name of Paul Revere is remembered chiefly because Longfellow made him the hero of his celebrated nineteenth-century poem; nevertheless, Revere, courageous, resourceful, and strong, was typical of the American revolutionary spirit.

➤ The American victory at Lexington and Concord was badly flawed by a lack of discipline and leadership; however, it inflamed the spirit of rebellion, and it proved to the colonists that the British army was hardly invincible.

➤ King George III and the conservative majority in Parliament, refusing to see in Lexington and Concord a demonstration of the colonists' will and ability to fight, persisted in their belief that force of arms would bring a quick end to the rebellion.

# Chapter 9

# Green Mountains and Bunker Hill

King George III had no interest in reconciling with his American colonies, but his minister, Lord North, whose policies had done so much to alienate Americans in the first place, was having second thoughts. Even before Lexington and Concord, he had obtained George's grudging consent to present a plan for reconciliation. The House of Lords received it on February 20, 1775, and Commons endorsed it a week later. The day after the Lexington and Concord battles, the plan arrived in Boston by ship.

North's plan compromised on Parliament's right to tax the colonies, allowing colonies to tax themselves to support civil government, the judiciary, and the common defense. Parliament still retained regulatory taxing authority, but this wasn't the principal reason why the Continental Congress rejected North's plan on July 31, 1775. The problem was that the plan authorized Parliament to deal with individual colonies only, which meant that no union of colonies or a Continental Congress was to be recognized.

At this point in history, colonists saw themselves as Americans, not citizens of the colony of Massachusetts or Virginia or Connecticut, and, therefore, North's plan for reconciliation was a little too late. It was a new *nation* that was coming to birth.

# "In the Name of Jehovah and the Continental Congress"

Thoughtful generations have marveled at the good fortune that blessed the American Revolution with an abundance of brilliant, idealistic, practical, and insightful men who instinctively grasped just what it took to create a country. We have seen that, from the beginning of the revolutionary movement, with the passage of the Stamp Act in 1765, the activists emphasized the key importance of unified action. Recognizing that America was a place of vast spaces and thinly broadcast settlements, they created the Sons of Liberty and the Committees of Correspondence, working them into an intercolonial network linked by such couriers as Paul Revere.

Reporting to George's secretary of state for war, Lord Barrington, on April 22, 1775, Gen. Thomas Gage dismissed Lexington and Concord as nothing more than "an affair that happened here on the 19th."

*Gen. Thomas Gage, British commander in chief of North American forces and royal governor of Massachusetts. (Image from the National Archives)*

Gage failed to grasp that "the affair" did not just happen in Massachusetts. By 10 A.M. on the 19th, just after the first American fell at Lexington, Committee of Safety couriers were riding for all points north and south. Within hours, news of the battle had reached New York, Philadelphia, and most points in between. Within days, it had penetrated to Virginia and the rest of the southland. The twin battles were a national affair in the most profound sense: Their impact carried throughout the nation even as it created that nation.

## Meet Ethan Allen

The significance of Lexington and Concord was not lost on the leaders of Connecticut. They had dispatched Benedict Arnold, a prosperous New Haven merchant and now captain of militia, to Massachusetts. He arrived 10 days after the "Lexington alarm" and persuaded the Massachusetts authorities to appoint him colonel of militia and put him in charge of a "bold enterprise": the capture of Fort Ticonderoga.

Ticonderoga is an Iroquois word meaning "between two waters." The fort, in northeastern New York, stood at the point where Lake George drains into Lake Champlain. Strategically positioned on the main route between Canada and the upper Hudson Valley, it was the gateway to all Canada. Moreover, it harbored a cache of artillery, which the Americans badly needed.

**Voices of Liberty**

"Ever since I arrived to a state of manhood and acquainted myself with the general history of mankind, I have felt a sincere passion for liberty. ... [T]he first systematical and bloody attempt at Lexington to enslave America thoroughly electrified my mind and fully determined me to take part with my country."

—Ethan Allen, *Narrative*, 1779

Arnold returned to Connecticut, only to discover that the Connecticut assembly had approved a similar plan to take Fort Ticonderoga, but had given the assignment to Ethan Allen. Arnold, ambitious and eager to make a hero's name for himself, showed the Connecticut troops his commission from the Massachusetts Committee of Public Safety. They were unimpressed. The troops that had been gathered by authority of the Connecticut assembly were completely loyal to Ethan Allen. Many declared that they would "march home rather than serve under any other leader."

Just who was Ethan Allen? He had been born in Litchfield, Connecticut, in 1738, in the midst of a January blizzard. He grew into a man of 6-foot-4-inch height, a giant for those days, marched in the French and Indian War but saw no action, then worked as an iron monger, finally selling his blast furnace in 1765. He moved to Northhampton and used the proceeds of the sale to finance a stint of "riotous living," which included amusing himself by writing obscene jokes about the local clergy. This did not go unnoticed. In July 1767, the selectmen of Northhampton ejected Allen, his wife, and his child from town.

Leaving his family in the care of his brother in Salisbury, Allen secured a land grant in the wilderness of what would become the state of Vermont. Settling in Bennington, Allen sent for his family, and he became colonel of a local militia/vigilante force known as the Green Mountain Boys.

In the late 1760s and early 1770s, New York and New Hampshire both claimed present-day Vermont, and New York disputed New Hampshire's right to grant land west of the Green Mountains—the very land Allen lived on. The Green Mountain Boys were formed in 1770 to challenge a sheriff's party sent by New York to evict settlers who had received land grants from New Hampshire. Allen led the Boys in harassing the sheriff's men, on one occasion besting them in a fight, then administering to the New Yorkers a sound thrashing with birch rods.

Hard drinking, hard swearing, impious, irreverent, and intrepid, Ethan Allen was the stuff frontier legends are made of, and to the Connecticut assembly, he and his Green Mountain Boys seemed the natural choice for the mission to "Fort Ti." Benedict Arnold swallowed his pride (something, we shall see in Chapter 18, "Defeat and Disloyalty," that became increasingly difficult for him to do), and agreed to a joint command with Ethan Allen.

## The Taking of Fort Ti

At least Benedict Arnold thought of it as a joint command. But when it came time to set off for Fort Ti, Allen stepped in front of Col. Arnold (over whom, in any case, he towered) and made a speech:

> *I now propose to advance before you and in person to conduct you through the wicket-gate; for we must this morning quit our pretensions to valor, or possess ourselves of this fortress in a few minutes; and, in as much as it is a desperate attempt (which none but the bravest of men dare undertake), I do not urge it in any contrary to his will. You that will undertake voluntarily, poise your firelocks!*

The mission called for utmost stealth, and, just before dawn on May 10, two or three hundred volunteers waited for boats that would carry them to within a half mile of the fort. After considerable delay, only two boats materialized, and, not wishing to lose the element of surprise by waiting for more boats, Allen and Arnold jammed themselves and 83 men into the leaky vessels, crossing two miles over Lake Champlain in a fierce squall. With typical pluck, Allen insisted that the storm was a stroke of fortune, for it muffled their noise and made them utterly invisible to the enemy.

Allen, Arnold, and their small group charged the fort. A sentry spied them, leveled his musket, pulled the trigger, and the powder flashed in the pan—the weapon misfired. When another sentry pricked one of Allen's officers with his bayonet, the giant Vermonter raised his sword, but struck only with its flat, knocking the sentry out of the way without doing him any great injury. With Arnold close behind, Allen rushed up a staircase, where he was met by a Lt. Feltham, who, having hurriedly drawn on his breeches, held them up with

**Fightin' Words**

A **firelock**, **flintlock**, or **matchlock** is a musket or other firearm that uses a gunlock with a flint embedded in the hammer to produce a spark and ignite the gunpowder charge.

one hand. In this rather awkward state, he demanded by what authority Allen and his men had intruded on the property of the king. It was the kind of question Ethan Allen relished.

"In the name of the Great Jehovah and the Continental Congress," Allen bellowed, brandishing his sword over the lieutenant's head. Then he went on to demand the fort "and all the effects of George the Third."

The fort's commandant, a Capt. Delaplace, complied. For, as it turned out, the mission was never quite as "desperate" as Ethan Allen, Benedict Arnold, or their men had imagined and assumed. If the Americans had instantly realized how vital the fort was, it seems that the British had not. A mere 48 men garrisoned it, and many of these were *invalids*, disabled soldiers assigned light duty.

### Fightin' Words

**Invalids** were disabled soldiers assigned light duty, such as garrisoning forts. **Mortars** are thick, squat artillery pieces intended to fire projectiles into a high trajectory in order to assault forts and other stockaded or high-walled places. **Howitzers** are lighter, more portable artillery pieces, also used to deliver high-trajectory projectiles.

Ethan Allen had gained the gateway to Canada and a base from which he could dispatch Seth Warner, third in command behind himself and Arnold, to take the nearby post of Crown Point, also manned feebly. Together, the forts netted the patriot cause 78 artillery pieces, six *mortars*, three *howitzers*, a wealth of cannonballs, flints for flintlock muskets, and other war materiel. Just how the Americans made use of this artillery bonanza we will see in Chapter 11, "The Battle for Boston."

## "I Do Not Think Myself Equal to the Command"

The Revolution now stirring to life was bringing together a remarkable mix of individuals—physicians like Joseph Warren, artisans like Paul Revere, brilliant attorneys and political theorists like John Adams, politicians and orators like Sam Adams and Patrick Henry, well-to-do merchants like John Hancock and Benedict Arnold, and backwoodsmen like Ethan Allen. Waiting in the wings was perhaps the most remarkable figure of them all.

George Washington, master of a northern Virginia plantation called Mount Vernon, a lordly place on the wide Potomac, had earned his military reputation in the French and Indian War. Now he donned his colonel's uniform once again, serving the colony of Virginia and the cause of the Revolution as chairman of a committee to "consider ways and means to supply these Colonies with ammunition and military stores."

*Engraving after the familiar, unfinished portrait of George Washington by Gilbert Stuart. (Image from the National Archives)*

## Creation of the Continental Army

On the very day that Ethan Allen and Benedict Arnold took Fort Ticonderoga, delegates from 12 colonies—all the colonies except Georgia—met in a Second Continental Congress at the State House (later Independence Hall), Philadelphia. Speaking of remarkable people in this Revolution, the 342 delegates to the Second Continental Congress included, among others:

➤ **John Hancock**, who replaced Edmund Randolph as president of the Congress.

➤ **Benjamin Franklin**, almost 70, a delegate from Pennsylvania, famed as the author of the phenomenally popular *Poor Richard's Almanack* series, a scientist, an investigator into a mysterious thing called electricity, an inventor (of everything from the Franklin stove to the lightning rod), deputy postmaster of the colonies, and an agent representing the Pennsylvania colony in London.

➤ **Thomas Jefferson**, delegate from Virginia, a prosperous planter, and, like Franklin, a scientist-philosopher; he was also a brilliant architect (who would design his own magnificent residence, Monticello, as well the neoclassical buildings of the University of Virginia) and an incisive political author, whose works would include the Declaration of Independence.

➤ **John Adams**, a delegate from Massachusetts, a measured orator of conservative bearing, who nevertheless uttered the most radical of revolutionary sentiments; intensely devoted to the cause of Massachusetts, Adams was also the most continental-minded of the men who would come to be called the founding fathers; he worked tirelessly to keep the colonies united.

John Adams had proposed that Congress adopt the Boston militia (see Chapter 11) as the Continental army. His concern was to avoid regionalism. Even when an army acted locally, it was important that it do so as a national force. Ultimately, the Second Continental Congress called for the creation of a Continental army to be drawn from *all* the colonies —a truly national force. The Continental army was by no means expected to be the only American military asset in this Revolution. The colonies would raise and contribute their own militia forces as well. But Adams and the other members of Congress believed it was critically important to add to these forces an army of the United States of America—a name that would not appear on any official document until the Declaration of Independence was proclaimed on July 4, 1776.

**Sites and Sights**

Independence Hall is part of Independence National park in Philadelphia's Old City historic district. Located on Chestnut Street between 5th and 6th Streets, Independence Hall was built in 1732 as colonial Pennsylvania's seat of government. For information on hours, call 215-597-8974.

Most of all, the Continental Congress knew that, while militia forces could harass the British army, only a regular army could engage the British on equal terms. The Continental army was to be a European-style regular army, which would fight in very different ways from the militias and the frontiersmen.

On June 14, John Adams proposed a commander in chief for the Continental army. John Hancock, sitting in the president's chair, doubtless, expected to hear himself, a fellow Bostonian, named. But Adams spoke of a "gentleman from Virginia who is among us here, and who is George Washington of Virginia."

After naming the commander in chief, the Congress selected his lieutenants: Artemas Ward (already commanding the Boston militia); Israel Putnam, of Connecticut; Philip Schuyler, a wealthy New Yorker; and two recently retired officers of the British army, Charles Lee and Horatio Gates, both of whom had served with Braddock and Washington in the French and Indian War. These Britons were strong opponents of George III and Lord North, and Congress wanted their military expertise to create a truly professional army in the forthcoming war with Great Britain. Their appointment demonstrates both the lack of professional military experience among the colonists, and the complexity of allegiances in the Revolutionary War, where Britons sometimes fought with the rebels, and Americans with the British. As to the army that Washington would command, it did begin with the men of the Boston Army, to which would be added companies of riflemen recruited in Pennsylvania, Maryland, and Virginia. By the end of 1775, Congress had 27,500 Continental soldiers on its payroll, from all the colonies.

# Yankee Doodle Versus a War Machine

That Congress could raise an army of 27,500 by the end of 1775 is impressive, given that in 1774 no national army existed—indeed, there was no standing army anywhere in the colonies. However, even though in 1774 the British had an effective army of some 17,500 men and a navy of 16,000, the next year Parliament authorized an army of 55,000 and a navy of 28,000. The United States had a single naval vessel in 1775, compared to the 270 warships of the Royal Navy. Great Britain had a population of 8 million people in 1775, of whom 2,350,000 could be considered military manpower. The colonies had a population of about 2,256,000 in 1775, excluding Indians and including 506,000 slaves. Assuming about 10 percent of the non-slave population could bear arms, the potential military manpower of the colonies was 175,000.

How meaningful are these figures? In terms of the numbers of men actually involved in the war, not very. Both Britain and America were internally divided in this war, and neither could call upon the full strength of its population for support. Many Britons thought George III's actions against the colonies were unjust, and refused to fight against fellow Englishmen who were defending their liberty Britain's Lord Shelburne complained that whereas 300,000 Englishmen had entered the army during the Seven Years' War (in America, the French and Indian War), an army of only 30,000 could be raised to put down the colonial rebellion—and this number included German mercenary troops (the Hessians) as well as Britons. As for the Americans, the combined forces of the Continental army and all of the militias at any one time never approached 175,000.

Many Americans continued to support Great Britain throughout the Revolutionary War, while the majority of colonists were lukewarm in their allegiance to either side. Some colonists were neutral, while others were concerned only with local issues, and not with the major question of whether the United States would win its independence from Great Britain. Therefore, Congress could draw on only a minority of the colonies' population for wartime support.

But consider these numbers from the perspective of the patriots and the British government in 1775. Surely, a contest between the colonies and the mother country must have seemed extremely lopsided. Compare their financial resources, and America's prospects had to look worse than bleak. If Britain commanded five times the military resources of the colonies, it enjoyed a *thousand* times the financial resources. Whereas Britain had a "sinking fund"—essentially, ready cash—of 2 to 3 million pounds per year, the total annual revenue of the American colonies (which had little power to tax) was a paltry £75,000 annually. Many Americans might not have been impressed with the way the British fought the French and Indian War, but they had to take seriously the amount of money the Crown had sunk into that war. In a single 12-month period, 17 million pounds were spent.

The Americans did enjoy important advantages, too, although these are more difficult to quantify:

➤ They were fighting for a cause they believed in. In contrast, the brutally treated British soldiers often felt little loyalty to their government or leaders and scant sense of purpose. Furthermore, sentiment regarding the question of colonial independence varied greatly among Englishmen, and as the war dragged on, public opinion increasingly favored independence.

➤ The colonists were fighting on their own ground.

➤ They were fighting under familiar conditions of climate and terrain, which were decidedly unfavorable to European methods of warfare.

➤ The Continental army and the colonial militias lacked trained artillerists, military engineers, cavalrymen, and men with military administrative experience; however, a significant number of colonial army officers were veterans of the French and Indian War and other Indian conflicts. They had more tactical experience fighting under frontier conditions than their British counterparts had.

➤ It is a myth that the typical American revolutionary soldier was handy with a gun. Many were town dwellers who rarely, if ever, handled firearms. Likewise, many farmers who lived near larger settlements hunted little. Nevertheless, the American forces did include a significant number of frontiersmen who were excellent marksmen.

## General Washington

There was one other asset in the Americans' favor. Whereas British military leadership was fragmented (and often inept), the American forces (with rare exception) looked to a single man for leadership. George Washington was not a profound military genius, but he had a reasonably sound grasp of military strategy and tactics. More important, he possessed the powerful character of a leader. He commanded great loyalty and confidence.

To be more precise, he possessed the character of a leader *suited to a democracy*. To be sure, Washington was no Ethan Allen. He was no frontiersman or man of the people. Born in Westmoreland County, Virginia, in 1732, he was raised by his eldest brother, Lawrence, after the death of his father in 1743. From Lawrence, who died in 1752, George Washington received a substantial inheritance, the jewel of which was Mount Vernon, a fine plantation estate on the Potomac. Washington became a prosperous gentleman planter, further solidifying his financial position by his 1759 marriage to Martha Custis, a wealthy widow. By this time, Washington had earned a military reputation as colonel of the Virginia militia in the French and Indian War and was elected justice of the peace for Fairfax County, serving from 1760 to 1774.

As the Revolution approached, Washington became a key member of the first Virginia provincial congress in August 1774 and was chosen as one of seven Virginia delegates to the First Continental Congress the following month. He was a delegate to the Second Continental Congress as well.

Landed and prosperous, Washington does not, by modern standards, seem a likely candidate for revolutionary activist. We think of revolutions, such as the French Revolution, the Bolshevik Revolution, the Cuban Revolution of 1958, as actions of the disadvantaged and downtrodden against the ruling class. While it is true that, in the American Revolution, many frontier settlers considered themselves disadvantaged and even downtrodden, it was the colonial elite, people like Washington, Hancock, and Franklin who led the Revolution. To be sure, they were animated by much advanced political thought, but they fought to *regain* what they believed were ancient rights—"inalienable" and "self-evident," not radical or innovative. It was the taxation and trade policy of King George's government, not the idea of liberty, that disturbed the status quo. As men like Washington saw it, the Revolution would be fought not so much to change their world, but to restore to it a balance and justice perceived as natural.

Ensconced in his white-columned mansion above the Potomac, served, as others of his station were, by slaves, Washington might have embraced command with haughty grandeur. Instead, in accepting the call of the Continental Congress to lead the Continental army, Washington, on June 16, 1775, wrote to President Hancock of his "great distress from a consciousness that my abilities and Military experience may not be equal to the extensive and important Trust ...." Nevertheless, he pledged to do his utmost, and he went on to decline in advance any offer of salary, save reimbursement of his expenses.

# Gallantry at Bunker Hill

In Chapter 11, we will look at the details of the siege of Boston, headquarters of the British army in America. For now, it is enough to know that a stream of New Englanders were pouring into Cambridge and adjacent towns with the purpose of laying siege to Boston. By the end of May, some 10,000 colonial troops surrounded the city.

In the meantime, on May 25, HMS *Cerberus* sailed into Boston Harbor, bearing three major generals to assist Thomas Gage in crushing the rebellion. They were William Howe, the senior officer, John Burgoyne, and Henry Clinton. Born in 1729, Howe was well connected, but he earned his rank serving in the War of the Austrian Succession and in the French and Indian War, playing a key role in Wolfe's victory at Quebec. An advanced military thinker, as British commanders went, he made a genuine effort to adopt tactics suited to wilderness warfare. Moreover, he was openly sympathetic to the American cause, but declared that "a man's private feelings ought to give way to the service at all times," and he eagerly embraced the assignment to quell the rebellion.

Burgoyne and Clinton, *Cerberus'* other two passengers, were very different in character from Howe and from one another. "Gentleman Johnny" Burgoyne was a member of Parliament, a playwright, a man of fashionable wit, and a notorious lady killer. His troops had affection for him, because he treated them as human beings—a novelty in the British service. Yet he grossly underestimated the military prowess of the colonials. Told that a mere 10,000 provincials had bottled up 5,000 British regulars in Boston, he cavalierly remarked, "What! Well, let us get in and we'll soon find elbow room." It is said that when he disembarked at Boston, the populace greeted him with shouts of "Make way for General Elbow-Room!"

In contrast to both Burgoyne and Howe, Henry Clinton was a humorless, colorless, by-the-book commander, whose signal strength was as a planner of military operations rather than a leader of troops.

General Gage greeted the arrivals and quickly assigned Howe to crush the American army in a single blow. Howe decided on an amphibious landing at Dorchester Point, to the right of Cambridge, in coordination with Clinton's landing at Willis Creek, to the left. This would secure the high ground at Charlestown: Bunker Hill. The twin operations would be well covered by fire from the men o' war in Boston Harbor, and, with the high ground secured, the forces of Howe and Clinton could crush the American flanks in a pincers movement converging on Cambridge.

The only flaw in this plan was that the Americans knew about it. The local Committee of Safety had a well-developed network of spies, and Gen. Artemas Ward, in command of the Boston Army, called a hasty council of war. The Committee of Safety wanted the army to seize, occupy, and fortify Bunker Hill before Gage could attain it. Both Ward and Joseph Warren objected, pointing out that the Boston army was desperately short of ammunition and that Bunker Hill, projecting out on Charlestown Peninsula, was totally exposed to the guns of the British fleet. Moreover, the only way off the hill was via Charlestown Neck, a narrow isthmus that flooded at high tide.

To these objections, Maj. Gen. Israel Putnam, 57-year-old veteran of the French and Indian War, replied with cryptic wisdom. "Americans are not at all afraid of their heads, though very much afraid of their legs. If you cover these, they will fight forever." In that era of crude medicine, leg wounds almost always resulted in amputation, if not agonizing infection and death. Dug in, the men would fight.

And so it was decided. Putnam led 1,200 men to the heights beyond Charlestown. The issue of just how Americans, whether fearing for their heads or legs, would "fight forever" with only 11 barrels of gunpowder was left unanswered.

## Prescott Occupies the "Wrong" Hill

In company with "Old Put" was Col. William Prescott, another French and Indian War veteran. Putnam argued that it was better to occupy Breed's Hill, which was closer to Boston, than Bunker Hill. The two argued for a time, and ultimately decided to concentrate on Breed's Hill, leaving some men to fortify Bunker Hill to cover any retreat. It was a tactical error. Higher, steeper, and farther from the ships of the Royal Navy, Bunker Hill could have been made virtually impregnable. In contrast, Breed's Hill was lower, not as steep, more exposed, and far more vulnerable.

Twelve hundred Americans dug furiously into Breed's Hill. Gage and Howe had 2,500 troops ready to attack. They were supported by land-based artillery and by the cannon of the 68-gun ship of the line *Somerset,* two floating artillery batteries, the frigate *Glasgow*, the armed transport *Symmetry*, a pair of gunboats, and two sloops of war, *Falcon* and *Lively.*

At dawn on June 17, a Royal Marine sentry on the *Lively* first saw the Americans at work on Breed's Hill. *Lively* opened fire. British admiral Samuel Graves ordered the firing to stop, but soon the entire fleet opened up on the American position.

The naval bombardment surprised Gage, Clinton, and Howe far more than it did the Americans, who were expecting it. The British generals called a hasty council of war. Clinton, the great planner, wanted to attack across Charlestown Neck, moving against the rebel rear. But Gage and Howe had command of the attack, and they proposed to disembark from the Mystic River side of the peninsula and march around to the American rear. This required waiting for a favorable tide, and it meant that the Americans had an additional six hours to continue digging in.

**Sites and Sights**

Visit Charlestown, just across the Charlestown Bridge from Boston's North End, and you will find the Bunker Hill Monument, designed by Solomon Willard, precisely where it should be—perched atop Breed's Hill, where the battle was actually fought. From the monument, you can appreciate the strategic importance of Bunker/Breed's Hill. Call 617-242-5641 for information.

**Fightin' Words**

A **redoubt** is a small, usually temporary defensive fortification. A **breastwork** is an even more modest fortification, reaching no higher than a man's chest—hence the name.

## The British Attack

It was also six hours of naval bombardment. One shot took the head off a soldier named Asa Pollard, a sight that struck terror into the patriot defenders. Col. Prescott leapt to the parapet of the fortification, deliberately exposing himself to fire, to prove that Pollard had simply gotten in the way of a lucky shot.

From his position on Bunker Hill, Gen. Putnam issued commands, twice leaving the fortification to venture across exposed Charlestown Neck to demand reinforcements from Artemas Ward. At last Ward released 1,200 New Hampshiremen under the command of John Stark and James Reed. Steely cool, Stark marched his troops through four miles of incoming shot and shell at the stately marching tempo of the period. Urged by a subordinate to rush the cadence, he declined to do so, replying that "one fresh man in action is worth ten fatigued men."

At 1:00, 2,300 redcoats disembarked at Moulton's Point, at the tip of Charlestown Peninsula. But, suddenly, the assault didn't look so easy to Howe. Vulnerable as Breed's Hill was, Prescott had put up a formidable *redoubt* on top of the hill and a *breastwork* alongside the hill. Glimpsing the men also occupying Bunker Hill, to the rear of Breed's Hill, Howe assumed that the Yankees had a substantial reserve. Looking along the ridge leading to Breed's Hill, Howe now saw Stark's sharpshooters marching to reinforce the American position. All this gave the British general pause. He delayed again, to await reinforcements of his own.

Once more, Prescott was given the gift of time, which he used to improve his position. During this interval, dashing young Dr. Joseph Warren joined the defenders of Breed's Hill. With a major general's commission, he outranked Col. Prescott, who offered to defer command to him. "I shall take no command here," Warren cordially replied. "I came as a volunteer with my musket to serve you." Such was the spirit of the rebellion.

Now reinforced up to a full strength of about 2,500 men between himself and Brig. Gen. Sir Robert Pigot, Howe was ready to attack. Howe's objective was a breastwork and a rail fence on the Mystic River slope of the hill—the latter defended by Stark's sharpshooters. Pigot was to attack the redoubt, the earthwork defenses at the top of the hill.

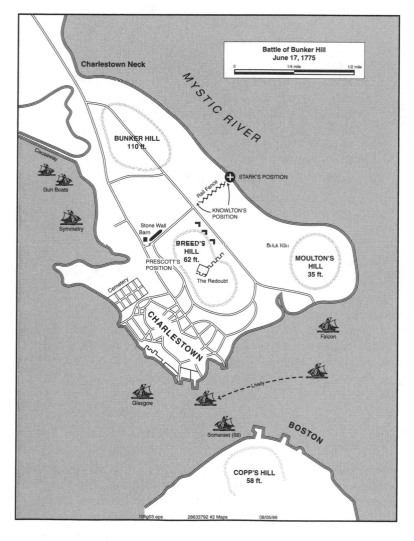

*The Battle of Bunker Hill.* (Map by Kevin D. Smith)

British military doctrine called for any assault on a fortification to be preceded by concentrated artillery bombardment. Howe accordingly ordered his artillery to commence firing. Shots rang out—then suddenly fell silent. It seems that the artillerists had mistakenly supplied the 6-pounder cannons with 12-pound balls. They wouldn't fit.

In the meantime, to Howe's left, the troops under Pigot were being raked by rifle fire from houses in Charlestown. Pigot called to Admiral Graves for help. He responded by bombarding the town, using solid cannonballs heated red hot and hollowed-out cannonballs known as *carcasses*. Pierced with holes, these were filled with flammable pitch, set ablaze, and fired. On impact, they broke apart, spewing flames. Soon, all of Charlestown was engulfed.

**Fightin' Words**

**Carcasses** are hollow cannonballs filled with pitch, ignited, and then fired. Shattering on impact, they spread the burning pitch, igniting whatever they hit.

Against this backdrop, the battle continued to rage. Howe positioned 350 of his best troops, the light infantry, along the Mystic River beach and ordered them to make a bayonet charge into the Yankee position fronting the Mystic. At this point, Israel Putnam issued one of the most famous battle commands in American military history: "Don't fire until you see the whites of their eyes! Then, fire low."

And he meant it. When a few nervous militiamen let fly prematurely, Putnam roared that he would kill the next man who fired.

Stark, the New Hampshire frontiersman, made his firing orders even more specific. Dashing out 40 yards from behind the rail fence that terminated at the Mystic beach, he drove a stake into the earth. "Not a man is to fire until the first regular crosses that stake," he barked.

The British assault was courageous, but the steady, close-range fire of the Putnam's and Stark's men was deadly. Incredibly, 96 redcoats lay dead on Mystic's sands, the victims of three American volleys. Every member of Howe's personal staff was either killed or wounded. Howe, courageous, always in the forefront, was unscathed—physically. Emotionally, however, he was in shock. Gazing on his own dead and wounded, then learning that Pigot had also been thrown back, he experienced (as he later wrote) "a moment that I never felt before."

## "Greater Than We Can Bear"

The Americans were ecstatic. They had won! But Prescott tempered his own jubilation. While praising the defenders of Breed's Hill, he cautioned that the battle was not yet over. Nevertheless, a number of men, without authorization, began to leave. There *were* reserves at Bunker Hill, but Gen. Putnam was unable to get them to go forward to Breed's Hill, where he knew they were still needed. Most serious of all, ammunition was dwindling.

And Gen. Howe, though stunned, was a seasoned veteran. Repulse, shock, and death, he knew, were part of combat. Within 15 minutes of his first disastrous assault, he was set up to attack again. This time, his main force would join Pigot in a head-on attack of the redoubt atop the hill, while a smaller secondary force would keep the Mystic flank occupied.

Again, the redcoats were cut down. John Pitcairn, the major of Royal Marines who had fought at Lexington and Concord, was among the slain. Once again, Pigot and Howe were forced to withdraw. Yet the American defenders were also beginning to buckle under the pressure of the assaults.

Reinforcements arrived, but some of these men avoided battle by huddling *behind* Bunker Hill. Thrown into the thick of combat, the fresh troops found it hard to maintain courage under fire. If a man fell wounded, 20 would rush to "volunteer" to carry him to the rear. There was plenty to be afraid of. If reinforcements were in short supply, powder was down to almost nothing. The men had sufficient musket balls to repulse a third assault, but not enough powder. So they broke apart the prepared paper powder cartridges that formed the charge that fired the ball. The contents were divided, which meant that every man would get powder, but the result would be a reduction of their muskets' effective range by half.

While the American troops suffered a crisis of nerve, 400 Royal Marines and army regulars instantly responded to Howe's call for a fresh assault. Again, shaken though they were, the Americans poured on the fire. But, this time, the redcoats breached the Yankee positions on Breed's Hill. Combat was now hand-to-hand. Because most of the Americans lacked bayonets, Prescott ordered his men to use their muskets as clubs in order to "twitch their guns away."

At last, as more and more scarlet-coated men poured over the parapet, Prescott shouted, "Give way, men! Save yourselves!" Prescott and Putnam conducted a fighting retreat, backing down Breed's Hill, moving across Bunker Hill, running over Charlestown Neck, and moving back onto the mainland. It was in the retreat that the Americans suffered their heaviest casualties, about 450, including 140 dead—among them the brilliant Joseph Warren, physician, major general of volunteers, and, in this action, foot soldier.

But the British, technically the victors, had the most to mourn. Of 2,400 men actually engaged in combat, 1,054 had been shot, of whom 226 died. Against any enemy, such losses would have been staggering. But these were suffered by the elite troops of Europe fighting a ragtag army of provincials, whom they significantly outnumbered and vastly outgunned. Certainly, these were not the battle numbers one associated with victory. To his diary, Henry Clinton confided: "A dear-bought victory; another such would have ruined us."

### We Hold These Truths

"My Lord: You will receive an account of some success against the Rebels, but attended with a long list of killed and wounded on our side; so many of the latter that the hospital has hardly hands sufficient to take care of them. These people shew a spirit and conduct against us they never shewed against the French, and every body has judged of them from their formed appearance and behaviour when joyned with the Kings forces in the last war; which has led many into great mistakes.

" ... A small body acting in one spot will not avail. You must have large armys, making divertions on different sides, to divide their force.

"The loss we have sustained is greater than we can bear .... I wish this cursed place was burned ...."

—Thomas Gage to Lord Barrington, Secretary of State for War, June 26, 1775

## *The Vanquished Triumph*

The Americans were no longer in possession of Bunker Hill, but, as at Lexington and Concord, they came away from battle feeling that they had given better than they got. They had made another dent, a bloody, gaping gash, in the British war machine.

The veterans of the misnamed Bunker Hill battle had much to be proud of, but the outcome did give some false confidence. To be sure, the Americans had held their own against the finest soldiers in the British army *and* a naval bombardment. But it is also true that they enjoyed the immense advantage of fighting from a height and from cover. True, too, that, while much of the American performance depended on the independence of spirit of the individual American fighting man, the troops of Bunker Hill had also shown the dangers of a lack of discipline. Desertion was plentiful, as was outright refusal to fight. Dissension among the commanders, Putnam, Prescott, and Stark, was intense.

*Neither* side could afford many battles like this one. But Bunker Hill gave the Americans the impetus to go on the offensive with a plan, more bold than prudent, to take the war to British Canada, and that is the subject of the next chapter.

## The Least You Need to Know

➤ Fort Ticonderoga, weakly defended, fell easily to Ethan Allen, gaining for the patriot cause a strategically important outpost and major cache of badly needed artillery.

➤ The Second Continental Congress created a *national* army in the hope of increasing colonial unity; George Washington reluctantly accepted command of this Continental army.

➤ In general, British military and economic resources dwarfed those of the Americans; however, the patriots enjoyed certain advantages of geography, frontier military experience, unity of purpose, and faith in the leadership of Washington.

➤ The Battle of Bunker Hill ended in a British victory so costly that it seemed almost a defeat, and convinced the British commanders that the American Revolution would be a hard-fought affair.

# Chapter 10

# Canadian Sunset

### In This Chapter

➤ Canada spurns Congress's offer of union

➤ Congress authorizes an invasion of Canada

➤ Ethan Allen fails to take Montreal and is captured

➤ Benedict Arnold's epic march to Quebec

➤ Disastrous withdrawal from Canada

➤ Arnold's heroism on Lake Champlain

A ragtag collection of minutemen had beaten the best of Britain at Lexington and Concord, and although the redcoats prevailed at Bunker Hill, they had done so at a cost that felt to them much more like defeat. On July 3, 1775, George Washington assembled on Cambridge Common troops of the Boston militia, called them the "Continental army," and formally assumed command.

Feeling like a winner, with two battles under its belt and an officially constituted national army decreed (if not yet fully created), America decided to take the offensive and bring its new war to Canada.

## The Fourteenth Colony?

Many Americans took for granted that Canada would want to join the revolution they had started. Maybe it was wishful thinking, but it was by no means unreasonable:

➤ Canada was overwhelmingly French, not British. It was a conquered nation.

➤ Surely the French Canadians had to resent British tyranny even more strongly than the Anglo-Americans did.

➤ Canada shared a continent with the 13 colonies. And, like them, Canada was separated from England by a vast ocean. It should be obvious that Canada and the lower colonies had more in common with one another than with the mother country.

## Congress Resolves—and Reverses

Drifting with the prevailing sentiment, Congress resolved on June 1, 1775, that there should be no expedition against Canada. Instead, it would create a commission to carry the gospel of liberty and rebellion to our northern neighbors, who would be invited to join the struggle.

To the surprise and consternation of Congress, however, the Canadians were not interested. The Quebec Act—which, as we saw in Chapter 7, "Tea Parties and Sons of Liberty," had so outraged the colonists—worked wonders of reconciliation on the Canadians. The crown's treatment of Canada was as sensitive and enlightened as its policy toward the lower 13 colonies was obstinate, oafish, and autocratic. The royal governor of Canada, Gen. Guy Carleton, was guided by both common sense and humanity. The deeply Catholic French Canadians typically looked to their clergy for guidance, and the bishops and fathers uniformly counseled their flock to remain loyal to King George, who, after all, had granted them a freedom of worship that only two of the 13 colonies, Maryland and Pennsylvania, were willing to extend. Canadian Catholics also enjoyed access to political office, which was closed to Catholics in all of the 13 rebellious colonies.

**Fightin' Words**

The **Articles of Confederation** were the first constitution of the United States. Adopted in 1777 and ratified in 1781, they created a weak federal government and were soon supplanted by the Constitution (1788).

Congress never quite abandoned the idea of Canada's voluntary union with the colonies. The *Articles of Confederation,* which were drafted in 1776 and approved the following year, included a provision to allow Canada's immediate membership in the union, should it so desire (see Chapter 27, "A New Order for the Ages"). On June 27, 1775, however, less than a month after it had resolved not to invade Canada, Congress authorized doing just that.

## Allen and Arnold, Again

Ethan Allen and Benedict Arnold, uneasy comrades in arms, competitive co-conquerors of Fort Ticonderoga, had lobbied Congress for just such a resolution of invasion. The headstrong and impetuous Allen enjoyed being a hero, but Arnold seemed to be after even more. Just look at his behavior after the taking of Ticonderoga. On May 17, 1775, a week after Ticonderoga fell, Arnold had led a quick raid on St. Johns, Canada (about 20 miles southeast of Montreal) and captured a 70-ton, 16-gun British warship. On

June 1, Arnold was given command of American forces on Lake Champlain, but, two weeks later, was ordered to relinquish command to another. Arnold had swallowed his pride when Ethan Allen was given command over the Ticonderoga expedition, but this was too much. He nearly defied the order and was on the verge of leading a mutiny, but ultimately backed down. To add insult to his injury, however, Massachusetts authorities accused him of misappropriating funds—a charge of which he was eventually cleared.

These first weeks of the Revolution revealed Benedict Arnold's problematic character as a soldier. Bold, resolute, beloved by his men, and always tactically inventive, he was also egomaniacal, impetuous, quick to take offense, and supremely arrogant in dealing with those of superior or equal rank. Even the fact that his finances were questioned was all too typical. Arnold habitually spent freely, worrying about the consequences only after they had overtaken him.

In working to persuade Congress to authorize a full-scale invasion of Canada, Benedict Arnold believed that his only competition in this enterprise was Ethan Allen. Presumably, Allen felt the same way about Arnold.

Imagine the consternation of both men when, on June 27, Congress chose neither Allen nor Arnold, but Maj. Gen. Philip Schuyler, to lead the invasion. A wealthy and patrician New Yorker, Schuyler had been named by Congress as one of the Continental army's four major generals. Selecting him to lead the Canadian expedition was a logical choice, but not the best one. During the French and Indian War, Schuyler demonstrated skills as an administrator, not as a battle commander. Worse, he was in ill health. Fortunately, however, Schuyler had made a good choice of second in command. Tall, handsome, dashing Richard Montgomery had been a British regular in the French and Indian War. Instead of returning with his regiment after that conflict, he married a wealthy young woman and settled in America.

Authorized at the end of June to invade Canada, Schuyler dithered and delayed. At last, urged on by the exasperated Montgomery, he was ready to move in September. Before he could get under way, however, he received word that George Washington had authorized the ever-persuasive Benedict Arnold to lead a simultaneous operation. While Schuyler attacked Montreal, Arnold would take Quebec.

Learning that, during Schuyler's delay, an enemy expedition was preparing to recapture Fort Ti (as it was familiarly called) and Crown Point, Montgomery decided to take matters into his own hands. Montgomery sent Schuyler a polite message that, much as it disturbed him to move without his orders, he nevertheless believed that "prevention of the enemy is of the utmost importance." Montgomery moved out of Fort Ticonderoga and headed for Canada with about 1,200 men, including Ethan Allen and his Green Mountain Boys.

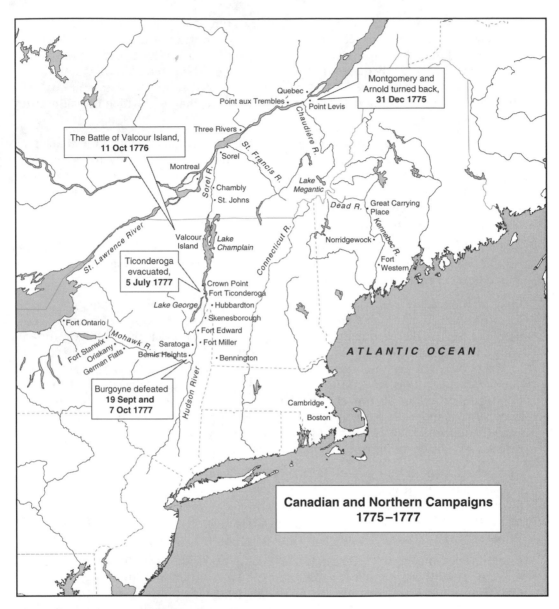

*Canadian and northern campaigns, 1775–77.*
(Map by Kevin D. Smith)

## Success and Failure

Like Arnold, Allen had suffered his share of disappointment. Having taken Fort Ti, Allen returned to his rustic hometown of Bennington expecting a hero's welcome. What he got was a windy sermon by Rev. Jedediah Dewey, who spent two hours

**136**

thanking God for the victory Allen had achieved. "Parson Dewey," Allen finally piped up, "aren't you going to tell the Lord about me being there, too?" Dewey derided Allen as a "great infidel" and admonished him to "be quiet."

But this affront was nothing compared to what happened next. His Green Mountain Boys, preparing for the anticipated invasion of Canada, voted Allen out and elected one Seth Warner to lead them instead. Allen's deselection, it seems, had been engineered by sober-sided citizens who were appalled by the frontiersman's hard-drinking godlessness. To Allen's credit, he responded to this blow as Benedict Arnold would not have; he accepted it. And when some of his men offered to quit the Green Mountain Boys, Allen persuaded them to remain in service and show loyalty to their new leader. Furthermore, he appealed directly to Gen. Schuyler to permit him to join the Canadian expedition—not as a commissioned officer, but as a scout.

On September 4, Gen. Schuyler, ailing, caught up with Montgomery, and the two led the assault on St. Johns—site of a British fort and barracks defended by about 200 regulars and a contingent of Indians. The Americans had hoped for a rapid assault but soon found themselves battling a well-entrenched enemy. By mid September, Schuyler was so ill that he had to be invalided to the rear, and, once again, Montgomery was in sole command. While laying prolonged siege to St. Johns, about half his troops fell ill and were increasingly miserable as the autumn weather turned increasingly cold. In the meantime, British general Carleton reinforced St. Johns, bringing the strength there to about 700 men.

### We Hold These Truths

As in most wars, disease claimed far more lives than bullets did. For every battle death on both sides, there were nine from disease. Dysentery, smallpox, venereal disease, and "camp fevers" (mainly typhus and typhoid) were the chief scourges. In the south, malaria was added to this list. Smallpox inoculation was not a new idea by the 1770s, but many doctors as well as patients still resisted it. Little wonder, for, in the eighteenth century, inoculation consisted of deliberately infecting the patient with what was hoped would be a mild form of the disease. After the first two years of the war, the incidence of smallpox fell, due, in part, to inoculation. Enteric diseases—such as dysentery—were always more prevalent and virulent in American camps than in British camps, which were better disciplined and more sanitary. British regiments also included trained surgeons among their personnel. Although Congress created an Army Medical Department as early as May 1775, it was hampered by scant funding.

While he suffered in the siege, Montgomery dispatched Ethan Allen and a militia officer named John Brown to recruit a handful of rebellious Canadians. While Brown traveled to the settlement of La Prairie to gather volunteers, Allen recruited along the Richelieu River. Allen was immediately heartened by his success and, realizing that Montreal was weakly defended, impetuously decided to invade the town. Unfortunately, his new recruits were also impetuous, and as quickly as they had decided to join Allen, they drifted away. Without an army to take Montreal, Allen turned back toward St. Johns with the 110 volunteers who had remained with him and rejoined Brown, who had some 200 recruits in tow. Together, the pair decided to take the town. Allen would cross the St. Lawrence River with his 110 men below Montreal, and Brown would cross the river above it. The two groups would attack simultaneously from opposite sides.

Allen successfully crossed the river during the night of September 24–25, but Brown did not. Once again caught short, Allen retreated, but could not get all of his men back across the river before Gen. Carleton, with 35 regulars and 200 volunteers, took him and 20 of his men captive. The Vermonter was clapped in irons and shipped back to England for trial. But then the government thought better of it. Allen's first loyalty was to Vermont, and he wanted the Continental Congress to recognize Vermont as a separate state. Since the rebel government of New York claimed the territory of Vermont, the Continental Congress was unlikely to grant Vermont independent status. Therefore, Allen decided to negotiate with the British, who held out the promise of granting Vermont an elected assembly like those of the other colonies. Instead of being hanged as a traitor, in June 1776, Allen was returned to Halifax, Nova Scotia, and in October, was paroled in New York City.

Ethan Allen was lucky, but his ill-advised attempt on Montreal had done significant damage to the American cause in Canada. It solidified popular Canadian sentiment against any participation in the Revolution and, even worse, moved many vacillating Indians to side with the victorious British.

While Allen and Brown were failing against Montreal, Montgomery was finally making headway against St. Johns. He sent a force downriver to Chambly, where a small British fort held a cache of gunpowder. Montgomery captured Chambly and the powder on October 18. Slowly, too, St. Johns was wearing down. But not until a siege mortar arrived—called the Old Sow—was Montgomery able to pummel the British fort into final surrender, on November 2, 1775.

**Fightin' Words**

A **brigantine** was a two-masted, square-rigged sailing vessel.

# Target: Quebec

But what, exactly, had Montgomery gained? The army he had defeated was better clothed and better fed than his own miserable men, who now begged to be allowed to go back home. Worse, two precious months had been lost in this first leg of the invasion.

Montgomery pulled his soldiers together with a promise that warm clothes and food awaited in Montreal. The ragtag band took the town, which was defended by a mere 150 British regulars and a smattering of militia, on November 13. A British *brigantine,* two other armed craft, and some smaller vessels also fell to the Americans. And, yes, the weary, chilly band found food and clothing to cheer them. Now Montgomery had nothing to do but wait for word from Benedict Arnold in Quebec.

## "Our Fatigues Seemed Daily to Increase"

Arnold and his men were undergoing an epic of endurance and suffering. He had left with 1,100 volunteers from Cambridge—men bored with the siege of Boston—on September 12. Maine was freezing, and the *bateaux* that were supposed to carry them up the Kennebec River from Fort Western (present-day Augusta, Maine) had been hurriedly cobbled together out of green—uncured—wood. They fell apart in the icy water. At one point, Arnold and his men were forced to wade in the frigid river for some 180 miles.

Then the food gave out. The men ate their soap, and when the soap ran out, they boiled anything made of leather: moccasins, breeches, whatever. Men dropped out along the way—at one point, an entire division of 350 left with its lieutenant colonel—and men died. On November 9, 600 of the original 1,100 reached the south bank of the St. Lawrence River. The journey was supposed to have taken 20 days. It took 45. Arnold's trip had been estimated at 180 miles. The actual distance was 350.

Quebec, Arnold knew, was held by a small number of Royal Marines, a few regulars, and perhaps 400 militiamen. Even with his ragged force, Arnold believed he could take the fortress town. But, once again, fortune frowned on the American commander. A frigid wind kept the men from crossing the St. Lawrence for two nights. During this delay, British reinforcements arrived, bringing Quebec's body of defenders to 1,200.

Still, Arnold was bent on achieving glory. On two nights, November 13 and 14, Arnold's column crossed the St. Lawrence. Marching over the Plains of Abraham, Arnold overwhelmed the militia there, then sent emissaries toward the town with a flag of truce.

Flag or no flag, the British let loose cannon fire from behind their walls, driving the emissaries back to Arnold. The *Lizard,* a British *frigate,* sailed

**Fightin' Words**

**Bateaux** (singular, **bateau**) were long, flat-bottomed boats with sharply pointed bow and stern, used to navigate rivers in the north country.

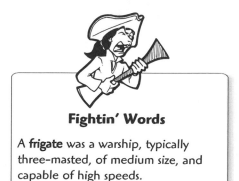

**Fightin' Words**

A **frigate** was a warship, typically three-masted, of medium size, and capable of high speeds.

**139**

up the St. Lawrence, behind the Americans, cutting off Arnold's route of retreat. Eight hundred troops under Col. Allen Maclean prepared to attack the invaders, who withdrew to Pointe aux Trembles to shiver and wait.

## The Attack

At last, on December 2, Montgomery came to the rescue. Together, the forces of Montgomery and Arnold numbered about 1,000 men. Much heartened, they marched back to Quebec, but, within sight of the town, the iron once again left the Americans' spines. They lacked the artillery needed for a rapid siege, and they could not expect to survive a Canadian winter camped outside of the town. Moreover, the terms of enlistment for all of Arnold's New Englanders would expire at the end of the year. They would be free to go home. Gen. Carleton had continued to build up his defenses; 1,800 men now prepared to repel an attack. But to turn back after all they had been through was unthinkable. Generals Montgomery and Arnold decided to attack at once.

**Fightin' Words**

**Grapeshot** was a cluster of small iron balls fired from a cannon as an antipersonnel weapon.

**Voices of Liberty**

"In about eight weeks we completed a march of near six hundred miles."

—Benedict Arnold, probably to Gen. Schuyler, November 27, 1775. (Arnold and his men had actually marched 350 miles—an astounding feat nevertheless.)

On December 31, with a blizzard in full force, the Americans attacked. On the left, Montgomery's men slogged through the snow, dragging their siege ladders. On the right, Arnold's 600 men advanced but were caught under a hail of bullets. Catching a bullet in the leg, Arnold fell and had to turn over command to feisty Daniel Morgan. Remarkably, Morgan was able to lead a group of attackers into the Lower Town, where they hunkered down to await the arrival of Montgomery.

Montgomery was leading his men tortuously over barricades and other obstacles. The British defenders watched and waited. When Montgomery and most of his fellow officers were at point-blank range, the British fired *grapeshot* and a musket volley. Montgomery and most of his officers were cut down, as by a scythe; his men panicked and fled.

In the meantime, Carleton had sent reinforcements to the Lower Town. Morgan's position was hopeless, and his men began to surrender. Morgan himself fought on, but, at last, seeing a priest among the crowd of Quebec's defenders, he called out: "Are you a priest?" Receiving a nod in reply, Morgan offered him his sword: "Then I give my sword to you. But not a scoundrel of these cowards shall take it out of my hands."

# A Swarm of Misguided People

The invasion of Canada had started out as misery and ended in disaster. Not counting the men of Arnold's forces who dropped out or died en route to Quebec, more than half of the invasion force were casualties: 48 dead, 34 wounded, 372 made captive. Still, the painfully wounded Arnold refused to give up. For five months, from January to May 1776, he and his command lingered on the outskirts of Quebec.

## Flight from the North

Congress and Gen. Washington struggled to scrape together a force to send to the relief of Benedict Arnold. By April 2, 1776, troop strength outside of Quebec hovered at around 2,000. Arnold, promoted by Congress to brigadier general, went to Montreal to take command of forces there. Gen. David Wooster arrived from Montreal to take over at Quebec. Another commander, Maj. Gen. John Thomas, arrived on May 1. Nominally, the forces around Quebec now numbered 2,500, but disease, desertion, and expiration of enlistment reduced this number to about 600 men actually fit for duty—a number far too small to attempt to storm the fortressed town.

Then, on May 2, as the ice on the St. Lawrence River broke up, Gen. Thomas learned that ships were carrying a major force to Quebec under Gen. John Burgoyne. Soon, some 13,000 men—among them 4,300 German mercenaries in the British service—would arrive. Thomas and his small army decamped and fled, harassed by Royal Marines. Discipline fell apart. To make matters worse, smallpox, which had plagued the army for months, now became a raging epidemic. Gen. Thomas succumbed to the disease on June 2.

## Cowardice at the Cedars

The American invaders were no longer an army, but a disease-ridden mob. Col. Timothy Bedel was ordered to defend the Cedars, an outpost on the St. Lawrence 40 miles west of Montreal, with 390 Continental army troops. What happened next was typical of the demoralized state of the army.

Learning of the approach of 600 of the enemy, Bedel left the outpost in the hands of Maj. Isaac Butterfield, and then set off for Montreal to summon reinforcements. Before they could arrive, Maj. Butterfield surrendered the entire garrison without putting up a fight. The 100-man relief column marched into an ambush and was likewise forced to surrender. Immediately, a handful of prisoners were tortured to death by the Indian allies of the British. When the British commander learned of the approach of a much larger relief force under Benedict Arnold, he warned Arnold that all the prisoners would be turned over to the Indians if he attacked. Arnold agreed not to attack, and the surviving prisoners were turned over to him, in exchange for the later promised release of British captives.

## "No One Thing Is Right"

On June 1, 1776, a bewildered and distraught Continental Congress received a message from Gen. John Sullivan, who had been dispatched with reinforcements to try to salvage something of the whole sorry operation.

**141**

> *I have done everything I possibly could in time to get information of the true state of affairs, and can in a word inform you that no one thing is right. Everything is in the utmost confusion and almost everyone frightened as they know not what. The report is that [British] General Carl[e]ton has advanced to Three Rivers and the ships [bearing Burgoyne and his massive reinforcements] are coming up the River St. Lawrence.*

Sullivan called the retreat from Quebec "infamous" and the surrender at the Cedars "still more scandalous."

## Shock at Trois Rivières

In an attempt to carry out the orders of Congress and push back toward Quebec, Gen. Sullivan directed Gen. William Thompson to take 2,000 of his best troops to Trois Rivières, on the north bank of the St. Lawrence, halfway between Montreal and Quebec. Sullivan reckoned that the place was held by no more than 800 troops. It was a fatal miscalculation; Burgoyne's regulars had begun arriving, and 6,000 of them, under Brig. Gen. Simon Fraser, were already at Trois Rivières.

On June 6 and 7, by night, Thompson moved his men in bateaux to a point 10 miles north of his objective. Leaving a detachment of 250 to guard the boats, he and his four regimental commanders—Arthur St. Clair, William Irvine, William Maxwell, and "Mad" Anthony Wayne—began the approach to Trois Rivières. Their French-Canadian guide managed to get them lost—perhaps on purpose—and the troops were exhausted as they neared their objective.

Wayne spotted a clearing with British troops and whipped his tired men into a vigorous attack that routed a numerically superior force. Thompson came up with the rest of his command to press the pursuit, but then the Americans encountered a line of entrenchments harboring the main body of Simon Fraser's soldiers. Doubtless unaware of just how badly outnumbered he was, Thompson attacked, only to be repulsed. He tried unsuccessfully to muster his scattered forces for a second attack but soon had to retreat.

Gen. Carleton could easily have cut off the retreat of the American forces, but he didn't know what he would do with perhaps as many as 2,000 prisoners. So he left them to the mercy of the swamps, where they were ambushed by Indians and Canadian militiamen. Eleven hundred American soldiers eventually straggled into Sorel by June 11. At least 400 troops were wounded, killed, or captured. British losses numbered eight killed and nine wounded.

## Escape from Valcour Island

The final phase of America's Canadian venture was potentially the most catastrophic. Once it was clear that the invasion of Canada had totally collapsed, the British began preparing a counteroffensive, an invasion *from* Canada. It was critical to gain control of the waterway straddling Canada and America, Lake Champlain, and both sides scrambled to cobble together shallow-draft fleets to ply the lake's waters.

Here is where the resourceful genius of Benedict Arnold blossomed. Using any tools available and felling local trees, Arnold supervised construction of four large galleys— the *Washington, Congress, Trumbull,* and *Gates.* The *Washington,* which we can assume was typical, measured 72 feet, 4 inches on deck, with a 20-foot beam. Carrying a crew of 80, it mounted two 18-pound guns, two 12-pounders, two 9-pounders, four 4-pounders, and a 2-pounder and eight swivel guns on the quarterdeck. In addition, eight or nine smaller *gundalows* were built, each having a single 12-pound gun in the bow and two 9-pounders amidships, and carrying a crew of 45.

The British also set out to build a fleet for Lake Champlain. They dismantled an ocean-going vessel, the *Inflexible,* and rebuilt it at St. Johns. (They did the same for two smaller schooners and a large gundalow.) At St. Johns, the British built a mammoth *radeau*—or sailing scow—called the *Thunderer.* This improvised vessel carried a crew of 300, two large howitzers, six 24-pound guns, and six 12-pounders. The *Thunderer* was 92 feet long and 33 feet in beam, but it was quite unmaneuverable and did not take part in battle. The British also had numerous smaller vessels, including longboats and gunboats.

Arnold left Crown Point with 10 craft on August 24, 1776, and anchored the boats off rocky Valcour Island. By the time of the battle, which began on October 11, Arnold was in command of 15 vessels. When he saw the size of the approaching British fleet—20 gunboats, 30 longboats, and larger vessels—he pulled back all his boats. It was too late, however. Over the next three days, the two makeshift fleets fought it out, the American vessels taking the worst of it.

**Fightin' Words**

A **gundalow** was a flat-bottomed, open boat with pointed prows on either end. The word is derived from *gondola.*

**Voices of Liberty**

"Thus was the country 'round Quebec freed from a swarm of misguided people, led by designing men, enemies to the libertys of their country, under the specious title of the Assertors of American Rights."

—May 6, 1776 journal entry of Thomas Ainslie, Collector of Customs of the Port of Quebec, regarding the American withdrawal from Canada

By the morning of the 13th, Arnold had two large vessels left, the *Congress* and the *Washington,* in which he made his escape, keeping up a running fight with the pursuing British fleet all the way to Buttonmould Bay on the Vermont shore of Lake Champlain. There, he beached and burned the wrecks of his two ships and made his way overland to Crown Point. Realizing that he could not hold this position, he burned the buildings of Crown Point and retreated to Fort Ticonderoga—the point from which the Canadian venture had begun two years earlier.

Benedict Arnold lost 11 of the 15 vessels that were at Valcour Island. Of the 750 men engaged in the battle, about 80 were killed or wounded. None of the 17–20 British gunboats engaged—or the two larger vessels, the *Carleton* and the *Inflexible*—was damaged.

Valcour Island was the crowning defeat in a disastrous campaign. And yet, by building the Champlain squadron and keeping Carleton occupied, Benedict Arnold took the momentum out of the British advance. "The season is so far advanced," Carleton reported to Lord George Germain, "that I cannot yet pretend to Your Lordship whether anything further can be done this year." The approaching winter put an end to plans for Carleton's forces to link up with those of William Howe, and, therefore, the cause of the Revolution was spared what surely would have been a crushing blow—a thrust that would have cut the colonies in two, severing the north from the south.

Although Benedict Arnold had suffered a decisive tactical defeat, by delaying an invasion from Canada, he had achieved a great strategic victory. In the time he had bought for the patriot cause, His Majesty's troops would become that much wearier, and America would begin to receive aid from France. Benedict Arnold, whose later actions would make his name a synonym for "traitor," had saved the Revolution—not by winning, but by losing a battle.

---

### The Least You Need to Know

➤ Many Americans, including members of Congress, assumed that Canada would be sympathetic to the American cause and would join the revolution. When Canada declined, Congress authorized an invasion—despite a shortage of men and equipment.

➤ The glory-seeking Ethan Allen and the ambitious Benedict Arnold vied for the opportunity to lead the Canadian invasion, but Congress assigned the mission to Maj. Gen. Philip Schuyler.

➤ The American invasion, aimed chiefly at Montreal and Quebec, was defeated by a combination of the harsh Canadian elements and British forces that were far superior in numbers.

➤ During the protracted retreat from Canada, Benedict Arnold fought a delaying action on Lake Champlain that prevented British forces from invading the lower 13 colonies and, quite likely, bringing an abrupt end to the Revolution.

# Chapter 11

# The Battle for Boston

> ## In This Chapter
>
> ➤ Boston: life under siege
>
> ➤ The "Boston army" and its problems
>
> ➤ The Royal Navy takes revenge—sort of
>
> ➤ The patriots fortify Dorchester Heights
>
> ➤ The redcoats evacuate Boston

Bunker Hill left Gen. Thomas Gage in a panic. Although he had forced the Americans from the high ground, he had suffered heavy casualties and was now hemmed in, held under siege in Boston by a revolutionary army that grew daily.

Fortunately for the American cause, Gage was not one of history's great commanders. Had he really *looked* at the rebel army springing up around him, he would have seen that it was no army at all, but a rabble, and he would have taken the offensive after his victory at Bunker Hill—for, however costly, it *was* a victory. Gage could have driven the Americans from their lines, and the siege taking shape would have been broken. Gage lacked the brute numbers to push a frontal attack, but he controlled the coastal waters. Using the Royal Navy, he might have flanked—and crushed—the "Boston army" by sea. If this hadn't ended the rebellion, it would have crippled it.

George Washington, who *was* about to prove himself one of history's great commanders, saw what Gage failed to see. Early in July 1775, he arrived in Cambridge to take command of the Boston army. By this time, the numbers were impressive—16,000–17,000 men—but they had almost nothing a "real" army has: no unified command, little discipline, few military supplies, and very little money. The task, as Washington saw it, was to create an army before the British realized that he had none and decided to attack.

# Woes of a City on a Hill

From the earliest days of its settlement, Boston had seen itself as the "city on a hill." The phrase was from the Old Testament and implied that Boston, chief city of the "New Israel," would stand as a shining example to guide the world to righteousness. What had seemed true in the seventeenth-century Puritan Boston seemed even truer now that the city was the focus of revolution. The people of Boston felt that the eyes of the nation—indeed, of the world—were focused on them. Here, the revolution would move forward—or fail.

## *Life Under Occupation*

For Boston, revolutionary strife had begun as early as 1768, when the first British troops were quartered there. The Boston Massacre of 1770 was a symptom of the tensions created by the occupation (see Chapter 6, "Regulators, Rioters, and a Massacre in Boston"). Following the Boston Tea Party of 1773 (see Chapter 7, "Tea Parties and Sons of Liberty"), Boston was singled out for punishment, which mainly took the form of an import-export blockade. By July 1775, after Lexington and Concord and Bunker Hill, some 10,000 of the city's civilian citizens had fled, leaving a civilian population of about 7,000.

Some who stayed behind were loyalists, but most were not. They were just victims of war: people who had too little money or too few friends and family to go elsewhere, people who had businesses and property to protect, and people who just could not bear to leave home. Those who stayed in Boston suffered acute shortages of food and were in some danger from bombardment. More destructive were the British soldiers, who freely took whatever they wanted—typically without bothering to distinguish between loyalist and rebel.

As a Bostonian named John Andrews wrote in a letter to one William Barrell:

> We have now and then a carcase offered for sale in the market, which formerly we would not have picked up in the street .... Was it not for a triffle of salt provissions that we have, 'twould be impossible for us to live. Pork and beans one day, and beans and pork another, and fish when we can catch it.

## *Besieged*

The siege of Boston began on April 19, 1775, when the "embattled farmers" of Lexington and Concord drove the British troops back to Boston, and then prepared to *invest* the city. On April 23, 1775, the Massachusetts Provincial Congress voted to raise an army of 30,000, including 13,600 to be organized immediately in Massachusetts. Until George Washington arrived to convert the Boston army into the core of the Continental army, Artemas Ward was commander in chief of the besieging force.

Gen. Gage was quite right in his perception that the besieging forces were steadily growing. Rhode Island voted a brigade of three regiments, 1,500 men under Nathanael Greene. New Hampshire set a quota of 2,000, and Connecticut 6,000. Although these colonies fell short of their quotas, by June 1775, some 15,000 provincial troops were positioned just outside Boston. A third of this force was designated the right wing and was positioned at Roxbury, Dorchester, and Jamaica Plain. The center was headquartered at Cambridge and constituted 9,000 men directly under Ward's command. On the left was the balance of the troops: a Massachusetts regiment and militiamen from New Hampshire.

Most militiamen brought their own muskets, but they had little else, and gunpowder was in short supply. More serious was the matter of command. The Provincial Congress appointed Artemas Ward to lead the Boston army, but most militia forces would take orders only from their own officers.

With only 6,500 men as of June 15, Gen. Gage was badly outnumbered, but he had a well-supplied and well-disciplined force under unified command.

**Fightin' Words**

In military parlance, to **invest** a place is to surround it and hold it under siege. The payoff of this "investment," if successful, is the fall of the besieged town or fortress.

## Work of the Boston Army

Washington took command of the Boston army on July 2, 1775, and set about transforming it into a unified and disciplined Continental army. Although his mere presence went a long way, he immediately was faced with the problem of short-term militia enlistments. The terms of the entire Connecticut militia were due to expire on December 10, and Washington had to figure out how to replace them.

There was even worse to contend with. Our schoolbooks teach us that the American revolutionary soldiers were idealists, one and all, brave champions of liberty, motivated by a single-minded passion for liberty.

Doubtless, this was true of many. But many more were all too human. With an acute shortage of gunpowder, in the midst of a siege, and a significant portion of his army about to disband, Washington also had to deal with politicians back in Philadelphia, who had been quick to authorize an army and quick to give Washington command of it, but who were now agonizingly slow in voting the funds for it. In the meantime, the commander in chief was continually hounded by office seekers—wannabe majors and colonels who saw the Continental army as a ticket to future influence and advantage.

**Sites and Sights**

In 1636, North America's first college, Harvard, was founded in Cambridge, across the Charles River from Boston. Today, Harvard University is the central presence of Cambridge, along with Radcliffe College and the Massachusetts Institute of Technology (MIT). Cambridge also features museums, including the Fogg Art Museum, the Arthur M. Sackler Museum (specializing in ancient Greek, Roman, Egyptian, Islamic, and Asian art), the Busch–Reisinger Museum (central and northern European art), and others. Little of Cambridge's revolutionary heritage remains.

## We Hold These Truths

On July 27, 1775, Washington wrote to his brother John Augustine Washington:

*I found a mixed multitude of People here, under very little discipline, order, or Government. I found the enemy in possession of a place called Bunker's Hill, on Charles Town Neck, strongly Intrenched, and Fortifying themselves ....*

*... Their Force, including Marines, Tories, &c., are computed, from the best accounts I can get, at about 12,000 Men; ours, including Sick, absent, &c., at about 16,000; but then we have a Cemi Circle of Eight or Nine Miles, to guard to every part of which we are obliged to be equally attentive; whilst they, situated as it were in the Center of the Cemicircle, can bend their whole Force (having the entire command of the Water), against any one part of it with equal facility ....*

## Voices of Liberty

"Such a dearth of public spirit, and want of virtue, such stock-jobbing, and fertility in all the low arts to obtain advantages of one kind or another ... I never saw before, and pray God I may never be witness to again .... Could I have foreseen what I have, and am likely to experience, no consideration upon earth should have induced me to accept this command."

—George Washington in a letter, November 28, 1775

By January 14, 1776, only 8,212 men of the 20,370 authorized by Congress had been enlisted, and, of that number, only 5,582 were present and fit for duty. The 5,000 militiamen called in to replace the Connecticut troops who left on December 10 would end their brief terms of service on January 15. Of the men present, about 2,000 lacked muskets, and the rest had no more than 10 rounds of ammunition each.

"Search the vast volumes of history through," Washington wrote in a letter, "and I much question whether a case similar to ours is to be found; to wit, to maintain a post against the flower of British troops for six months together, without powder, and then to have one army disbanded and another to be raised within the same distance of a reinforced enemy."

Then the news got even worse. The Boston garrison, by this time under Gen. Howe, was being reinforced. Washington convened a *council of war* on January 16 and made a persuasive case for attacking the British before additional reinforcements made attack impossible. A call went out for 13 militia regiments to serve during February and March, and Washington's hopes rose. The very next day, he received word of the failure at Quebec (see Chapter 10, "Canadian Sunset"), and Congress detached three of the promised militia regiments for service up north. Nevertheless, on February 16, with 16,000 troops, Washington proposed a surprise attack against Boston over the ice.

The commander in chief's officers objected to this plan. According to accepted tactical doctrine, any assault should be preceded by artillery bombardment. Instead, they proposed seizing a lesser objective, with the hope of drawing the British into open battle. Reluctantly—for he believed that the ice presented a golden opportunity for a surprise attack on the main objective—Washington accepted a plan to occupy Dorchester Heights.

**Fightin' Words**

A **council of war** is a meeting among the commander in chief and his field officers and immediate subordinates to establish tactics and strategy for a critical operation.

## Garrison Life

While Washington planned, Gage and Howe presided over the reinforcement of the Boston garrison. At the start of 1775, Gage had some 4,500 combat troops. By mid June, reinforcements brought the garrison's strength to about 6,500. With British naval personnel, by the end of the Boston siege, Gage and Howe commanded about 11,000 troops—all bottled up in Boston.

Garrison duty is typically dull, and garrison duty under siege is excruciating. The redcoats passed the time with amateur theatricals and with some of the more cooperative girls of the town. The officers ate well and enjoyed comfortable quarters, but the men were poorly fed and indifferently housed. Scurvy and smallpox assumed epidemic proportions. Supplies came by sea, either from Canada, the West Indies, or all the way from England. The longer the route, the greater the chance of misfortune, as when a major supply of 5,000 oxen, 14,000 sheep, 10,000 butts of beer, oats, hay, and flour was delayed by storm and the action of American *privateers*. Only a fraction of the provisions shipped reached the garrison, and the British troops suffered just as the civilian population of Boston suffered.

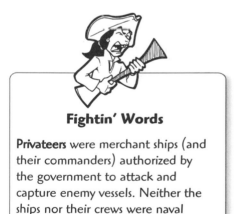

**Fightin' Words**

**Privateers** were merchant ships (and their commanders) authorized by the government to attack and capture enemy vessels. Neither the ships nor their crews were naval personnel.

## A "Noble Train" of Artillery

While Washington planned and Gage languished, Boston bookstore-owner Henry Knox was about to earn his appointment as colonel of the Continental Regiment of Artillery. On November 16, 1775, he proposed to Gen. Washington a plan to transport the artillery captured at Fort Ticonderoga (see Chapter 9, "Green Mountains and Bunker Hill") more than 300 miles to Cambridge, to bombard Boston in preparation for an attack on the British garrison. Three hundred miles was a formidable distance in an era when transportation was supplied exclusively by human and animal muscle. Three hundred miles through the American wilderness, where roads were often little more than wishful thinking, was truly stupendous.

Knox left Cambridge immediately and reached Fort Ti on December 5. He chose 50–60 cannons and mortars, and then directed construction of 42 sledges, which would be pulled by 80 yoke of oxen (that is, 160 oxen yoked into 80 pairs). The first leg of the journey, to the southern tip of Lake George, was tedious and time-consuming. It was January 7, 1776 before what Knox called the "noble train of artillery" reached that point. But then the men and beasts got the hang of it, and the almost 300 miles through the rugged Berkshires nearly flew by. The artillery began arriving in Cambridge on January 24—no one knows just how many pieces in all, but 59 is a good guess, including 14 mortars, 2 howitzers, and 43 cannons. Three of the large siege mortars (including one dubbed the "Old Sow") were 13-inchers weighing more than a ton each. The total weight of the guns transported was 119,900 pounds—and then there was the additional 2,300 pounds of lead the convoy carried.

*Henry Knox, the father of American artillery, as painted by Gilbert Stuart. (Image from the National Archives)*

In a war in which everything was in short supply for the patriots, the presence of heavy artillery was almost beyond expectation. Its timely arrival at the Boston lines would make the capture of Boston a reality—driving out of the city the "flower of British troops."

# To Annoy the Rebels

If Sam Adams, John Hancock, Patrick Henry, and the rest had stopped to think about the Royal Navy, they probably wouldn't have pushed so eagerly for a revolution. By the second half of the eighteenth century, the Royal Navy was the most powerful navy in the history of the world. Moreover, the American colonies, stretching up and down the Atlantic coast and dissected by navigable rivers and estuaries, were ideal targets for naval warfare.

## *Might of the British Navy*

As we will see in Chapter 23, "'I Have Not Yet Begun to Fight,'" the Royal Navy was not as mighty at the outbreak of the Revolution as it had been during the French and Indian War. It was nevertheless formidable, consisting, in 1775, of 131 ships of the line (the largest warships) and 139 vessels of other classes. By the end of the Revolution, the British had a total of 468 ships, of which 100 nimble frigates and lighter warships were committed to the American theater of operations. With these and a quantity of marines, the British should have been able to crush the Revolution quickly. For even if the Americans could rapidly raise an army of sorts, instantly conjuring up a world-class navy was impossible.

What went wrong for the British? On August 20, 1775, Gen. John Burgoyne wrote a flaming letter to Lord George Germain, secretary of state for the American colonies, complaining that he could not answer the question "What is the Admiral doing?" (referring to Adm. Samuel Graves, who commanded the naval forces in and around the colonies), but that he could "only say what he is *not* doing":

> *He is* not *supplying the troops ....*
>
> *He is* not *defending the other islands in [Boston] harbour, for the enemy landed in force ....*
>
> *He is* not *employing his ships to keep up communication and intelligence with the servants and friends of Government at different parts of the continent ....*

To the suggestion that Graves was "surely intent on greater objects," Burgoyne responded, "Alas! He is *not!*" Burgoyne criticized the "supineness" of the navy, which, added to the "defects of Quartermaster General, Adjutant General, Secretaries and commissaries ... make altogether a mass of insufficiency that I am afraid would counteract and disappoint the ablest counsels in the world."

The British army and navy were bogged down by laziness, corruption, and bureaucracy, like massive weapons too heavy to wield swiftly, decisively, and effectively.

# Buying Off a Bombardment

Adm. Graves protested that he "zealously continued to exert every power and exhaust every resource to annoy the Rebels," including a naval bombardment of coastal towns. Had Graves vigorously pursued a program of such action, the Americans would surely have been brought to their knees. But Graves' program of destruction was hardly vigorous.

On October 7, 1775, a small fleet operating in Newport harbor materialized off Bristol, Rhode Island. An officer was sent ashore to warn that if a town delegation did not come out to the ships within an hour to hear the demands of Capt. James Wallace, Capt. Wallace would level the town by naval bombardment. With typical rebel defiance, Governor William Bradford informed Wallace's emissary that it would be more fitting and proper for the captain to come ashore to him.

### Voices of Liberty

*With all their firing and their skill
They did not any person kill,
Neither was any person hurt
Except the Reverend parson Burt.
And he was not killed by a ball,
As judged by jurors one and all,
But being in a sickly state,
He frightened fell, which proved his fate.*

—Anonymous verse by a citizen of Bristol, Rhode Island, 1775

By 8 P.M., a downpour began, and, in the deluge, Wallace's small fleet opened fire. "The shrieks of the women, the cries of the children and groans of the sick," wrote a correspondent to the *New York Gazette,* "would have extorted a tear from even the eye of a Nero."

After a pounding of about an hour and a half, a militia colonel rowed out to Wallace's ship and asked that Bristol be given a respite of time in which to select a delegation. Wallace granted the time, and a delegation met with him. In exchange for 200 sheep and 30 cattle, Wallace told the group, he would cease fire. The delegation, like the Yankee traders they were, haggled and cajoled Wallace until he declared, "I have this one proposal to make: if you will promise to supply me with 40 sheep, at or before twelve o'clock, I will assure you that not another gun will be discharged." And so the bargain was struck, and Bristol bought off destruction.

# Falmouth Flames

Falmouth, Maine—near present-day Portland—was not so fortunate. Capt. Henry Mowat set out from Boston on October 6, 1775, and trained his guns on Gloucester, Massachusetts. He held his fire, however, deciding that the houses were too far apart to be destroyed effectively by naval gunfire. He then moved up the coast and, on October 16, anchored off Falmouth.

Like Capt. Wallace, Mowat came with demands. He wasn't after sheep and cattle, however. The captain wanted "cannon and hostages." When his demands were rejected, he bombarded the town with two ships, the 8-gun *Canceau* and the 6-gun

*Halifax,* firing both solid cannonballs and flaming "carcasses" (see Chapter 9). The cannonade lasted all day on October 18, from nine in the morning until six in the evening. American resistance was feeble and disorganized. The patriots managed to inflict two casualties, both wounds. Warned by Mowat, most of the townspeople had fled, so there were no American casualties—but the town was almost entirely destroyed: 139 homes and 278 other buildings burned to the ground. Fifteen merchant ships had been riding at anchor for Falmouth; four were taken as prizes, the rest put to the torch.

George Washington received word of the Falmouth bombardment, and on October 24, he wrote to Congress: "It appears the same desolation is meditated upon all the Towns on the coast." Looking at a map, Washington concluded that Portsmouth, New Hampshire would be the Royal Navy's next target. He detached Gen. John Sullivan from siege duty at Boston to defend Portsmouth from the anticipated attack. But Adm. Graves lacked both the stomach and the initiative to continue the program of devastation, and Portsmouth, as well as the rest of the coastal towns, was spared.

The Americans gave the British no credit for compassion. Instead, the Falmouth bombardment was taken as a measure of just how ruthless the British could be and just how little they valued colonial lives and property. Doubtless, the raid created more rebels than it discouraged.

## This Unhappy Town Relieved

Through the fall and winter, the two armies—the motley besiegers and the red-coated besieged—eyed each other across Boston Neck and the Charlestown peninsula. On October 10, 1775, by order of the Crown, Gen. William Howe replaced Thomas Gage, who returned to England. On January 27, 1776, Adm. Samuel Graves was replaced by Adm. Richard Howe, brother of the new commander in chief of the army. There was fresh blood at the top, and the British garrison had swelled to 7–8,000 men. But 16,000 or more Americans also were firmly entrenched—poorly equipped, to be sure, with many about to depart as their militia commitments expired. The British knew none of this and did nothing but sit it out in Boston.

### Dorchester High Ground

The standoff ended when Col. Knox delivered his "noble train of artillery" from Fort Ticonderoga. Washington was persuaded to fortify Dorchester Heights, which neither side had occupied. The idea was to erect fortifications while preserving the element of surprise, as had been done at the Battle of Bunker Hill.

This would be no mean feat in the frozen New England March. The icy ground would yield to nothing but painstaking and time-consuming

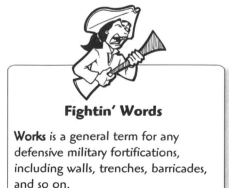

**Fightin' Words**

**Works** is a general term for any defensive military fortifications, including walls, trenches, barricades, and so on.

work with pick and shovel. Then, Rufus Putnam (no relation to Israel Putnam of Bunker Hill) hit on the idea of building the fortifications above ground, using prefabricated parts. Quickly, colonial carpenters hammered together great timber frames (called "chandeliers"), into which hay bales were thrust to provide cover. The *works* were then surrounded with barrels filled with earth. These would not only supply additional protection from enemy fire but could be rolled down the hill at attacking troops.

Knox's artillery was to be positioned within the fortification. Under the command of Gen. John Thomas, during the night of March 4, 1776, a labor detail of 1,200 men, covered by 800 of the Continental Army's best troops, moved a train of 360 ox carts, burdened with the prefabricated fortification materials, up Dorchester Heights. A full moon gave sufficient light for the work, while a ground fog shielded it from enemy eyes. At 10:00 a British officer reported the fortification activity to his commander, the portly and lethargic Gen. Francis Smith, who did nothing. By 3:00 the next morning, the colonials had fortified Dorchester Heights. Although 1,200 men had been directly involved in the work, Howe estimated that it must have taken 12,000, and a military engineer attached to Howe upped that estimate to 20,000.

**Voices of Liberty**

"The rebels have done more in one night than my whole army could do in months."

—Gen. William Howe, British commander in chief, remarking on the fortification of Dorchester Heights, 1776

Occupying the Heights was a brilliant move. British artillery could not be sufficiently elevated to bombard the position, and the commanding height left the British fleet exposed to bombardment. Initially, Howe decided to attack the position with 2,200 men but then called off the operation at the last minute because of a storm.

Wishing to extend their control of the high ground, the Americans stealthily moved to occupy nearby Nock's Hill during the night of March 9, but were quickly driven off with a few casualties.

It hardly mattered. Despite the loss of face that would be suffered, the British had already decided to abandon Boston, since there was no local support for the British cause in that city. Given that decision, Gen. Howe decided that a battle against Dorchester Heights would be futile; he would take the war elsewhere. Howe ordered the withdrawal of British forces from Boston.

## The British Decamp

Howe's decision was made on March 7. At 9:00 on the morning of March 17, the ships were loaded. To keep it from falling into patriot hands, the 64th Regiment placed charges in and about the main British headquarters at Castle William. Then they blew the fortress up.

Eleven thousand British soldiers and sailors, together with perhaps 1,000 colonial loyalists, boarded the ships for evacuation. The Americans held their fire. By secret agreement, the British had been granted leave to depart in safety, provided they did not do to all of Boston what they had done to Castle William. Washington and others had figured on the British evacuating to New York. Instead, they retreated to the relative safety of Halifax, Nova Scotia.

For eight months, the colonials had held what Washington called the "flower of British soldiers" under siege. A mere 20 patriot soldiers had been killed. Boston and the entire province of Massachusetts, singled out for a martyr's fate in the years, months, and days leading up to the Revolution, would not see another redcoat for the remainder of the war.

*The remainder of the war.* That phrase must have lingered in Howe's mind as he and his command sailed in convoy up to Halifax. The general realized what his predecessor, Thomas Gage, had failed utterly to believe. This American Revolution would be a long war, much longer than any British politician or soldier might have imagined.

---

### The Least You Need to Know

➤ Thomas Gage, commanding the British garrison in Boston, failed to recognize how poorly organized and equipped the American forces were. Instead of attacking them, he let his army fall under siege.

➤ Gen. Washington's problems included disciplining and supplying the army around Boston. His worst problem was the withdrawal of militia troops who signed up for two-month commitments and then were released.

➤ The arrival of captured artillery from Fort Ticonderoga, 300 miles away, gave the Americans a way to bring the siege of Boston to an end.

➤ Once Washington's troops occupied and fortified Dorchester Heights, British general William Howe (who replaced Gen. Gage) realized that his position in Boston was untenable and ordered his troops to evacuate.

# Chapter 12

---

# Common Sense and a Bold Declaration

---

### In This Chapter

➤ Galloway's Plan of Union

➤ The Olive Branch Petition: a last-ditch attempt at reconciliation

➤ Paine's *Common Sense* unifies the forces of independence

➤ The writing of the Declaration of Independence

➤ The document

---

Most historians would fix the beginning of the American Revolution at April 19, 1775, the date of the battles of Lexington and Concord. July 4, 1776, is the date on which the Declaration of Independence, the birth certificate of the United States and one of history's greatest documents, was enacted by the Continental Congress. The American Revolution was transformed by the document signed in Philadelphia into a War of Independence. This chapter moves the focus from the conflict fought with powder and lead to the war waged with pen and ink.

## A War of Documents

As Thomas Hutchinson, the bitter royal governor of Massachusetts, saw it, American agitators had been working toward revolution since the Stamp Act of 1765. John Adams, however, one of the chief architects of independence, recalled in his later years that, while there was general discontentment, Americans had no desire for independence from the Crown before 1775–1776.

"For my part," Adams wrote, "there was not a moment during the Revolution when I would not have given everything I ever possessed for a restoration of the state of things before the contest began."

Adams's statement is revealing. It tells us that the American Revolution wasn't turned on suddenly as if by a switch, and it tells us that doubts, regrets, and a desire for reconciliation with the mother country were present at the beginning and throughout the conflict. It tells us, too, that a revolution cannot be fought with bullets alone but is propelled and perpetuated as much by ideas and emotions conveyed in words.

## Plan of Union

History loves ultimatums and absolutes. Everyone remembers the words of Patrick Henry that rang in the ears of Virginia's legislators on March 23, 1775: "Give me liberty, or give me death!" But there were others who looked for alternatives to those extremes.

Among these moderates was Joseph Galloway. Born in Maryland about 1731, Galloway was a leading Philadelphia attorney, vice president of the prestigious American Philosophical Society, and a close friend of Benjamin Franklin. From 1757 to 1774, he was a member of the Pennsylvania Assembly, serving as its president from 1766 to 1774.

On September 28, 1774, Galloway introduced the Plan of Union to the First Continental Congress. It would have given the colonies a large measure of home rule, although ultimately leaving them subject to the king's pleasure. A royally appointed president-general would preside over the united colonies, which would be represented by a popularly elected Grand Council of members from each colony. Although the president-general could veto acts of the Grand Council, the united colonial government would have direct authority in commercial, civil, criminal, and police matters.

**Fightin' Words**

The **Suffolk Resolves,** adopted by the First Continental Congress on September 17, 1774, declared the Intolerable Acts unconstitutional, urged withholding taxes from the Crown, and recommended economic sanctions against Britain.

The Continental Congress, which had just endorsed the radical *Suffolk Resolves*—the Massachusetts documents that declared the Intolerable Acts unconstitutional, urged the withholding of taxes from the Crown, and recommended economic sanctions against Britain—voted to postpone consideration of Galloway's Plan of Union by a single vote. This was late in 1774, just months before Lexington and Concord; a single vote might have averted the Revolution.

# An Olive Branch Offered—and Spurned

Richard Henry Lee, a delegate from the frontier backcountry of Virginia, wrote of the Second Continental Congress, which convened in Philadelphia on May 10, 1775: "There never appeared more perfect unanimity among any sett of men."

The operative word was *appeared*. Very soon into the deliberations of the Congress, it became apparent that the delegates were deeply divided over the issue of separation or reconciliation with England. John Dickinson was a Maryland-born Pennsylvania and Delaware politician whose *Letters from a Farmer in Pennsylvania to Inhabitants of the British Colonies*—14 essays published in the *Pennsylvania Chronicle* during 1767–68—was the most widely read and influential indictment of the Townshend Acts. Dickinson now drafted what came to be called "The Olive Branch Petition."

The petition reiterated all the colonial grievances but professed attachment "to your Majesty's person, family, and government, with all devotion that principle and affection can inspire." The petition spoke of being "connected with Great Britain by the strongest ties that can unite societies" and went on to "beseech your Majesty, that your royal authority and influence may be graciously interposed to procure us relief from our afflicting fears and jealousies."

Adams and the other New Englanders objected to the Olive Branch Petition; in a letter Adams observed that it "gives a silly cast to our doings." Nevertheless, he and the other members of the Continental Congress endorsed the petition—but as individuals, not on behalf of the Congress. The document was put into the hands of Richard Penn—a descendent of the great William Penn, founder of Pennsylvania—who carried it to London and King George III. But the monarch refused even to receive Penn, who had arrived on August 14, 1775, and, on August 23, George proclaimed "our Colonies and Plantations in North America, misled by dangerous and designing men," to be in a state of rebellion. He ordered "all our Officers ... and all our obedient and loyal subjects, to use their utmost endeavours to withstand and suppress such rebellion." Given the leisurely pace of transportation and communication in the eighteenth century, it was November before Congress learned that its olive branch had been so rudely cast aside.

Although King George III spurned the Olive Branch Petition with nary a glance, his prime minister, Lord North, whose insensitive policies had done much to bring the colonies to the brink of revolution in the first place, suddenly turned conciliatory. North secured parliamentary and, grudgingly, royal approval of a plan for reconciliation, which would concede much of the power of taxation to the colonies. On July 31, 1775, the Second Continental Congress, two days before adjourning, rejected North's plan.

On November 16, however, statesman Edmund Burke, always a friend to the American cause, made a speech in support of his "Motion for a Bill to Compose American Troubles." His bold proposition was to assert parliamentary supremacy over royal prerogative where the colonies were concerned. In short, having given up on persuading King George to reconcile with the colonies, Burke hoped to give Parliament the direct authority to do so. The bill failed to pass.

**Voices of Liberty**

"Magnanimity in politics is not seldom the truest wisdom; and a great empire and little minds go ill together."

—Edmund Burke, speech to the House of Commons, urging reconciliation with the colonies, March 22, 1775

# Indecision on Independence

The tide had not yet turned universally toward independence, however. On November 4, 1775, the Assembly of New Jersey simply declared reports of colonists seeking independence "groundless," as if the idea could be legislated out of existence. On November 9, the very day that word was received of King George refusing even to receive the Olive Branch Petition, the Pennsylvania Assembly instructed its delegates to the Continental Congress to "dissent from and utterly reject any propositions … that may cause or lead to a separation from our mother country or a change of the form of this government."

While New Jersey and Pennsylvania temporarily recoiled from independence, Congress played for time. On December 6, after much wrangling, Congress issued a response to the rejection of its petition, reaffirming allegiance to the Crown but disavowing the authority of Parliament, because the colonies did not (and could not) enjoy representation in that body.

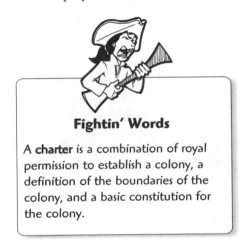

**Fightin' Words**

A **charter** is a combination of royal permission to establish a colony, a definition of the boundaries of the colony, and a basic constitution for the colony.

In the meantime, some colonies were eager to write constitutions for themselves—each one, in effect, a de facto declaration of independence. Massachusetts was first, its Provincial Congress suggesting that the Continental Congress write a model constitution for it and the other colonies. Fearing that this would be too bold a move toward independence, the Continental Congress declined, and Massachusetts reinstituted its *Charter* of 1691—modified to replace the royal governor with a 28-member elected council—as the first state constitution in America.

On October 18, 1775, New Hampshire, eager to press the Continental Congress for something approaching a declaration of independence, asked the same question Massachusetts had asked earlier. Once again, Congress dodged the issue. Because New Hampshire had no colonial charter to fall back on, however, it added the advice that New Hampshire "establish such a government, as in their judgment will best produce the happiness of the people." On January 5, 1776, New Hampshire became the first colony to write a new state constitution.

South Carolina followed New Hampshire with a constitution approved on March 26, 1776. All three of these first constitutions were half-hearted and tentative, none of them making a full break with the mother country. The other colonies would follow with constitutions throughout 1776, but, by then, there was no room for half-heartedness. By the time the Declaration of Independence was adopted on July 4, 1776, seven states were already fully constituted.

# Mr. Paine's Pamphlet and Its Progeny

King George's rejection of the Olive Branch Petition convinced many that separation from the mother country was just a matter of time. A pamphlet published on January 9, 1776 and written, according to the title page, "by an Englishman," finally crystallized popular opinion in favor of complete and immediate independence.

Benjamin Rush, the most highly respected physician in America, a delegate to the Continental Congress, and a man who had no doubts about independence, persuaded Thomas Paine, a newly arrived immigrant from England (he settled in Philadelphia in November 1774), to write a popular pamphlet on the subject of independence. When Paine had finished with it, Rush was mightily impressed and gave it the title by which it has entered history: *Common Sense.*

## A Man of Uncommon Sense

Thomas Paine was born in England in 1737, the son of an impoverished farmer and corset maker. At 13, he was apprenticed to the latter trade, took to the sea for a year at 19, and then spent the next 17 years more or less failing at one pursuit after another, including exciseman (tax collector), corset maker, school teacher, tobacconist, grocer, and husband.

Yet those years were not spent in vain. Paine devoured books on "natural philosophy" (as the sciences were called in the eighteenth century) and political philosophy. He became so informed and eloquent that his fellow excisemen chose him, in 1772, to petition Parliament on their behalf for higher salaries. His efforts proved less than successful. Paine was fired and went bankrupt—though not before meeting and befriending Benjamin Franklin, then serving as a colonial agent in London. In November 1774, Paine, frustrated and discouraged, resolved to make a new start in America, bringing with him letters of recommendation from Franklin, who commended him as an "ingenious, worthy young man."

In Philadelphia, Paine quickly established himself as an able journalist. Since he often wrote about the latest scientific discoveries, it is no wonder that he soon came into contact with Dr. Benjamin Rush, who judged that Paine could write the pamphlet promoting independence that he himself would like to write, but feared to. "I suggested to him," Rush recalled in his autobiography, "that he had nothing to fear from the popular odium … for he could live anywhere, but that my profession and connections … forbade me to come forward as a pioneer in that important controversy."

## A Bestseller

A 47-page pamphlet, *Common Sense* sold for two shillings. It was neither lawyerly nor statesmanlike. Although it contained no original political theory, it made the argument for independence more simply, thoroughly, and persuasively than any document that had come before it.

Paine used every argument at his disposal. Recognizing the strongly anti-Catholic sentiment that prevailed in the colonies, he compared King George III to the pope; he portrayed the notion of the hereditary succession of the monarchy as an evident absurdity rather than as a product of the natural order; he demolished, one after the other, all arguments favoring reconciliation with England; and he underscored the economic benefits of independence. Always, though, Paine returned to two central themes:

**Voices of Liberty**

"I know not whether any man in the world has had more influence on its inhabitants or affairs for the last 30 years than Tom Paine."

—John Adams, 1805

➤ That republican government was inherently and inescapably superior to government by hereditary monarchy.

➤ That equality of rights was the chief birthright of humanity, which no just government could fail to support and defend.

Then Paine did even more. And in this, perhaps, is the truest genius of *Common Sense*. "O ye that love mankind!" Paine concluded his pamphlet:

> *Ye that dare oppose not only the tyranny but the tyrant, stand forth! Every spot of the old world is overrun with oppression. Freedom hath been hunted round the globe. Asia and Africa have long expelled her. Europe regards her like a stranger, and England hath given her warning to depart. O receive the fugitive, and prepare in time an asylum for mankind!*

Paine transformed a quarrel between the colonies and the mother country not only into an international event, but into an event of central importance to humankind. The outcome of the American struggle for independence, he argued, would determine the fate of a humanity historically—and even now—bound by the chains of tyranny. The American Revolution was a revolution for the world, for history, and for the future.

In less than three months, 120,000 copies of *Common Sense* were sold. Probably better than half a million copies were distributed before the end of the Revolution.

# The Great Debate

Rural New Englanders were quite familiar with the phenomenon of the spring freshet—the quiet stream that freezes in winter and, with the spring thaw, swells into a roiling torrent. Such was the course of the independence movement in the spring that followed the publication of *Common Sense*—and Washington's victory in the siege of Boston (see Chapter 11, "The Battle for Boston"). That's the way John Adams put it in a letter of May 20, 1776: "Every post and every day rolls in upon us Independence like a torrent."

The Continental Congress shook off its ambivalence. On February 18, it authorized privateers—merchant ships given permission to raid and capture British vessels. On February 26, it embargoed exports to Britain and the British West Indies. On March 3, Congress sent Silas Deane to France to negotiate for aid. On March 14, Congress moved against the loyalists, ordering that they be disarmed. On April 6, it opened all American ports to the trade of all nations save Britain.

One after the other, the colonies, which now considered themselves states, voted for independence.

### We Hold These Truths

Virginia's resolution for independence is the most eloquent and famous of all the colonial independence resolutions. It was enacted on May 15, 1776:

> *... Instead of redress of grievances [the king has given] increased insult, oppression and a vigorous attempt to effect our total destruction .... Our properties are subjected to confiscation, our people, when captivated, compelled to join in the murder and plunder of their relations and countrymen, and all former rapine and oppression of Americans declared legal and just ....*

> *Wherefore, appealing to the SEARCHER of HEARTS for the sincerity of former declarations, expressing our desire to preserve the connection [with England], and that we are driven from that inclination by their wicked councils, and the eternal law of self-preservation:*

> *Resolved unanimously, that the delegates appointed ... declare the United Colonies free and independent states, absolved from allegiance to, or dependence upon, the crown or parliament of Great Britain ....*

On May 15, the Continental Congress enacted a resolution recommending to "the respective Assemblies and Conventions of the United Colonies, where no Government sufficient to the exigencies of their affairs has been hitherto established, to adopt such Government ...." Less than a month later, on June 7, Richard Henry Lee of Virginia introduced another resolution:

> *That these United Colonies are, and of right ought to be, free and independent States ... and that all political connection between them and the State of Great Britain is, and ought to be totally dissolved.*

*That it is expedient forthwith to take the most effectual measures for forming foreign alliances.*

*That a plan of confederation be prepared and transmitted to the respective Colonies for their consideration and approbation.*

Because it was felt that the Middle Atlantic colonies were "not yet ripe for bidding adieu to the British connection," debate on the resolution was postponed three weeks. (In that time, Delaware, Connecticut, New Hampshire, New Jersey, and Maryland all instructed their congressional delegates to vote for independence.)

**Voices of Liberty**

"I arrived in Congress (tho detained by thunder and rain) time enough to give my voice in the matter of Independence."

—Delaware Delegate Caesar Rodney, to his brother Thomas, July 4, 1776

The debate got under way on July 1; Pennsylvania's Dickinson urged delay, whereas John Adams and Richard Henry Lee urged immediate action. On that day, South Carolina and Pennsylvania voted against independence, while the Delaware delegation was divided, and New York, reorganizing its government, abstained. The vote, then, stood at nine to four in favor of independence.

Not content with less than an overwhelming majority, the radicals of Delaware dispatched Caesar Rodney on a Paul Revere–like midnight ride from Dover to Philadelphia. Breathless after his 80-mile gallop, Rodney arrived in time to swing the Delaware vote to independence. At this, South Carolina's delegation was moved to change its vote to favor independence, as did Pennsylvania. New York again abstained, but the majority, on July 2, was indeed overwhelming. And the word went forth.

# Authors of Independence

Congress did not waste the three-week interval between the introduction of Lee's resolution of independence and the start of the debate. In this interim, it appointed a committee to draft a declaration of independence, naming to it John Adams, Benjamin Franklin, Robert Livingston, Roger Sherman, and Thomas Jefferson.

Adams, of course, was a prime mover of revolutionary activity in the very cradle of the Revolution—Massachusetts. Franklin, at 70 the oldest of the committee, already had an international reputation as a scientist, inventor, writer, editor, politician, and emerging statesman. Livingston, scion of a distinguished New York family, carried into the work assigned him his colony's reservations regarding independence. Sherman, of Connecticut, had been trained as a cobbler but educated himself through omnivorous reading and became a legislator, economic theorist, and the author of a series of almanacs based on his astronomical calculations.

# The Remarkable Mr. Jefferson

Then there was Thomas Jefferson. Classically educated at the College of William and Mary and a successful lawyer by profession, he earned a reputation as an uninspired speaker but a great writer. His 1774 *View of the Rights of America* was a direct attack on the Crown and was considered too radical by most of the early leaders of the independence movement. No one could deny its eloquence, however, and it earned Jefferson a place in the vanguard of revolutionary activists.

Like the other members of the committee—and like many of the other founding fathers—Jefferson was a man of many talents and interests. Perhaps only Franklin achieved Jefferson's degree of greatness in so many fields. In addition to being a great political writer, Jefferson was an inventor, a scientist, a naturalist, and an extraordinary architect, whose own home, Monticello, and the old buildings of the University of Virginia are among the sublime gems of early American building design. Jefferson, of course, would later serve as the third president of the United States, introducing a vigorous liberal element into American government and vastly expanding the nation through the Louisiana Purchase.

**Voices of Liberty**

"Reason first—You are a Virginian, and a Virginian ought to appear at the head of this business. Reason second—I am obnoxious, suspected, and unpopular. You are very much otherwise. Reason third—You can write ten times better than I can."

—John Adams, persuading Jefferson to write the Declaration of Independence

*Charcoal drawing of Thomas Jefferson, author of the Declaration of Independence.* (Image from the National Archives)

Such was Jefferson's reputation as a writer that the other members of the committee delegated the actual drafting of the Declaration of Independence entirely to him. It was an honor, but perhaps not as great as we might imagine. Nobody believed the Declaration of Independence would be—or had to be—a particularly momentous document. It had to be legally defensible, something that would stand up to the scrutiny of the foreign powers, especially France, to which the United States would have to appeal for aid in battling an empire that commanded the world's mightiest army and navy.

## "An Expression of the American Mind"

Years later, writing to Henry Lee in 1825, Thomas Jefferson recalled that his purpose in writing the declaration was not to "find out new principles, or new arguments, never before thought of ... but to justify ourselves in the independent stand we are compelled to take" and to "appeal to the tribunal of the world ... for our justification."

> *Neither aiming at originality of principle or sentiment, nor yet copied from any particular previous writing, it was intended to be an expression of the American mind, and to give to that expression the proper tone and spirit called for by the occasion. All its authority rests on the harmonizing sentiments of the day, whether expressed in conversation, in letters, printed essays, or in the elementary books of public right, as Aristotle, Cicero, Locke, Sidney, etc....*

Of the authors Jefferson enumerated, Jefferson's declaration owed its most direct debt to the seventeenth-century British philosopher John Locke. Locke had enumerated the basic rights of human beings as life, liberty, and property. In his very first draft, Jefferson wrote of "inalienable rights" to life and liberty, but he changed Locke's "property" to "the pursuit of happiness." In eighteenth-century England, "happiness" was often used in the narrow sense of material prosperity, but it also included general well-being. Jefferson significantly slanted Locke's list of basic rights by using a far broader and more resonant term than "property."

## Rough Draft: The Question of Slavery

The first draft Jefferson offered included a condemnation of King George III for having "waged cruel war against human nature itself, violating its most sacred rights of life & liberty in the persons of a distant people who never offended him, captivating & carrying them into slavery in another hemisphere, or to incur miserable death in their transportation thither." Jefferson's paragraph on slavery was medicine too strong for the Virginian's fellow slaveholders—and for some Yankee traders as well, who thrived on the so-called triangle trade—selling goods financed by the slave trade. Moreover, it was clearly unfair to blame George III for the slave trade, and inclusion of such an unfair accusation would only discredit the rest of the Declaration.

The clause was stricken. The United States of America would fight for its liberty and for the inalienable rights of humankind, but it would do so as a slave nation.

# "The Bells Rang All Day and Almost All Night"

In a letter dated July 9, 1776, John Adams wrote to Samuel Chase, a Maryland signer of the Declaration, that "the river is passed, and the bridge cut away .... The Declaration was yesterday published and proclaimed .... The bells rang all day and almost all night."

All over the new nation, there was rejoicing and celebration. But people like Adams himself, one of those most directly responsible for this call to independence, best understood that rejoicing and celebration are mostly empty noise. Well into the Revolution, Adams was in Holland, drumming up international support for the cause. He was asked what proportion of Americans truly supported independence. Adams replied that less than one-twentieth of the American population did *not* support it. Years later, however, in 1815, he admitted that the divisions even after the Declaration had been far deeper: "I should say that full one-third were averse to the revolution" and another third, "the yeomanry, the soundest part of the nation, always averse to war, were rather lukewarm."

Even if the nation were 100 percent behind the push to break the bonds that held it to England, the struggle would be daunting. How much grimmer must it have appeared on July 4, 1776 to John Adams and to others with eyes for reality and stomachs for the truth.

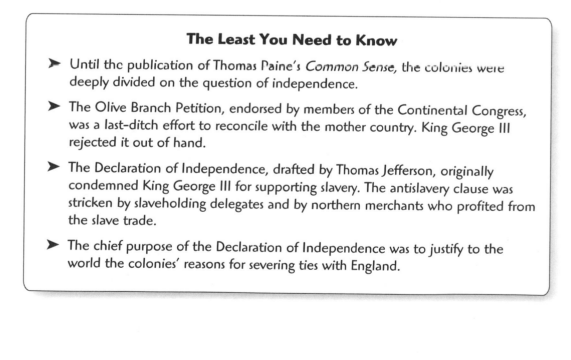

### The Least You Need to Know

➤ Until the publication of Thomas Paine's *Common Sense,* the colonies were deeply divided on the question of independence.

➤ The Olive Branch Petition, endorsed by members of the Continental Congress, was a last-ditch effort to reconcile with the mother country. King George III rejected it out of hand.

➤ The Declaration of Independence, drafted by Thomas Jefferson, originally condemned King George III for supporting slavery. The antislavery clause was stricken by slaveholding delegates and by northern merchants who profited from the slave trade.

➤ The chief purpose of the Declaration of Independence was to justify to the world the colonies' reasons for severing ties with England.

# Part 3
# Times That Try Men's Souls

*Except for the Canadian fiasco, the initial clashes of the Revolution were greatly encouraging to the Americans. Then things began to go wrong. Very wrong. In this section, we see how Washington lost Long Island, New York, and the Hudson River forts. But, in defeat, Washington demonstrated the full strength of his character and resolve. After making a fighting retreat across New Jersey and into Pennsylvania, Washington launched two surprise attacks back across the Delaware, stunning the British and Hessians at Trenton and Princeton.*

*After finding the American rebels surprisingly difficult adversaries, British general Burgoyne formulated a grand plan for a convergence of forces that would sever New England from the rest of the colonies—a decapitating blow that would end the rebellion. The last three chapters of this section detail the fate of Burgoyne's plans and include a great patriot defeat, the loss of Philadelphia, and victory, the surrender of an entire British army at Saratoga.*

# Chapter 13

# The Battle for New York

## In This Chapter

➤ The British target New York

➤ Washington manages a miraculous evacuation of Long Island

➤ The British invade Manhattan

➤ Martyrdom of Nathan Hale

➤ Manhattan in British hands

With defeat in Boston came a new line of British reasoning. If Massachusetts was the fountainhead of the revolution, it was also the most formidable fortress of rebellion—the toughest nut to crack. Wouldn't it make more sense to attack first where the spirit of revolution was at its weakest?

Public opinion at home was governing British strategy. Many Britons thought the war could not be won, since Americans were totally alienated from the British Crown. King George III and Lord North had to convince these doubters that many, if not most, Americans were still loyal. British troops in loyalist areas such as New York would receive a great deal of local support, making it easier for King George III to convince the British public that he was fighting with, not against, most Americans. The soldiers of the Crown now turned their attention to two places where Tories (loyalists) abounded: South Carolina and New York. The South Carolina campaign will be covered separately in Chapter 21, "Southern Exposure." Here, we look at the fate of New York and the beginning of George Washington's long retreat to victory.

# The British Eye the Big Apple

Boston, for the time being, was lost to the British. New York City might not be the heart of the Revolution, but it was a critical prize. Whoever controlled the city and its harbor also controlled the lordly Hudson River, principal avenue into the American interior. Seize this, and the colonies, so adept at communication and the coordination of action, would be completely divided. Thus isolated, New England could finally be defeated, and the rebellion would surely collapse.

The big picture was this: Gen. Howe had withdrawn from Boston to the safety of Halifax, Nova Scotia, and would sail southward with a much bigger army. He would take and occupy New York City, then spread his control of the Hudson River north to Albany, isolating New England from the other colonies. From Canada, a British force led by Gen. Guy Carleton would join Howe at Albany. Together, the two could operate at will and defeat the remnants of rebellion in detail. Divide and conquer.

## *Patriot Defenses*

Charles Lee had been reared in England and entered his father's British regiment as an ensign in 1747. In 1755, he served with Edward Braddock in the disastrous assault on Fort Duquesne during the French and Indian War. His reputation as a "colorful" officer was enhanced by his adoption into the Mohawk tribe and his "marriage" to the daughter of a Seneca chief. Lee came to America to live in 1773 and immediately joined the most radical wing of the revolutionary cause. Well before the Continental Congress created the Continental army, Lee urged the patriots to raise a military force—doubtless with the intention of obtaining command of it. Since leaving the British army in 1765, he had collected an officer's pension, and he saw no reason to stop even after Congress appointed him major general, subordinate only to George Washington and Artemas Ward. When Congress pledged to pay for any property the British might confiscate from him, he wrote a letter to the authorities requesting the discontinuance of his half pay.

Detached from Boston siege duty by Washington in January 1776 to see to the defense of New York, he did not arrive in the city until February 4. What he saw on his arrival did not give him much hope for successfully securing the city against attack. "What to do with the city … puzzles me," he wrote in a letter dated February 19, 1776. "It is so encircled with deep navigable waters that whoever commands the sea must command the town." And there was no question who commanded the sea.

Lee's idea for the defense of New York was to place 4–5,000 troops on Long Island and fortify Brooklyn Heights, which overlooked lower Manhattan. Uptown, he placed troops for the defense of Kings Bridge, which connected Manhattan with the Bronx on the mainland. Lee understood that, given the naval superiority of the British, he could not hold Manhattan as a fortress. He believed, however, that once the British invaded Manhattan, it would serve as "a field of battle so advantageous, indeed, that if our people behave with common spirit, and the commanders are men of discretion, it might cost the enemy many thousands of men to get possession of it."

The plan and the words were characteristically bold. Yet, when Washington arrived to establish his headquarters in the city on April 13, Lee had built virtually none of the fortifications he had planned. (Indeed, Lee had been dispatched to the defense of Charleston, South Carolina some five weeks before Washington's arrival.) The commander in chief set his army to digging up the island, throwing up great earthen works.

Fortunately for the Americans, the British moved at their customary stately pace. It would be September before Manhattan was attacked. The 19,000 Continentals and militiamen gathered for the defense of the island had a full five months to dig and build. That they were mostly untrained, poorly armed, and sorely short of artillery doubtless encouraged the men to dig deep, build the earthen walls high, and pack them solidly.

**Voices of Liberty**

"The rebels have very good marksmen, but some of them have wretched guns, and most of them shoot crooked."

—Hessian officer, 1776

## Staten Island Arrival

On June 25, 1776, William Howe landed off Sandy Hook, a spit of land projecting from New Jersey into Raritan Bay, opposite Staten Island. He had three ships, the vanguard of 130 vessels that would arrive on the 29th, carrying 9,300 troops. An American sentinel, Daniel McCurtin, sighted them—looking (he reported) like "a fleet of pine trees trimmed ... the whole Bay was full of shipping ... I thought all London was afloat."

It was only the beginning. On July 12, Lord Richard Howe, William's admiral brother, arrived with 150 more ships and reinforcements from England. Soon, additional British troops and German mercenary forces followed, and, on August 12, yet more soldiers arrived from the failed expedition against Charleston, South Carolina.

By the last week of August, Howe had mustered 31,625 troops, of whom 24,464 were fit for duty. In addition to the troop transports, Howe was prepared to support the land forces with 30 combat ships, including 10 *ships of the line* and 20 frigates—a total of perhaps 1,200 guns. According to some historians, it was the largest expeditionary force England, which wielded the mightiest army and navy in the world, had ever sent overseas.

**Fightin' Words**

A **ship of the line** is any warship big enough to take a position in the line of battle. In practice, these were typically vessels with more than 74 guns.

## The Trap Is Set

Washington faced this gathering onslaught with 6,500 troops on Long Island, many of which were concentrated on fortified Brooklyn Heights under Gen. Israel Putnam. Below the fortifications, in the woods and farmlands to the southeast and south (the present-day Brooklyn neighborhoods of Sunset Park, Parkville, and Flatbush), Gen. William Alexander (of New Jersey) and Gen. John Sullivan were posted with contingents of some 1,600 and 1,500 men, respectively. Another group of troops was posted on Governor's Island in New York Harbor, off the lower tip of Manhattan, and various divisions of Continentals and militia outfits were dispersed in and around New York City. These included a brigade of 2,400 troops under Thomas Mifflin, a prominent Philadelphia Quaker turned general. Mifflin and his troops occupied Fort Washington, which overlooked the Hudson near the north end of Manhattan, at about the present location of 180th Street. East of this, on the Harlem River side of the island, 1,800 of Gen. George Clinton's men were assigned to hold Kings Bridge, the link to the mainland. In all, Washington had just under 20,000 troops in and around New York City. At the time, these troops constituted the very backbone of America's military strength. George Washington could ill afford to squander them.

The Continental Congress pressed Washington to hold New York City, but the decision was ultimately a military, not a political, one. Although more experienced than most of his senior officers, Washington was still learning, and he had precious little time to ponder strategy. He was short on soldiers and field officers, and had almost no staff officers—the people who attend to the myriad details of the execution of strategy, who see to it that the principal commander's orders are carried out properly. Without a staff, much of Washington's time and attention were absorbed in minute and mundane detail.

Washington could have chosen the strategically viable course of withdrawing northward onto the mainland, into what was then the wilds of Westchester County. There, of course, the great British fleet could not follow, and Howe would have to seek and pursue—operations that did not favor the British. Unfortunately, he split his forces between Manhattan and Long Island—with the East River and Long Island Sound between them—exposing them to the formidable British fleet, whose warships could bombard and whose transports could deliver soldiers anywhere along Manhattan and Long Island. Howe could strike at will, and would have plenty of naval strength to prevent the arrival of any reinforcements.

### Fightin' Words

Dragoons are mounted infantrymen. Like the cavalry, they ride to battle; unlike the cavalry, upon arrival, they dismount and fight as infantry.

## The Battle of Long Island

The British began to land on Long Island on the night of August 26. The 17th Light *Dragoons*, the 33rd West Ridings, the kilted 71st Highlanders (under the particularly dashing Lt. Col. James Grant), the Guards, and a dozen more regiments took positions in the area of southeast Brooklyn still called today the "Flatlands." The officers who led them bore grudges: Henry Clinton, smarting from the costly Battle of Bunker Hill; Charles Cornwallis, fresh from defeat at Charleston; and Lord Hugh Percy, who had seen the humiliation of the redcoats at Lexington and Concord.

The British in America had so far shown little flair for surprise. This time things were different. By night, the three commanders led their 10,000-man column in a broad movement to the northeast so that the attack, when it came on the morning of the 27th, rushed in on Gen. Sullivan's left flank—precisely the opposite side from which it had been expected. While Clinton, Cornwallis, and Percy attacked from the northeast, 5,000 *Hessians*—the German mercenary troops—pressed in due north from the Flatlands, and 7,000 kilted Highlanders attacked from the west. The effect of an attack from three sides with 22,000 men overwhelmed the 3,100 Americans positioned before the Brooklyn Heights fortifications. They had counted on the accuracy of sharpshooting riflemen, but in the onslaught, rifles could not be reloaded fast enough.

There was heroism nevertheless. Gen. Alexander—popularly called Lord Stirling in deference to an inherited Scottish title—held out long enough to exact a toll on Grant's Highlanders and then to retreat in an orderly fashion. But by noon it was over, and those who survived the attack were falling back on the works at Brooklyn Heights, defeated.

For all the Britons' stealth, vigor, and overwhelming numbers, Howe's commanders had accomplished remarkably little. The American army on Long Island was still intact, ensconced behind the heavily fortified works of the Heights—works more formidable than any at Breeds Hill, a place Howe knew only too well. Worse, the winds were against the British fleet, so Howe's brother was unable to help from the water. The British commander decided to dig in. When it came time to assault the Brooklyn Heights fortress, he wanted to be able to do it from the closest possible range.

### Fightin' Words

**Hessians** were mercenary troops in the British employ. While some were from the German principality of Hesse, they came from various German states. Three of their principal commanders were, however, Hessian.

### Voices of Liberty

"Rejoice, my friends, that we have given the Rebels a d----d crush .... It was a glorious achievement, my friend, and will immortalize us and crush the rebel colonies."
—British officer, September 3, 1776

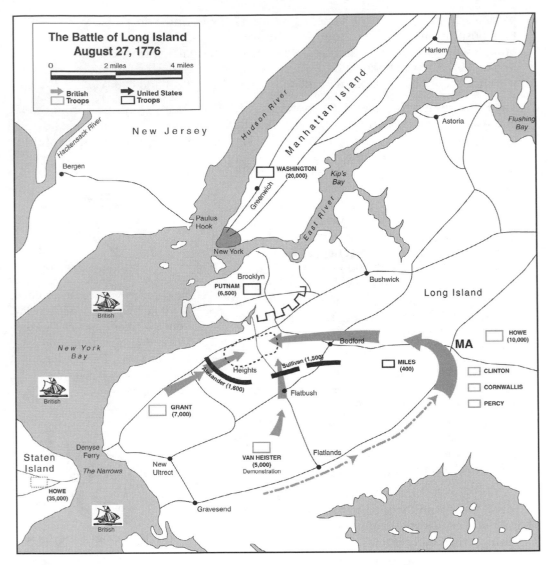

*The Battle of Long Island. Note the brilliant movement of the British forces.*
(Map by Kevin D. Smith)

## Escape to Manhattan

George Washington's presence did much to compose the badly shaken troops. At first, the commander in chief remained confident that Brooklyn could be held, and so brought some of his Manhattan units into the fortifications at Brooklyn Heights.

It was a bad move, and Washington soon realized it. The shooting had stopped for now, but by the 28th he understood that his position was untenable, and he ordered preparations for evacuation. Washington's army had never been in greater danger. If Howe had realized that an evacuation was under way, he would have attacked with everything he had, and the colonials would have been cut to ribbons. Yet, at times of gravest crisis and peril, George Washington demonstrated his greatness as a leader and a military commander. He had blundered badly, so far, in the defense of New York, yet he refused to panic. With great skill, Washington now managed the stealthy retreat of thousands of troops, a handful at a time, together with precious stores, in small boats across the East River to Manhattan during the stormy and foggy night of August 29–30. The evacuation was managed so skillfully that, as a Hessian major reported to his patron in Europe, "We had no knowledge of this [evacuation] until four o'clock in the morning."

### We Hold These Truths

David Bushnell was a student at Yale who demonstrated to his doubting professors that gunpowder could be detonated underwater. This gave him the idea for what he called a *water machine*—the world's first combat submarine. A pear-shaped vessel made of oak and reinforced with iron bands, the water machine was called the *Turtle*. It was $7^1/_2$ feet long by 6 feet wide and was operated by one man who controlled two hand-driven screws and could submerge the vessel by pulling a valve that flooded a compartment in the hull and then surface again by operating a foot pump. It was equipped with an explosive mine that could be attached to the hull of an enemy ship and timed to explode after the *Turtle* had retreated to safety.

On September 6, 1776, in New York Harbor, Sergeant Ezra Lee, trained by Bushnell, used the *Turtle* in an attempt to sink the British warship HMS *Eagle*. Lee could not attach the mine and was forced to withdraw; the explosive detonated harmlessly in the East River. The *Turtle* was tried a few more times but proved unsuccessful.

# Fight for New York

As if George Washington's strategic dilemmas were not enough, he faced the problem of expiring militia enlistments. The remaining troops were frightened and depressed, with little confidence in the officers who led them. Poorly supplied, as usual, plagued by miserable weather, raw nerved, perhaps a quarter of the 20,000 defenders lay ill.

In view of the desperate and apparently deteriorating situation, Gen. Nathanael Greene advised Washington to burn and abandon New York. Congress weighed in on September 3 with a resolution that the city be spared from the torch. If lost to the British, the delegates argued, it could always be recaptured. On September 7, Washington decided to leave the men of Knox and Putnam downtown, post another 9,000 troops to defend the ground between Harlem and Kings Bridge, and deploy militiamen under Gen. Greene along the East River to repel further landings.

It was a terrible plan: It dispersed the American troops thinly over 16 miles and left the weakest position right in the middle. On September 12, the general's top officers urged him to consolidate troop strength by evacuating everyone south of Fort Washington. Washington complied, but it was too late. The storms of late August had given way to the hazy heat of September, and, on the 15th, calm weather and favorable winds allowed the British fleet to sail up the Hudson and East Rivers, flanking Manhattan Island. The gun ports of the warships stood menacingly open, and the transport barges that accompanied them landed at Kip's Bay—where 34th Street today ends at FDR Drive.

Preceded by a brief cannonade beginning at 11:00 in the morning, the troops landed unopposed in 85 flatboats. The handful of militiamen fled, spreading panic to other units in what is now Midtown. Gen. Washington, alarmed by the sound of cannon fire, rode south from Harlem and attempted to rally the troops. When this failed, the commander in chief lashed out in a rage with his riding crop at officers as well as ordinary soldiers. Washington took flight only at the last possible moment, when an aide grabbed the bridle of his horse and led him away, just steps ahead of the approaching Hessians.

As the American troops moved hurriedly northward to the protection afforded by Harlem Heights and Fort Washington (just north of present-day 125th Street), the British and Hessian forces marched inland and uptown toward today's 42nd Street. Generals Howe, Clinton, and Cornwallis set up headquarters in the elegant Murray house—in the neighborhood known today as Murray Hill. From here, they would advance northward.

The British landings could have been a lot worse. Gen. Henry Clinton had urged Howe to move boldly against Kings Bridge in upper Manhattan—a move that would have put the British in position to destroy Washington's spread-out forces. Howe demurred, however, arguing that so direct an assault on the city would damage too many houses needed for winter quarters. Besides, landing farther down at Kip's Bay would present much less resistance. Washington had given the British a chance to annihilate his army, but the cautious and slow-moving Howe failed to take advantage of it.

## The British Attack—and Blink

At the opening of the Revolution, New York was emerging as a major commercial center, with a population approaching 30,000, mostly concentrated at the southern tip of the island, below Wall Street. Greenwich Village, in those days, really was a country village, punctuated by the summer estates of some of the city's wealthier residents. To the north lay hilly farmland with meandering streams. Many decades of development have flattened most of Manhattan's topography, but in the eighteenth century it was an island of hill and dale, and the most commanding heights—unflattened even today—lay above the present location of 125th Street. From Harlem Heights, the American defenders had a clear view of the drama that unfolded on September 15.

Along the eastern road, a line of brilliant scarlet flowed in stately fashion, making its way to the American position. At the same time, along the western road, Aaron Burr, a young New Jersey man who was among Washington's handful of staff officers, led the columns of Knox and Putnam up from the Battery to join the main body of troops on the Heights. The observers on the Heights saw the parallel advance of the two columns, but neither column could see or hear the other. A notch called McGowan's (or McGown's) Pass pierced the hilly, wooded tract running down the center of Manhattan. If British troops were to scout the pass, the advancing Americans would be cut off and lost. But luck was with the desperate patriots, and the men of Putnam and Knox reached and scaled the Heights of Harlem, where they were welcomed into the ranks of the defenders.

By nightfall on September 15, Howe had established forward posts from McGowan's Pass (at the northeast corner of Central Park today) southwest to the Hudson River (at about the location of 105th Street).

Before dawn of the 16th, Lt. Col. Thomas Knowlton, a tall, handsome, dashing soldier from Connecticut, led 100 handpicked Connecticut *Rangers* down the so-called Hollow Way—a steep descent from the Harlem Heights to the Hudson. He ran into elements of the famed Black Watch Highland troops and engaged them, but was forced to retreat as more Highlanders arrived. The British took the retreat as the beginning of a general flight, and the advance elements of Howe's invading force attacked, anticipating a rout.

What they got was a fight. Gen. Washington, who had made one strategic blunder after another, again showed true leadership genius. He committed to battle the very militiamen who had fled from the British at Kip's Bay and against whom he had wielded his riding crop. The Highlanders, who moments before were jeering contemptuously, fled in full retreat across the buckwheat field that fronted the Hudson (on the site of today's Barnard College). Although the popular Knowlton had fallen in battle, the victory heartened the troops.

The effect on Gen. Howe should have been negligible. After all, he had thousands of well-equipped troops and a naval fleet. He could have struck Washington's position from the flanks or the rear, if the experience in the buckwheat field discouraged him. Instead, he did nothing.

Washington realized that with each passing day the afterglow of the battle in the buckwheat field faded. Fear and chagrin were again setting in.

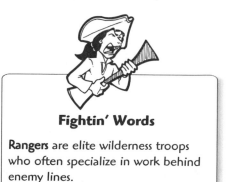

**Fightin' Words**

**Rangers** are elite wilderness troops who often specialize in work behind enemy lines.

# One Life to Lose

It was difficult to be heroic sitting behind the walls of a fort. Connecticut's Knowlton, who had gone out in a blaze of glory, had earlier selected another earnest and dashing young Connecticut man, a 21-year-old schoolmaster-turned-captain named Nathan Hale, to command a company of his rangers. When Washington asked for a volunteer to spy behind the enemy lines shortly before the Battle of Harlem Heights, Hale stepped up. "I wish to be useful," he explained to a friend, "and every kind of service, necessary to the public good, becomes honorable by being necessary."

But Hale became far more famous for what he said on September 22, after he was captured and sentenced to execution. He had been collecting information on enemy troop disposition since September 12. It is said that Hale's Tory cousin, one Samuel Hale, betrayed the young schoolmaster to the British. Perhaps, but the courageous Hale was not a very good spy. Tall, plump, pocky, and with flaming red hair, he stood out in a crowd. Even less discreet was his practice of writing down the information he collected and carrying the paper with him in his coat. Captured on the 21st, he was not accorded a trial but condemned to hang on Sunday. At least he was given the opportunity to speak some stirring last words: "I only regret that I have but one life to lose for my country."

### Voices of Liberty

"What a pity is it
That we can die but once to save
our country."

—Joseph Addison, *Cato* (1713), act 4, scene 4 (often cited as the inspiration for Nathan Hale's famous last words)

# New York in Flames

While Howe and his officers were occupied with Nathan Hale uptown, other British soldiers were dispatched to extinguish a blaze downtown. Sometime after midnight on September 20–21, a fire broke out in a house near Whitehall Slip, at the tip of the island, and then spread north and west, consuming 493 houses before it was brought under control. The British accused the Americans of having started the fire, but no proof ever surfaced. In a day when houses were built of wood, huddled closely together, and lit by various open-flame devices, it hardly required arson to start a catastrophic fire.

The fire probably contributed to Howe's delay in pushing the attack on Harlem Heights. Certainly, it caused the British army great inconvenience, since they needed all the billeting space they could get. Forbidden by Congress from burning the city to keep it out of enemy hands, George Washington remarked that "providence, or some good honest fellow, has done more for us than we were disposed to do for ourselves."

# Retreat to White Plains

By the middle of October, Howe had still not moved against Fort Washington and Harlem Heights. Washington observed, however, that Howe's barges were probing for

Hudson landings in Westchester, above his position, obviously preparing for an encirclement. On October 16, Washington decided it was high time to evacuate Manhattan. The progress north to White Plains, in Westchester County, was slow and straggling. Yet Howe moved even more slowly, several times engaged by small American forces that cost him time and not a few casualties.

Washington's main body reached the village of White Plains in advance of Howe, and he placed his troops on three hills there. Again, he made a tactical error, however, by failing to fortify Chatterton Hill—the highest and, therefore, most important of the three hills. Only 1,600 men, all militia, held the position—under Gen. Alexander McDougall of New York.

Howe might not have been an aggressive or bold commander, but he had a good eye for weakness, and he instinctively threw his main attack against Chatterton Hill. An artillery bombardment was followed by a clumsy infantry assault, and then, far more devastating, a cavalry charge by the 17th Dragoons—the very first cavalry charge of the war. At this point, cavalry was virtually unknown to the American army, and the untried militiamen panicked at the ferocity of the onslaught. Behind them, the more experienced soldiers of the Maryland and Delaware lines offered stout resistance, ultimately retreating, but in good order.

Howe took Chatterton Hill, yet once again the main chance had eluded him. Had he pressed his advantage, he might have destroyed Washington's army; as it was, he let the Americans withdraw farther north. Taking a position at North Castle, Washington now had free access to supplies from New England. Fed and in possession of some new equipment, his troops felt refreshed and saw White Plains as a victory, which wasn't entirely wrong. Although they had lost White Plains, the Americans had suffered perhaps 150 killed and wounded, whereas the British suffered 214 casualties and the Hessians 99.

## The Fort Washington Trap

Then Washington and his men were in for a stunner. Early in November, Howe turned back toward Manhattan. A counsel of war was hastily convened. Washington and his officers concluded that Howe had decided to invade New Jersey.

They were dead wrong. Washington evacuated Manhattan, leaving a garrison of 2,000 at Fort Washington, perched on a rocky reef at what is now West 180th Street. With reinforcements, their number rose to nearly 3,000. On the night of November 14, the British moved 30 flatboats into position for an assault on Fort Washington. On the 15th, the British demanded surrender of the fort. Refused, they attacked the next day from three directions.

Washington rushed back to Fort Lee, New Jersey (across the Hudson), ventured across the river, and, with generals Putnam, Greene, and Hugh Mercer, made a personal reconnaissance. Seeing there was nothing he could do to save the fort, he retired to Fort Lee, and, at 3:00 that afternoon, Fort Washington was given to the British. Howe's forces captured 2,818 American officers and men. Fifty-three Americans fell in battle; the number of wounded is unknown. British and Hessian losses were heavy: 458 killed and wounded.

The loss of so many men was a serious blow to the American cause, as was the loss of the fort and its equipment. Four days later, Fort Lee also fell to the British. These defeats accounted for the loss of 146 cannon, 12,000 shot and shell, 2,800 muskets, 400,000 cartridges, and miscellaneous other military equipment. The loss to patriot morale is impossible to calculate, coupled with the hard truth that all of Manhattan and a substantial swath along the Jersey bank of the Hudson were in British hands, splitting the American army in three. Charles Lee was up in North Castle, Westchester County; Gen. William Heath was at Peekskill, up the Hudson from Manhattan; and Washington took the main body of troops on a long, drizzling November retreat through New Jersey.

---

### The Least You Need to Know

➤ The British turned their attention from the strongly rebellious New England to South Carolina and New York—colonies with a significant Tory population.

➤ The battles on Long Island, Manhattan, and Westchester revealed many weaknesses in Washington's grasp of strategy and tactics, but each of these desperate battles also showed him as a personally inspiring leader of great courage.

➤ Gen. Howe used superior numbers and equipment, as well as the guns of the Royal Navy, to defeat Washington on Long Island, Manhattan, and White Plains. Howe never exploited his costly victories, however, and Washington escaped each trap with the bulk of his army intact.

➤ The loss of Forts Washington and Lee, and of Manhattan, were serious blows to the American army in terms of men and material lost and in general morale and resolve.

# Chapter 14

---

# Crossing the Delaware

---

## In This Chapter

➤ General Lee's treachery

➤ The Continental army at low ebb

➤ Cornwallis fails to destroy Washington's army

➤ The Delaware crossing

➤ The Battle of Princeton

---

Manhattan and the Hudson River forts, Fort Washington and Fort Lee, had been lost. But whatever his shortcomings as a strategist and tactician, Washington's effectiveness as a leader lay in great part in his refusal to yield to defeatism or panic.

The Americans were defending their homeland. The British soldiers were far from home. Washington understood that he might lose cities and he might lose battles, but he could still win independence—or, at least, a favorable settlement from the Crown. He needed to keep his army alive and together, and to maintain among its soldiers, Congress, and the people, the will to continue. In the meantime, for the British, the costlier the war became and the longer it lasted, the more impatient the British public would become. George III and Lord North could only fight on as long as they could persuade British voters to contribute taxes for the armed forces.

So Washington moved the battle to New Jersey.

## Jersey Winter

Casualties, the expiration of enlistment, and capture had reduced Washington's command to about 16,400 troops. Washington had anticipated the retreat to New Jersey, and on November 10, 1776, after the Battle of White Plains, but before the loss of the Hudson River forts, he had communicated with Gen. Charles Lee: "If the enemy should remove the whole, or greatest part of their force, to the west side of Hudson river, I have no doubt of your following with all possible dispatch …."

Ten days later, after Forts Washington and Lee had fallen, the commander in chief again asked Lee to join him in Jersey, then repeated the request the next day—"unless some new event should occur, or some more cogent reason present itself." The calm, courteous letters to Lee were more typical of George Washington's command style than was his lashing out, with riding crop, against the militiamen who had fled before the British invasion at Kip's Bay (Chapter 13, "The Battle of New York"). Washington believed in giving his senior commanders as free a hand as possible.

**Fightin' Words**

**Amphibious operations**, during the nineteenth century, were attacks in which troops were carried into battle by boat rather than by overland march.

**Fightin' Words**

In Washington's army, the **adjutant general** was the chief administrative officer of the army.

## Jealous Generals

Forty-four hundred of Washington's troops were with the commander in chief at Newark, New Jersey. A mere thousand, under Gen. William Alexander ("Lord Stirling"), were stationed at New Brunswick and Rahway, to intercept any *amphibious operations*. Up in Peekskill, New York, Gen. William Heath, a fifth-generation resident of Roxbury, near Boston, com-manded 4,000 men to defend the Hudson highlands. In White Plains, Lee had fully 7,000 troops, including some of the best regiments in the Continental army.

Why did Lee delay in sending Washington the troops he knew were so desperately needed? Pushed, he replied lamely to Washington's *adjutant general,* Joseph Reed, that he could not cross the Hudson at Dobbs Ferry in time to help Washington, so he ordered Gen. Heath to send 2,000 men by way of Kings Ferry, closer to Heath's position, but farther from Washington's. Clearly, the "colorful" Lee had his own agenda, which apparently included a burning ambition to take Washington's place as commander in chief. The defeat of troops under Washington's personal command might well bring about such a succession.

## The Reluctant Hunter

It was not a good time for a crisis of command. In retreat, Washington's forces were vulnerable, dispirited, poorly supplied, and, many of them, nearing the expiration of their enlistments. Gen. Howe's troops, well fed and in for the duration, were in an excellent position to bring the war to a conclusion.

Howe had many options. With the bulk of Washington's army retreating through New Jersey, he could have moved against Heath up the Hudson, which would have cleared the way for more troops to invade from Canada, while leaving his own forces free to invade New England. Or he might have elected to proceed directly to the capital of the rebellion, Philadelphia, which he could have captured, while destroying Washington's retreating army in the process.

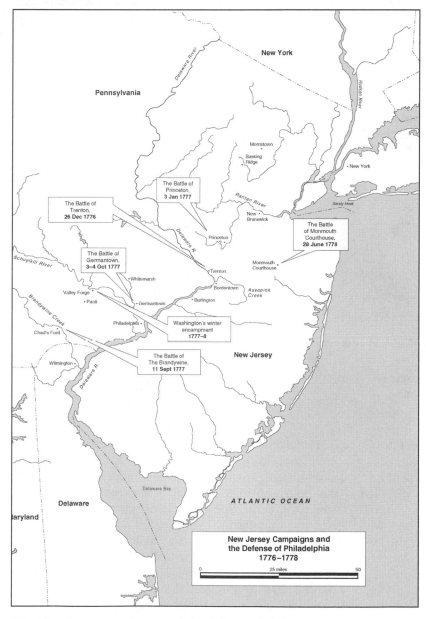

*The New Jersey campaigns and the defense of Philadelphia.*
(Map by Kevin D. Smith)

But Howe was neither aggressive, imaginative, nor flexible enough to contemplate a winter campaign. Winter warfare was unpleasant and inconvenient, so instead of vigorously hunting down Washington's undermanned and highly vulnerable army, Howe bedded down for the season, ordering that *winter quarters* be established in Amboy, New Brunswick, and Princeton on the eastern front, and in Bordentown and at Trenton, the main post, on the Delaware River.

**Fightin' Words**

Winter quarters were camps established to shelter armies during the winter; in the eighteenth century, armies typically avoided combat during the entire winter.

**Voices of Liberty**

"The Cry of want of Provisions comes to me from every Quarter ...."

—George Washington, winter, 1776–1777

## A Naked Army

While establishing these posts, Howe dispatched Gen. Henry Clinton from New York with some 6,000 men to occupy Newport, Rhode Island, preparatory to a spring campaign against New England. He sent Gen. Charles Cornwallis to pursue Washington beyond New Brunswick, to give the British elbow room for their winter hibernation.

Cornwallis boasted that he would bag Washington and his tattered army as a hunter bags a fox. Whereas Howe was slow and deliberate, Cornwallis drove his troops swiftly and unsparingly. He was closing in on Newark by November 29th, which sent Washington and his headquarters force of 4,000 running to New Brunswick just steps ahead of Hessian advance guards. Washington lamented the condition of his army, but they outran Cornwallis, leaving his troops panting with exhaustion after a daylong 20-mile forced march through the rain. The Hessians and British were loaded down with 60-pound packs. The impoverished American troops had no such burdens.

Washington left Alexander at Princeton to delay the British advance, and reached Trenton with his main force on December 3 hoping that Charles Lee would meet him there. But Lee was days distant. Washington, who had already prepared for an evacuation across the Delaware River into Pennsylvania, sent his troops across on December 7, and deployed them across some 25 miles of Pennsylvania river front. As a precaution, he sent troops to find and destroy every boat of any size for some 75 miles up and down the lower Delaware. Survival of the army was uppermost in Washington's mind, and he meant to make it very difficult for the British to give chase. Cornwallis knew when he was beaten. He readily secured permission from Howe to halt at the Delaware—Howe believed the rebels would keep until spring, anyway—and Howe set about installing his army in their various New Jersey posts for the winter.

## Damnably Deficient

By early December, Charles Lee and his command were in New Jersey, but even as he made his way to join Washington, he wrote to Heath that he didn't believe the commander in chief would benefit from his support on the Delaware, and then he revealed the true scope of his ambition: "I am in the hopes here to reconquer (if I may so express myself) the Jerseys."

Establishing a *bivouac* for his troops a few miles below Morristown, Lee himself rode off another three miles to Basking Ridge, where he found comfortable quarters in the tavern of the Widow White. With him were four other officers and a guard of about 15 men. On November 13, Lee rose and set about completing some paperwork, including a letter to Gen. Horatio Gates:

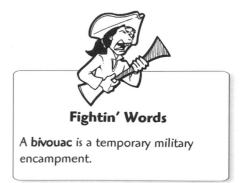

**Fightin' Words**

A **bivouac** is a temporary military encampment.

> *The ingenious manoeuvre of Fort Washington has unhinged the goodly fabrick we had been building. There never was so damned a stroke. Entre nous [between us], a certain great man is most damnably deficient. He has thrown me into a situation where I have my choice of difficulties. If I stay in this Province I risk myself and army, and if I do not stay the Province is lost for ever. I have neither guides, cavalry, medicines, money, shoes or stockings. I must act with the greatest circumspection. Tories are in my front, rear and on my flanks. The mass of the people is strangely contaminated.*
>
> *In short unless something which I do not expect turns up we are lost ….*

Just as he finished the letter, a detachment of British dragoons burst in on Charles Lee and took him prisoner.

Given his self-serving ambitions and his loss of confidence in Washington, Lee's capture may actually have been a great service to the patriot cause. His army, three miles away, near Morristown, marched on to join Washington on the Delaware. Lee was ordered returned to England for trial as a deserter—but Howe, always a fair-minded man, was convinced that Lee had resigned his half-pay commission before joining the rebel cause. He sent Lee as a prisoner to New York instead of London.

## Providence Smiles at Trenton

Thomas Paine, author of *Common Sense* (Chapter 12, "Common Sense and a Bold Declaration"), joined Washington's army and retreated with it through New Jersey. In Newark (it is said), he used a drumhead for a desk and a campfire for illumination to write the first of the papers collected in 1783 as *The American Crisis*. The initial essay, published on December 19, 1776, begins:

> *These are the times that try men's souls. The summer soldier and sunshine patriot will, in this crisis, shrink from the service of his country; but he that stands it now, deserves the love and thanks of man and woman. Tyranny, like hell, is not easily conquered.*

**187**

Paine's eloquence shamed the summer soldiers and helped revive the flagging cause. Gen. Thomas Mifflin, a popular Philadelphian, traveled quickly throughout his home state, where he rallied the militia. Immediately, Washington started getting reinforcements. By Christmas time, he still had no more than 6,000 troops fit for duty, however. If he waited for more, two things might have happened: First, enlistments were set to expire on New Year's Eve—which could reduce the forces on the Delaware to a mere 1,400. Second, a hard freeze of the river would make it possible for the boatless British to cross—not that the hibernating Howe necessarily would. For both of these reasons, Washington decided on a counteroffensive.

## Another Crossing

For the British and Hessian troops lodged at Trenton and the other posts Howe had established, the approach of Christmas was welcomed with food and drink "liberated"

### Fightin' Words

**Durham boats** were designed to carry iron ore, grain, whiskey, and similar bulk freight between Philadelphia and New Jersey. Forty to 60 feet long, they drew only 20 inches of water when fully loaded to their 15-ton capacity.

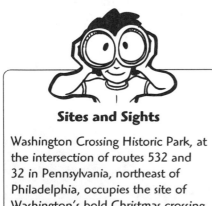

### Sites and Sights

Washington Crossing Historic Park, at the intersection of routes 532 and 32 in Pennsylvania, northeast of Philadelphia, occupies the site of Washington's bold Christmas crossing into New Jersey. Telephone 215-493-4076 for park information.

from the citizens of New Jersey, and enjoyed in warmth and comfort. Outside, the weather was miserable. The Delaware had frozen, then melted under warm rains, then frozen again. On Christmas night of 1776, great sheets of broken ice whirled in the swift current. Washington loaded 2,400 veteran troops and 18 cannon into *Durham boats*. One officer recalled how the icy snow on the riverbank was "tinged here and there with the blood from the feet of men who wore broken shoes." The officer continued, "It will be a terrible night for the soldiers, but I have not heard a man complain."

While Washington crossed at McKonkey's Ferry (modern Washington Crossing), nine miles above Trenton, another 1,000 militiamen, commanded by Gen. James Ewing, were to cross at Trenton Ferry to block any retreat of Hessians who occupied Trenton. Col. John Cadwalader was to cross the Delaware at Bordentown in a diversionary move. But it is no surprise that Ewing never made it across and that Cadwalader was so delayed that he was of no real help. The night was bitter and stormy, and the current raging.

The plan was for Washington's men to disembark at midnight, but the weather caused so many delays that the men were not all across before 3:00 on the morning of the 26th. It took another hour before they were all ready to march, which meant that the attack, which depended entirely on surprise, would not occur before daybreak. Yet Washington did enjoy certain advantages. Col. Johann Rall, commander of the Hessian brigade holding Trenton, had proven himself a courageous and able soldier at White Plains and at the taking of Fort

Washington. However, he was a notorious drunkard, who badly underestimated the American soldiers; "country clowns," he called them. So contemptuous was he of the colonials that, although ordered to construct fortifications and dispatch scouting parties, he declined, remarking that "we want no trenches. We will go at them with the bayonet." On Christmas night, Rall had to be carried to his bed, dead drunk.

*Engraving of Emanuel Leutze's celebrated painting,* Washington Crossing the Delaware. *(Image from the National Archives)*

## Merry Christmas

Washington insisted on quiet and the absence of lights to preserve as much surprise as possible. When the snow and freezing rain soaked muskets and rendered them useless, Washington directed Gen. Sullivan to order his men to fix bayonets. "I am resolved to take Trenton," the commander in chief said. As the day eerily dawned, the men broke into a trot, doing their best to outpace the rising sun.

Groggy from Christmas libation, the last thing the Hessians expected was a sentry's cry: *"Der Feind! Heraus! Heraus!"* ("The enemy! Get up! Get up!") American units closed in from the northwest, the north, the northeast, the south and the southeast. Even without Ewing and Cadwalader, the attack went remarkably well and was over quickly. Roused from his stupor, Rall tried to rally his panicked men, but was himself cut down and mortally wounded. Trenton belonged to Washington, along with 918 prisoners and a wealth of equipment and stores. The Americans had suffered no more than four wounded, and some authorities claim no American was killed, while others report two killed in action and two frozen to death. Of the 1,200 Hessians engaged, 106 were killed or wounded.

Because Ewing and Cadwalader had failed to carry out their missions, Washington could not press the offensive on to Princeton and New Brunswick and had no choice but to withdraw across the Delaware, back into Pennsylvania. If anything, conditions on the river had become even worse. The withdrawal from Trenton began at noon on the 26th, and some of Washington's men were not back in their Pennsylvania bivouacs before noon of the 27th. Many of the troops had been continuously engaged for as much as 50 hours. Some had marched at least 40 miles, round-trip, on top of the difficult river crossing. But as the historian Hugh Trevelyan wrote, "it may be doubted whether so small a number of men ever employed so short a space of time with greater or more lasting results upon the history of the world." George Washington and a few thousand ragged soldiers had revived the imperiled Revolution.

*Washington accepts the surrender of the Hessians after the Battle of Trenton. (Image from the National Archives)*

# Triumph at Princeton

Victory at Trenton had an immediate salutary effect on the Continental army. Generals Henry Knox and Thomas Mifflin pleaded with their men to extend their enlistments, ending on December 31, six more weeks. Washington added his voice to the pleas, and by December 30 was able to write to Congress that, "to a man," the regiments had extended their enrollment by six weeks.

With six more fighting weeks at his disposal, Washington crossed into New Jersey once again, taking up a position at hard-won Trenton. But British Gen. Cornwallis, grumbling that the defeat of the Hessians had thrust upon him an unwanted winter campaign, rushed almost 8,000 fresh troops from Princeton to Trenton. Washington sent a covering force under Gen. Edward Hand, who, with help from more miserable weather, managed to delay Cornwallis's advance.

## Withdrawal and Advance

Washington had hurriedly erected works along the Assumpink Creek just south of Trenton. He left a skeleton force of 400 with orders to make noise and keep the fires lighted, so that Cornwallis would think he was about to bag his fox after all. Cornwallis reached Trenton on January 2. His officers urged an immediate attack. But the din of men digging trenches and the flicker of campfires assured the commander that Washington's army would be there on the next day, when his own troops were refreshed and ready for a quick battle. So he waited, and at 1:00 on the morning of January 3, 1777, the main body of Washington's army moved out in silence. Their plan was not to retreat back into Pennsylvania, but to boldly attack Princeton and New Brunswick.

In his advance on Trenton, Cornwallis had left 1,200 troops under Lt. Col. Charles Mahwood as a rear guard. On the morning of January 3, Mahwood was marching to join the main force at Trenton, when, through the fog, he saw the glint of bayonets. He thought they belonged to a column of Hessians, then realized they were Americans—presumably retreating after inevitable defeat at Trenton.

## Victory and the Spoils Not Taken

In fact, they were a detachment under Gen. Hugh Mercer, sent by Washington to destroy Stony Brook Bridge, for the British a vital link on the Trenton road. In any case, Mahwood suddenly wheeled his men about, and the Battle of Princeton was on. At the orchard of William Clark, near a Quaker meetinghouse, the fighting was fierce. And, at first blush, the American militiamen panicked, unable to load faster than Mahwood's men could ply their bayonets.

Fearing another Kip's Bay rout, Washington rode to the scene and, amid a hail of musket lead and the flash of enemy sabers, Washington rallied the troops—long enough for the guns of Henry Knox to speak and for Daniel Hitchcock's brigade of Rhode Islanders and Massachusetts men, along with Pennsylvanians under Edward Hand, to come pounding to Mercer's aid. Soon, Mahwood and his men were running back in panic along the Trenton road.

Hugh Mercer, like Washington, was a man of unbounded courage, but he was not so fortunate this day. He fell in that orchard battle, mortally wounded.

Washington resisted the impulse to pursue the fleeing attackers, for he knew they would lead him straight to Cornwallis. Instead, he advanced into Princeton and engaged the few British soldiers remaining there. Washington had taken Princeton, but he could not afford to occupy it. Cornwallis, with far superior numbers, would counterattack soon. Worse, Washington had to abandon his plan to capture New Brunswick. There, he knew, the British stored massive quantities of supplies, together with a war chest of some £70,000. Such a stroke, Washington believed, might be sufficient to end the war—or, at least, prompt the British to treat on very generous terms.

**191**

But it was not to be. After Trenton and Princeton, Washington's tattered forces had no more to give. Instead of advancing to New Brunswick, Washington set off to the west, for winter haven in the New Jersey highlands.

# Stalemate

Having learned much through hard experience, George Washington chose his winter quarters wisely. Morristown was situated on a steep-sided plateau, making for a highly defensible position. From here, he could observe enemy movements. But he could do little more. The victories at Trenton and Princeton had salvaged the Revolution, turning the long retreat from Long Island and Manhattan into a pair of stunning victories that emboldened New Jersey patriots to renew their resistance to British rule.

However, most of these patriots preferred to fight an irregular, guerrilla war, rather than join the Continental army, thus creating a civil war in northern New Jersey, where local patriots and Loyalists fought each other in a bloody conflict that lasted for years. Neither side could win, but the longer the conflict continued, the more likely it was that the British public would become disillusioned with paying taxes to support a hopeless war in America. Trenton and Princeton aided the American cause not so much by destroying British troops or reconquering territory, as by weakening George III's position with his own people.

Washington's recruiters found they could not replenish the army that dwindled away at Morristown. Having already extended their enlistments six weeks beyond year's end, many Continental regiments were now greatly reduced. Fortunately for the American cause, Howe, Cornwallis, and Baron Wilhelm von Knyphausen, commander in chief of the Hessians, stunned by failure, holed up in the little piece of New Jersey left to them, apparently unaware of just how weak and reduced Washington's encamped forces were. Stalemate would endure until spring.

**Sites and Sights**

Morristown National Historic Park, just outside of suburban Morristown, New Jersey, is the site of Washington's winter quarters during 1777 and during 1779-1780. Visitors can explore the Ford Mansion, Washington's headquarters in 1779-80, and reconstructed soldiers' huts. Call 201-539-2085 for information.

## The Least You Need to Know

➤ The loss of Long Island, Manhattan, and the Hudson River forts had left the Continental army and the American cause at low ebb, yet, at precisely this nadir, Washington decided to take the offensive.

➤ As he had done during the invasion of Manhattan, Howe acted ponderously and with too much caution, missing an opportunity to annihilate Washington's army in New Jersey, which was reduced by casualties, capture, and the expiration of enlistments.

➤ After withdrawing to Pennsylvania, Washington made a stealthy, storm-tossed crossing of the Delaware on Christmas night, 1776, and surprised the Hessians at Trenton.

➤ Following victory at Trenton, Washington took Princeton, but exhaustion and a shortage of men and supplies prevented his going on to capture New Brunswick, which harbored a wealth of supplies and the British war chest.

# Chapter 15

# Gentleman Johnny

## In This Chapter

➤ The character of John Burgoyne

➤ A grand strategy to break the Revolution

➤ The patriots lose Fort Ticonderoga

➤ The "martyrdom" of Jane McCrea

➤ A bloody draw at Oriskany

➤ Burgoyne loses most of his Indian allies

The victories at Trenton and Princeton saved the Revolution. But encamped for the winter in frigid Morristown, what did George Washington have to ponder? An army barely clothed and poorly provisioned, its ranks ravaged by a smallpox epidemic—one of the scourges of eighteenth-century camp life. The commander in chief set his men to work building a totally useless fort—christened Fort Nonsense—for the sole purpose of keeping them active and disciplined.

With early spring came an influx of new troops, and, better still, the veterans were no longer so eager to leave when their terms of enlistment expired. Thanks to the persuasive charm of Benjamin Franklin and the acuity of Silas Deane, congressional emissaries, the French were slowly being won over to the cause of American liberty. King Louis XVI, always eager to tweak the British nose, was not quite ready for an official alliance with the emerging republic, but private firms were beginning to furnish supplies. In March, the brig *Mercury* arrived from France with a load of muskets, munitions, and clothing; it was the first of more than 30 French cargo vessels to arrive that spring. In June, Marie Joseph Paul Yves Roch Gilbert du Motier, Marquis de Lafayette arrived with a party of other idealistic adventurers (including Baron de Kalb), eager to impart European military expertise to the officers and men of the Continental army. (The European contributions to the American Revolution are discussed in Chapter 19, "Valley Forge".)

As the spring of 1777 budded in New Jersey, the Revolution once again seemed viable. But spring brought renewed resolve to the British forces as well, and "Gentleman Johnny" Burgoyne, as dashing and flamboyant as William Howe was timid and conventional, had a brand new plan for crushing the rebellion.

# "Thoughts for Conducting the War"

"Gentleman Johnny," his officers and men called Gen. John Burgoyne, and he was the perfect eighteenth-century British gentleman. Born of ancient lineage in Lancashire, Burgoyne received a first-class education at Westminster School, which instilled in him a love of learning and letters—a passion matched only by his romantic regard for women. Commissioned a *cornet* in 13th Light Dragoons in 1740 and promoted to lieutenant the following year, he suddenly eloped with the daughter of the Earl of Derby (she was the sister of a Westminster school chum) and seemingly torpedoed his military career. Hard up for cash, he sold his commission (at the time, gentlemen officers of the British army purchased their commissions for substantial sums) and moved to France in 1746.

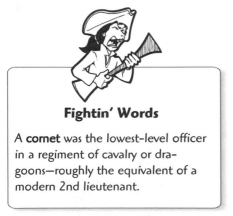

**Fightin' Words**

A **cornet** was the lowest-level officer in a regiment of cavalry or dragoons—roughly the equivalent of a modern 2nd lieutenant.

Fortunately, Derby's heart softened, and he exerted his influence to gain for Burgoyne, in 1757, a captaincy in the 11th Dragoons during the Seven Years' War. Proving himself an able officer, Burgoyne was elected to Parliament in 1762 (and compiled a liberal record with regard to the rights of the American colonies), but then his regiment was dispatched to Portugal to counter the Spanish invasion there. Again, he acquitted himself admirably and, on his return to London, found himself welcomed as a hero.

By September 1774, he had achieved the rank of major general and was assigned as subordinate to join Gen. Thomas Gage to counter the incipient rebellion in North America. He returned to England in November 1775, but was again sent to North America to reinforce Britain's Canadian forces. After triumphing at the Battle of Trois-Rivieres (June 8, 1776, and discussed in Chapter 10, "Canadian Sunset"), Burgoyne wintered back in England.

In London, "Gentleman Johnny" revived and perfected the plan Gen. Guy Carleton had attempted the previous year: the division of the state of New York along the Hudson, the isolation of New England, and the decapitation of the Revolution. Burgoyne submitted a document titled "Thoughts for Conducting the War from the Side of Canada" to Lord Germain, secretary of state for the American colonies, on February 28, 1777, outlining a three-pronged attack on New York:

➤ A principal force would advance southward down Lake Champlain and the upper Hudson.

➤ Simultaneously, a smaller force would operate through the New York frontier country, from Oswego through the Mohawk Valley.

➤ These two operations would be coordinated with Howe, who would send another major force up the Hudson, meeting Burgoyne's principal force at Albany in a pincers movement that would amputate New England from the rest of the colonies.

*"Gentleman Johnny" Burgoyne.*
(Image from the National Archives)

King George endorsed the plan, scrawling on the margin of Burgoyne's manuscript, "the force from Canada must join [Howe] at Albany," and Lord Germain authorized Burgoyne to carry it out. Yet Germain failed to ponder the details. First, giving command of the expedition to Burgoyne was an affront to Gentleman Johnny's superior, Guy Carleton. Worse, it compelled Gen. Howe, the commander in chief of British forces in America, to subordinate his actions to those of Burgoyne, junior to him as well as to Carleton.

But Germain had been careful not to offend Howe. On March 3, immediately after approving Burgoyne's plan, Germain also approved Howe's plan for attacking Philadelphia (discussed in Chapter 16, "Philadelphia Falls"). He assumed that Howe would capture the American capital city, then rush up to rendezvous with Burgoyne—although Germain didn't tell Burgoyne any of this. For years, historians believed that

Germain had simply forgotten to tell Howe that he was supposed to join forces with Burgoyne in Albany to deliver the knockout blow to the Revolution. In fact, before he left Canada, Burgoyne saw a letter from Howe to Carleton, informing him that unless Washington attempted to unite his army with forces in north, Howe had no intention of helping Burgoyne.

While Germain had been foolish enough to approve two mutually exclusive plans, Burgoyne should have protested. But he seemed little disturbed by the news that the essential third prong of his attack would likely fail to materialize. Had he the seniority of Carleton, perhaps Burgoyne could have prevailed upon Howe to put the Philadelphia assault on ice. But Burgoyne was a British gentleman, who understood what it meant to be a junior dealing with seniors. He decided to carry on, presumably in the hope that Howe would find the time to join him in Albany.

We begin the story of Burgoyne's grand strategy here, and Chapters 16 and 17 take it to its conclusion.

# Ticonderoga Tragedy

Burgoyne began his move south from St. Johns, Newfoundland, to Lake Champlain on June 17, 1777. He commanded a force of 7,000 infantrymen, British regulars as well as German mercenaries, in addition to a small force of English and German artillerists, 400 Indian auxiliaries, and a few Canadian and Tory adventurers. His baggage train included 138 artillery pieces, and he made use of the flotilla of vessels Carleton had used against Benedict Arnold in 1776, augmented by boats captured from Arnold.

The capture of lightly defended Fort Ticonderoga by the Americans in May 1775 had been an important early triumph. Situated on the western shore of Lake Champlain, it commanded fleet movements on the lake. The fort had been built by the French during the French and Indian War, and Washington ordered John Trumbull, a Connecticut painter, to upgrade its fortifications. In this he was aided by Tadeusz Kosciuszko, a Polish officer and military engineer who had joined the American cause in August 1776. An ingenious system of log booms and iron chains was built across the quarter-mile water gap across Lake Champlain, between the fort and an outcropping of land. This made passage of enemy vessels impossible. Yet no amount of fortification could substitute for manpower, and Gen. Arthur St. Clair, commanding the Lake Champlain region, could afford only about one fifth of the strength necessary to defend Fort Ticonderoga adequately. Mount Defiance, an 800-foot hill just to the southwest of the fort, was left completely undefended.

The American commanders guessed that the British offensive, when it came down from Canada, would not come by way of Lake Champlain, but via the Mohawk Valley or perhaps by sea. If the worst did happen, the American commanders resolved to hold out at the fort as long as possible, then withdraw to Mount Independence, across the lake. It was a hare-brained plan, of course, since any force strong enough to threaten Fort Ticonderoga would certainly be strong enough to keep its defenders from crossing over to Mount Independence.

On July 1, Burgoyne divided his forces at Lake Champlain. The British contingent went down the west side of the lake, while the Brunswick mercenaries, under Baron Friedrich von Riedesel, took the east. Von Riedesel's mission was to secure Mount Independence. The mercenaries were accustomed to fighting on open battlefields, not traipsing through a thick, swampy forest, fetid with the July heat. They struggled in painful slow motion toward their objective.

*Baron Friedrich von Riedesel, commander of German mercenaries. (Image from the National Archives)*

On the west shore, however, the British moved swiftly, clearing the forest for the artillery with which to bombard Fort Ti. Burgoyne was anticipating a conventional siege, but then a Lt. Twiss of the Royal Engineers took note of Mount Defiance, the wholly undefended commanding position southwest of the fort. American commanders had felt relatively safe in leaving the position undefended, because, high and steep, it seemed practically inaccessible. Twiss alerted Maj. Gen. William Phillips, the chief artillery officer, who remarked that "where a goat can go a man can go and where a man can go he can drag a gun." Phillips hauled guns to the summit of Mount Defiance, but his exertions must have alerted Arthur St. Clair within the fort. On July 6, Brig. Gen. Simon Fraser, commanding the British Advance Corps, reported that the Americans had abandoned Fort Ticonderoga, not a shot having been fired. Fraser further reported fires on Mount Independence, opposite Fort Ti across Lake Champlain.

Gen. St. Clair had decided not even to attempt to hold the fort. But neither would he defend Mount Independence, as the American fallback plan called for. Instead, St. Clair withdrew to Mount Independence, gathered up the garrison, and marched and sailed to Skenesboro, at the south end of Lake Champlain. Given the force aligned against him, this was not a bad move, but the fires Fraser had seen were the blazing barracks and military stores, which St. Clair had ordered destroyed lest they fall into enemy hands. Worse, St. Clair forgot to destroy the bridge, supported by boats, across the lake. The British Advance Corps used this to pursue the retreating Americans.

It was no easy pursuit, and the difficulty was compounded by the failure of Riedesel's Germans, hopelessly bogged down in the swampy woods, to join forces with Fraser. Then, on July 7, Fraser's men stumbled into a New Hampshire regiment, a fight broke out, and the New Hampshiremen, fleeing to Hubbardton, Vermont, quickly surrendered.

But it wasn't over. The rear guard of St. Clair's main force, commanded by Col. Seth Warner, rallied and struck at Fraser. In contrast to the New Hampshire militia, Warner's men fought with a fierce coolness, firing into Fraser's lines with deadly accuracy. Fraser was about to withdraw when Baron von Riedesel arrived. His men readily flanked the American position, then charged in with a devastating bayonet attack. St. Clair ordered a militia unit to the rescue, but the men refused. Col. Warner had no choice but to order his troops to scatter. The survivors—about 600 of 1,000 troops engaged (300 men were captured, about 50 killed)—straggled to rejoin St. Clair's main column at Fort Edward, a tumbledown outpost on the Hudson.

# The Death of Jenny McCrea

The loss of Fort Ticonderoga, the "Gibraltar of America," was profoundly depressing to the patriots and exhilarating to the British. It was said that, hearing the news of the victory, King George ran into his wife's dressing room shouting, "I have beat them! I have beat all of the Americans!"

But he had not. St. Clair—subsequently court-martialed and acquitted for abandoning Fort Ti—had managed to preserve his army, which meant that Gentleman Johnny Burgoyne had failed in his primary mission. Yet he didn't see it that way. What he saw was that he was now only about 20 miles from Albany and a victorious union (for so his grand plan had prescribed) with the forces of Gen. Howe and Barry St. Leger.

Burgoyne had admonished Britain's Indian allies to confine their attacks to soldiers, even issuing "certificates of protection" to all Tories who requested them. But fancy speeches and paper documents meant nothing to Indians given license to kill the white invaders of their land, and who made little distinction between patriots and Tories.

Jane McCrea was a Tory girl who lived with her brother on the Hudson, between Saratoga and Fort Edward. She was engaged to David Jones, a Tory in the service of Gen. Burgoyne's army. Jane McCrea went to join her fiancé at Fort Edwards, where, on July 27, 1777, just two days before Burgoyne's main body of troops reached the fort, she and a Mrs. McNeil (an American cousin of Simon Fraser) were captured by

Burgoyne's Indian allies, traveling ahead of his army. The Indians started back to Fort Ann, where Burgoyne was headquartered. By the time they arrived, they had only Mrs. McNeil in tow—and the scalp of Jane McCrea. Lt. Jones identified it as that of his fiancée.

## We Hold These Truths

The murder of Jane—affectionately called Jenny—McCrea was the subject of much American anti-British propaganda and entered into folklore. It is believed that the unfortunate girl had been shot after her captors, drunk, argued over who should guard her—although another story holds that she was accidentally shot by a member of an American rescue party.

She was between 18 and 23 at the time of her death and has been variously described as "a country girl ... without either beauty or accomplishment"; a pretty lass possessed of "clustering curls of soft blonde hair"; and a stunning young woman with tresses "of extraordinary length and beauty, measuring a yard and a quarter ... darker than a raven's wing."

McCrea's killer was identified as a Wyandot named Panther, but Burgoyne dared not act against him for fear of alienating his Indian allies. Gen. Horatio Gates, commander of American forces at Bennington, Vermont, sent Burgoyne an indignant letter, which the Americans publicized for its propaganda value:

> That the famous Lieutenant General Burgoyne, in whom the fine Gentleman is united with the Soldier and Scholar, should hire the savage of America to scalp Europeans and the descendants of Europeans, nay more, that he should pay a price for each scalp so barbarously taken, is more than will be believed in Europe, untill authenticated facts shall, in every Gazette, convince mankind of the truth of the horrid fate.
>
> ... The miserable fate of Miss McCrea was particularly aggravated by her being dressed to receive her promised husband, but met her murderer employed by you.

Burgoyne, who was clearly pained by the atrocity, had more than personal guilt to worry about. Local outrage over the killing of Jane McCrea—though she was the Tory fiancée of a Tory in Burgoyne's service—stirred the patriot cause and called to the colors the farmers of Bennington, which would prove the undoing of Burgoyne's grand strategy.

# Reversals of Fortune

Following the McCrea tragedy, Burgoyne could take comfort in the completion, on July 29, of the road through the wilderness. Carving it out, and building no fewer than 40 bridges, had consumed almost a full month—time for the Americans to regroup and resupply themselves. Now Burgoyne's officers were eager to make a dash to Albany, meet up with St. Leger and Howe, deliver the crushing blow to the rebels, and return to England in triumph.

Instead, Burgoyne ordered his troops into camp around Fort Edward to wait until his full forces were assembled. He intended to arrive in Albany at full strength—making a fitting union with Howe. But on August 3, he received a dispatch from that general, congratulating him on the capture of Fort Ticonderoga and casually informing him that his "intention is for Pennsylvania, where I expect to meet Washington, but if he goes to the northward … be assured I shall soon be after him to relieve you."

Of course, this shouldn't have come as a surprise to Burgoyne, but he had hoped—*wished* is probably more like it—that Howe would follow his plan. He comforted himself that at least Gen. St. Leger would meet him and that, together, they could still wreak havoc on the rebels. As for the news about Howe, he kept that to himself. No use imperiling the morale of his troops.

## *Oriskany Rout*

On June 18, 1777, one of the colonels attached to St. Leger's force, Daniel Claus, dispatched a dozen *Iroquois* braves, mostly Cayugas, under Mohawk and Cayuga chiefs, to scout out the American stronghold at Fort Stanwix and to take some prisoners to be brought back for questioning. The Indians ambushed a tree-cutting party and a sod-cutting party outside of the fort, killing eight men and capturing five. Under interrogation several days later, the prisoners painted a picture of Fort Stanwix as so formidably garrisoned that St. Leger decided to delay his attack on the fort.

St. Leger should not have assumed that the prisoners were telling the truth. Fort Stanwix, in fact, was falling down with neglect and disrepair, and its 29-year-old commandant, Col. Peter Gansevoort, feverishly urged his small 750-man garrison to repair whatever they could.

In the meantime, the feisty militia general Nicholas Herkimer unsuccessfully attempted to assassinate Joseph Brant, the most highly skilled and most dangerous pro-British Indian leader. At Herkimer's invitation, Brant came out for a peace parley in an open square in the wilderness village of Unadilla, at the junction of the Unadilla and Susquehanna rivers, about 60 miles south

**Fightin' Words**

The **Iroquois** were not (and are not) an Indian tribe, but an ancient (dating to the sixteenth century) cultural and political confederation of tribes—the Mohawks, Oneida, Onondaga, Cayuga, Seneca, and (after 1722) the Tuscaroras.

of Fort Stanwix, which was on the Mohawk River. The plan was for four of Herkimer's men to draw pistols hidden in their cloaks and shoot Brant dead. As it turned out, only one assassin even attempted to draw his pistol, but it became entangled in his shirt. A war whoop went up from the Indians who accompanied Brant, and they leveled their weapons. Both sides stood at a standoff, then departed the field.

*Joseph Brant, Mohawk chief and ally of the British.*
(Image from the National Archives)

Col. Gansevoort was luckier in his covert action. He dispatched Ahnyero, a prominent Oneida warrior known to the Americans as Thomas Spencer, to infiltrate the large Indian council convening at Oswego toward the end of July. Ahnyero learned of St. Leger's plan to attack Fort Stanwix, and he furnished full details concerning troop strength.

In the meantime, St. Leger sent 30 riflemen, commanded by Lieutenant Harleigh Bird, and 200 Iroquois under Chief Hare to intercept a supply party to Fort Stanwix. That party, however, under Lt. Col. Robert Mellon, reached the fort before Bird and unloaded the supplies. Only as Mellon was returning from this mission did Hare and his Indians attack, killing one *bateauman* and capturing four more. Bird's mission was not a total

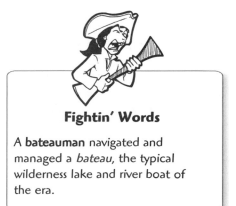

**Fightin' Words**

A **bateauman** navigated and managed a *bateau*, the typical wilderness lake and river boat of the era.

disappointment, however, because he was able to assess the true strength of Fort Stanwix and reported to St. Leger that it was quite weak.

On August 3, St. Leger began his advance on Fort Stanwix with full military pomp, intending to overawe the outpost's defenders with the might of the British army. He set up his position just out of range of the American artillery and demanded Gansevoort's surrender. Whether or not he was impressed with St. Leger's display, the American commander ignored the surrender demand, and on August 4, St. Leger commenced artillery bombardment. For all its fury, the bombardment killed only one man and wounded six. Far more effective was the work of Indian snipers, who calmly picked off soldiers as they desperately worked to cover the fort's interior roofs and parapets with sod.

## *"To the Last Extremity"*

On August 6, three messengers from Gen. Herkimer managed to penetrate the Indian lines surrounding the fort. Herkimer was at the Indian town of Oriskany, 10 miles southwest of Fort Stanwix, with 800 militiamen. The message asked Gansevoort to join him in a combined assault on St. Leger's lines. Gansevoort fired three cannon shots as a signal that he had received the message and would comply, then sent out 200 men under Lt. Col. Marinus Willett. They quickly encountered one of St. Leger's encampments and attacked, killing 15 to 20 British and Indians and taking four prisoners. This minor patriot victory came at the expense of alerting St. Leger to Willett's presence, which meant that Willett would be unable to reinforce Herkimer.

### Voices of Liberty

"I have only to say that it is my determined resolution, with the forces under my command, to defend this fort, at every hazard, to the last extremity, in behalf of the United States, who have place me here to defend it against all their enemies."

—Peter Gansevoort, in response to a British demand that he surrender Fort Stanwix, August 3, 1777

Herkimer's combination of military skill and prudence was rare in a militia commander. He insisted on waiting for a sortie from Fort Stanwix before he attacked. But his subordinate officers, lacking their commander's military virtues, demanded immediate action, taunting Herkimer with accusations of cowardice and even of harboring loyalist sympathies. The latter accusation hit home; for one of his brothers was fighting on the side of St. Leger.

Facing the prospect of mutiny, Herkimer decided, against his better judgment, to proceed. One of St. Leger's Indian scouts brought the British commander word of the advance. St. Leger dispatched Joseph Brant with 400 Indians and an equal number of loyalist troops—John Butler's Tory Rangers and John Johnson's Royal Greens—to ambush Herkimer's force. Unfortunately, the Indian scouts Herkimer employed, some 60 Oneidas, failed to detect the ambush. Six miles from Fort Stanwix, where a wide ravine was crossed by a log causeway, Brant, Butler, and Johnson struck at 10:00 on the morning of August 6.

Most of the American officers were killed in the opening minutes of the Battle of Oriskany. Herkimer was severely wounded, his leg shattered by a musket ball. Propped up against a saddle, smoking a pipe, bleeding to death, he calmly tried to direct the chaos of panic and death that passed for a battle. One entire American regiment ran, but the others fought hand-to-hand. The Tory forces suffered serious losses, as did Brant's Indians, including the deaths of two chiefs and the wounding of another. Then nature itself intervened, as a sudden thunderstorm interrupted the battle, providing time for the forces to regroup on higher ground.

John Butler succeeded briefly in breaching the patriots' defensive positions by ordering his men to turn their green coats inside out, so that they resembled the American uniforms. Then he ordered an advance, directly into the American lines. But the deception did not long endure, and even this attack was beaten off.

## The Indians Bow Out

At last, the Indians, discouraged by their own heavy losses, retreated, and with that desertion, Butler and Johnson also had to withdraw. The American forces, however, were in no shape to pursue them.

The Battle of Oriskany was a disaster for all concerned. Half of the American forces were killed, wounded, or captured. The able militia commander Herkimer died of his wounds. The British lost 33, with 41 wounded, and the Indians' losses were the heaviest of all: 17 Senecas killed, including their chief warriors, and 16 wounded; 60 to 80 Indians from other tribes were also killed or wounded. In all, 23 war chiefs were killed or wounded. In an effort to whip the warriors into a frenzy, the British officers had given the Indians liberal doses of rum. As a result, many fought drunk, and not as well.

Although Oriskany was not a victory for either side, the battle did halt Herkimer's attempt to reinforce Fort Stanwix, and St. Leger again demanded Gansevoort's surrender, sending two officers to the fort for a parley. One of them declared to Gansevoort and Willett, "If the terms are rejected, the Indians, who are numerous and much exasperated and mortified from their losses in the action against Gen. Herkimer, cannot be restrained from plundering property and probably destroying the lives of the greater part of the garrison."

Willett replied with indignation: "Do I understand you, Sir, … that you come from a British colonel, to the commandant of this garrison, to tell him, that if he does not deliver up the garrison into the hands of your Colonel, he will send his Indians to murder our women and children[?]"

Gen. Philip Schuyler, encamped at Fort Dayton, 50 miles from Fort Stanwix, dispatched Gen. Ebenezer Learned and a Massachusetts brigade to the relief of the fort; a short time after this, he also sent the First New York Regiment under Gen. Benedict Arnold. An advance party from Learned's brigade happened to meet Maj. Walter Butler (the brother of Tory Ranger commander John Butler) and Hon Yost Schuyler, a prominent Tory, and took both men captive. Arnold promised Hon Yost Schuyler pardon and restoration of his property if he agreed to return to St. Leger's camp and tell the Indians that Walter Butler, Joseph Brant's close friend, had been captured and would be hanged. A fearful Hon Yost Schuyler not only complied, but also obligingly exaggerated reports of the strength of Arnold's force.

The ruse worked. Perhaps as many as 600 Indian warriors promptly deserted St. Leger, and the British general, himself alarmed by the fabricated report of Arnold's strength, hastily lifted the siege of Fort Stanwix on August 22. He withdrew, leaving behind a large store of equipment and artillery. This convinced Joseph Brant and other Indian leaders that if this was how whites fought a war, they would have no more of it. For his part, Burgoyne found a new use for the Indian allies who still remained. The British commander was lately plagued by desertions, and he now gave his Indian auxiliaries permission to take the scalps of any deserters they found.

# The Hessians

The Revolution was not fought exclusively between British and Continental soldiers. As we have seen—and will explore at greater length in Chapter 20, "White War, Red Blood"—Indians were involved in some of the ugliest combat of the war, and, as we have also seen, German mercenaries also played an important role. Some 30,000 mercenary troops fought against the Americans. They were men from various German states, misleadingly lumped together under the name Hessians, probably because their principal commanders, a succession of three men, all came from Hesse-Cassel and Hesse-Hanau.

In part because they were "foreign"—that is, spoke German rather than English—and in part because they fought for money rather than country, the "Hessians" were especially hated by American citizens and American troops.

## *Hired Guns*

There was nothing unique or new about hiring mercenaries; European powers had been doing it for years. During the Revolution, the Duke of Brunswick (Brunschweig) was the first German to conclude a treaty with the British to supply troops. The British crown was to provide the troops with the same pay, food, and wounded care it provided its own troops (which really was doing the mercenaries no great favor). The duke, of course, benefited far more. For each soldier furnished, he received more than £7 and an indemnity against various losses. Although the duke was given a percentage of this fee for each man wounded or maimed, he had to furnish replacements at no additional cost for men who had fallen ill or who had deserted. In addition to the per-man fee, the British paid him an annual subsidy of £11,517. As the war ground on, most fees were raised across the board.

On the face of it, the German mercenaries looked like terrific soldiers. They were well trained and had been rigorously disciplined in the tradition of Frederick the Great. They were feared for their cruelty in battle, but the British ultimately found this to be a liability. Gen. Howe's civilian secretary, Ambrose Searle, wrote that the "Hessians are more infamous and cruel than any. It is a misfortune we ever had such a dirty, cowardly set of contemptible miscreants." Yet, after a few years of experience against them, the Americans transformed them into objects of ridicule. Their adherence to European tactics and drill was ill suited to the American situation. The "Hessians" never won a fight in which they alone were pitted against American forces.

## Farmers Triumphant at Bennington

During eight years of war, about 5,000 German mercenaries deserted the ranks, and, indeed, by mid-August 1777, desertion had become a major problem for Gen. Burgoyne, among his British regulars as well as the Germans. The army had not only failed to score any definitive victories, it was running low on supplies. Accordingly, Burgoyne decided to raid Bennington, Vermont, where the patriots had a large store of provisions.

The first order of business was to assign Indian auxiliaries to steal much-needed horses, which they did—but when their demand for payment was not met, they cut the animals' hamstring muscles, rendering them useless. Among the many and growing complaints about Indian allies, the loudest issued from Lt. Col. Frederick Baum, the German mercenary commander detailed by Burgoyne to take Bennington. He felt fortunate, at least, that he would be facing nothing more than a few militiamen at Bennington. Certainly, an initial engagement at Cambridge, New York, on August 12, had gone well. Forty or 50 Americans were easily routed.

At Bennington, Gen. John Stark, who had distinguished himself at the Battle of Bunker Hill, was steadily accumulating reinforcements—many of them rallied to the cause by the fate of Jane McCrea. Others joined Stark, or at least refrained from joining loyalist forces, because of the news that New York's patriot government had finally agreed to recognize that Vermont was a separate state. (Once the British had surrendered at Saratoga, New York went back on its promise and continued to claim Vermont for another decade or more.) When he learned that Baum's Indian auxiliaries were looting and terrorizing the countryside, he dispatched 200 militiamen to drive the Indians off. However, they were met by Baum's main column, and were themselves sent running.

On the 15th, a rainstorm postponed any action and gave Stark time to receive 400 reinforcements, the Vermont militia, led by Seth Warner. Baum's men, in the meantime, decided to dig in. On the 16th, Stark and Warner waited for the rain to stop, then moved in to attack, with an enveloping movement to him in the front, rear, and flanks. Baum saw the detachments, but because they were

**Sites and Sights**

The Bennington Battle Monument (802–447–0550) marks the site of the Battle of Bennington, and the Bennington Museum (802–447–1571) contains a rich collection of early American and Revolutionary artifacts. It was also at Bennington that Ethan Allen put together his Green Mountain Boys (Chapter 9).

dressed in civilian clothing, the formally uniformed Baum assumed they were the local Tories Col. Philip Skene had promised would come to his aid.

With all the Americans in place, the attack began. In the shock of the initial assault, the Indians, Tories, and Canadians panicked and fled. The Germans and the British, dug in on a hilltop, held their ground and were joined by some of their fleeing comrades. For two hours, Stark and Warner kept up the pressure. With ammunition dwindling, Baum's troops began to flee, except for his faithful dragoons. Baum, determined to save the day, ordered his men to draw sabers and charge into the Americans. It was a gesture both futile and fatal. Baum fell, mortally wounded, whereupon his men surrendered.

In the meantime, more German mercenaries arrived, led by Lt. Col. Heinrich von Breymann. They were met at the outskirts of Bennington by Stark's troops, who were poorly organized. Fortunately, more of Warner's Vermont militiamen reached Bennington from Manchester and, with Stark's regrouped men, counterattacked Von Breymann's forces.

Of the combined British and German forces, 207 lay dead and another 700 were taken prisoner. Thirty Americans fell in battle, and perhaps 40 more were wounded. It was, by any measure, a great victory. Not only did it greatly boost American morale, it deprived Burgoyne of supplies he badly needed—putting him in a position of dire need with which the Americans were all too familiar. To the Americans, the bounty of weapons, including rifles and four brass cannon, was most welcome. As for Gentleman Johnny Burgoyne, the grand strategy that, in London's palatial corridors of government, had seemed so certain of success, all but disintegrated in the forests, hills, and watercourses of New York and Vermont.

### Voices of Liberty

"We'll beat them before night, or Molly Stark will be a widow."

—Gen. John Stark, predicting victory at the Battle of Bennington

---

### The Least You Need to Know

➤ Gen. Burgoyne was a bold strategist, but a mediocre leader, whose appreciation for the realities of wilderness combat was highly deficient.

➤ The American loss of Fort Ticonderoga was a serious blow to morale; however, the subsequent victory at the Battle of Bennington did much to redress the loss.

➤ The murder of Jane McCrea, at the hands of Burgoyne's Indian allies, did much to consolidate local resistance against the British.

➤ The Battle of Oriskany was fought to a bloody draw, but it prepared the way for victory at the Battle of Bennington.

# Chapter 16

# Philadelphia Falls

The 13 colonies hugging the Atlantic coast were still a vast country. For Washington, chronically starved for manpower, weaponry, and supplies, trying to conduct a war in one part of the colonies meant failing to conduct it adequately in another part. But the collapse of Burgoyne's grand plan to seize New York state and divide and conquer the colonies revealed that the British, like Washington, were also starved. Lord Germain seemed not to appreciate this dilemma when he approved Burgoyne's "Thoughts for Conducting the War from the Side of Canada" *and* Howe's plan for attacking Philadelphia.

In Chapter 15, "Gentleman Johnny," we saw what happened to Burgoyne up north. Here is the progress of Howe in Pennsylvania.

## The Lure of Philadelphia

The historian Troyer Anderson has commented that the "American Revolution was won and lost during the first three years," the period of Gen. William Howe's command, and that "any explanation of British failure … becomes a verdict upon the conduct" of Howe and his brother, Adm. Richard Howe.

Anderson wrote his opinion in 1936, when William Howe had been in his grave for 122 years. Yet, having lost Boston and failed repeatedly thereafter to use the men and equipment of the greatest army in the world to destroy a ragtag force of rebels fighting in a wilderness, Howe must have felt the weight of history bearing down on him. He wanted—he *needed*—a decisive victory. Let Burgoyne fight in the wilds of New York and Vermont. He, William Howe, would attack and take Philadelphia, the leading metropolis of the American continent.

It was an attractive prize. Not only was it the center of colonial wealth and culture, it was also the rebel capital, the seat of the upstart Continental Congress, the place where the insolent Declaration of Independence had been signed. Paradoxically, though, Philadelphia was also a stronghold of loyalism. Philadelphia had grown rapidly during the eighteenth century, and by the time of the Revolution it was the second largest city in the British Empire. Philadelphians had prospered under British rule, and were worried about their future if the United States became independent. Moreover, the Quakers, who still wielded great influence in the city, were generally loyalists, because they were pacifists and they blamed the rebels for the bloodshed that was now overtaking America. Unlike Boston, in which revolutionary sedition loitered on every street corner and caroused in every tavern, Philadelphia had a host of prominent citizens who embraced the government of King George III.

But what about Burgoyne's plans? Commander in chief Howe rationalized his decision this way:

➤ Public opinion in and about Philadelphia and all of Pennsylvania would favor the British cause, so taking the rebel capital would be quick and easy.

➤ The capture of Philadelphia would deal a decapitating blow to the Revolution.

➤ An attack on Philadelphia would draw Washington's forces away from Burgoyne, so that the Philadelphia campaign would not be an abandonment of his colleague, but would actually help him.

In many ways, it was a good plan. In some ways, it even worked. Howe had shown a flash of his former brilliance in guessing accurately what Washington would do. Washington, Howe knew, was a provincial commander. He had shown a tactical and personal flair for leadership, but he had repeatedly made strategic blunders. Howe decided to offer Washington a gambit, tempting him to make the obvious move, to defend Philadelphia. By doing this, Washington would forsake the less obvious and far more effective move to the north, where, joining with Gen. Horatio Gates, he could have made a more effective force against Burgoyne.

As Howe had hoped, Washington made the strategically obvious and faulty move of throwing everything he had into the defense of Philadelphia. What Howe hadn't counted on was how costly, on the one hand, the defense would be and, on the other hand, that the colonials in New York and Vermont would beat Burgoyne even without the help of George Washington's army.

## On the Banks of the Brandywine

To the Continental army, which had moved from its encampment in Morristown, New Jersey, to the banks of the Neshaminy Creek in Pennsylvania, the waning summer of 1777 brought much speculation and many rumors about what the British would do next. On August 22, definitive news came. As John Adams put it in a letter to his wife, Abigail, "It is now no longer a secret where Mr. Howe's fleet is ... it is arrived at the head of Chesapeake Bay .... His march by land to Philadelphia may be about sixty or seventy miles."

Howe had altered the plan he had originally presented to Lord Germain in that he had elected to move not overland, but by sea. As usual, however, Howe proved unable to move expeditiously. In April he began the process of readying the expedition from New York to a landing near Philadelphia, but his fleet, laden with 15,000 troops, didn't embark until July 23.

And Howe not only moved slowly, he moved stupidly. The direct water route between New York and Philadelphia is via the Delaware River. Instead, Howe chose to take the much longer route around Cape Charles and then up the Chesapeake. His reasoning perhaps reveals his central weakness as a commander. He worried that navigating the Delaware was too hazardous (it was not) and that the river was too well defended (it was not). In his caution, Howe demonstrated that he was far more focused on *not losing* than he was on *winning*. Caution is admirable in most walks of life. In a military commander, however, it can be a fatal flaw.

**Voices of Liberty**

"... The army is not yet in motion, though preparing to move .... We may venture to think that, by the blessing of Providence, this ungrateful rebellion will be crushed in the course of the present campaign [against Philadelphia]."

—Ambrose Serle, cMilan secretary to William Howe, writing to the Earl of Dartmouth, May 20, 1777

And Howe compounded his error. Even by the roundabout route he chose, Howe could have put in at Delaware Bay, disembarking at New Castle, just 33 miles from Philadelphia. Instead, he sailed a great deal further down the coast to the mouth of the Chesapeake Bay, then sailed up it and unloaded at Head of Elk in Maryland, about 55 or 60 miles from his objective. Moreover, after more than a month (from July 23 to August 25) packed aboard troop transports beneath the blazing summer sun, Howe's soldiers were sickly and weak when they got off the boats. The commander would need time to rest and refit his troops—and to scour the Maryland countryside for cavalry mounts. The horses fared worse than the men on the meandering voyage: Most had died.

The long delays gave Washington plenty of time to assemble and move his army. On August 24, the commander in chief and his Continental army—at this point numbering about 11,000 men—paraded through Philadelphia, marching southward to meet Howe, Cornwallis, and Wilhelm, Baron von Knyphausen, the new commander in chief of the German mercenaries. Knyphausen, slender, upright, "a grim and silent man," had replaced Leopold Philip von Heister, who was relieved after the Hessian disaster at Trenton (Chapter 14, "Crossing the Delaware").

On September 11, early in the morning, four little girls were playing "close by Polly Buckwalter's Lane," near the road to Kennett Square, Pennsylvania. Approaching them came a group of horsemen.

"Girls," one of the riders called out, "you'd better go home!"

"Why?"

"Because the British regiments are coming up the road."

One of the girls, looking up the road, saw the redcoats "in great numbers," and all four ran off to their homes.

They were mistaken about the "great numbers"; for what they saw were not the British in their multitudes, but a mere diversionary force. Of course, little girls have a right to be wrong. The American commander should have known better. Tricked, Washington left many of the upstream fords across Brandywine Creek undefended. Across these fords, Howe's main force splashed across, putting them in a perfect position to surprise the Americans from the right rear. It was practically a replay of what had happened on Long Island, when the British forces approached from precisely the opposite direction anticipated (Chapter 13, "The Battle for New York").

The New Hampshire forces, under the command of Gen. John Sullivan, took the first surprise blows, and did not take them well. All along the placid Brandywine, the thin American line began to give way. Howe threw Von Knyphausen's Germans squarely against the American center at Chadd's Ford, while he and Cornwallis crossed the Brandywine at two other unguarded fords, *outflanking* Washington's army. The beleaguered Sullivan, in response, sent generals Adam Stephen and William Alexander ("Lord Stirling") to check the British advance. In so doing, however, they left a broad gap between their lines, which, at about 4:00 in the afternoon, Howe exploited with a fierce bayonet attack. Washington, made aware of this action, sent Gen. Nathanael Greene to fill the breach.

What had begun as panic now became furious confusion. The Americans fought fiercely, but ineffectively. Their belated determination could not repair the damage done by the early surprise. Worse, just as Howe and Cornwallis crossed the Brandywine, Von Knyphausen broke through the American center, braved the patriots' desperate fire, and captured the Continental artillery. He made deadly use of it, turning the guns on the retreating Americans.

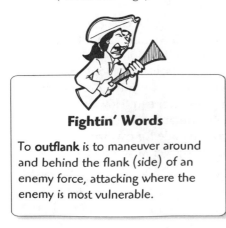

**Fightin' Words**

To **outflank** is to maneuver around and behind the flank (side) of an enemy force, attacking where the enemy is most vulnerable.

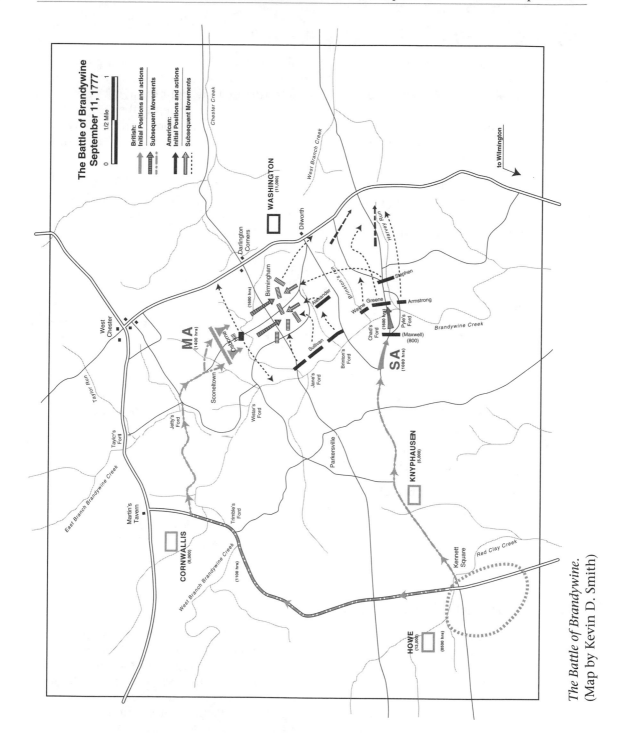

*The Battle of Brandywine.*
*(Map by Kevin D. Smith)*

**213**

## *"Our Army Was Something Broke"*

The Battle of Brandywine lasted all day, ending only with nightfall. Washington withdrew to Chester, Pennsylvania, still interposed between Howe and Philadelphia, but certainly the loser at Brandywine. "It was fortunate that night came on," Col. Timothy Pickering of Massachusetts recorded in his journal for September 11. Joseph Clark, a young New Jerseyan fighting in the American ranks, recorded in his diary how, as "night was spreading its dusky shade through the gloomy valley … our army was something broke."

Of some 11,000 American troops engaged at Brandywine, 1,200 to 1,300 were casualties, perhaps 400 of this number taken as prisoners. Eleven precious artillery pieces were captured. Howe, in overall command of 12,500 men, lost 577 killed and wounded. All but 40 of this number were British regulars.

### We Hold These Truths

John Sullivan was competent and courageous, but also one of the patriots' unluckiest generals. His troops were stunningly outflanked at Long Island and, in an almost identical maneuver, again at Brandywine. As historian Mark Boatner III put it, "After Long Island and Brandywine, it is not likely that Gen. Sullivan will ever be nominated as defensive end on anybody's All-American team."

After the battle, members of the Continental Congress initiated a movement to suspend Sullivan from command. Washington refused to act against him and officially acquitted him. As the commander in chief's great biographer, Douglas Southall Freeman concluded, "Washington conducted the Brandywine operation as if he had been in a daze."

## Massacre and Humiliation

During the rapid retreat to Chester, some semblance of order was restored to the American ranks. After resting the night, Washington fell back closer to Philadelphia. Howe marched into Chester and occupied it—15 miles from the new nation's capital. A torpor had stolen over Congress—or, at least, an unwillingness to accept reality. In any case, it took all of Alexander Hamilton's persuasive power to convince Congress to evacuate, leaving on September 18, first for Lancaster, Pennsylvania, and then to the village of York. The Liberty Bell, cracked when it rang in celebration of American independence on July 8, 1776, and already regarded as a kind of sacred relic of the

Revolution, was carefully packed and sent via army baggage train to Allentown, Pennsylvania. There it was hidden in Zion Reformed Church.

In the meantime, on September 16, at White Horse Tavern and at Malvern Hill, both west of Philadelphia, Washington briefly engaged Howe. Washington's nascent cavalry—just getting organized by the Polish patriot Casimir Pulaski (see Chapter 19, "Valley Forge")—began to duel with the Hessians. Washington then dispatched forces under generals Anthony (best known later as "Mad Anthony") Wayne and William Maxwell to fight in earnest, but a torrential storm soaked the combatants, bringing the battle to an abrupt halt. The Americans, whose ammunition was stored in jerry-built cartridge boxes, found that their powder had been drenched and was useless. The troops trudged through the mud to Reading Furnace, where they could be resupplied.

## Butchery at Paoli

The ruined powder was only the beginning. A detachment of Von Knyphausen's troops, foraging along the Schuylkill River, just west of Philadelphia, discovered Valley Forge on September 18, a completely unguarded patriot supply depot. A large quantity of flour, horseshoes, tools, and other supplies were captured. Howe established a post.

A few days later, disaster struck "Mad Anthony" Wayne. Washington had sent him with 1,500 men and four cannon to Warren's Tavern, near the town of Paoli, to harass the British rear guard. Wayne, usually an alert and canny commander, did not count on the activity of local Tories. They spied on Wayne and reported his presence to the British. Howe responded by sending Maj. Gen. Charles Grey to surprise Wayne's camp during the night of September 20–21.

*"Mad Anthony" Wayne, in a portrait engraved and published in 1796.* (Image from the National Archives)

The attack would earn Grey the nickname "No-Flint" among his men; for he ordered them not to load their muskets, and if their muskets were already loaded, to remove the flints from the locks, so that they could not fire. He would have no firing, he explained, but a bayonet attack instead, silent and swift. The tactic worked. The British fell upon the unsuspecting Americans like assassins. Only after the quick action was practically over did Grey's men load and fire; for Wayne's panic-stricken soldiers carelessly ran about in front of their campfires, offering perfectly silhouetted targets.

Howe claimed 500 kills, but Wayne counted 150 bodies—150 bodies so mangled by British bayonets that local residents dubbed the encounter the Paoli Massacre. The only bright spot in the horrific affair was that Wayne managed to save his cannon and lead most of his men to safety.

## The Loss of Philadelphia

Shaken by Paoli, Washington moved his troops to Pott's Grove (modern Pottstown), Pennsylvania, whereupon Howe, changing direction, started his main body of troops across the Schuylkill. On September 23, Lord Cornwallis marched four British and two Hessian units into Philadelphia, unopposed. After taking possession of the city, he bedded down his forces in Germantown, just to the north of the city.

# Glorious Victory Shamefully Lost

There is no denying that the loss of Philadelphia came as a severe psychological blow to the Americans. Some officers and others began openly to question Washington's fitness for command. Yet, just how serious was the loss?

➤ Congress had escaped and continued to operate in York, Pennsylvania.

➤ Howe had wasted so much time getting to Philadelphia that it was impossible for him to help Burgoyne in the north.

➤ The capital had fallen, but the Continental army was still intact, and the Revolution was still on.

Washington resolved to recover from the disasters of Brandywine, Paoli, and Philadelphia itself. He had learned from experience never to admit defeat, even in defeat. So he proposed to attack—and attack precisely the position at which the British were strongest: Germantown.

## The Germantown Disaster

After marching 16 miles during the night from an encampment at Skippack Creek, Washington attacked Howe's advance units at dawn of October 4. Washington had a force of 8,000 Continentals and 3,000 militiamen versus 9,000 British troops camped at Germantown. The advance troops, the British 40th Regiment, retreated to the large house of Benjamin Chew, a formidable stone structure that made a most convenient impromptu fortress. From its cover, the British poured fire on Gen. Sullivan's troops. Washington considered bypassing the house, but was persuaded by Gen. Henry Knox to halt the advance and bombard the house.

The artillery barrage had no effect on the Chew house, and cost the Continentals casualties as well as an hour's delay. In the meantime, Gen. Adam Stephen, hearing the fire, rushed his men into the battle, but, confused by the morning fog, ended up firing on and colliding with the rear of Mad Anthony Wayne's column. The result was paralysis and panic. To make matters even worse, Gen. Nathanael Greene's advance bogged down. All hope of a coordinated attack evaporated, and Washington had no choice but to order a general withdrawal.

## Defeat or Victory?

From a strictly military point of view, Germantown was a disaster, the result of a combination of bad weather, bad luck, and a bad plan. Its cost had been heavy. Washington lost 152 men killed and 521 wounded. At least 400 were captured. Howe's casualties were 535 killed and wounded.

And yet, from a political and psychological point of view, Germantown was not an unmitigated catastrophe. French observers were impressed by the fact that Washington, having lost Philadelphia, made bold to attack. What they saw moved their government a step closer to outright alliance with the patriots. As for the American army, officers and men did not view Germantown so much as a defeat, but as a narrowly missed victory. As Gen. John Armstrong reported to Gen. Horatio Gates, it was a "glorious victory fought for and eight tenths won," only to be "shamefully but mysteriously lost."

### Sites and Sights

Like all great English-style houses, the Chew residence had a name, Cliveden. Built in 1763, it still stands at 6401 Germantown Avenue, now a part of Philadelphia, and may be visited; call 215–848–1777. During part of his presidency, George Washington lived in Germantown, in the Deshler Morris House at 5442 Germantown Avenue (phone 215–596–1748). Germantown, occupying higher ground than Philadelphia proper, was believed to offer some protection from the yellow fever epidemics that periodically plagued the city.

Even the British command seemed unable to accept the victory with unalloyed pleasure: They had won by retreating and taking refuge. "Tho we gave away a complete victory," T. Will Heth, a Continental officer, wrote to Col. John Lamb, on October 12, "we have learned this valuable truth: [that we are able] to beat them by vigorous exertion, and that we are far superior [in] point of swiftness. We are in high spirits .... Another bout or two must make [the British] situation very disagreeable."

Certainly, up north, in New York, at a place called Saratoga, John Burgoyne was just now finding out how "disagreeable" the British situation could be.

### The Least You Need to Know

➤ Howe had sound reasons for targeting Philadelphia as a military objective; however, his campaign compromised Burgoyne's operations in the north, the operation took much too long, and it ultimately failed to "crush the rebellion."

➤ Washington's defense of Philadelphia was poorly planned and poorly executed, yet the army endured, and the Revolution stubbornly survived the fall of its capital city.

➤ From a military perspective, Washington's counterattack at Germantown was a poorly planned failure; yet the audacity of the attack helped win over the French government to wholehearted support of the American cause and also gave the Continental army a surprising morale boost.

➤ The loss of Philadelphia was a serious psychological blow to the patriots, but it was a strategic error for the British, who temporarily gained a city, but lost an opportunity to destroy Washington's capacity to continue the Revolution.

# Chapter 17

# Saratoga Saga

## In This Chapter

➤ Burgoyne blunders at the Battle of Freeman's Farm

➤ The second Saratoga battle: Bemis Heights

➤ Benedict Arnold—hero again

➤ Burgoyne's surrender

➤ National and international significance of the Saratoga victory

As fall colors appeared along the Hudson, Gentleman Johnny Burgoyne received one bad piece of news after another. First came Howe's letter, letting him know that only if Washington turned north would he join Burgoyne in Albany. Next came word of the British disasters covered in Chapter 15, "Gentleman Johnny": Baum and Breymann were beaten at Bennington, and Barry St. Leger failing to take Fort Stanwix.

With each pillar of his grand plan crumbling, Burgoyne thought of falling back to Fort Edward or Fort Ticonderoga. But, as he interpreted his orders from London, he did not have the option of falling back. Regardless of others' success or failure, he was to "force a junction with Sir William Howe." Never mind that Howe was preoccupied in Pennsylvania. Burgoyne saw no alternative to marching into Albany. Besides, as he shouted to his troops when they crossed to the west bank of the Hudson on September 13, "Britons never retreat!"

With that, Burgoyne ordered the boat-borne bridge spanning the river dismantled. The way back to Canada was thus symbolically severed. This chapter tells what happened when Burgoyne tried to advance to Albany.

# The Bravery of Benedict Arnold

The redcoats' march along the Hudson's west bank was painfully slow. Local patriots had wrecked many small bridges spanning countless streams. Burgoyne's army was encumbered by guns and carts, which required decent roads and bridges. These had to be built as needed, often slowing progress to a mile or less per day.

If Burgoyne was hobbled by patriot sabotage, he was also blinded by the desertion of most of his Indian allies after the Battle of Bennington and the withdrawal before Fort Stanwix. The Indians were his scouts, and, without them, the army could only grope its way along. Advance parties, foraging for food, were continually sniped at. One entire party of 30 was captured. On September 16, Burgoyne still *saw* nothing, but he heard the distant rat-a-tat of reveille drums. Somewhere to the south, then, the main strength of the enemy must lay, and Burgoyne dispatched a party to reconnoiter. They found tracks leading to an abandoned farm.

## Voices of Liberty

"I am sorry the Canada army will be disappointed in the junction they expect with Sir William Howe, but the more honour for Burgoyne if he does the business without any assistance from New York."

—Lord Germain to William Knox, undersecretary of state for the colonies, September 29, 1777

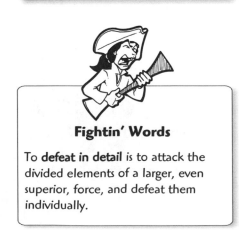

## Fightin' Words

To **defeat in detail** is to attack the divided elements of a larger, even superior, force, and defeat them individually.

## *Freeman's Farm*

The forlorn farm, its unharvested wheat rippling in the breeze, belonged to a man named Freeman. Burgoyne, doubtless heartened by the prospect of a battle on an open field—where he could use his troops to best advantage—decided to draw the Americans out. In his eagerness to do so, however, he made a classic tactical blunder. A prime commandment of military tactics is never to divide your forces in the face of the enemy. Even though Burgoyne believed he was "in the face of the enemy"—he hadn't seen them, but the drums told him they were near—he divided his forces into three.

On September 19, he assigned Gen. Simon Fraser to lead 2,200 men along a path that led to Freeman's western fields. Burgoyne would take 1,100 men south and then west to meet up with Fraser on Freeman's Farm. He assigned the east column, another 1,100 men in three Brunswick regiments commanded by Baron von Reidesel, to move south, down the river road. The three columns were out of sight of one another, their movement to be coordinated by means of a signal gun. In truth, there was no reliable means of coordinating movement through such broken terrain. Burgoyne had divided his forces, inviting *defeat in detail*.

The Americans saw everything, yet their overall commander, Horatio Gates, a cautious and conventional officer, did nothing to exploit the vulnerable disposition of Burgoyne's divided command. His subordinate, the dashing and imperious Benedict Arnold, urged him to action. At last, Gates ordered riflemen under the wily Daniel Morgan and light infantry led by Henry Dearborn to make contact.

The British and German troops began their advance before dawn, but the terrain was so rugged that it was nearly one in the afternoon before Burgoyne's center column broke through to the clearing that was Freeman's Farm. From the woods on the south edge of the clearing, shots rang out. Every British officer in the advance line fell, victims of Morgan's riflemen.

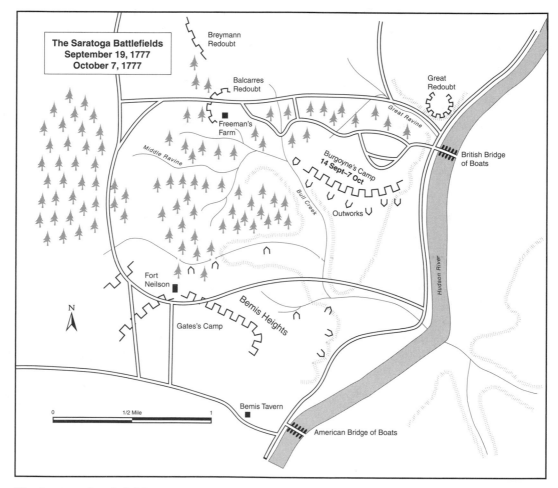

*The Saratoga battlefields.*
(Map by Kevin D. Smith)

## We Hold These Truths

Daniel Morgan's background as a frontiersman included a first cousin named Daniel Boone. Morgan fought alongside Washington in the French and Indian War, during which the tough 200-pounder endured 500 lashes for hitting a British officer who had struck him with the flat of his sword. Morgan remarked that he owed the British one stripe, because the drummer had miscounted. He also survived an Indian bullet through the face, losing his teeth on one side. After the French and Indian War, he served against Pontiac and in Lord Dunmore's War (1774).

During the Revolution, he led a Virginia rifle company, serving with Arnold in Canada and Gates at Saratoga. Morgan resigned in July 1779, ostensibly for his health, but probably because he was not given the brigade command he believed he deserved. Ordered by Congress in June 1780 to report to Gates in the Southern theater, he declined, but then rushed south when he realized his services were badly needed.

Morgan resigned again in February 1781, became a prosperous frontier farmer after the war, and won election to Congress in 1797.

Astounded by their success, Morgan's riflemen gave chase to Burgyone's advance line, stampeding to the rear in panic. Suddenly, Morgan's men collided headlong with the main body of the British center column. In complete disarray, Morgan's troops scattered back into the woods. The American commander endured a moment of panic, fearing that the British had mauled his elite troops, but he sounded a turkey call—his idiosyncratic substitute for a bugle—and his men instantly reassembled. As for the British, the encounter had so shaken them that, as the survivors ran toward them, many in the main body opened fire indiscriminately, wounding and killing their own men.

Seeing all this, Burgoyne decided not to wait for a signal from Fraser's column, but fired his own signal gun and moved his main body of troops onto Freeman's Farm, forming his lines along its northern edge.

Although there is some controversy, the evidence is that Benedict Arnold assumed command of the next phase of the battle. With Burgoyne's ranks neatly formed, European style, in the clearing, Morgan and Dearborn took positions along the southern edge of the clearing, and seven more regiments were sent down from Bemis

Heights, just south of the farm. For the next three or four hours, a firefight pitted American tactics against European. Firing from cover, the Americans cut through the ranks of the three British regiments standing shoulder to shoulder. The British suffered severe losses, but, with discipline and artillery, returned effective fire. Each time the Americans attempted to charge out of cover to take the battle to a conclusion, the British would drive them back.

Both sides were aware of the critical passage of time. Burgoyne knew that if he could hold out, Reidesel and Fraser would arrive with reinforcements. The Americans wanted to destroy the British forces in detail before the arrival of those fresh troops. Reidesel at last broke through from the east and opened up with cannon. Arnold had returned to Bemis Heights to get more troops, so he was absent from the field when the Germans arrived. Essentially leaderless, the Americans held their ground for a time, but fell back as darkness settled over Freeman's Farm.

Fraser did not reach the vicinity of the battle until it was nearly over. His men exchanged fire with an American brigade, but contributed little. At the end of the day, Burgoyne's men—those left standing—felt fortunate to have survived. The British general had lost some 600 men. Of the 800 troops in the three regiments that absorbed the brunt of the combat, 350 were killed, wounded, or captured—a staggering 44-percent casualty rate. American losses totaled 319, including 65 killed, 208 wounded, and 36 missing. One regiment, the 62nd, was reduced from 350 to 60 men, a loss of 83 percent.

### Voices of Liberty

"Colonel Morgan, you and I have seen too many redskins to be deceived by that garb of paint and feathers; they are asses in lion's skins, Canadians and Tories; let your riflemen cure them of their borrowed plumes."

—Benedict Arnold directing Daniel Morgan to open fire on Burgoyne's advance guard at Freeman's Farm, September 19, 1777

### Voices of Liberty

"While the American must look on these figures as a testimony of rebel marksmanship, he must also see in them a badge of British courage."

—Mark M. Boatner III, *Encyclopedia of the American Revolution*

## In a Huff

Burgoyne could claim a technical victory, in that he possessed Freeman's Farm. Had he possessed sufficient resolve to resume the battle over the next day or two, he might have beaten Gates, who had performed not so much poorly as with utter passivity. Gates had more than sufficient men at Bemis Heights—4,000 versus 900— to swoop down on the men Von Reidesel had left to guard Burgoyne's supplies. With his supplies gone, Burgoyne would have been faced with the choice of surrender or starvation.

But neither Burgoyne nor Gates had seized the initiative. Arnold quarreled bitterly with Gates, whose report of the battle to Congress conspicuously left Arnold out of the action. At this insult, Arnold asked Gates for a "pass to Philadelphia ... where I propose to join Gen. Washington, and may possibly have it in my power to serve my country, tho I am thought of no consequence to this Department." Gates relieved Arnold of command and barred him from headquarters. Only after a number of Gates's other officers protested was Arnold persuaded to stay on, although Gates did not officially ask him back.

It was not the first time the difficult Arnold had to be talked out of resignation. After his performance at Valcour Island (Chapter 10, "Canadian Sunset") in October 1776, he returned a popular hero, but his overweening arrogance had incited the envy and enmity of several other officers. In February 1777, Congress created five new major generalships, deliberately insulting Arnold by passing him over in favor of his juniors. Only Washington's personal intervention prevented him from resigning at that time.

# A Silver Bullet

It was fortunate for the American cause that Arnold stayed on. The Battle of Saratoga, which began with Freeman's Farm, was about to enter a second phase, at Bemis Heights, and Arnold would perform even more heroically.

Saratoga's second phase came just as Burgoyne was tensely anticipating the arrival of reinforcements. He had given up on Howe, but he took some comfort from a message he had received earlier from Sir Henry Clinton, the general Howe had left in charge of New York City when he took his main contingent on its expedition to Philadelphia. If Howe repeatedly failed to perform with the brilliance and dash he had shown during the French and Indian War, behaving instead with a depressing lack of imagination and an excess of caution, Clinton was even less bold, describing himself, quite remarkably, as "a shy bitch." He had at least 7,000 troops in New York, whom he might have dispatched up the Hudson to remove Burgoyne from his predicament. Instead, after much debate, he sent 3,000, informing Burgoyne in a secret message in late July or early August. The document was unintelligible until it was covered by a specially cut hourglass-shaped mask, which was delivered by a separate messenger. Decoded, it read:

> *Sir W. Howe is gone to the Cheasapeak Bay with the greatest part of the army. I hear he is landed but am not certain. I am left to command here with too small a force to make any effectual diversion in your favour. I shall try something at any rate. It may be of use to you. I own to you I think Sir W.'s move just at this time the worst he could take.*

Well, "something" was better than nothing—and it was considerate of Clinton to offer his opinion on "Sir W.'s" move.

It was October 3—and Burgoyne's situation was probably already beyond hope—before Clinton finally sent those 3,000 men up the Hudson. They took a series of patriot river forts—Fort Montgomery, Fort Clinton, and Fort Constitution—then Clinton sent Burgoyne a message. It was, in part, a reply to an urgent letter of September 28th from

Burgoyne, asking whether Clinton would be able to reinforce him. Burgoyne wanted to know whether he should proceed to Albany or retreat, pointing out that he could not stay where he was beyond October 12. Clinton's message read:

> *Nous voici—and nothing between us but Gates. I sincerely hope this little success of ours may facilitate your operations. In answer to your letter of the 28th of September by C.C. I shall only say, I cannot presume to order, or even advise, for reasons obvious. I heartily wish you success.*

But this message never reached John Burgoyne. The journal of Dr. James Thatcher, serving with the Continental army, explains why:

> October 14, 1777: *We have been trembling alive to [the] menacing prospect [of the arrival of Clinton's forces in Albany], but our fears are in a measure allayed by the following singular incident. After the capture of Fort Montgomery, Sir Henry Clinton despatched a messenger by the name of Daniel Taylor to Burgoyne with the intelligence [that he was not rushing to Albany]; fortunately, [Taylor] was taken away as a spy, and finding himself in danger, he was seen to turn aside and take something from his pocket and swallow it. General George Clinton [the Patriot commander], into whose hands he had fallen, ordered a severe dose of emetic tartar to be administered. This produced the happiest effect as respects the prescriber, but it proved fatal to the patient. He discharged a small silver bullet, which being unscrewed, was found to enclose a letter from Sir Henry Clinton to Burgoyne. "Out of thine own mouth thou shalt be condemned." The spy was tried, convicted and executed ....*

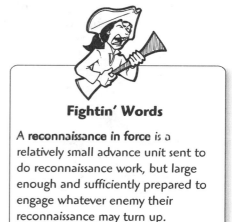

### Fightin' Words

A **reconnaissance in force** is a relatively small advance unit sent to do reconnaissance work, but large enough and sufficiently prepared to engage whatever enemy their reconnaissance may turn up.

Ironically, by the time the message was intercepted, Burgoyne had already begun surrender negotiations with Gen. Horatio Gates at Saratoga.

# The Battle of Bemis Heights

Soon after sending the intercepted silver-bullet message to Burgoyne, Howe sent Clinton a request for reinforcements. Clinton stopped his advance up the Hudson, abandoned the three forts he had captured, reversed course, and left Gentleman Johnny to twist slowly in the wind.

Two weeks had elapsed since the Battle of Freeman's Farm. Burgoyne had nervously used the time to construct elaborate entrenchments and redoubts on the high ground called Bemis Heights. For his part, Gates had been reinforced by the arrival of troops under Gen. Benjamin Lincoln. Some of Lincoln's forces were already harassing

Burgoyne's rear positions, and the British commander knew he was in trouble—although he didn't know how much. He was now outnumbered, 11,000 to 5,000. On October 7, feeling that he could no longer wait for destruction to come, Burgoyne sent a *reconnaissance in force* of 1,650 men to determine just what he was facing.

He didn't have to wait long to find out. Gates dispatched Daniel Morgan to attack the right flank of the reconnaissance and Gen. Enoch Poor to attack the left. Morgan's men rushed wide around Burgoyne's troops to take up positions in the woods, from which they could fire on both flank and rear. In his account of the battle, Col. James Wilkinson entirely omitted the role Benedict Arnold played, just as Gates had omitted Arnold from his report on Freeman's Farm.

Officially barred from headquarters, Arnold had nevertheless allowed brother officers to persuade him to stay in camp after Freeman's Farm. Now, with neither orders nor authorization, he gathered up a detachment to attack the breastworks behind which some of Burgoyne's men had taken shelter. Next, seeing Continental troops under Gen. Ebenezer Learned marching toward the British right, Arnold galloped directly across the line of fire to lead them away from the right and instead into a frontal assault against "Breymann's redoubt," an enforced position occupied by Hessians. Arnold did not escape this attack unscathed. His horse was shot from under him, and then he took a bullet in the leg. Unable to continue, he had to be carried from the field. On the British side, however, the officer corps fared far worse. Among the casualties was Gen. Simon Fraser, one of British army's most dashing and capable commanders, who fell mortally wounded while trying to cover the redcoats' retreat.

### Sites and Sights

The most dramatic way to gain an appreciation of the difficulties of war in Hudson-area wilderness is to visit the six–million–acre Adirondack Park, which encloses 1,000 miles of rivers and some 2,500 lakes. Hikers and river enthusiasts who think the American West has a corner on spectacular wilderness need to explore this region. Contact the Visitor Interpretive Center at 518-327-3000.

# Gentlemen Johnny Packs It In

Without Arnold to lead it, the American charge quickly petered out, although they could hardly have done much more damage to Burgoyne's army. Burgoyne suffered 600 killed or wounded; American casualties were fewer than 150. He fell back with his survivors on Saratoga, with Gates continually harassing him in pursuit. On October 12, Gates maneuvered around Burgoyne, cutting off all access to the Hudson and, therefore, any hope of withdrawal north to safety.

On October 13, with the unanimous concurrence of his officers, Burgoyne sent Gates a message, asking for surrender terms. Gates replied with a demand for unconditional surrender, which Burgoyne—now outnumbered more than two to one, hopelessly cut off, and without access to provisions—rejected. Even more remarkably, Gates, in a position to demand whatever he wanted, essentially allowed Burgoyne to dictate terms. On October 16, the two commanders drew up the Saratoga Convention—Burgoyne would agree only to a "convention," not a "surrender"—by which the troops were permitted not only to avoid becoming prisoners of war, but to return to England "on condition of not serving again in North America during the present contest." As Burgoyne explained to Lord Germain, in a letter of October 20, he had saved the army, "because if sent home, the State is thereby enabled to send forth the troops now destined for her internal defence"; that is, by using these particular troops for European service, an equivalent number of troops, currently in European service, could be freed up for duty in North America.

On the 17th, at two in the afternoon, the British marched out of their fortifications, and Gen. Burgoyne formally surrendered his army to Gates, on the terms concluded the day before. The two commanders then dined together, during which Burgoyne gallantly toasted Gen. Washington, and Gates, in return, responded with a toast to King George III.

Burgoyne accompanied his troops back to England. Keenly aware that his military reputation hung by a very frayed thread indeed, he demanded a court martial in an effort to redeem it. This he was never given—nor was he ever given another army to command. "Thus ended all our hopes of victory, honour, glory, etc.," wrote Lt. William Digby of the Shropshire Regiment. For his part, Gates, summed up in a letter to his wife what he took as the meaning of Saratoga: "If old England is not by this lesson taught humility, then she is an obstinate old slut, bent upon her ruin."

But both Digby and Gates missed the full meaning of the Saratoga campaign, as did Burgoyne, who saw it only as a personal loss. The fact was that an American force had not merely defeated a British force, driving it from the field, but that an American army had defeated a British army, driving it from the country. This validated the Revolution not only in America, but in much of the international community—most significantly in France, which was at last moved to declare itself a full ally of the United States.

The war would drag on, but America, clearly, was in it to stay—and would no longer fight it alone.

---

### The Least You Need to Know

➤ Without aid from either Howe or Clinton, Burgoyne was doomed.

➤ The Saratoga Campaign consisted of two major battles—Freeman's Farm and Bemis Heights; both were fought under the nominal command of Continental general Horatio Gates, but it was the reckless (and officially unacknowledged) heroism of Benedict Arnold that achieved ultimate victory.

➤ Gen. Gates granted Burgoyne generous surrender terms, permitting him and his army to return to England.

➤ The defeat of Burgoyne was a turning point in the Revolution, one which finally convinced the French to make a full alliance with the United States.

# Part 4
# Winter of Discontent

*The British regulars, the Tories, the Hessians, and the British-allied Indians were only one set of enemies Washington and his forces faced. A lack of supplies, clothing, and food threatened to destroy the army. Another threat came in the form of challenges to Washington's leadership, which are detailed in this section.*

*The Revolution was really at least two wars. There were the battles, primarily along the seaboard, between formed armies, patriots versus redcoats, and there was the ongoing convulsion of violence farther inland, between British-allied Indians and the patriot settlers of the frontier. Chapter 21 treats the role of Indians in the American Revolution. The war was also sharply divided into northern and southern theaters. Chapter 22 tells how the British took control of the two leading port cities of the South, Savannah and Charleston.*

*Finally, you'll read the story of how one of the boldest heroes of the Revolution, the dashing and impetuous Benedict Arnold, turned traitor, making his name a synonym for turncoat in the American lexicon.*

# Chapter 18

# Defeat and Disloyalty

Revolutions are dangerous things, not just to the powers that be, but also to the powers that come into being. Once the status quo has been attacked, power becomes a commodity and is up for grabs. Congress had enthusiastically approved George Washington as commander in chief of the Revolution's armed forces, but not everybody was happy about this, and discontent with Washington's command grew most intense after the loss of Philadelphia.

This chapter begins with the British and Americans struggling for control of the Delaware River, and ends with the struggle for power within the Revolution itself.

## Colonial Engineering: The Delaware Defenses

Gen. Howe had taken Philadelphia. The cost to the forces immediately under his command was significant, but the operation actually cost a lot more. Tied down by his campaign in Pennsylvania, Howe had been unable to help Burgoyne in Saratoga. The result, as we saw in the last chapter, was the defeat and "deportation" of an entire British army.

Having gained Philadelphia at so great a price, Howe needed to clear a supply route to the occupied city. It would not do to create the conditions of another Boston, leaving his troops in possession of a town but vulnerable to siege. The threat to Howe came from two mighty patriot forts on the Delaware River, Fort Mifflin on the Pennsylvania side of the river, and Fort Mercer on the Jersey side. Lest the British should try to run their ships past these forts, defying their guns by swift movement, patriot engineers constructed spiked barricades, called *chevaux de frise*, across the river, to block shipping.

*Forts Mifflin and Mercer were located opposite one another. Fort Mercer was at Red Bank, New Jersey, and Fort Mifflin was in the river, on Port Island, between Mud and Hog Islands. Together, they covered, with their cannon, the system of chevaux de frise.*

## Two Glorious Days

Mention French aid in the American Revolution, and the name of Lafayette naturally leaps to mind. Lafayette was a brave and dashing officer committed to the cause of liberty and possessed of a profound regard for George Washington. Such men are an asset to any cause. But the Americans were also badly in need of hard, nuts-and-bolts know-how, and this was supplied by a number of French *military engineers*. One of these, the Chevalier de Mauduit du Plessis, arrived in October 1777 to help Col. Christopher Greene, commandant of Fort Mercer, more effectively organize the defense of this important installation. Du Plessis could do nothing to augment the 400 Rhode Islanders who garrisoned the fort, a large earthwork mounting 14 cannon, but his professional eye immediately detected a problem. The fort was too big for its garrison. He had a new interior wall built, cutting off the northern wing of the fort. This simple stroke of engineering knowledge would make all the difference.

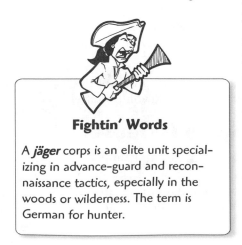

On October 21, 1777, Col. Carl Emil Kurt von Donop was detached by Howe with 2,000 Hessians to capture Fort Mercer. His command consisted of two elite groups, a *jäger* corps and grenadiers, and an additional unit, the Regiment von Mirbach, plus two cannon. Von Donop camped at Haddonfield, New Jersey, and, at 3:00 on the morning of the 22nd, marched off to the fort. He reached it by noon and began deploying his forces. At 4:30, he sent an officer to demand surrender, informing Col. Greene that he would give "no quarter."

The commandant refused to surrender. With what must be called calculated contempt, the Hessian mounted his attack at a leisurely pace. It was nine in the evening before he attacked in two columns, two battalions of grenadiers and the Regiment von Mirbach from the north, and the others from the west. "Vittoria!" shouted the northern column as they stormed the breastworks—only to find themselves in an empty compound, confronted by du Plessis's interior wall. In the meantime, Von Donop himself led the western column through the *abatis* and across the ditch, only to find his progress halted at the *berm*. He had mounted an assault against a walled fortress without thinking to bring ladders.

Up to now, Greene had yet to fire a shot. Calmly, he gave the order, and a hail of grapeshot and musket fire poured down on the massed ranks of the Hessians. Von Donop was among the first to fall, severely hit in the leg with a wound that proved mortal. Nevertheless, the Hessians withdrew and reformed, this time for an attempt on the south wall of the fortress. Thus far, the German mercenaries had shown great courage but little brains in their assault on Fort Mercer. Attacking from the south, after taking a beating north and east, required even more courage and perhaps even less brains. For the troops now exposed themselves not only to gunfire from the fort, but also from *rowing galleys* stationed out on the river. Of 1,200 Hessian troops actively engaged in storming Fort Mercer, 400 or so became casualties. American losses numbered 14 killed and 23 wounded.

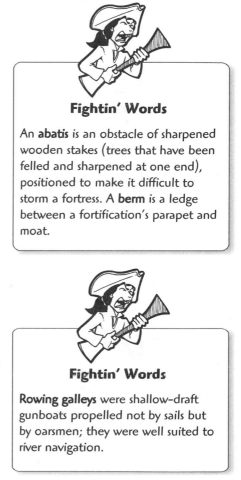

### Fightin' Words

An **abatis** is an obstacle of sharpened wooden stakes (trees that have been felled and sharpened at one end), positioned to make it difficult to storm a fortress. A **berm** is a ledge between a fortification's parapet and moat.

### Fightin' Words

**Rowing galleys** were shallow-draft gunboats propelled not by sails but by oarsmen; they were well suited to river navigation.

The next day, October 23, the British ships *Augusta*, mounting 64 guns, *Roebuck* (44 guns), *Merlin* (18 guns), and what one witness described only as two frigates approached the *chevaux de frise* and began to fire on the American galleys and "floating batters" (additional obstructions placed to block river passage). The galleys, together with guns on Fort Mifflin, returned fire, the combat becoming so furious (according to Col. William Bradford of the Continental army) that the very "elements seemed to be in flames."

At noon, the *Augusta* suddenly exploded. "Here presented a glorious sight before she blew," Bradford wrote to the president of the Pennsylvania Executive Council, "she laying broadside-to aground, and the flames issuing thro every port she had." By three, *Merlin,* having run aground, also burst into flame and exploded. "Thus ended two glorious days," Bradford wrote.

## Fort Mifflin Falls

Working in concert with the rowing galleys stationed on the Delaware, the defenders of Fort Mifflin sunk the *Augusta* and *Merlin*, defeating the assault on Fort Mercer.

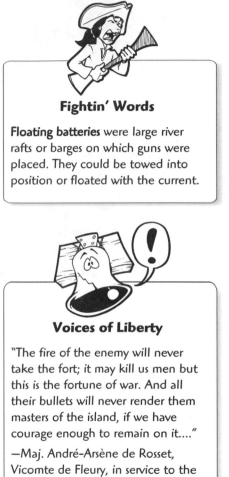

### Fightin' Words

**Floating batteries** were large river rafts or barges on which guns were placed. They could be towed into position or floated with the current.

### Voices of Liberty

"The fire of the enemy will never take the fort; it may kill us men but this is the fortune of war. And all their bullets will never render them masters of the island, if we have courage enough to remain on it...."

—Maj. André-Arsène de Rosset, Vicomte de Fleury, in service to the Continental army, writing of the bombardment of Fort Mifflin, October 14, 1777

The damage inflicted by the fort's guns made Howe all the more anxious to take Fort Mifflin. It was indeed vulnerable. Garrisoned by 450 men, Fort Mifflin was not as well engineered as Fort Mercer. Its land side was especially exposed. On November 10, the British commenced a severe bombardment by five *floating batteries* from Province Island and a huge floating battery, mounting 22 24-pound cannon, which was positioned a mere 40 yards from the fort.

Maj. André-Arsène de Rosset, Vicomte de Fleury, was the French engineer assigned to assist Lt. Col. Samuel Smith to defend the fort. Fleury kept a journal during the bombardment, which was kept up for five days.

"The enemy keep up a firing of cannon every half hour," Fleury recorded at 11:00 on the night of the 12th. "Our garrison diminishes, our soldiers are overwhelmed with fatigue—they spend nights in watching and labour without doing much on account of their weakness."

Fleury directed continual repair and reinforcement, but was forced to work with few tools and a shortage of materials. "Fort Mifflin," he wrote on the 14th, "is certainly capable of defence if the means be furnished...." But these means were unavailable, and, by the 14th, Col. Smith, badly injured, had been evacuated, and command fell to Maj. Simeon Thayer, who refused to capitulate. By nightfall, the fort was virtually reduced to rubble.

"We must have men to defend the ruins of the fort," the ever-resolute Fleury recorded in his journal. "Our ruins will serve us as breast-works, we will defend the ground inch by inch, and the enemy shall pay dearly for every step.... I repeat it—their fire will kill us, because we have no cover, but it will never take the fort."

## The Americans Lose Forts, the British Lose Time

On October 15, Maj. Thayer at last evacuated Fort Mifflin, having lost 250 of his 450-man garrison. He moved them to Fort Mercer, which fell under bombardment from

November 20–21 and also finally had to be abandoned. The flotilla of rowed galleys was likewise abandoned and burned, to keep the vessels out of enemy hands.

In an act of some desperation, during January 1778, David Bushnell, inventor of the submarine (see Chapter 13, "The Battle for New York"), was employed to create what might be described as floating combustibles. The British name for them was "infernals." They were arrangements of kegs packed with gunpowder and sent floating down the Delaware. Really, they were floating mines: On coming into contact with an object, such as a British ship, they exploded.

At first, Bushnell's "infernals" caused great alarm among the British, some of whom believed the kegs were like Trojan horses, filled not with gunpowder but actually packed with rebel soldiers, ready to spring into action. Soon, however, the British understood that they were explosive devices. They started simply firing at any object seen floating in the river. A lot of ammunition was thereby wasted, but any "infernals" hit were also safely detonated.

The loss of the Delaware forts was a serious blow to the patriots, compounding the loss of Philadelphia. But the effort of clearing those forts had cost the British heavily.

# The Conway Cabal

The Delaware River forts were not the only patriot assets under siege at this time. Washington's performance at Brandywine and Germantown had been poor—there was no denying that—whereas the performance of the army at Saratoga had been spectacular. Gen. Horatio Gates, overall commander in the north, claimed credit for the Saratoga victory, although he had, in fact, conducted the campaign passively. It was thanks to Benedict Arnold and Daniel Morgan that the Battle of Bemis Heights, culmination of the Saratoga campaign, ended with Burgoyne's surrender.

## *Office Politics*

There were plenty of voices raised in doubt about Washington's fitness for command. However, certain politicians—most prominent among them, Samuel Adams, Richard Henry Lee, Thomas Mifflin, and Dr. Benjamin Rush—saw the discontent over Washington as an opportunity to regain for New England leadership of the Revolution. These politicians disapproved not only of Washington's conduct of the war, but also of how Benjamin Franklin and Silas Deane, both associated with the Washingtonian political faction, were conducting affairs abroad. They feared entangling the United States in dangerous foreign alliances.

Moreover, many members of Congress feared Washington's attempt to shape his Continental troops into a European-style, regular army. Such armies were widely believed to be instruments of tyranny. Washington was trapped in what seems to modern interpreters a classic Catch-22 situation: The more successful he was at creating the disciplined, professional force that was essential to winning the Revolutionary War, the more his enemies suspected him of aiming at military dictatorship.

The dissident politicians began undermining Washington in subtle ways, mainly through hints dropped here and there, and by an anonymous paper called "Thoughts of a Freeman," which opined that "the people of America have been guilty in making a man their God."

Into this cauldron of simmering intrigue crept one Thomas Conway. Born an Irish Catholic in 1733, Conway was taken to France at age 6, was given a French education, and joined the French army in 1747. He sought and received permission to go to America, as a fighter for liberty, and arrived in Morristown on May 8, 1777. On Washington's recommendation, he was made a *brigadier general* on May 13.

The most junior of the 24 brigadier generals in the Continental army at the time, Conway lusted after a promotion, bombarding Congress with importunate letters, remarking in one that Washington (who had recommended his commission in the first place) was a fine man, but "his talents for the command of an Army ... were miserable indeed."

**Fightin' Words**

**Brigadier general** is the junior-most general officer rank, the equivalent of a modern one-star general. A brigadier commands a brigade, a military formation consisting of two or more regiments. (In the Continental Army, a full-strength regiment consisted of 728 officers and men.)

General Conway did not, in fact, form a "cabal"—a secret conspiracy—to overthrow Washington. But it was his name that adhered to the nascent anti-Washington movement. Here's how that came to happen.

On October 28, 1777, James Wilkinson was tarrying in York, Pennsylvania, taking his sweet time in delivering the urgent news from Gates that Burgoyne had surrendered at Saratoga (see Chapter 17, "Saratoga Saga"). Wilkinson was courting a young woman in York, but took time off to speak with Maj. William McWilliams, aide-de-camp to Gen. William Alexander ("Lord Stirling"). Wilkinson told McWilliams that Horatio Gates had received a letter from Conway stating that "Heaven has been determined to save your country; or a weak General and bad Councellors would have ruined it."

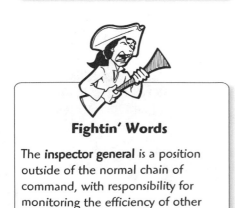

**Fightin' Words**

The **inspector general** is a position outside of the normal chain of command, with responsibility for monitoring the efficiency of other units.

McWilliams dutifully passed on Wilkinson's indiscreet gossip to Gen. Alexander, who informed Washington of what he considered "wicked duplicity of conduct."

When Washington confronted Conway with this letter, Conway denied having used the phrase "weak General" and protested that he had only meant to congratulate Gates on his victory. Then, as if to register his indignation at Washington's accusations, Conway abruptly resigned his commission on November 14.

But this would not be the end of it. Thomas Mifflin, most vocal of Washington's critics in Congress, became president of the congressional Board of War at this time. He quickly pushed through a promotion for Conway, making him not only a major general, but *inspector general* of the Continental Army.

## Showdown

Washington was disgusted by the baldly political promotion of the scheming Conway, and was concerned about the impact this promotion, over 23 other brigadiers, would have on morale. Nevertheless, he coolly informed Conway that he would always respect the decisions of Congress. Conway unwisely refused to let the matter rest and now accused Washington of intending to undermine him as inspector general. Washington in turn protested this accusation to Congress. In the meantime, intrigue over what was now being called a "secret correspondence" between Conway and Gates intensified.

## Gates Plays Dumb

Sensing that the tide of public and congressional opinion was turning against him, Gates attempted to imply that Alexander Hamilton, serving as Washington's aide, had secretly gained access to and copied some of Gates's correspondence, including Conway's letters. In feigned alarm, Gates wrote to Washington, suggesting that he investigate the breach.

Washington responded with a letter to Gates, explaining that he had learned of the contents of Conway's letter to Gates through Gates's very own aide, James Wilkinson! To give the knife an added twist, Washington sent this news to Gates via no less a body than the Continental Congress.

Wilkinson scrambled to put the blame on another of Gates's aides, Lt. Col. Robert Troup, but the mortified Gates was not deceived. He gave Wilkinson a severe dressing down, to which the wily young officer responded not with contrition, but a challenge to a duel. Fortunately, both men calmed down and reconciled before the duel could be fought.

## The Commander Pulls It Together

Washington's having sent the reply to Gates through Congress had been a brilliant stroke. As historian Mark Boatner III remarked, the evidence clearly demonstrated that the candidates for leadership, that some in Congress supported, were "pygmies coping with a giant." Worse for the Gates-Conway faction, publicizing the affair rallied Washington's many devoted supporters. Nine brigadiers and a host of colonels drafted a formal protest to Congress, objecting to Conway's promotion and to Wilkinson's promotion; he had

**Fightin' Words**

A **brevet** promotion is a promotion in rank but not pay, usually of a temporary nature, and typically for bravery or other distinction in the field.

been *breveted* a brigadier merely for bringing to Congress (and by the slowest means possible at that!) the news of Saratoga.

In the end, Washington emerged with the equivalent of a vote of confidence. Never one to hold a grudge, the vindicated commander in chief was quick to establish a smooth working relationship with Gates, whom he considered unspectacular but competent and, therefore, useful.

Conway, far less valuable than Gates, tendered his resignation in April 1778, expecting, perhaps, that his congressional friends would not accept it. But accept it they did, immediately and without question.

On July 4, 1778, John Cadwalader, a Pennsylvania militia general devoted to Gen. Washington, challenged Conway to a duel. The two met on the field of honor, and Conway was wounded—with a degree of symbolic irony—in the mouth.

### We Hold These Truths

Perhaps believing that he had been mortally wounded, the ailing Conway wrote a letter to Washington on July 23:

> I find myself just able to hold the pen during a few minutes, and take this opportunity of expressing my sincere grief for having done, written, or said anything disagreeable to your Excellency. My career will soon be over; therefore justice and truth prompt me to declare my last sentiments. You are in my eyes the great and good man. May you long enjoy the love, veneration, and esteem of these States, whose liberties you have asserted by your virtues.

Washington never responded. As for Conway, he fully recovered from his wound and returned to France, where he served in the French army until his royalist affiliations made life highly dangerous in the wake of the French Revolution. He fled the country, and it is believed that he died, in exile, about 1800.

## Year's End, 1777

As 1777 came to a close, Washington had survived an incipient assault on his authority, an entire British army had been defeated and driven from the country, the capital of the rebellion was still in the hands of its enemies, and Washington faced the grim prospect of getting his army—as always, ill-clothed and poorly fed—through the winter. Yet he knew that, if he did get the army through, it would no longer be facing the mighty British unaided. France was about to join the war, and a formal treaty of alliance was only weeks away.

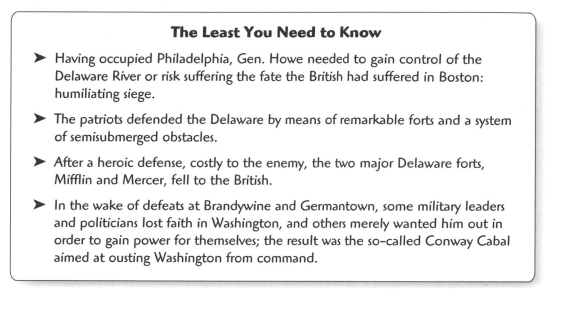

**The Least You Need to Know**

➤ Having occupied Philadelphia, Gen. Howe needed to gain control of the Delaware River or risk suffering the fate the British had suffered in Boston: humiliating siege.

➤ The patriots defended the Delaware by means of remarkable forts and a system of semisubmerged obstacles.

➤ After a heroic defense, costly to the enemy, the two major Delaware forts, Mifflin and Mercer, fell to the British.

➤ In the wake of defeats at Brandywine and Germantown, some military leaders and politicians lost faith in Washington, and others merely wanted him out in order to gain power for themselves; the result was the so-called Conway Cabal aimed at ousting Washington from command.

# Chapter 19

# Valley Forge

## In This Chapter

➤ How French support was won

➤ The arrival of Lafayette

➤ The ordeal of Valley Forge

➤ The Continental army takes the initiative

➤ The first major Franco–American operation fails

➤ The British unsuccessfully seek reconciliation

As far as some people were concerned at the end of 1777, George Washington could do nothing right. His choice of Valley Forge, Pennsylvania, on the west side of Schuylkill River, as winter quarters was criticized as too exposed to the elements. Washington knew, however, that it was centrally located and easily defended.

Contrary to historical myth, the winter of 1777–78 was not particularly harsh, but Washington had gone into winter quarters late, and there was a race against the elements to build adequate huts. Worse, the state of supply was poorer than ever. Many soldiers really were half-naked and shoeless. Starvation was a real possibility; although it didn't come to that for the men, many of the army's horses did starve to death.

Yet the army at Valley Forge was never in serious danger of disintegrating. A forge, of course, is a place where tools and weapons are heated, formed, and hammered out. And with the exertions of Lafayette, Baron Friedrich von Steuben, and other foreign officers, Washington's ragged army was indeed pounded into shape, ready to reclaim the initiative, come spring, in the Middle States.

# The French Connections

Most of the battles of the American Revolution were fought on a relatively small scale. Many of them (as we will see in Chapter 20, "White War, Red Blood") were short, sharp, brutal exchanges in obscure corners of the wilderness. Yet the American Revolution loomed for the nations of Europe as part of an ongoing *world* war, which had begun in the seventeenth century and, with intervals of uneasy peace, had consumed much of the eighteenth as well, most recently in the Seven Years' War, of which the French and Indian War was the American phase.

In each of these wars, England and France had always been on opposite sides. Would this happen again? Could France be drawn into the American Revolution as an ally of the United States against its ancient adversary? The answer was not obvious. France, after all, was a monarchy. Could it support a revolution against another monarch? Congress, therefore, began its approach modestly, by seeking aid short of out-and-out war.

## *Vive la Figaro!*

As early as September 1775, the French had sent a secret agent, Achard de Bonvouloir, to report on the situation in the colonies. Benjamin Franklin, with three other members of a five-man Committee of Correspondence set up by Congress in November 1775 to make contact with "our friends abroad," met with Achard de Bonvouloir, and Congress was encouraged, in April 1776, to send Silas Deane, congressman from Connecticut, to Paris for the purpose of purchasing—on credit, of course—clothing and equipment for 25,000 men, as well as artillery and munitions. He was also instructed to open a dialogue on a possible alliance.

*Benjamin Franklin in the royal court of France.* (Image from the National Archives)

It would, ultimately, prove a lively dialogue. Charles Gravier, comte de Vergennes, the French foreign minister, doubtless had many reservations about assisting a revolutionary government to break away from a royalist power, but his hatred of England and his burning desire to avenge his nation's defeat in the Seven Years' War blew away all doubts. As early as 1775, he was persuaded that the colonists were serious about winning their independence, and Vergennes sent Achard de Bonvouloir on his exploratory mission in North America.

By May 1776, Vergennes' interest in the Revolution had become even more serious. He approached a young man who had started life as a watchmaker and became famous to all the world as the creator of a fictitious barber/valet, a delightful schemer named Figaro. Pierre Augustin Caron de Beaumarchais wrote *Le Barbier de Séville* in 1775 and would follow this with another wildly successful comedy, *Le Mariage de Figaro*, in 1784. Both plays were huge successes in their own time and remain fresh today, in opera form, as Gioacchino Rossini's *The Barber of Seville* and as Wolfgang Amadeus Mozart's *The Marriage of Figaro*.

Vergennes asked the creator of Figaro to create another fiction, a firm Beaumarchais christened Roderigue Hortalez & Cie, to function, in part, as a real company, but its principal role was to launder money both France and Spain would supply in support of the American Revolution. At this point, the government of Louis XVI was not willing to declare open allegiance with America—a move that would invite out-and-out war with Britain—but, through Beaumarchais' company, it was willing to funnel a million *livres* to the Americans, and, what's more, Spain would do the same. Beaumarchais was instructed to raise an equivalent amount from among private investors. Hortalez & Cie. would draw military supplies from French stocks, which the Americans would pay for (as best they could) with rice, tobacco, and other commodities. The French government would assist Hortalez to sell these items in France.

In June 1776, the French government paid Beaumarchais his million, in August he acquired the Spanish money and raised funds from investors. Beaumarchais was already acquainted with Arthur Lee (youngest son of the prominent Virginia family), with whom he had discussed the Hortalez idea. In July, Beaumarchais contacted Silas Deane, and the pipeline from France to America was opened. It has been estimated that the victories at Trenton and Princeton owed much to French supplies, and 90 percent of the war materials that made the Saratoga victory possible had come through the Beaumarchais scheme. Millions of dollars worth of military aid were funneled to the Revolution well before France concluded an official alliance.

## The Mission of Benjamin Franklin

Many Americans would earn their reputations in the Revolution. Benjamin Franklin, nearly 70 when it began, had already earned his. He was world famous as a scientist, inventor, author, editor, entrepreneur—even as a favorite with the ladies. One place in which his reputation was especially strong was France, which he had visited in 1767 and 1769. It was natural that Congress would choose Franklin to join Arthur Lee and Silas Deane as commissioners to negotiate a formal treaty of alliance with that nation.

On December 4, 1776, Franklin reached Paris, where Arthur Lee (described by some historians as psychotic) snubbed him, but where he got on famously with Silas Deane. With the arrival of Franklin, serious and persuasive negotiations for a full-scale treaty of alliance moved ahead.

## The Good Marquis

While Lee, Deane, and Beaumarchais worked out the details of covert French financial aid to America, other young Frenchmen were already talking about direct military involvement. We've already met the most famous of these, the Marquis de Lafayette, in Chapter 16, "Philadelphia Falls."

Born into a noble family, Lafayette, orphaned by age 13, had already inherited a huge fortune when he married the daughter of the wealthy and powerful duc d'Ayen in 1774. The union brought him into the intimate circle of Louis XVI's young courtiers, but this did not satisfy the restless spirit of the marquis. On August 8, 1775, he was a guest at a dinner during which the Duke of Gloucester expressed his sympathy with the cause of American liberty. Suddenly, a spark was struck. Young Lafayette resolved to go to America. A confidant, the Comte de Broglie, introduced Lafayette to Johann Kalb (who would become known to the Americans as the Baron de Kalb), a Bavarian by birth who was serving with de Broglie's French corps. Kalb also yearned to fight in America, and, taking the younger Lafayette in tow, he approached Silas Deane, who concluded written agreements with both men, promising them commissions as major generals.

*The Marquis de Lafayette, in an engraving after a painting by George E. Perrine.*
(Image from the National Archives)

A suspicious Congress greeted Lafayette coolly, but when he insisted on serving at his own expense and starting as a volunteer, he was commissioned a major general on July 31, 1777. He was introduced to Washington the very next day, and the two formed an immediate bond.

Yet what was Washington to do with Lafayette? True, he was a trained European officer with a passion to lead troops against the British. But he was only 20 years old, had never been in battle, and spoke but a smattering of English. The young man's baptism under fire came not in a triumph, but in an American defeat, the Battle of Brandywine (see Chapter 16). Lafayette's conspicuous gallantry in checking the enemy's advance—he was wounded in the thigh—dispelled any doubt about his value to the cause. After recuperating in Bethlehem, Pennsylvania, for two months, he rejoined Washington's army at White Marsh, after the Battle of Germantown, and, on November 25, he prevailed against a force of Hessians in a skirmish at Gloucester, New Jersey.

In response to Washington's request that Lafayette be given "a command equal to his rank," Congress voted him command of a division of Virginia light troops on December 1, 1777.

### Voices of Liberty

"After the sacrifices I have made, I have the right to expect two favours; one is to serve at my own expense,—the other is to serve, at first, as volunteer."

—Lafayette to the Continental Congress, 1777

## Saratoga Dividend: Amity and Commerce

In the meantime, Lafayette's country was drifting toward formal alliance. On December 17, 1777, after learning of the victory at Saratoga and impressed by Washington's spirit at Germantown—despite his defeat there—French authorities informed Franklin and the other American envoys in Paris that the government of Louis XVI would recognize American independence. On January 8, 1778, Vergennes told the envoys that France was prepared to conclude a formal alliance.

Two treaties were ratified by the Continental Congress on May 4. A treaty of "amity and commerce" formalized French recognition of American independence, and a second treaty pledged an alliance to become effective if war should break out between France and England. For this eventuality, the signatories did not have long to wait. After the French ambassador to England informed the British government of the treaties, on May 13, the British ambassador was recalled from Paris, thereby severing diplomatic relations. Spain offered to mediate, but war between France and England broke out following a minor naval exchange on June 20. France and the United States were full military allies.

## "What Is to Become of the Army?"

Valley Forge has become synonymous in the American experience with courage, endurance, and determination. The encampment there was not well planned, however. The ill-fated Philadelphia campaign had kept Washington's army in the field late into the winter, until December 11, by which time the men were exhausted, their supplies dwindling, and their clothing in tatters. Valley Forge was well chosen for tactical and strategic reasons—squarely between Philadelphia, where the enemy was located, and York, to which Congress had evacuated. Valley Forge presented terrain that was easily defended; it was a site with good drainage, and it was close to woods, which supplied lumber for building huts and stockades. Yet, as Washington biographer Douglas Southall Freeman points out, Valley forge offered "no village, no plain, and little valley," and Baron de Kalb was so appalled at the inhospitable nature of these winter quarters that he assumed the site had been selected by a corrupt speculator, a traitor, or a "council of ignoramuses."

For six months, from December 19, 1777, to June 18, 1778, 10,000 men huddled in makeshift huts, some dolefully chanting "no pay, no clothes, no provisions, no rum." Some 4,000 of the 10,000 men quartered at Valley Forge were so destitute of clothing that they dared not venture out of their huts. About 2,500 men, out of 10,000, died during the six months in camp.

### Sites and Sights

Valley Forge National Historical Park is located at the intersection of routes 23 and 363 in Bucks County, Pennsylvania (phone 610-783-1077). A wealth of exhibits serve as monuments to the endurance and sacrifice of American soldiers during the Revolution.

Perhaps the deepest horror of Valley Forge was that the suffering and death had little to do with the weather and even less to do with the enemy. Those in the government responsible for supplying the army were inefficient, incompetent, and often corrupt. Local farmers, who might have helped, instead sold their produce to the British, who were warm and snug in Philadelphia. Washington pleaded with Congress in a letter from Valley Forge of December 23, 1777: "What then is to become of the Army this Winter? and if we are as often without Provisions now, as with it, what is to become of us in the Spring...?"

Massachusetts colonel John Brooks wrote to a friend in January how hard it was to see "our poor brave fellows living in tents, bare-footed, bare-legged, bare-breeched, etc., etc., in snow, in rain, on marches, in camp, and on duty .... Nothing but virtue has kept our army together."

# Foreign Aid

Lafayette shared the hardships of Valley Forge, as did Kalb and an officer from Prussia, Friedrich Wilhelm Augustus von Steuben.

## The Prussian Officer

Steuben was born into the army, at Magdeburg fortress, where his father was an engineer. By age 17, he had become an officer in the Prussian army, served in the Seven Years' War, and rose in the staff of Frederick the Great's headquarters. At the time, staff work—the business of ensuring that the orders of high command are carried out in every detail—was little known among the French and British, and Steuben's knowledge would prove invaluable to the American army.

Steuben left the Prussian army in 1763 (for reasons that are unclear) and became chamberlain in the court of the petty prince of Hohenzollern-Hechingen. When Steuben's prince went broke in 1775, the ex-Prussian officer had to look for other work and, after being turned down by the armies of France, Austria, and Baden, he met a friend of Benjamin Franklin, who suggested the American service. Franklin wrote a letter of recommendation to Washington, Beaumarchais' Hortalez & Cie. provided travel funds, and Steuben arrived in Portsmouth, New Hampshire, on December 1, 1777. On February 23, 1778, he reported to Valley Forge, where, with the help of Gen. Nathanael Greene and Alexander Hamilton, he drafted a training program for the Continental army.

Steuben picked 100 men, whom he trained intensively, then turned them loose on the rest of the shivering, ragged army. Each of these first 100 trained a certain number of men, who, in turn, passed on what they had learned, so that, quite rapidly, as if by geometric progression, the Continental army gained a healthy dose of Prussian discipline. Washington was convinced this not only helped maintain morale through the miserable winter, but greatly improved performance during the Monmouth campaign and subsequent actions.

**Voices of Liberty**

"With regard to military discipline, I may safely say no such thing existed [in the Continental army]. The formation of the regiments was as varied as their mode of drill, which consisted only of the manual exercise."

—Baron von Steuben, 1778

## Baron de Kalb

Johann Kalb was known as *Baron* de Kalb only in America. In truth, he was no baron; he had been born to Bavarian peasants in 1721 and became a lieutenant in a German regiment of the French infantry in 1743. He distinguished himself and in 1768 was sent on a secret visit to the 13 British colonies in North America to analyze their attitude toward Great Britain. Kalb liked America, and, securing the promise of a commission in the Continental army from Silas Deane, he set off for revolutionary service in 1776, taking Lafayette along with him. Like the other foreign officers, Kalb became an ardent admirer of Washington and was of great assistance during the torturous Valley Forge winter.

In April 1780, Kalb was sent to command the relief of Charleston, South Carolina, but the city fell to the British before he arrived. As we will see in Chapter 24, "Backcountry Battles," Kalb tried to persuade Gen. Horatio Gates to make a preemptive attack on the British at Deep River, North Carolina, but Gates's characteristic caution intervened, he delayed, and the element of surprise was lost. In the subsequent Battle of Camden, Kalb was mortally wounded.

# The Poles

Two more remarkable foreign officers made great contributions to the American cause. Unlike the peasant Kalb, Tadeusz Kosciuszko had been born into the nobility and was sent to a military academy in Warsaw. After this training, he went to Paris to study military and civil architecture and painting. After returning home in 1774, he taught drawing and mathematics to the daughters of a general, Józef Sosnowski—and tried unsuccessfully to elope with one of the girls.

In part to escape the general's wrath, Kosciuszko returned to France, learned of the American Revolution, and in 1776 set sail for America. In August, he went to work for the Pennsylvania Committee of Defense in Philadelphia, where he helped plan fortifications to defend the residence of the Continental Congress against the British. In the spring of 1777, he joined Horatio Gates and supervised construction of fortifications that prevented the retreat of Gen. Burgoyne and helped bring about his capitulation at Saratoga. After this, Kosciuszko worked on the fortification of West Point, New York, where, in March 1780, he was appointed chief of the Continental army's engineering corps. After this, he served in the South, under Gen. Nathanael Greene, and performed with dash and brilliance.

### We Hold These Truths

After the war, Congress voted Kosciuszko U.S. citizenship and commissioned him a brigadier general in the United States Army. He returned to Poland, however, as a freedom fighter. Despite success in several important battles, he was defeated by Russian forces in 1794, wounded, and held prisoner for the next two years. He returned to the United States in 1797 and was greeted with wild enthusiasm by Philadelphians. Before leaving for France the following year to promote Polish freedom, Kosciuszko set aside a portion of his estate to pay for the well-being and education of his slaves, whom he set free.

In December 1776, Casimir Pulaski, another Polish freedom fighter in Parisian exile, met Benjamin Franklin, who persuaded Pulaski to join the cause and wrote a letter of recommendation to Washington. Although he was a man of difficult temperament, Pulaski was especially valuable to the Continental Army because of his experience with cavalry, a service arm almost totally lacking before he created the Pulaski Legion in 1778. In May 1779, Pulaski was instrumental in the defense of Charleston. Wounded in a heroic—but suicidal—cavalry charge at Savannah on October 9, 1779, he died aboard the *Wasp,* which was carrying him back to Charleston.

# Action in the Middle States

The alliance with France and the training rendered by experienced foreign officers not only enabled the Continental army to survive Valley Forge, it helped the army emerge from the terrible winter as a much-improved fighting force. Equally important, of course, was the new alliance with the French. True, some in the American government were not totally thrilled. They understood that the French were in it primarily to gain an advantage over the British, and they feared that France would try to reestablish a North American empire. But the immediate impact of the alliance on Britain was dramatic.

In February 1778, William Howe asked to be relieved of his duties as commander in chief. Lord Germain asked him to stay on until a replacement could be installed, and on March 7, Sir Henry Clinton was chosen to replace him. Clinton accepted the new command with great reluctance. On March 21, Germain issued orders to Clinton. The alliance between the Americans and the French had shifted the focus of the war to France, and Clinton was instructed to send 5,000 men to the island of St. Lucia in the West Indies, and another 3,000 to reinforce St. Augustine and Pensacola, Florida. The men in Philadelphia were to be transferred to New York City. Hard-won Philadelphia was being given back to the rebels!

## *Fought to a Stand: Monmouth Court House*

Before dawn on June 16, 1778, Clinton began removing artillery from the redoubts around Philadelphia. This signaled to Washington that the British were preparing for some operation, and he figured it might well be a march through New Jersey. He convened a council of war on June 17, in which he allowed Charles Lee to convince him to keep his troops at Valley Forge until there was a more definite indication of the enemy's intention.

Surprisingly, Clinton moved faster than he—or probably any British commander—had ever moved before. By the 18th, his troops, 10,000 strong plus another 3,000 local Tories, were out of Philadelphia and moving toward Haddonfield, New Jersey. Washington now started his men on the move, but quarreled with Lee over who should command the striking force aimed directly at Clinton's column. Washington wanted to give the assignment to young Lafayette, but Charles Lee, second only to Washington in seniority, demanded command, and Washington felt he could do no less than acquiesce.

In the meantime, on June 28, an advance unit of New Jersey militiamen had engaged some of Clinton's best regiments and was in desperate need of assistance. When Lee did nothing, Washington ordered him to attack at once. But Lee made the mistake of scattering his troops, and the attack was, therefore, worse than useless. Lee ordered a retreat, temporarily stranding the small command of Mad Anthony Wayne, who narrowly averted disaster.

Then into the retreat rode George Washington. Lafayette later described how the commander in chief, having relieved Lee to assume personal command, "stopped the

**249**

retreat" by the mere fact of his presence and "calm courage." Yet, through Lee's indolence and incompetence, the momentum of this battle had been irretrievably lost. The two sides fought it out in the vicinity of Monmouth Court House, in punishing midsummer heat (sunstroke killed at least 37 Americans and 60 British), until both the Americans and the British withdrew, mutually near collapse. Casualties were almost even on both sides: 356 Americans were killed, wounded, or missing, and 358 British were killed or wounded—though some historians believe that British losses were much higher. While the Americans held the field, the British kept their army intact, accomplishing the evacuation from Philadelphia.

### We Hold These Truths

The name "Molly Pitcher" was applied to several Revolutionary heroines, the most famous of which took part in the Battle of Monmouth. (Most historians now believe that "Molly Pitcher" was a generic name bestowed on women who carried water—in a pitcher—to the thirsty combatants on the field.) A soldier named Joseph P. Martin relates:

> A woman whose husband belonged to the Artillery, and who was then attached to a piece [gun] in the engagement, attended with her husband at the piece the whole time. While in the act of reaching a cartridge and having one of her feet as far before the other as she could step, a cannon shot from the enemy passed directly between her legs without doing any other damage than carrying away all the lower part of her petticoat. Looking at it with apparent unconcern, she observed that it was lucky it did not pass a little higher, for in that case it might have carried away something else, and continued her occupation.

In many later versions of this story, Molly takes over firing the artillery piece after her husband is wounded or slain.

In only one respect might Monmouth be called a clear American victory. It resulted in the court martial of the incompetent, but all too highly placed, Charles Lee, who was finally removed from service.

## Yankee Doodle in Rhode Island

After Monmouth, Washington pressed his pursuit of Clinton as best he could, vainly hoping to trap him. To this end, a Franco-American amphibious operation was launched against Newport, Rhode Island. It was the first operation under the new alliance, and it was spearheaded by Adm. Charles Hector Théodot, Comte d'Estaing. A French historian remarked that the French "navy did not credit him with natural ability when the war broke out, and it is safe to say that its opinion was justified by his conduct during it."

D'Estaing sailed from Toulon on April 13, 1778, and managed to make an extraordinarily slow crossing of 87 days, which made him too late to bottle up the British fleet in the Chesapeake. From July 11–22, he lingered uselessly before Sandy Hook bar, an obstruction across New York bay, to prevent his huge ships of war from running aground—at least, that was D'Estaing's fear. The delay meant that he would not engage the British in New York City. On July 29, he sailed to Newport, where he was to disgorge the 4,000 troops he carried to join about 10,000 Americans under John Sullivan (with Nathanael Greene and Lafayette serving as his subordinate commanders). By the time New England militia reinforcements made the rendezvous, however, Clinton had sent troops to reinforce Gen. Robert Pigot, who commanded the Newport defenses.

This was only the first of many failures during the maiden Franco-American operation. Sullivan and D'Estaing distrusted one another to begin with, and relations only grew worse. The operation suffered repeated delays, and by the time D'Estaing was disembarking his troops, a reinforced British fleet was sighted. Against Sullivan's bellows of protest, D'Estaing reloaded his troops and put out to sea to meet the enemy, but a storm on the night of August 11 scattered both the British and the French squadrons. Adm. Richard Howe returned to New York for repairs, then slipped off to the West Indies, to which his fleet had been ordered. D'Estaing sailed to Boston to refit his storm-battered fleet, leaving Sullivan's men, unreinforced, to face the reinforced British. An African-American unit, commanded by Christopher Greene (a white Rhode Island officer), fought so fiercely that Sullivan was able to withdraw from Pigot's forces and save his army—although some 5,000 discouraged militiamen quickly left the American service when their enlistments expired.

251

## Mad Anthony Triumphs

Sullivan and others may have been disappointed and disgusted with America's French allies at this point, but France's entry into war with England had already produced a profound impact. Sir Henry Clinton's forces were greatly weakened, not by patriot action, but by London, which felt it necessary to meet the French threat in the West Indies. Clinton had no huge force to invade from Canada, but he did decide to make use of the assets that remained in New York. On May 30, 1779, he moved about 6,000 troops in 70 sailing ships and 150 flatbottom boats up the Hudson. His objective was to seize West Point, by which control of the lower Hudson could be achieved, thereby cutting off the flow of men and materiel to and from New England.

Clinton's force quickly took Stony Point, on the west bank of the Hudson, about 35 miles north of New York City, and Verplanck's Point, on the opposite bank. The British quickly dug in and fortified these positions.

Realizing the danger of yielding control of the Hudson, Washington responded by getting a spy inside the newly constructed British works at Stony Point. On July 2, militia captain Allen McLane, disguised as a local farmer, conducted a Mrs. Smith into the fortress to "see her sons" (presumably Tories serving with the British). McLane reported that the works were unfinished and vulnerable. McLane conducted further reconnaissance from the outside of the fortress, and, on July 17, Washington was ready to move. He sent Mad Anthony Wayne with a force of 1,350 picked men. They were assigned to carry out a surprise attack that, to Wayne, must have seemed fitting revenge for Paoli (see Chapter 16): To maintain stealth, bayonets would be used exclusively. Except in one battalion, not a single musket was even loaded.

The midnight attack was carried out with great skill, and although the British fired upon the Americans with cannon as well as muskets, Wayne's troops returned not a single shot, but advanced under fire, overran the fort, and captured it. Sixty-three British soldiers died, more than 70 were wounded, and 543 were taken prisoner—along with artillery and equipment. The cost to Wayne's unit was 15 killed and 80 wounded.

Although Washington once called Stony Point the "key to the continent," he decided that he could not spare the men required to hold it and, therefore, dismantled the works before abandoning them. Clinton would subsequently reoccupy the position, but, by then, its strategic value had been largely lost. Washington gained no great strategic advantage by the operation, but he and Wayne scored a great psychological triumph, which supplied in abundance the emotional fuel that kept the Revolution in motion.

## *"The Greatest Enterprise"*

Prima donnas are no rarity among military commanders, and the Continental army was no exception. Mad Anthony Wayne was prima donna enough to have omitted mention of Maj. Henry "Lighthorse Harry" Lee in his report of the action at Stony Point. Lee's corps had played a dashing, if minor, role in that engagement, and Lee was inspired by it. He willingly accepted an assignment to raid Paulus Hook, an isolated British post on the site of present-day Jersey City, New Jersey, just across the Hudson from Manhattan.

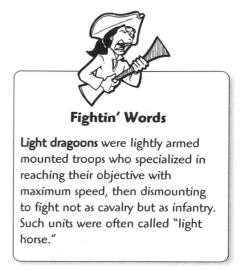

### Fightin' Words

**Light dragoons** were lightly armed mounted troops who specialized in reaching their objective with maximum speed, then dismounting to fight not as cavalry but as infantry. Such units were often called "light horse."

"Lighthorse Harry" Lee was one of the remarkable Lees of Virginia (the incompetent Gen. Charles Lee was no relation—although another Charles Lee, a Revolutionary naval officer, was), which produced a half dozen young men of significance to the war. Lighthorse Harry's grandson, Robert E. Lee, would emerge, in the Civil War, as the most illustrious member of this military family. The Lighthorse nickname acknowledged service with the *Light Dragoons*, a lightly armed, highly mobile, elite force.

Allen McLane, another hero of Stony Point also unsung by Wayne, scouted Paulus Hook, determined that the British garrison numbered a mere 200, and, on August 18, 1779, guided Lee and his detachment of 400 through the complex approach to the fort, which had to be approached at low tide, because a moat protected the only route in or out. Lee planned to attack at half past midnight on the 19th, when the tide would be low. McLane somewhat misdirected Lee, putting him behind schedule. When Lee finally assembled the troops at the edge of a salt marsh some 500 yards shy of their objective, he discovered that half of the Virginia contingent, about 100 men, had simply wandered off. Lee proceeded with the attack, ensuring stealth by ordering his men to refrain from priming their muskets. Any man who tried to fire without orders was to be shot. The attack would be exclusively with bayonets.

The fort fell within 30 minutes. Fifty British soldiers were "put to the bayonet"—presumably, some were killed, some wounded—and 158 prisoners were taken, of a total of 250 men garrisoning the position. Lee lost two killed and three wounded. Alarm guns soon aroused the British on the New York side of the Hudson, however, and Lee had to beat a hasty retreat with his POWs in tow. Congress presented Lee with a gold medal for this exploit, which one participant grandiosely referred to as "the greatest enterprise ever undertaken." Some of Lee's fellow officers, however, were jealous and demanded Lee's court-martial for a number of errors, including taking precedence over senior officers. In the end, the court-martial not only vindicated Light Horse Harry, but heaped upon him additional praise.

## The Springfield Raid

In the Middle States, Washington's army was now performing well, but the commander in chief lacked the resources to do more than harass and raid. For the most part, the British merely responded to these jabs, but took no initiative beyond this. At last, in June 1780, Baron Knyphausen—temporarily in command of the New York City region while Clinton campaigned in the South (see Chapter 21, "Southern Exposure")—decided to stage a raid of his own.

Knyphausen had been hearing rumors that Washington's army was on the verge of mutiny and that the civilian population in the vicinity of Springfield, New Jersey (in present-day Union County) was sufficiently discontented to rally to the loyalist cause. On June 7, 1780, with 6,000 men, Knyphausen crossed from Staten Island to Elizabethtown (present-day Elizabeth, New Jersey) and advanced on the village of Connecticut Farms—present-day Union, about two and a half miles southeast of Springfield—intending to gather local support for an attack on Washington's encampment at Morristown.

Perhaps the intelligence concerning civilian discontent was faulty or just wishful thinking. For, instead of support, Knyphausen was met by stiff opposition from the New Jersey militia, which was soon reinforced by Continental troops. After burning a church and some other buildings—and accidentally killing the wife of Rev. James Caldwell—Knyphausen hastily retreated to Elizabethtown. Regrouping, Knyphausen staged a second raid, this time against Springfield proper, on June 23. Nathanael Greene, with a thousand troops, opposed the 6,000 men in Knyphausen's column, which succeeded in taking Springfield, but was then fought to a standstill. The Hessian commander burned all but four of Springfield's 50 houses before withdrawing back to Staten Island. This violent raid was typical of the civil conflict that had engulfed northern New Jersey since the campaigns of 1776.

# British Peace Feelers

By the end of the 1770s, the entry of France into the war had yet to have a direct effect on any particular engagement, but it had a profound effect on the conduct of the war, drawing off much of Clinton's manpower to the West Indies. The Crown was now in a humor to negotiate an end to the war, and, in early spring of 1778, Frederick Howard, 5th Earl of Carlisle, was appointed to head a new peace commission, which had the king's authority to deal directly with Congress and even to suspend any act of Parliament passed since 1763.

The Carlisle Commission was ill-timed, to say the least. With the British evacuating Philadelphia, Congress was in no mood to negotiate anything short of total British withdrawal and recognition of independence. On April 22, Congress resolved that any individual or group that came to terms with the commission was thereby an enemy of the United States. The commission responded to congressional resistance with attempts to bribe individual congressmen, a move that put the commission in increasingly bad odor, despite offers of general pardons and a generous degree of independence and autonomy. At one point, Lafayette challenged Carlisle to a duel for having defamed France in letters to Congress. Nothing came of the fiery young man's challenge.

At last, on November 27, 1778, the Carlisle Commission admitted failure. What they were offering would have averted revolt back in 1774 or even 1775, but the tide of history had risen well beyond that point. The war would be fought to its conclusion.

---

### The Least You Need to Know

➤ Winning French support for the Revolution was a delicate matter. Although France was happy to support action against its longtime enemy, it did not want to provoke an all-out war until it was persuaded that the American Revolution would actually succeed.

➤ Before a formal alliance was concluded with France, Lafayette and Baron de Kalb offered their services to the United States, and Beaumarchais set up Hortalez & Cie., a dummy corporation by which France covertly funneled supplies and munitions to the Americans.

➤ The American army suffered terribly at Valley Forge during the winter of 1777–78, largely due to the incompetence and corruption of government officials responsible for supplying the army. Despite the hardships, the army emerged stronger and better trained.

➤ France's entry into the war prompted the British to send troops to the West Indies; Gen. Clinton was forced to abandon Philadelphia and consolidate his strength in New York.

➤ After the British abandonment of Philadelphia, the Americans took the initiative in the Middle Atlantic states and flatly rejected the Carlisle Commission, a British peace proposal.

# Chapter 20

---

# White War, Red Blood

The American Revolution lasted nearly eight years and exacted from Americans and British alike profound sacrifices. Yet the "set battles" between American and British (as well as Hessian) armies, represent only part of the Revolution. Some of these battles spanned days, but most were over in a matter of hours. What was going on the rest of those eight years?

In many ways, the War of Independence merely continued the violence that had been present on the North American frontier since the days of Columbus. As the Indians saw it, the Revolution was no different from the previous wars, with much of the fighting, suffering, and dying happening among Indians and settlers in obscure corners of the American frontier. This wilderness war was as much a part of the Revolution as the formal combat between men in red coats and in the blue and buff.

## Indian Alliances

After the French and Indian War, British colonial authorities began to realize the importance of better relations with the Indians. Recall from Chapter 5, "All the King's Men," that the falling out between the colonies and the mother country can be traced, in part, to King George's Proclamation of 1763, an attempt to woo Indian friendship by temporarily restricting white settlement to the land east of the Appalachian divide. The very next year, British colonial authorities created an Indian Department to formalize dealings with the Native Americans. As soon as hostilities broke out in 1775, the Continental Congress created an Indian Department of its own.

But personal relationships, not bureaucratic decree, typically formed alliances during the Revolution. Well before the battles of Lexington and Concord, William Johnson, a British hero of the French and Indian War, and Thayendanegea, a Mohawk better known to the English as Joseph Brant, forged a powerful personal and political alliance. Johnson had come to America from Ireland at age 15, settled in the Mohawk Valley northwest of Albany, and quickly established a friendship with the Mohawks. After the death of his first wife, he married Degonwadonti—Molly Brant—daughter of his friend Nichus Brant and Nichus's Indian wife, Owandah. Molly was at least 25 years younger than Johnson and had an even younger brother, Joseph, whom Johnson informally adopted as a son. Through his bravery in the French and Indian War, on the side of the British, Brant earned prestige among the Mohawks as well as the colonists. When Johnson died suddenly in 1774, Brant continued a close relationship with Johnson's son Guy. This friendship would be the core of an expanding British-Indian alliance through the early part of the war. The Mohawks, most powerful of the mighty Iroquois confederation, persuaded other member tribes, the Senecas, Cayugas, and Onondagas, to side with the British.

Only the Oneidas and the Tuscaroras from the Iroquois confederation allied themselves with the Americans. Samuel Kirkland, a teacher and Presbyterian minister who worked among the Oneida tribe, earning their friendship. They were joined in supporting the Americans by the Mahicans—also called the Stockbridge Indians—who were the remnants of a tribe, once quite powerful, that had been decimated by the Mohawks. Finally, through the efforts of an American Indian Department agent, James Dean, the Tuscaroras also sided with the Americans.

**Voices of Liberty**

"It is ... His Majesty's pleasure that you do lose no time in taking such steps as may induce [the Iroquois] to take up the hatchet against His Majesty's rebellious subjects in America ...."

—Earl of Dartmouth, Secretary of Colonial Affairs and Board of Trade, to William Johnson, July 24, 1775

Beyond these basic alliances, the British generally enjoyed more Indian support than the Americans did. The British were more willing to keep their treaties with the Indians than the colonists were, and most tribal authorities reasoned that if the British authorities remained in power, there was some hope of stemming the invasion of their lands. King George had attempted to limit white settlement and promised to continue to do so. If, on the other hand, the Americans should throw off the British yoke, there would be no government authority to limit the invasion.

# Havoc in the Borderlands

As we have seen (especially in Chapters 15, "Gentleman Johnny," and 17, "Saratoga Saga"), Indian warriors sometimes served as auxiliaries to the regular army, but they also fought on their own. By September 1776, the entire American frontier throughout Virginia, Pennsylvania, and New York was in a state of panic. Taking advantage of this, throughout New York's Mohawk Valley, numerous loyalists, evicted from their lands by the rebels, disguised themselves as Indians and raided settlers.

Often, Britain's Indian allies were less than impressed by the fighting prowess of the redcoats. Joseph Brant and Gu-cinge, a powerful Seneca chief, often led raids against the patriots in the New York border country—with the blessing of William Tryon, Tory governor of New York, who urged British military authorities to "loose the savages against the miserable Rebels in order to impose a reign of terror on the frontiers." Officially, British prime minister Lord North repudiated such action, condemning it as "unconstitutional, inhuman, and unchristian." Nevertheless, the use of Indians as instruments of frontier terror became unofficial British policy.

## *Cherry Valley Massacre*

By the end of 1777, hit-and-run raids were commonplace horrors throughout the New York and Pennsylvania frontier, particularly in the Cherry, Mohawk, and Wyoming valleys. Casualties in these wilderness battles were not merely killed, but were typically mutilated, scalped, and burned. Captives were tortured and often burned alive. Raids provoked counterraids, and a deadly rhythm of action and vengeance developed. In March 1778, Gen. Philip Schuyler warned Congress that the western frontiers were about to erupt, and by April 1778, a major build-up of Tory and Indian forces was well under way along the upper Susquehanna.

Col. John Butler, commanding 400 Rangers and Tories, was joined at the Indian town of Tioga by some 900 Senecas and Cayugas. Their target was the Wyoming Valley of northern Pennsylvania. While Butler and his Indian allies constructed boats for the trip down the Susquehanna, the Seneca chief Gu-cinge took 400 warriors in advance to attack settlements among the west branch of the river. In the meantime, Joseph Brant, with 450 Indians and Tories, was planning an attack on New York's Cherry Valley at the headwaters of the Susquehanna.

Cherry Valley had been subject to raids since 1776, but its settlers did little to defend themselves. Col. Samuel Campbell pathetically augmented his small militia force by outfitting 26 boys with wooden rifles and pointed hats made of paper. The ruse fooled Joseph Brant—at least for a time—persuading him to attack nearby Cobleskill instead of Cherry Valley. This small settlement defended by 20 local militiamen under Capt. Christian Brown and a 37-man detachment from Col. Ichabod Alden's Seventh Massachusetts Regiment of Continental troops was set upon by Brant's 450 men. Thirty-one Americans were killed and six wounded; Cobleskill was burned.

Pennsylvania's Wyoming Valley was defended by a collection of *wilderness forts* that were little more than fortified houses, including Wintermoot's (or Wintermot's), Forty Fort, Jenkins' Fort, Wilkes-Barre Fort, and Pittston Fort. The Wintermoots were Tory sympathizers, who "surrendered" without a shot. Jenkins' Fort fell to a Tory-Indian force on July 2, 1778. Forty Fort, garrisoned by 450 Continental troops and militiamen commanded by Col. Zebulon Butler (no relation to John Butler), a Continental army officer, and Nathan Denison, a colonel of the militia, refused to surrender.

Over Helmut Wintermoot's objections, John Butler put the fort to the torch on July 3 to trick the commanders of Forty Fort into thinking he had withdrawn. Zebulon Butler tried to dissuade Denison and the other militiamen from venturing out to pursue John Butler's force. But he was overruled, Denison took the bait, the entire garrison ventured out—and was promptly ambushed. Of the 450 Americans involved, 300 died or were wounded. Of the 1,200 Tories and Indians, only 11 were lost.

**Fightin' Words**

**Wilderness forts** were typically not military structures, but private homes that had been reinforced so that they might be used by militia for purposes of defense.

With Forty Fort gone, the defenseless Wyoming Valley was burned and looted, while, to the northeast, Joseph Brant turned his attention to Cherry Valley, raiding Andrustown, seven miles west, on July 18. With 50 warriors and a few Tories, he captured 14 settlers and killed 11 before burning the town. On September 12, with a much larger party of Indians, Brant attacked German Flats (present-day Herkimer) on the Mohawk River. Most of the town's inhabitants had fled to nearby forts, so Brant destroyed a virtually deserted village. This was the kind of fighting he preferred. Unlike his more bloodthirsty Indian brethren—or sadistic Tories—he preferred to destroy property and hit military objectives rather than murder noncombatants. There are many stories of his efforts to spare women and children.

## Vengeance on All Sides

Various militia groups set out to destroy Indian settlements in retaliation for the raids. Usually, everyone was killed—men, women, children—and the village burned to the ground. Brant, surveying the devastation, returned to Cherry Valley in November 1778. Lt. Col. Ichabod Alden and 250 Continental soldiers of the Seventh Massachusetts Regiment had been sent to defend the valley. But Alden blithely ignored warnings from friendly Indians, who told him that a large force of Indians and Tories was planning to attack Cherry Valley again.

On November 10, 800 Tories and Indians charged the fort garrisoned by 250. Alden and many others perished. By 2:00 in the afternoon, Cherry Valley had been virtually destroyed. Some of the Senecas and Mohawks indulged not only in scalping and mutilation, but also in *ritual cannibalism*. Patriot propagandists made use of these Indian practices to greatly exaggerate native and Tory brutality. In fact, Tories, Indians, and patriots alike employed similar practices to terrify their opponents and exact vengeance.

George Washington did more than send relief to the beleaguered valley: He authorized a massive campaign of retaliation—to the point of extermination—against the Iroquois confederation. He authorized the campaign early in 1779, but it was June 18 before the ever-cautious Gen. John Sullivan began marching his force of 2,500 men from New Jersey, New York, and New Hampshire from their rendezvous at Easton, Pennsylvania, to the Susquehanna. Washington had a three-pronged strategy: Sullivan would cut through the valley of the Susquehanna to the southern border of New York; Gen. James Clinton and 1,500 troops would move through the Mohawk Valley to Lake Otsego and then down the Susquehanna; and Col. Daniel Brodhead would lead 600 men from Fort Pitt up the Allegheny. At Tioga, Pennsylvania, Sullivan and Clinton would join forces, move north to Niagara, and meet Brodhead at Genesee.

Even before Sullivan got under way, however, Clinton had launched a six-day raid from his base of operations at Canajoharie on the Mohawk River. On April 21, 12 Onondagans were killed and 34 captured; 50 houses were destroyed, and food and supplies plundered. The *"longhouse,"* in which representatives of the Iroquois confederation met, was burned. The raid was highly significant: Because the Oneidas, an Iroquois tribe, participated in the operation, it signaled the beginning of the dissolution of the Iroquois confederation as a major military and political force.

**Fightin' Words**

**Ritual cannibalism** was common among the Indians, whereby captors would eat a small piece of their victim's flesh or internal organs to symbolize the absorption of the victim's strength, courage, and skill. In Native-American culture, ritual cannibalism expressed respect for a vanquished opponent; they did not engage in full-scale cannibalism by making a meal out of their opponents.

**Fightin' Words**

The **longhouse** was a ritual meeting house for Iroquois leaders; figuratively, the longhouse also represented the six Iroquois nations.

In the meantime, Joseph Brant hit the Mohawk Valley town of Minisink, about 20 miles above the juncture of New York, New Jersey, and Pennsylvania. Sixty Indians and 27 Tories disguised as Indians torched the settlement in the dead of night, as the settlers—mostly women, children, and men too old for militia duty—slept. Minisink's small fort, its mill, and 12 houses were destroyed, along with orchards and farms. A few settlers were killed or taken prisoner. The local militia retaliated, but was badly beaten: Of 170 militiamen, perhaps as many as 140 were lost in the attack by a combined Indian-Tory force of 87.

On August 9, Sullivan finally reached Newtychanning, a deserted Seneca village, and put its 28 buildings to the torch. When he arrived in Tioga, where he would rendezvous with Clinton, he established Fort Sullivan. Throughout August and September 1779, Sullivan's forces devastated the Indian settlements throughout the region, causing great hardship for the Indians. The coming winter starved many, and the Iroquois confederation was torn apart. Yet most of the Indians were still at large after the long and arduous campaign. As Maj. Jeremiah Fogg observed in his journal when the army returned to Fort Sullivan on September, "The nests are destroyed, but the birds are still on the wing."

Although the winter of 1779–80 was eerily calm, spring brought renewed Indian raids, driven not only by a thirst for vengeance, but a sense that there was nothing more to lose.

**Voices of Liberty**

"I flatter myself that the orders with which I was entrusted are fully executed, as we have not left a single settlement or field of corn in the country of the [Iroquois], nor is there even the appearance of an Indian on this side of the Niagara."

—Gen. Sullivan to the Continental Congress, September 1779

**Fightin' Words**

In the eighteenth and early nineteenth century, the "Northwest" was the frontier area lying north of the Ohio River and east of the Mississippi. Historians call this the **Old Northwest**.

# Trouble in the Old Northwest

While raids and vengeance raids burned across the borderlands of Pennsylvania and New York, terror also visited the thinly settled *Old Northwest* and Kentucky.

Around July 2, 1775, chiefs and subchiefs of the five Shawnee septs (bands) met at the Shawnee "capital," Chillicothe, on the Little Miami River in Ohio, to deliberate a response to white incursions into Kentucky. Chief Cornstalk, a principal Shawnee leader, advocated neutrality in the Revolution, but by fall 1775, Shawnees began raiding the new Kentucky settlements, which did not stem the tide of immigration.

In June 1776, seeking help in resisting the Indian raids, George Rogers Clark journeyed to Williamsburg to appeal to Virginia authorities, who had jurisdiction over frontier Kentucky. In the meantime, a Shawnee subchief named Pluck-kemeh-notee, known to the whites as Pluggy, renewed attacks in Kentucky. On his way to attack Harrodsburg, Pluggy was killed, and his death incited Chief Black Fish to organize 200 warriors in a campaign to annihilate white Kentucky once and for all. On or about July 4, 1776, at a grand Indian council among the Shawnees, Iroquois, Delawares, Ottawas, Cherokees, Wyandots, and Mingos, Chief Cornstalk abandoned neutrality and threw in with the British.

By the end of January 1777, raids had driven most settlers from the country, so that only Harrodsburg and Boonesboro could muster a body of men—just 103—to oppose Black Fish. The chief moved against Harrodsburg on March 18, 1777, but had to withdraw because of a severe snow, ice, and rain storm. On April 24, he turned against Boonesboro. During a four-day siege, one settler was killed and seven wounded, including Daniel Boone, founder of the settlement. Yet Boonesboro survived, and Black Fish withdrew, periodically returning to attack this and other settlements.

By this time, George Rogers Clark had persuaded Virginia authorities to make Kentucky a county of that state, and he was commissioned to raise and command a Kentucky militia. He decided to attack the British western forts at Kaskaskia, Cahokia, and Vincennes, then taking the principal fort of Detroit. While these forts were far north of Kentucky, Clark knew that these outposts served as Indian sanctuaries and points of supply. It was futile to fight Indian raiders; destroy the sources of supply, however, and the raids would stop.

### Voices of Liberty

"It is better for the red men to die like warriors than to diminish away by inches. Now is the time to begin. If we fight like men, we may hope to enlarge our bounds."

—Cornstalk, chief of Shawnee, July 1776

### We Hold These Truths

Brother of William Clark, who would serve as cocaptain of the Lewis and Clark expedition, George Rogers Clark (1752–1818) was a surveyor on the Kentucky frontier in the 1770s. He fought against the Shawnee chief Cornstalk during Lord Dunmore's War and against the Shawnees and British in Kentucky and the southern Ohio Valley during the American Revolution. In 1778 he led a spectacular militia action against the western forts of the British and their Indian allies, and between 1780 and 1782 he became commander of the American defense on the Ohio frontier.

After the Revolution, Clark helped establish U.S. sovereignty over the Ohio country. Unfortunately, prematurely aged and infirm, Clark had taken to heavy drinking. Bitter over the refusal of Virginia and the federal government to pay for his long service, Clark became involved in Spanish and French colonization schemes in the Mississippi Valley and accepted a commission as French commander on the Ohio. When these schemes collapsed, Clark's reputation suffered, and in 1794, he retired to private life in Jefferson County, Kentucky, where he ran a mill and steadily declined in health. He died in obscurity.

Early in June 1777, Clark discovered that the British garrison at Kaskaskia had been withdrawn to Detroit and that the surrounding settlements up to Cahokia were virtually defenseless. While Clark formulated his plan of attack and assembled the necessary forces, Cornstalk, the Shawnee chief, was talking neutrality with the Americans even as he was preparing to war against them. The young Shawnee warriors were impatient. In concert with Wyandots, Mingos, and Cherokees, a group of Shawnees raided the area of Wheeling (in present-day West Virginia) during midsummer 1777, and Congress dispatched Gen. Edward Hand to recruit Pennsylvanians, Virginians, and Kentuckians for an attack on a British Indian supply depot on the Cuyahoga River, near present-day Cleveland.

Under a flag of truce, Cornstalk went to Fort Randolph at Point Pleasant on the confluence of the Ohio River and the Kanawha to warn the Americans that, if Hand attacked, all the Shawnee and allied nations would retaliate. Capt. Matthew Arbuckle, commandant of the fort, ignoring both the warning and the flag of truce, imprisoned Cornstalk, his son Silverheels, and another warrior, intending to hold them hostage to ensure the Shawnees' good behavior. On November 10, 1777, a party of white hunters, having heard that the chief was being held under light guard forced their way into the fort and killed, then mutilated, Cornstalk and the other two Shawnees. The Shawnee then turned their wrath full force on the frontier, and Gen. Hand's efforts to contain the violence proved ineffectual.

# Frontier Heroes and Villains

On February 8, 1778, the Shawnee chief Blue Jacket, with 102 warriors, captured a salt-making party of 27 at Blue Licks, Kentucky. Among the captives was Daniel Boone, destined to become one of the legendary figures of the early American push westward.

## Dan'l Boone, Woodsman

Born in 1734 to a lapsed Quaker in southern Pennsylvania, Daniel Boone moved with his family to Yadkin County, North Carolina, when he was 19. He first heard about a place called Kentucky from one of his fellow volunteers under George Washington at Fort Duquesne during Gen. Edward Braddock's disastrous operation there. After the French and Indian War, Boone wandered the game-rich wilds of Kentucky seeking deerskins to make ends meet. Like most pioneers, Boone was plagued by debt, and he developed the conviction that there was a fortune to be made beyond the mountains.

He led settlers into Kentucky and founded Boonesboro. Captured near the settlement by Blue Jacket, Boone pretended to turn traitor, accepted adoption into the Shawnee tribe, and offered to cooperate with Henry Hamilton, England's ruthless liaison with the Indians. The Indians called Hamilton "Hair Buyer," because he paid bounties for patriot scalps, and he was probably the most hated man in the West. By feigning cooperation, Boone managed to delay an attack on Fort Pitt (Fort Duquesne during the French and Indian War) at the forks of the Ohio and to gather information on a planned attack on Boonesboro. With this information, Boone escaped to mount a successful resistance at his settlement. Boone's ruse was so thorough that some accused him of cowardice and collaboration, but a postwar court-martial exonerated the frontiersman and credited him with helping to save the frontier during the American Revolution.

## We Hold These Truths

After the Revolution, Boone became a hero in the popular literature read by Easterners. A Pennsylvania schoolteacher turned land promoter named John Filson traveled to Kentucky in 1782 and wrote *The Discovery, Settlement, and Present State of Kentucke*, which included a section subtitled "The Adventures of Col. Daniel Boone," an "autobiography."

By the time Filson's book was published, Boone had suffered considerable misfortune. His son Israel died in an Indian ambush during the last major frontier conflict of the Revolution. In 1780, Boone headed for Virginia with $50,000—mostly his friends' money—to buy land warrants to keep Eastern speculators from gobbling up Kentucky. The money was stolen. Although he had become a successful surveyor, trader, and landowner, he lost everything through his own carelessness and the legal chicanery of land speculators. In the 1790s, he packed up his family and moved to present-day Missouri, where he died, a poor man, little noticed, in 1819.

## The Depredations of Black Fish

Boone had taken an enormous risk in deceiving Black Fish, a man who knew no mercy. On September 8, 1778, with 444 warriors, while Boone was a captive, Black Fish laid siege to Boonesboro for almost two weeks before finally giving up and returning to Chillicothe.

In May, Black Fish and 400 warriors laid siege to Fort Randolph, where Cornstalk had been imprisoned and killed. When this, too, proved unsuccessful, the chief withdrew and divided his forces for scattered raids along the Kanawba River, east into Virginia, and into the Shenandoah Valley. Spurred by Black Fish, Shawnee, Wyandots, Mingos, Delawares, Miamis, and some Kickapoos raided throughout the West.

## Fightin' Words

**Flatboats** varied greatly in their dimensions, but all shared one characteristic in common: their flat bottoms. This enabled these vessels to navigate often shallow and vegetation-clogged rivers. Typically, a flatboat was propelled and maneuvered by a long pole thrust into the river bottom.

## Clark Presses His Campaign

While Black Fish and other Indians terrorized the frontier, George Rogers Clark struggled to recruit troops. By the end of May 1778, he had managed to muster only 175 men to march against Kaskaskia and Cahokia, the first leg in a planned assault on British-held Detroit.

On June 26, 1778, Clark embarked from Corn Island in *flatboats*, shot the rapids, and reached the mouth of the Tennessee River in four days. At Fort Massac, he and his men proceeded overland to Kaskaskia (in what is now southwestern Illinois). With great stealth, Clark captured a farm near the Kaskaskia River, collected boats, and ferried his troops across the river. Dividing his band in two to give the impression of greater numbers, he surrounded and surprised the fort, which surrendered without a shot. From this new base, Clark easily took Cahokia—again without having to fight.

Clark knew that taking Vincennes would be more difficult. "Hair Buyer" Hamilton was based there, and his forces would easily overwhelm Clark's diminutive army. Clark's only chance was to act with lightning speed. On February 5, 1779, he began the 150-mile march to Vincennes through a hostile wilderness in the dead of winter. He and his men reached Vincennes on February 23 and took a few prisoners in the settlement, from whom they learned that Fort Sackville (the British outpost at Vincennes) was now defended by only a few hundred men.

"A few hundred men" was still more than 150. A siege would only bring British reinforcements. Once again, Clark resorted to pure brass. He sent one of his prisoners back into town with a letter announcing his intention to take and occupy Vincennes and inviting those loyal to the king to repair the fort, as no quarter would be given. To create the impression of greater numbers, Clark signed the letter with the names of several officers—who weren't there. He also paraded some of his men in the fading light with counterfeit regimental colors and generally deployed his troops to make it look as if there were far more of them. It worked. No sooner did he begin the attack than most of the British-allied Indians deserted, and a group of Kickapoo and Piankashaw Indians actually ventured out to *help* Clark.

The fall of these forts did make life harder for the raiding Indians, some of whom at last made peace. Others, however, fought on even more desperately. Raiding became so severe in 1780 that Clark had to turn his attention from taking Detroit to raising a militia force to oppose the raiders. With about 1,000 men, he managed to disperse the Shawnees, but his plans to take Detroit were spoiled by the need to oppose other raids mounted by Indians and Tories—many directed by Joseph Brant—throughout the region.

Violence in the Old Northwest outlasted the Revolution and wasn't resolved until 1795, when Mad Anthony Wayne prevailed against Blue Jacket, Tecumseh, and Little Turtle in the conflict known as Little Turtle's War. Following Wayne's victory at the Battle of Fallen Timbers (August 20, 1794), the Treaty of Greenville (1795) established a boundary to white settlement that brought relative peace to the frontier until the outbreak of the War of 1812.

# Fighting on the Northern Frontier: Late Phase

In upstate New York, settlers were discovering to their horror that Gen. Sullivan's campaign of destruction had only inflamed the Indians. In the spring of 1780,

Col. Daniel Brodhead led 500 to 600 men in a month-long campaign along the Allegheny River and deep into Indian territory, destroying 10 Mingo, Wyandot, and Seneca towns as well as some 500 acres of corn in retaliation for raids.

On May 21, 1780, Sir John Johnson organized a massive assault on the forts and strong houses of the Mohawk Valley. With 400 Tories and 200 Indians, he burned Johnstown on May 23. During the summer, Joseph Brant hit the settlements of Caughnawaga and Canajoharie, then started down the Ohio, where he intercepted and ambushed a Pennsylvania militia force under Archibald Lochry. Out of 100, 5 officers and 35 men were killed and 48 men and 12 officers captured. The victorious Brant and his men turned back to New York, where they rejoined Johnson's Tories and a Seneca chief named Cornplanter. With a combined force of 1,800, they descended upon the Scoharie Valley on October 15 and then progressed up the Mohawk River, burning everything they encountered.

On October 19, Gen. Robert Van Rensselaer, with a militia force augmented by Oneidas, at last drove Johnson out of Scoharie. But by that time, in a five-day raid, Johnson and his Indian allies had destroyed as much as Gen. Sullivan had in a month-long campaign. Brant was wounded during Johnson's raid, and was out of action until early 1781, when he returned to harry the Mohawk Valley and Cherry Valley. With patriot fortunes in crisis, Col. Marianus Willett was assigned command of the region. He had only 130 Continental troops and a handful of militiamen, but his vigorous and skillful action put an end to raiding for the rest of the summer of 1781.

When attacks resumed in October, Willett battled Tories and Indians led by Walter Butler, who was fatally wounded. With his death, the raiders dispersed. In the meantime, Joseph Brant met with Abraham, chief of the so-called *Moravian Indians*, members of the Delaware tribe who had been christianized by Moravian missionaries. When Brant failed to recruit Abraham and his followers to fight the Americans, British authorities ordered them removed from Pennsylvania to the Ohio country. They set out for the Sandusky River, but by early 1782 a harsh winter famine compelled them to seek permission to move back temporarily to their western Pennsylvania mission towns on the Tuscarawas River.

The Moravians arrived just after the Mohawks and Delawares conducted a series of particularly brutal raids in the area. In February, Col. Brodhead, now commander of the Continental army's Western Department, dispatched Col. David Williamson to "punish" the hostiles. At Gnaddenhutten, Ohio, Williamson told Abraham and the 48 men, women, and boys gathered in the settlement that he had been sent to take them back to Fort Pitt, where they would be protected from all harm. At Williamson's request, Abraham sent runners to a neighboring missionary-Indian town, Salem, to fetch the Indians there and bring them back to

**Fightin' Words**

**Moravian Indians** were members of the Delaware tribe in Pennsylvania who had been christianized by local Moravian missionaries.

Gnaddenhutten. No sooner was this done than Williamson had the wrists of each Indian bound behind him; when the 50 or so people from Salem arrived, he had them likewise bound. In the morning, Williamson announced that the Moravians would be put to death as punishment for what the Delawares had done. That night, each Moravian captive—90 men, women, and children—was killed by a mallet blow to the back of the head.

Two boys somehow escaped to tell the tale. The massacre was condemned, but Williamson was not punished, and the outrage, of course, triggered massive Indian retaliation, which pushed into Kentucky and nearly led to the abandonment of the Kentucky frontier. In November 1782, however, George Rogers Clark assembled a substantial militia force and gave pursuit.

Although the Indians eluded him, Clark destroyed Chillicothe and other Shawnee towns and destroyed some 10,000 bushels of corn. Faced with starvation, the Indians stopped raiding for a time.

Despite the efforts of Clark and other United States frontiersmen, the war in the Old Northwest generally went badly for the patriots. Britain still held the most important forts, and the natives controlled most of the region north of the Ohio River. With the signing of preliminary articles of peace between the United States and Great Britain on November 30, 1782, England ceded the Old Northwest to the new nation. Although this did not end Indian-white warfare in the area, it did bring temporary peace to a region that, while distant from the major Revolutionary battles history remembers, felt the ravages of war perhaps more cruelly than any other theater.

---

### The Least You Need to Know

➤ Both the British and Americans made Indian alliances; however, because most Indians believed that British government would limit westward settlement, most sided with the British.

➤ If Indians were greatly feared as warriors, they also suffered some of the worst devastation of the Revolution.

➤ Contrary to official policy, British commanders extensively employed Indians to terrorize the frontier, encouraging particularly brutal warfare.

➤ Frontier warfare, though distant from the best-remembered battles of the Revolution, was a major aspect of the war.

➤ American commanders such as George Rogers Clark scored brilliant victories in the frontier, but the territory of the Old Northwest would not be secured by the end of the Revolution and would repeatedly erupt, becoming most violent during the War of 1812.

# Chapter 21

---

# Southern Exposure

## In This Chapter

➤ Loyalists in the South and elsewhere

➤ First blood in Virginia

➤ Failure of a British attempt to capture Charleston

➤ The British take Savannah

➤ A new assault on Charleston

The colonies stretched from the border of Canada down to Florida. Frontier and wilderness settlements extended west into the Appalachian Mountains and, in some areas, as far as the Mississippi River. Distances between settled areas were often great, especially inland from the coast. For both sides in the war, American space meant forces that were inadequate to begin with had to be spread even more thinly. Wherever the locals favored the Revolution, the patriots enjoyed a great advantage. However, in many places, local support for the Revolution was weak or even nonexistent. In parts of the South, loyalism ran high, and, early in the war, the British sought to exploit any softness of patriot sentiment.

This chapter deals mainly with the early phases of the Revolution in the South, concentrating on the coastal, or Tidewater, region. Chapter 24, "Backcountry Battles," deals with the later phases, primarily in the low country and Piedmont.

# The South: A Different War

Even today, most would agree that Boston, New York, and Philadelphia are quite different from Savannah and Charleston. In the eighteenth century, the differences were so profound and the distances so great that Massachusetts and the Carolinas, for example, were essentially different countries. For much of the war, action in the North and South was almost unrelated—except that, especially for the British, fighting in the one region reduced the available manpower for fighting in the other. Yet, in the earliest phases of the rebellion, when colonists protested taxation without representation (Chapters 5–8), British authorities were dumbfounded by the degree to which the colonies, North and South, communicated effectively and coordinated actions. The Howe brothers and other commanders believed that defeat in any region would also be rapidly communicated and, therefore, weaken the rebellion.

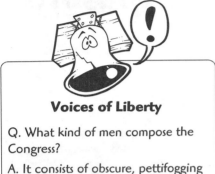

**Voices of Liberty**

Q. What kind of men compose the Congress?

A. It consists of obscure, pettifogging attorneys, bankrupt shopkeepers, outlawed smugglers, etc., etc.

—"A Loyalist Catechism," 1778

## Southern Loyalists

People supported the Revolution for a variety of reasons, many of which are summed up in the Declaration of Independence. Similarly, other people remained loyal to the Crown for various motives.

There were no clear class distinctions between patriots and loyalists. Rich merchants, large landowners, tradesmen, small farmers, seamen, and fishermen ended up in both camps. Economics played some role, but it was not a question of the rich versus the middle class and the poor. Those whose livelihoods depended on trade with Great Britain or with other British colonies tended to prefer continued membership in the British Empire. Humble seamen, fishermen, and those who supplied the seaports with manufactured or agricultural goods were therefore loyalists. On the other hand, those whose livelihoods depended on trade inside the 13 colonies, or on smuggling with places outside the British Empire, felt that their economic prospects would be unaffected or improved by independence.

Patriots were drawn to rebellion by the fear of tyranny. Loyalists disliked Parliament's taxation of the colonies, but believed that American rights could be safeguarded without armed revolt: After all, Great Britain's parliamentary government guaranteed many individual liberties. According to the loyalists, the present war had been provoked by rebels seeking a complete breakdown of law and order for sinister purposes of their own: In the chaos of revolution, ambitious patriots could use the army or the mob to seize power for themselves. Loyalists, like patriots, loved liberty, and they loved America. Loyalists simply believed that the greater threat to liberty came from revolt.

In any event, by the most pessimistic pro-Revolution estimates, fully one-third of the American population was loyalist. Optimistic loyalists put that proportion much higher. Judging by the number of persons who chose to leave America during and after the Revolution, the loyalists did constitute a large minority. About 80,000 persons took up new homes in Canada or Britain—one of every 30 white American families—and these represented a small proportion of all loyalists, most of whom chose to stay in the United States, since exile involved separation from family, friends, and birthplace, as well as economic hardship.

In all, perhaps 30,000 Tories served the British as combat troops. In the lower South, the brunt of the fighting in the Carolinas was borne by loyalists. In contrast to many British regular soldiers and "Hessians," loyalist combatants were powerfully motivated. The patriots hated them, and they suffered persecution and especially harsh treatment in combat. This motivated them to win—at all costs. As we saw in Chapter 20, "White War, Red Blood," the terror visited upon the northern frontier was chiefly the work of Indians *and* Tories, and, sometimes, of Tories disguised as Indians.

# Virginia Rises

Lord Dunmore, royal governor of Virginia, took a hard line against his rebellious colony in 1775 by raiding coastal towns and plantations. Seeking to drive Dunmore out of Norfolk, the Virginia Council of Safety recruited and stationed 1,000 militiamen at Great Bridge, a causeway spanning a sluggish, swampy stretch of the Elizabeth River some 10 miles from Norfolk.

Dunmore, leading 200 British regulars, some Tories, a few marines, and a band he called the Loyal *Ethiopians*—runaway black slaves—was attacked when he tried to cross the bridge. Some 60 of Dunmore's troops fell in battle—only a single patriot was killed—and Dunmore retreated to Norfolk. Loading as many Tories as he could onto British vessels in the harbor, he abandoned the town to the rebels.

Riding off the coast, Dunmore demanded that the people of Norfolk furnish provisions. When they refused, on January 1, 1776, he opened fire on the town, then sent landing parties to torch houses and warehouses along the shore. The patriots responded by setting fire to the homes of prominent Norfolk Tories.

**Fightin' Words**

In "polite" eighteenth-century white society, Africans and African Americans were frequently referred to generically as **Ethiopians,** even though the vast majority of African-American slaves came from West Africa, not the northeast.

**Voices of Liberty**

"They have destroyed one of the first towns in America .... They have done their worst, and ... to no other purpose than to give the world specimens of British cruelty and American fortitude, unless it be to force us to lay aside that childish fondness for Britain, and that foolish, tame dependence on her. ... How sunk is Britain!"

—*Virginia Gazette*, January 2, 1776

# Highlanders at Moore's Creek Bridge

In February 1776, Scots Highlander immigrants in North Carolina rallied to the Crown's cause. Some 1,500 of them marched toward the coast to join with British regulars to meet and destroy a rebel force on the move northwest. Anticipating the advance of the Scots, colonels Richard Caswell and John Alexander Lillington instructed about 1,000 patriot militiamen to dig shallow trenches and prepare an ambush. The work was finished when somebody realized that they had dug in with the creek at their backs, leaving no easy retreat. They repositioned themselves, dug in again, and waited.

On February 28, just before sunrise, the Scots encountered the abandoned trenches and assumed that this meant the defenders had deserted. They advanced across the bridge and were met by devastating rebel fire. Some 850 Highlanders became prisoners of war, and the patriots netted £15,000 in gold, 13 wagons, 1,500 rifles, 350 muskets, and 150 swords. About 30 Highlanders died and another 50 were wounded. Two patriots were wounded, one fatally. It was not a momentous battle, in and of itself, but Moore's Creek Bridge took the wind out of the Tories' sails throughout the Carolinas and up into Virginia.

# Charleston: First Pass

The fiasco at Moore's Creek Bridge did not discourage the British from attempting to exploit loyalism in Charleston, South Carolina. British command was encouraged that South Carolina had made no overtly hostile moves and was believed to harbor a good deal of loyalist sentiment. On June 4, 1776, 10 British men o' war and 30 troop transports dropped anchor off Charleston Bar.

### Voices of Liberty

*"The behaviour of the garrison, both men and officers, with Colonel Moultrie at their head, I confess astonished me. It was brave to the last degree. I had no idea that so much coolness and intrepidity could be displayed by a collection of raw recruits."*

—Gen. Charles Lee, 1776

But Henry Clinton, who had accompanied the fleet, should have taken notice: Charleston did not *welcome* these military representatives of the mother country. Forts had been built on Sullivan's and James islands, which controlled the approaches to the inner harbor and to Charleston proper. Warehouses on the waterfront had been torn down, to provide a clear field of fire against invaders. Two regiments had been raised and equipped to man the new forts, commanded, respectively, by Charles Cotesworth Pinckney and William Moultrie. Moultrie's second in command was a man from the low country, Francis Marion, whom we shall formally meet, as the Swamp Fox, in Chapter 24. The regiments were augmented by North Carolina infantry, and Gen. Charles Lee had come down from Cambridge, Massachusetts, to oversee defenses. Always arrogant and condescending, Lee was impressed in spite of himself by the assembled militia.

Britain's Clinton planned to close in on Sullivan's Island and bombard the fort, built of stout *palmetto* logs. During this bombardment, the troop transports would unload onto Long Island, a short distance from Sullivan's Island. The infantry would then march onto Sullivan's Island and take the fort. Once that was done, invading Charleston itself would be a simple matter.

British intelligence failed in two respects. First, it misread the sentiment in Charleston. Most Charlestonians were very willing to resist invasion. Second, the body of water separating Long Island from Sullivan's Island, which at first looked inconsiderable, proved to be unfordable. Men were picked off one by one as they tried to cross. The seaborne arm of the assault was not going well, either. In the treacherous shallows around the island, British ships ran aground, and their cannon fire was strangely ineffective against the *palmetto* walls of the fort. The tough wood seemed to soak up the balls like a sponge.

If British guns had little effect against the American fort, the South Carolinians' return fire was devastating. The British ships, trying to navigate difficult waters, were sitting ducks. Abandoning one frigate, which had run aground, Adm. Peter Parker withdrew his remaining ships, all of them badly damaged, although he had 100 guns versus only 21 in the fort. Sixty-four Royal Navy sailors died, and 131 were wounded. "No slaughterhouse could present so bad a sight with blood and entrails lying about, as did our ship," one British officer recalled. American losses were 17 dead and 20 wounded. The British were disappointed in their efforts to take the city, and years passed before Charleston was attacked again.

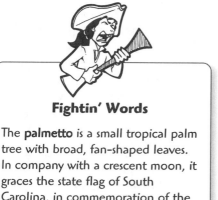

**Fightin' Words**

The **palmetto** is a small tropical palm tree with broad, fan-shaped leaves. In company with a crescent moon, it graces the state flag of South Carolina, in commemoration of the defense of Charleston. (The flag that was flown over Fort Sullivan bore a crescent moon above the word LIBERTY.)

# Savannah Falls

After the fiasco at Charleston, the British ignored the South for a couple of years. After the U.S.-French alliance of 1778, however, British strategy changed. From the end of 1778, the South became the main focus of British hopes and energies for a number of reasons:

➤ The southern colonies, which produced lucrative cash crops like tobacco and rice, were more valuable than the northern colonies. If Britain, now threatened with war against France, could only retain part of its American empire, they wished to hold the South.

➤ Loyalism in the South had increased, thanks to the concessions made by the Carlisle Commission early in 1778 (see Chapter 19, "Valley Forge"). Britain's promise not to tax America played an important role in winning support in places like Charleston.

➤ If Britain could keep the southern and West Indian colonies, the North would still be economically subservient to the British, who would control all of the North's main trading partners.

On November 27, 1778, Lt. Col. Archibald Campbell was dispatched from Sandy Hook, New Jersey, with 3,500 troops and a naval escort. On December 23, Campbell's command anchored off Tybee Island at the mouth of the Savannah River. Defending Savannah were 900 Continental soldiers and a militia force of perhaps 150, all commanded by Gen. Robert Howe (no relation to the British Howe brothers). Worse for the Americans, Gen. Augustine Prevost was marching north from Florida with his contingent of British troops to cooperate with Campbell in the capture of Savannah.

However, after obtaining what he called "the most satisfactory intelligence concerning the state of matters at Savannah," Campbell decided not to wait for Prevost, but to attack immediately. He landed his men at Girardeau's Plantation, about two miles south of the town. Waiting for him just a half mile south of Savannah were 700 of Howe's Continentals, plus the 150 militiamen. The battle, on December 29, quickly went to Campbell. The American units retreated in good order, except for a unit of Georgia militia, which, cut off from the causeway across Musgrove Swamp, had to make its way directly through the swamp. Among the 83 Americans who fell in battle that day, a large number drowned in the flooded swamp.

The British occupation of Savannah lasted through July 1782. In the early autumn of 1779, French admiral D'Estaing, having failed in the first Franco-American amphibious operation against Newport, Rhode Island (Chapter 19), and having withdrawn to the French West Indies, now decided to assist the Americans in the South—despite Washington's desire that he coordinate with Continental troops in the North. Some 33 warships, mounting 2,000 guns, and escorting transports carrying more than 4,000 troops, surprised the British off the Georgia coast. D'Estaing quickly captured two British warships and two store ships, one of which carried a £30,000 payroll intended for the British garrison at Savannah.

D'Estaing's fleet briefly disappeared, then, on September 9, the Frenchman began landing troops on Tybee Island. On September 16th, with American units having joined him, D'Estaing demanded the surrender of Savannah "to the arms of the King of France." British general Prevost asked for a 24-hour truce to ponder his options. D'Estaing agreed, and Prevost used the time to mount a defense employing some 3,200 troops. At the end of the truce, he sent word to the Frenchman that he would fight.

The battle did not begin until October 9. The combined French and American attack forces numbered under 5,000—more men than Prevost had, but the British commander had the advantage of defending from

**Fightin Words**

**Scurvy,** an extremely debilitating, sometimes fatal, disease, is characterized by bleeding gums, hemorrhages under the skin, and great weakness. Caused by a deficiency of vitamin C, it was a common scourge of sailors, who received no fresh fruit or vegetables on long voyages.

fortification. Prevost's men not only held, they counterattacked, killing or wounding 800 of the allies (of whom 650 were French), nearly a 20-percent casualty rate. Among the fallen was the dashing Polish officer who had virtually created the Continental cavalry, Casimir Pulaski. British losses were perhaps a hundred killed or wounded.

Gen. Benjamin Lincoln, in command of the American forces, wanted to give the attack a second try. D'Estaing would hear none of it. He feared being trapped by bad weather, *scurvy*, and the fleet of the enemy. After this, the second Franco-American amphibious disaster, D'Estaing withdrew again to Martinique in the Indies. Savannah would remain in British hands.

# Target: Charleston

Charleston was still in patriot hands. In the spring of 1779, Gen. Prevost drove Moultrie's American forces back upon the town, but when the British general reached the outskirts of Charleston, its defenses now appeared (deceptively, as it turned out) formidable. As Prevost stood with his forces outside the city, South Carolina's patriot governor, Edward Rutledge, offered to declare his state neutral—a very different stance from 1776. Taking this as a sign of weakness, Prevost insisted on unconditional surrender. Learning that Gen. Lincoln was approaching with a large American relief force, Prevost decided not to attack and retreated to Savannah, looting and pillaging all the way back.

Not until the end of 1779 did Henry Clinton put together a new force to strike at Charleston. He recalled 3,000 men to New York from Newport and added 3,500 British, Hessian, and Tory troops to this number. Ships' crews added an additional 5,000 men. This force set sail from New York on December 26, 1779. Because of violent weather, it was February 11, 1780, before the fleet, which had been scattered and reassembled, entered Edisto Inlet, where troops began to land on Johns Island, 30 miles below Charleston.

## Defenses

As indicated months earlier by Gov. Rutledge's offer of neutrality, the mood of Charleston had changed since 1776. Charlestonians had been able to sit out most of the war, and, indeed, they profited by it, doing a vigorous business in privateering. Patriotism had faded—as had the state of the city's defenses. The forts on Sullivan's Island and James Island had been abandoned. Only the Neck, the narrow isthmus connecting Charleston with the mainland, had been newly fortified. Along the sides of the town flanked by the Cooper and Ashley rivers, a line of makeshift forts had been hastily erected.

## Siege

Gen. Clinton moved with his customary deliberation against Charleston, slowly building up a siege force. In truth, he was also playing for time for personal reasons. He had submitted his resignation to London and was hoping he could soon turn over

### Sites and Sights

Charleston, South Carolina, is one of America's most beautiful cities, and a great many of its Revolutionary-era buildings still stand, especially below Broad Street. From the elegant Battery, at the southern tip of the city, it is easy to appreciate Charleston's strategic position at the confluence of two important rivers, the Ashley and the Cooper. Call the Charleston Area Visitor Information Center at 803–853–8000.

command to Gen. Cornwallis. The delay gave the Americans opportunity to rebuild decayed defenses. At last, on March 19, Clinton received word from London that his resignation had not been accepted. Realizing that he must now act against Charleston, he ordered even more troops for the attack. The next day, American commodore Abraham Whipple, realizing that his fleet (purchased from Adm. D'Estaing) was outgunned, withdrew up the Cooper River. Simultaneously, British admiral Marriot Arbuthnot crossed Charleston Bar and was in position to support the British assault.

During the night of March 28–29, Clinton's troops crossed the Ashley River and took up positions across the Neck. In effect, the American garrison was now almost completely sealed up in the town. On April 1, Clinton's engineers began to dig a series of trenches from which siege operations would be conducted. Although a force of 750 Virginia Continentals, having slipped past the British troops, arrived on April 6 to reinforce the garrison, the situation was becoming hopeless. The garrison could only watch as Clinton engineered his careful siege.

## Disaster

By April 10, with a major part of his siege works in place, Clinton demanded Gen. Lincoln's surrender. When Lincoln refused, the British began bombarding on April 13, using mainly incendiary shot, which set part of the city ablaze. Still, Lincoln held out,

### Voices of Liberty

"We fight, get beat, rise, and fight again."

—Patriot general Nathanael Greene, 1780

hoping that Gen. Isaac Huger, with a number of militiamen and 300 to 500 Continentals, would somehow provide a means of resistance or escape. On April 14, however, Banastre Tarleton and Patrick Ferguson led British and Tory forces in a surprise attack on Huger's encampment at Monck's Corner, South Carolina. American losses of men, supplies, and badly needed cavalry mounts were high, and Huger barely escaped with his life. With the defeat at Monck's Corner, Lincoln's garrison was left with no means of withdrawal from Charleston.

With Clinton's trenches steadily closing in, on April 19, Gen. Lincoln held another council of war, proposing that the garrison surrender Charleston. Christopher

Gadsden, lieutenant governor of South Carolina, vehemently objected to talk of surrender, threatening Lincoln with civil insurrection if he gave up. Nevertheless, on April 21, Lincoln did propose surrender terms. Clinton responded with a demand for unconditional surrender. Two nights later, a group of Americans sortied out against the British, but were quickly repulsed. It was a futile gesture. On May 8, Clinton issued another demand for unconditional surrender, which Lincoln rejected, holding out for better terms. Clinton's response the next night was a titanic artillery barrage, which so terrified the citizens of Charleston that they now petitioned Lincoln to give up.

Lincoln turned over Charleston to Henry Clinton on May 12, 1780. Five thousand American soldiers instantly became prisoners of war, and 400 precious artillery pieces and some 6,000 muskets also fell to the enemy. The loss of Charleston was the single greatest patriot defeat of the Revolution. Moreover, a key Southern port was now lost, and all of South Carolina thrown open to the British.

*Banastre Tarleton, British officer who commanded Tory forces with ruthless skill in the South.* (Image from the National Archives)

### The Least You Need to Know

➤ Loyalists were a powerful minority in the Middle States (especially New York) and in the lower South (especially in South Carolina).

➤ Loyalists, like patriots, were motivated by complex economic and ideological factors. Many loyalists were principled citizens who wanted the best for America.

➤ Savannah fell to the British at the close of 1778 and would remain in British hands until 1782.

➤ After Charleston proved not to be a pushover target in 1776, the British mounted a major, and successful, assault in 1780; the fall of Charleston was the worst patriot loss of the war.

# Chapter 22

# A Turncoat and the Mutineers

---

### In This Chapter

➤ Why Benedict Arnold turned traitor

➤ Arnold's plan: surrender West Point

➤ The mutiny of the Pennsylvania Line

➤ Washington suppresses a mutiny

➤ The war-profiteering crisis

---

It has been mentioned several times in this book that anyone reading about the American Revolution is struck by the nation's great good fortune in possessing men of extraordinary wisdom, courage, goodwill, and lofty character. Few revolutions have been so lucky.

Nevertheless, the American Revolution was a great human event, and no human event is without its share of greed, dissension, and selfishness. This chapter begins with the story of the most famous—or infamous—turncoat in American history, and concludes with trouble in the Continental Army and the menace posed by the war profiteers.

## Woes of a Married Man

In many ways, Benedict Arnold was just the kind of general George Washington badly needed. He played a big part in the bold capture of Fort Ticonderoga (Chapter 9, "Green Mountains and Bunker Hill"); performed heroically in the ill-fated invasion of Canada; probably saved the Revolution by his strategic delaying action at Valcour Island (Chapter 11, "The Battle for Boston"); and did far more to gain victory at Saratoga than did Horatio Gates, the overall commander there.

But, without question, Arnold was a difficult man, and an almost impossible subordinate. Born in 1741 in Norwich, Connecticut, he was *apprenticed* to a druggist as a youth, but bolted in 1758 to enlist in a New York militia company. After little more than a year, he deserted and had to be bailed out of trouble by his mother. Reenlisting in March 1760, he again deserted, and this time made his own way back to Norwich, via a wilderness trek. He then completed his pharmacy apprenticeship.

By the time he was 21, Arnold's parents were dead; he sold the family property and used the proceeds to move with his sister to New Haven, where he opened up a pharmacy and bookstore. He prospered and began operating his own trading vessels to Canada and the West Indies. As with such entrepreneurs as John Hancock, much of his prosperity came from smuggling—evading British taxation laws.

He married his first wife, Margaret Mansfield, in 1767 and, in 1775, arrived in Cambridge at the head of a Connecticut militia company. His wartime career began.

**Fightin' Words**

In eighteenth-century America, as in England at this time, **apprenticeship** was not only the chief method of learning a profession, it was the principal form of education in general. An apprentice was typically bound to a master for a certain period, working in return for room, board, and training.

## Ambitions Unrewarded

After his extraordinary wilderness march to Quebec and his return from the failed American assault at the end of 1775, Arnold was promoted to brigadier general. Then, following Valcour Island, he received a hero's accolades—from all but an important clique of fellow officers, who resented his impetuosity as well as his impatient energy and imperious tone. In February 1777, when Congress created five new major generalships, Arnold was passed over in favor of his juniors.

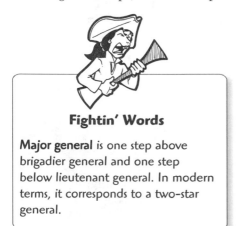

**Fightin' Words**

**Major general** is one step above brigadier general and one step below lieutenant general. In modern terms, it corresponds to a two-star general.

Arnold's response was hardly selfless, but it was understandable. He tendered his resignation. Only George Washington's personal persuasion kept him in the army. Just two months later, after he repelled a British attack on Danbury, Connecticut, Arnold was commissioned a *major general*. But even now, Congress handed him a slight. It still listed him as junior to the five men who had been promoted prior to him. This, in fact, had been Arnold's principal grievance, and, still feeling that his honor had been offended, he again tendered his resignation.

The exigencies of war stayed his hand, however. In July, he joined in the effort to block Burgoyne's advance into upper New York. In the fall, as was seen in Chapter 17,

"Saratoga Saga," he defied his commander, the overly cautious Gen. Horatio Gates, and became instrumental in achieving victory at Bemis Heights, the second of the two momentous Saratoga battles.

## Social Climbers

Although Gates did his best to cover up Arnold's heroism at Saratoga, Congress recognized his service by at last restoring his proper seniority. Crippled by a leg wound received at Bemis Heights, Arnold was given command of Philadelphia in June 1778.

Meanwhile, the U.S.-French alliance of February 1778 severely shook Arnold's loyalty to the American cause. Arnold, like many other religiously prejudiced Protestants of the era, deeply hated France because it was Roman Catholic, and because it was an absolute monarchy. Although many personal and selfish reasons lay behind Arnold's treachery, he also felt that the American Revolution lost its purity when it joined with the French. His anger helped him to justify his drift toward treason. Having suffered so much in wilderness campaigning, he quickly and extravagantly embraced the high life enjoyed by the city's prosperous Tories. There were, of course, significant differences between Benedict Arnold and his new Tory friends. First, he was a patriot general, and their sympathies were with the enemy. Second, they had a lot more money than he. The extravagant Arnold was soon deeply in debt.

In February 1779, Joseph Reed, president of the Pennsylvania Council and of the state, presented Congress with eight charges of official misconduct against Arnold, the most serious of which involved various forms of embezzlement, using government funds to purchase goods for personal speculation. Many years later the full extent of Arnold's corruption was revealed, but, in 1779, four of the eight charges were referred to Congress, and he was found guilty of only two of the least serious charges. Corruption and illegal trade were so widespread, so Arnold's actions were less shocking to his contemporaries than they are to us. Washington issued a reprimand so mild that it verged on praise, but, incredibly, the boundless arrogance of Benedict Arnold, who was guilty, did not permit him to accept anything less than a complete acquittal. However, he consoled himself in another quarter.

Having borne him three sons in five years, Margaret Mansfield died, leaving Arnold an eligible widower. On April 8, 1779, after an ardent—and costly—courtship, Arnold married Peggy Shippen, the 19-year-old daughter of one of Philadelphia's most prominent Tory families. Arnold, at 38, was more than twice his bride's age, but he was dashing, and she, if not ravishingly beautiful, was irrepressibly pert, pretty, and charmingly spoiled.

*The sprightly and spoiled Philadelphia Tory, Peggy Shippen Arnold, was Benedict Arnold's second wife.*
(Image from the National Archives)

# Just Business

If Arnold lived beyond his means before, he became even more extravagant as the husband of a girl born to wealth. As he struggled to make ends meet, American authorities kept questioning his conduct, and Arnold grew increasingly arrogant in his responses.

At about this time, British major John André, aide to Sir Henry Clinton, began receiving mysterious letters that hinted at a certain highly placed American officer's willingness to render "his services to the commander-in-chief of the British forces in any way that would most effectually restore the former government … whether by immediately joining the British army or cooperating on some concealed plan."

John André was titillated by the prospect of "turning" an American officer, and he greatly enjoyed the game of sending encrypted messages to and fro. Sir Henry Clinton was interested, but his proposition to Arnold was unimaginative. He wanted the American general to lead an American army into a trap, with Clinton paying two guineas a head for each soldier he captured. When Arnold asked for an additional £10,000 up front, negotiations broke down. They resumed in May 1780. Still embroiled in the court-martial over his conduct and misappropriation, Arnold was angling for command of the fortress at West Point. On June 15, he wrote Clinton that he expected to be given this assignment, and the discussion turned to how Arnold might surrender this key fortification to the British.

Always Arnold pushed for an agreement on price: £10,000, regardless of outcome, and £20,000 "if I point out a plan of cooperation by which Sir Henry shall possess himself of West Point, the garrison, etc., etc." After five weeks, Arnold received his reply. Clinton would pay £20,000, only if West Point was indeed surrendered. He would not pay £10,000 regardless of outcome, but, he assured Arnold, the general would not be "left a victim."

# A "Plan of Such Infinite Effect"

Arnold agreed and began sending Clinton important information concerning the battle plans for the campaign against the British in South Carolina and Georgia that Washington was drawing up with the French general, the Comte de Rochambeau. Arnold did not communicate directly, but through his wife, who "innocently" passed the information through additional intermediaries and finally to André.

Through most of the summer of 1779, Benedict Arnold was slated for command of a wing of the army in the forthcoming southern campaign. This would have spoiled his plans, so he complained that his wound (now three years old) prevented the exertion called for in an active campaign. He asked for a more sedentary assignment, and, on August 3, was given West Point.

Should West Point fall, so would control of the Hudson; Arnold's command encompassed not only the fortifications at West Point, but also those at Stony Point and Verplancks Point, as well as additional outposts and an infantry-cavalry force stationed at North Castle, east of Verplancks Point. To lose control of the Hudson, along with the military forces there, would likely spoil or at least delay the Yorktown campaign, because Washington would have to devote resources to repairing the breach. The outcome of the Revolution hung, at least to some degree, on the fate of West Point and its associated positions. To Lord George Germain, an excited Sir Henry Clinton wrote, on October 11, 1780, that great things were to be expected from "a plan of such infinite effect."

Assuming command of West Point, Arnold wasted no time preparing the fort to accommodate a British assault. He weakened the garrison by detaching 200 men for a wood-cutting party. Having been earlier informed that the chain stretched across the Hudson to impede the passage of ships was in urgent need of repair, Arnold made a point of not effecting the repairs.

Arnold also set about establishing a network of spies, largely through contact with Joshua Hett Smith, Tory brother of the former royal chief justice of New York. Arnold's intimacy with Smith drew the objections of his subordinate officers, yet none suspected treason. In the meantime, Arnold also maintained a correspondence with Clinton, continually pressuring him to reconsider paying the £10,000 originally requested.

Arnold and Clinton decided that Col. Beverly Robinson, a local Tory leader, would request a meeting with Arnold, supposedly to discuss the disposition of Tory household property in the area. André, in civilian garb, would come along, and, at an opportune time, Arnold would discuss with him his plans for the surrender of West Point. Arnold and Clinton would also use Joshua Smith as a messenger, and their means of transport would be the British sloop *Vulture*, which occasionally plied the Hudson's waters on reconnaissance missions. On September 21, *Vulture* carried André, who had assumed the named John Anderson, to a remote place in the woods, where he and Arnold plotted until after four in the morning. Too late for André to reboard the *Vulture*, he stayed the night at Smith's house.

# The Unraveling

Presumably, after their dead-of-night meeting in the woods, André and Arnold formulated their plans. Now those plans were about to unravel. Around dawn on September 23, Col. James Livingston, commander of local American forces, decided to attack the *Vulture*. The badly damaged sloop had all it could do to limp away. Major André was behind American lines. If he were captured in uniform, he would become a prisoner of war and would probably be exchanged by and by. But if he were taken in civilian clothes, he would be held, tried, and, doubtless, executed as a spy. Such were the immutable rules of war.

Arnold, unwilling to abandon his scheme, instructed André to put certain papers—apparently a full description of the West Point–area defenses—between his stockings and his feet. He gave the spy and his guide, Smith, passes to get them past the American guards. Smith and André set off for White Plains.

At the same time, Maj. Benjamin Tallmadge, Washington's chief of intelligence, was preparing for a meeting between Washington and Rochambeau, making certain that no Tory or British force would abduct the commander in chief. Patrolling the region, he pondered the recent strange behavior of Gen. Arnold: pumping officers throughout the area for information. He had asked Tallmadge the names and whereabouts of all secret agents in the area. Tallmadge knew better than to divulge such information, but he might not have thought more of it had not one of Arnold's letters also contained a request for the safe conduct of one John Anderson from Manhattan to West Point. This was a lot to ask: transporting an unknown man from British Manhattan to a key Continental army installation.

Returning from his patrol, Tallmadge learned that a John Anderson had been picked up by militiamen in Westchester. He had a pass signed by no less than Benedict Arnold, but the militiamen still brought him to Tallmadge's headquarters, where Lt. Col. John Jameson had him searched. In his stockings were found detailed plans of West Point, as well as summaries of various confidential orders issued by Gen. Washington. The handwriting precisely matched the handwriting on the passes Gen. Arnold had penned. In Tallmadge's absence, Jameson seized the documents and packed them off to Gen. Washington. Anderson was sent back to Benedict Arnold.

Tallmadge now acted quickly. He intercepted "Anderson," who now revealed himself as Maj. John André. On September 29, a board was convened to examine the major. André confessed everything, and the board recommended that he be executed as a spy. Washington issued the order personally. Tallmadge observed in a letter to his friend, Col. Samuel Webb, that André seemed "as cheerful as if he was going to an assembly. I am sure he will go to the gallows less tearful of his fate and with less concern than I shall behold the tragedy." John André was hanged on October 2, 1780.

*The execution of Benedict Arnold's contact, Maj. John André.*
(Image from the National Archives)

285

### We Hold These Truths

Sentenced to be hanged as a spy, André, on the eve of his execution, wrote the following appeal to George Washington, requesting a soldier's death (by firing squad) rather than a spy's (hanging):

> *Buoyed above the terror of death by the consciousness of a life devoted to honourable pursuits, and stained with no action that can give me remorse, I trust that the request I make to your Excellency at this serious period, and which is to soften my last moments, will not be rejected.*

> *Sympathy towards a soldier will surely induce your Excellency and a military tribunal to adopt a mode of my death to the feelings of a man of honour.*

> *Let me hope, Sir, that if aught in my character impresses you with esteem towards me, if aught in my misfortunes marks me as the victim of policy and not of resentment, I shall experience the operation of these feelings in your breast, by being informed that I am not to die on a gibbet.*

Washington neither answered André's request nor satisfied it. The major was hanged as a spy on October 2, 1780.

## Arnold: "Bound to Retaliate"

As for Benedict Arnold, Jameson's messenger reached him with the "news" about the papers found on André before the person Jameson sent had reached Washington. Thus Arnold, given timely warning, bade farewell to his dear Peggy, boarded his barge, and had it rowed down to HMS *Vulture*. The sloop took him to New York and into the service of His Majesty's army. Days later, hearing of death sentence pronounced upon André, Arnold, more arrogant and insolent than ever, wrote a letter to the commander in chief he had betrayed:

> *If after this just and candid representation of Major André's case the board of general officers adhere to their former opinion, I shall suppose it dictated by passion and resentment. And if that gentleman should suffer the severity of their sentence, I shall think myself bound by every tie of duty and honour to retaliate on such unhappy persons of your army as may fall within my power—that the respect due to flags and to the law of nations may be better understood and observed.*

*… If this warning should be disregarded, and he should suffer, I call heaven and earth to witness that your Excellency will be justly answerable for the torrent of blood that may be spilt in consequence.*

Washington, of course, was unmoved. He also ordered the immediate reinforcement of West Point. Although Arnold had slipped through his fingers, control of the Hudson had been preserved. As it later turned out, patriot control of the Hudson was a vital precondition for Washington's participation in the climactic Yorktown campaign, which took place in the following year, 1781 (see Chapter 25, "Yorktown: 'A Most Glorious Day'").

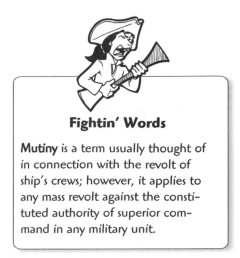

**Fightin' Words**

**Mutiny** is a term usually thought of in connection with the revolt of ship's crews; however, it applies to any mass revolt against the constituted authority of superior command in any military unit.

# Even Bigger Problems

Dramatic as it was, Arnold's treason, nipped in the bud, had no effect on the war. But the year of his treachery was also a year of *mutiny* in the Continental army.

## Grievances of the Pennsylvania Line

There had been a small-scale mutiny at Morristown in May 1780, when two Connecticut regiments defied their officers and demanded back pay. Pennsylvania troops disarmed them. But then, in January 1781, the Pennsylvania soldiers—the "Pennsylvania Line," rebelled. Their grievances were indeed serious:

➤ They had not been paid in many months.

➤ They had nothing to wear but rags.

➤ Their ration was bread and water.

➤ Many felt deceived by the terms of their enlistment. Having joined up for "three years or the duration of the war," many had been misled to believe that their term would constitute the shorter, not the longer, of the two. They wanted *out*.

The incident that touched off the mutiny was an instance of colossal insensitivity. On the night of January 1, 1781, recruiting agents appeared in their camp offering $25 in gold for new recruits. To these half-clothed, half-starved men, it was an outrage, and fully 2,400 of them revolted. On January 3, they made camp at Princeton and chose a spokesman to take their grievances to Congress. Fortunately, quick intervention by Joseph Reed, president of Pennsylvania, brought an end to the mutiny. He simply agreed to most of their demands.

Word of the mutiny spread, however, and soon reached Sir Henry Clinton. He dispatched two agents to provoke defections in the ranks. Once again, the British had misjudged the Americans. The mutiny was not about political allegiance, but about just treatment. Once just treatment was secured, the men of the Pennsylvania Line proved their allegiance to the cause of liberty by seizing Clinton's spies, who were quickly hanged.

A few weeks after the peaceful resolution of the mutiny of the Pennsylvania Line, three New Jersey regiments mutinied. This time, there was no one to intercede, and George Washington ordered the mutiny to be suppressed—immediately—by force of arms. The ringleaders were identified, tried, and hanged.

## And the Profiteers

The astounding fact is not that mutinies occurred in the Continental army, but that there were so few of them. Conditions for soldiers and even most officers were grim. Pay was irregular. Food was often not forthcoming. Clothing was always in short supply. In part, the supply problems were due to the inefficiency of the army's quarter-master corps. In part, they were the result of a chronic lack of funds. But Washington's army also faced problems with speculators, profiteering, and attempts to corner the market for certain goods.

Indeed, the temptation to profit from supplying the Continental army was great. Congress lacked the power to tax, which meant that the government could not count on having the fiscal muscle to buy goods at the best rates and even to claim priority in the purchase of goods. Without a centralized fiscal authority, or the authority to levy taxes, all Congress could do was "levy requisition" upon the states—in effect, *ask* them to pay. If the states were delinquent, Congress was powerless to act, except to print paper money, "Continental currency" popularly called "Continentals." Since it was not backed by *specie* (gold), the paper money depreciated almost immediately. A new expression entered the American vocabulary: "not worth a Continental."

**Fightin' Words**

**Specie** payments are payments in gold. Contrast currency payments, which are payments in paper money, that have no intrinsic value. **Impressment of goods** was a euphemism for the government seizure, without payment, of urgently needed supplies, food, or transportation.

Unscrupulous individuals—ranging from wealthy speculators to farmers (who, as Nathanael Greene complained to the governor of Rhode Island in 1775, "are extortionate")—could charge whatever the market would bear. Because the government lacked ready money, speculators could often corner the market for a particular good, driving up prices by buying up everything available. The relentless issuance of paper money provided some relief, but, in driving up inflation, it also exacerbated the situation. *Impressment of goods*—the seizure of supplies, food, and transportation—was sometimes the only alternative to failure in battle or starvation in camp. But it smacked of the very tyrannies that drove the colonists to war against Britain in the first place.

Foreign loans staved off bankruptcy, but one can only conclude that, despite mutinies and profiteering, an overriding belief in the rightness of the cause carried the Revolution through the hardest times.

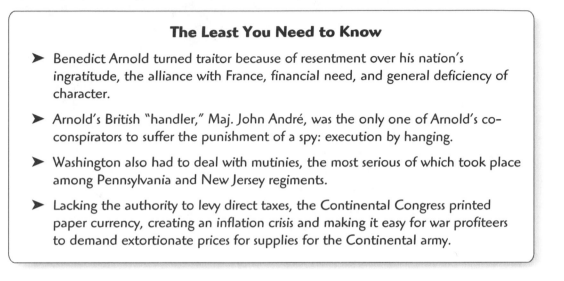

### The Least You Need to Know

➤ Benedict Arnold turned traitor because of resentment over his nation's ingratitude, the alliance with France, financial need, and general deficiency of character.

➤ Arnold's British "handler," Maj. John André, was the only one of Arnold's co-conspirators to suffer the punishment of a spy: execution by hanging.

➤ Washington also had to deal with mutinies, the most serious of which took place among Pennsylvania and New Jersey regiments.

➤ Lacking the authority to levy direct taxes, the Continental Congress printed paper currency, creating an inflation crisis and making it easy for war profiteers to demand extortionate prices for supplies for the Continental army.

# Part 5

# "The World Turned Upside Down"

*We now enter the endgame of the American Revolution, which includes a narrative of the war at sea, with special attention paid to America's single most daring naval hero, John Paul Jones, and a narrative of how the Patriots won back the South by fighting with stealth and wit through forest and swamp.*

*Chapter 26 is the story of the Siege of Yorktown, the battle in which Washington and his French allies on land and sea forced Lord Cornwallis and an army of Britain's best soldiers to throw down their arms, surrender, and, for all practical purposes, give the United States its independence.*

*We close with a narrative of how the Treaty of Paris was negotiated with England—finally behind the back of our French ally—and with an account of the effects of the Revolution, both immediate and enduring.*

# Chapter 23

# "I Have Not Yet Begun to Fight"

## In This Chapter

➤ The strength of the Royal Navy

➤ The birth of the American navy

➤ Victory in the Bahamas, defeat off Block Island

➤ The story of John Paul Jones

➤ British naval victories come too late to change the outcome of the war

"The Americans," declared Britain's secretary-at-war, Viscount Barrington, "may be reduced by the fleet, but never can be by the army."

Coming early in the conflict, it was a bold statement, and one few British military men wanted or were willing to hear. After all, this "rebellion"—for the British government would not officially dignify it with the term *revolution*—was a local conflict that could surely be squashed by the army. Naval operations were necessary to support the army's efforts, of course, but relying on massive fleet operations would be costly and would risk bringing the conflict onto the world stage.

Yet the American land victories, culminating in Saratoga (Chapter 17, "Saratoga Saga"), had already forced that issue, prompting France to enter the war in 1778 and, a year later, France's ally, Spain, as well. The army hadn't prevailed against the Americans after three years of combat, and now the American Revolution was, in fact, a world war, like the French and Indian War before it, in which navies *had* to play a major role.

# The Revolution at Sea

Deciding to counteract the Revolution with an army rather than a navy must have made the most sense to British military planners. As far as they could tell, there was something like an American army to fight, but nothing at all like an American navy.

## *Rule, Britannia!*

Britain had long possessed the most powerful navy in the world. In 1775, it included 131 ships of the line. These were the battleships of the era, which mounted a minimum of 64 guns—though the largest of these might have 90 or even more than 100 cannon. And firepower was half of what eighteenth-century naval operations were all about.

In an age of "wooden ships and iron men," enemy vessels fought by *broadsiding* one another. A ship's cannon were arranged in rows along the sides of the vessel. There might be a gun or two at the bow (front of the ship), the so-called bow chaser, but there were none at the stern (back). To bring one's firepower to bear against an enemy meant maneuvering so that the broadside of the ship, bristling with guns, was aimed against the target. Of course, this exposed a mighty big target. Therefore, the ship that won a battle was typically the ship that *survived*, by delivering the most shots before the enemy could deliver them in return. The better the ship was built, the better its chances, but more important was the number of guns. A vessel of 90 guns usually beat a vessel of 64 guns. It came down to the mathematics of firepower. Usually.

**Fightin' Words**

**Broadsiding** is the act of maneuvering so that a ship's main cannon can be fired effectively against a target.

But firepower was only half the equation. The other half was speed and maneuverability. If you could get your ship or ships to a target faster than your opponent or run rings around your opponent, and *cross the T*, you had a substantial advantage: Crossing the T meant maneuvering so that your guns were directed against the fore or aft of the enemy ship, where he had no guns (save, perhaps, for the bow chaser) to return fire, instead of against his broadside, where he could fire back.

**Fightin' Words**

**Crossing the T** was a basic naval battle maneuver in which one maneuvered so that one's guns were directed against the fore or aft of the enemy ship, where he had no guns (or almost none), instead of against his broadside, from which he could easily fire back.

So smaller, lighter, faster, and more maneuverable vessels were also important. The most significant of this class of ship was the frigate. If the ship of the line was analogous to a twentieth-century battleship, the frigate was a cruiser or destroyer. It typically served as the eyes of the fleet, a reconnaissance function, and it was also invaluable plying waters close to shore. These were shallow and treacherous, requiring a highly maneuverable ship that was light enough to ride high on the water. A heavy ship of the line might easily run aground.

In addition to its 131 ships of the line in 1775, the Royal Navy had 139 craft of other classes, many of them frigates. By the end of the Revolution, in 1783, the total number of vessels had swelled to 468. Impressive as these numbers are, they don't tell the whole story. At the end of the Seven Years' War (in America, the French and Indian War) in 1763, the Royal Navy was beyond challenge. But, in 1771, the Earl of Sandwich, a man infamous for his utter lack of principle, became first sea lord—the equivalent of secretary of the navy. Under him, the Royal Navy's ships were left to decay, and the morale of the service evaporated. Between 1774 and 1780, 60,000 sailors deserted or died from disease—and the Royal Navy during this time probably did not exceed 30,000 men in any one year. The chronic shortfall, as mentioned in Chapter 6, "Regulators, Rioters, and a Massacre in Boston," was made up by impressment.

## American Assets

A decayed navy was better than no navy at all, and that is what the United States had at the start of the war. In October 19, 1775, to James Warren, John Adams wrote a letter broaching the idea of an "American Fleet," observing, with irony, that "I don't mean 100 ships of the Line," but some small force. A proposal was pushed through Congress on October 30. The first vessels were a fleet of small craft brought together from various private sources during the siege of Boston (Chapter 11, "The Battle for Boston"). These managed to bring in 35 British supply vessels with valuable cargo and supplies. Congress's resolution authorized the construction of 13 frigates. By the end of the war, the United States Navy had had 53 ships in service—though not all survived the war.

The national navy competed for resources with state navies—11 states had their own navies—and with privateers and commerce raiders, which, with government authorization, preyed upon British shipping. The privateers, as we will see, performed a valuable service, but typical of the state navies' history was the 1779 expedition of the Massachusetts navy. This force consisted of 19 armed vessels, 20 troop transports, and 3,000 soldiers, and it was sent to Maine's Penobscot Bay. At the time, Maine was part of Massachusetts, and Penobscot Bay was known to be a haven for loyalists who had been driven out of Boston. The state navy commanders, like those heading many state militias, were amateurs.

At Penobscot Bay, the men who disembarked from the transports were unable to penetrate the loyalist fort, and the British had ample time to assemble a rescue fleet of 64 vessels. Overwhelmed, Massachusetts lost all of its vessels, either sunk by enemy fire or purposely scuttled to prevent capture. The Massachusetts treasury was put into the red to the tune of some $7,000,000, which nearly knocked that state out of the war.

# A Maiden Battle and a Bahamian Cruise

Despite its many problems, had the Royal Navy acted quickly, it might have crushed the Revolution. To be sure, it was a Goliath. And, in the makeshift American navy, it met a would-be David.

295

## The Massachusetts Navy Gets a Ship

On June 2, 1775, the British schooner *Margaretta* (four guns) and two sloops, the *Polly* and the *Unity*, entered Machias, a port in Maine, with the purpose of collecting timber for the British garrison in Boston. Local patriots hit upon the idea of capturing the vessels, not by catching them at sea, but in church. Learning that the pious crew of the *Margaretta* would be at worship on Sunday, June 11, the patriots rushed the chapel to capture them. The Brits, however, were not too lost in prayer to notice the attack and escape through the church windows. They ran from the chapel and down to their ship.

**Fightin' Words**

A **prize ship** is one that has been captured and, usually, put into service by the victors.

The patriots didn't give up. Taking to the few boats they had, about 40 volunteers pursued the *Margaretta*, and, after a skirmish, captured it and the *Unity* over the next two days. *Margaretta* was rechristened *Liberty*, and, a few weeks later, under the command of Jeremiah O'Brien, the *prize ship* captured the schooner *Diligent*, also off the coast of Machias. *Liberty* and *Diligent* became the first two ships of the Massachusetts navy.

## The Nassau Campaign

The action off Machias was on a small scale and was the work of locals. During March 3–4, 1776, the newly created Continental navy carried out its first—and only—*planned* major naval operation in the war.

Esek Hopkins, a Rhode Island farm boy turned sailor, was put in command of the first squadron of the ragtag navy. He surprised British forces on Nassau—then called Providence or New Providence—by landing a force of U.S. Marines in *their* first action of the war, an assault on Fort Montagu. Short and sharp, the raid not only took the fort, but netted 100 cannon and mortar—and captured the governor of the island, Monfort Browne. In a later prisoner exchange, Browne was swapped for an American officer and went on to command a unit of loyalists.

# The Exploits of John Paul Jones

Esek Hopkins commanded eight vessels, the largest of which were two merchant ships converted into small frigates of 24 and 20 guns. His officers included four men of the rank of captain, Dudley Saltonstall, Abraham Whipple, Nicholas Biddle, and John B. Hopkins, and a roster of young lieutenants, among them a young man named John Paul Jones.

Born John Paul in Scotland in 1747, the son of a Scottish squire's gardener, the youth was apprenticed to a shipowner. On his first voyage, Paul visited his brother, a tailor in Fredericksburg, Virginia. When his master went bankrupt, Paul was released from his apprenticeship and shipped aboard a slave ship. At 19, he became first mate on another slaver. But the young mariner was soon disgusted by the trade in human beings and booked passage for England. On the way home, the captain and mate of the ship on which he was a passenger took sick and died of a fever. Paul assumed command. For bringing the ship safely back to port, he was given a generous portion of the cargo as a reward, and he was immediately hired as captain of the *John*, out of Dumfries, Scotland.

Paul made two voyages to the West Indies. On the second, he flogged the ship's carpenter for neglect of duty. It was a common punishment of the day, but, this time, the victim died. The man's father charged Paul with murder; he was imprisoned briefly, tried, and acquitted. Back in the West Indies in 1773, as captain of the *Betsy*, out of London, Paul killed the ringleader of a mutiny that developed among his crew. Witnesses reported that the man actually impaled himself on Paul's sword when he rushed the captain.

Friends advised him to flee to America until a military court-martial could be convened, which would give him a more sympathetic trial than a civilian court. In America, Paul assumed the name Jones—John Paul Jones—and lived on the charity of friends. When the Revolution broke out, he went to Philadelphia to help fit out the *Alfred*, first of the vessels purchased by Congress. He got to know leaders of the Continental navy and, on December 7, 1775, secured appointment as first lieutenant aboard the *Alfred*, serving under Capt. Saltonstall. All thoughts of returning to the West Indies for a court-martial were forgotten.

On April 6, 1776, just a little over a month after his triumph at Nassau, Esek Hopkins was leading five Continental ships back from the West Indies when the 20-gun British frigate *Glasgow* attacked the flotilla around midnight, off Block Island, New York. *Glasgow* inflicted 24 casualties, severely disabled the *Alfred*, and handily escaped.

The American fleet began to fall apart. Officers and crew took up privateering or simply left the service. Hopkins, whose action in Nassau showed him to be an able seafarer, was no great leader, and he was censured by Congress. When the inactive fleet was blockaded by the British in December 1776, his subordinates complained to Congress of his incompetence, and Hopkins was relieved of command.

If anything good came out of the *Glasgow* encounter, it was the court martial of the captain of the *Providence*, for cowardice, and his replacement by Jones. Although the Scotsman was the most junior of the new navy's captains, he soon racked up a record unmatched by any other Continental officer. Given command of the *Providence* and a small flotilla, he captured or sunk 21 British warships, transports, and commercial vessels, as well as one loyalist privateer by the end of 1776.

**Fightin' Words**

**Spiking a cannon**—driving a spike through the barrel—rendered the gun inoperative beyond repair. It was a quick way of disarming an enemy.

## Aboard the Ranger

Jones had a streak of arrogance equal to his dash and skill. He was not popular with his brother officers, and he did not quietly acquiesce to being deemed junior to 17 other captains. Congress did not want to offend the other officers, but also was well aware of Jones's prowess. Accordingly, on June 14, 1777, he was given command of the sloop *Ranger* and was ordered to France to take command of the frigate *Indien*, which was being built in Amsterdam for the Continental navy. When he arrived in December, he found that the ship had been given to France by the American treaty commissioners, so he continued to sail in *Ranger*, leaving Brest on April 10, 1778, with a crew of 140.

During April 27–28, 1778, Jones raided Whitehaven on the Solway Firth in Scotland, *spiking* the guns of two forts and burning three British ships. Jones was unable to carry out his even more ambitious plan of burning all the ships in the harbor, but he had succeeded in carrying out the only American operation on British soil.

Jones's intention next was to kidnap the Earl of Selkirk and hold him hostage to assure good treatment for American prisoners of war, but Selkirk was not at home when the captain called. Undaunted, Jones crossed the Irish Sea to Carrickfergus, where he captured the British sloop *Drake* in a short, sharp action. He lost eight men killed or wounded, but inflicted 40 casualties on the British. By the time he returned to Brest, on May 8, he had seven prizes and a good many prisoners.

**Fightin' Words**

An **East Indiaman** was a merchant sailing ship specifically built for the long-haul trade with India (called East India to distinguish it from the Carribean islands of the West Indies).

**Fightin' Words**

**Convoying** is the grouping together of merchant vessels and/or troop transports with warships in order to protect the unarmed ships.

## Master of the Bonhomme Richard

In the summer of 1779, the French prepared five naval vessels and two privateers for Jones to lead, using a refitted *East Indiaman* called the *Duras*. At this time, the only American more popular among the French than John Paul Jones was Benjamin Franklin, whose *Poor Richard's Almanac* was eagerly read in the court of Louis XVI. With the court's enthusiastic approval, Jones renamed his new flagship *Bonhomme Richard*—the Good Man Richard.

The French court may have adored John Paul Jones, but the French naval officers who commanded most of the ships of the small flotilla Jones led resented the American upstart's authority. Nevertheless, in a sweeping voyage clockwise around the British Isles, Jones captured 17 vessels.

On September 23, 1779, off Flamborough Head, along the York coast, in the North Sea, Jones sighted two warships *convoying* 40 British merchant vessels. The warships were the 44-gun *Serapis* and the 20-gun *Countess of Scarborough*.

Now, the *Bonhomme Richard* was, in truth, not a very "good man" at all. It was a converted cargo vessel, not built as a warship. It was slow, not very seaworthy, and it mounted only 42 guns. Nevertheless, Jones decided to pursue *Serapis* while his three other vessels, *Vengeance, Pallas,* and *Alliance,* chased the *Countess.*

In the opening moments of this moonlit battle, two of Jones's largest cannon exploded, so that he was critically outgunned. But Jones hadn't lost his nerve or his superior seamanship. He outmaneuvered *Serapis,* and rammed her stern. Because this put *Bonhomme Richard* in a position from which none of her guns could be brought to bear, the captain of the *Serapis* called out: "Has your ship struck?"—meaning "struck colors," lowered its flag, surrendered. Jones replied with one of the most famous utterances in American history: "I have not yet begun to fight."

### Voices of Liberty

"I have not yet begun to fight."

—John Paul Jones, on being asked to surrender to HMS *Serapis,* September 23, 1779

### We Hold These Truths

After the fight with the *Serapis,* one of the most famous naval engagements in history, Jones made it to Texel, Holland, having left the badly crippled *Bonhomme Richard* at sea. It sank on September 25. Jones turned over his remaining vessels, except the *Alliance,* to the French. As captain of the *Alliance,* he continued to harass British shipping. In December 1780, as skipper of the *Ariel,* a French military transport, he returned to America, capturing the British ship *Triumph* along the way. (It subsequently escaped.)

On his return to the States, jealous brother officers blocked Jones's promotion to rear admiral, but he was given command of the largest ship in the Continental navy, the *America,* only to learn a year later that it was to be turned over to the French. Jones sailed with the French fleet until the end of the war.

After the Revolution, John Paul Jones went to Russia to serve Catherine the Great in her war against the Turks. Although successful, he again confronted jealous colleagues, and he returned to Paris in 1789, disappointed and broken in health. He died in 1793. Not until 1905 were his remains returned to the United States, where they were entombed, in 1913, at the naval academy in Annapolis, Maryland.

At this, the vessels separated, and *Serapis* now collided with *Bonhomme Richard*. Jones lashed on, tying the British vessel to his, then pounded it at pointblank range with his cannon. After two hours, it was *Serapis* that struck her colors.

# France Gains the Upper Hand

As we saw in Chapter 19, "Valley Forge," the early actions of the French fleet in the American Revolution were failures. Nevertheless, the French navy was a formidable asset. It had suffered badly in the Seven Years' War (the French and Indian War), but was rebuilt in a crash program that produced some beautifully designed warships. This was in dramatic contrast to the Royal Navy, which had gone into steep decline after the Seven Years' War.

## *Rodney's Moonlight Battle*

Because Adm. D'Estaing repeatedly fumbled and delayed, French engagements in American waters were either inconclusive or outright failures until 1781. Action elsewhere, however, was often more decisive.

George Brydges Rodney became a British naval hero during the Seven Years' War, but made an enemy of the corrupt Lord Sandwich, first sea lord. As a result, he was not given a command until 1779, when he was 61 years old and plagued by gout. More-over, the position he accepted, as commander in chief of the Leeward Islands in the West Indies, was one no other admiral would even consider. Rodney was instructed to relieve a Spanish siege against Gibraltar on his way to the West Indies. This he did, in a brilliant moonlight battle on January 16, 1781, in which he not only succeeded in temporarily relieving Gibraltar, but sank or captured seven Spanish warships.

## *French Successes*

Rodney was a national hero. Then something seemed to go wrong with him. On February 3, 1781, he captured the island of St. Eustatius, a possession of Holland, England's newest enemy in this revolution-turned-world war. He confiscated a rich treasure there, confident that, according to the law of the sea, a substantial portion of it would become his. He had forgotten that most of these riches had been taken by the Dutch from British merchants. Rodney soon saw his dream of fortune shattered under a hail of lawsuits in the British courts.

More immediately, his preoccupation with St. Eustatius kept him from making a scheduled rendezvous with Adm. Samuel Hood, who was blocking Fort Royal off Martinique. As a result, the French fleet succeeded in driving Hood off. It was a pattern that repeatedly frustrated English seapower in the Revolution. The British advocated offensive tactics at any cost. The

**Voices of Liberty**

"I require obedience only, I don't want advice."

—British admiral G. B. Rodney on the subject of consulting his subordinates

French believed in a strong defense. While most French commanders were inferior to their British counterparts, their defensive tactics repeatedly frustrated the British. Much energy was expended in a seesaw war in the West Indies. In 1778 and 1779, French naval victories seized the islands of Dominica, St. Vincent, and Grenada, while St. Lucia fell to the British. In 1781, Tobago became French as well.

In the meantime, another French admiral, Pierre André Suffren de Saint Tropez, was scoring French naval victories in far-flung theaters of the war, off the coast of the Portuguese-held Cape Verde Islands and off the coast of India. Adm. François Joseph Paul, comte De Grasse, having tangled with Rodney and other British commanders in a series of indecisive battles, sailed home in poor health in October 1780, but returned in 1781, with *discretionary orders* to assist George Washington and Rochambeau in the Yorktown campaign. In this momentous action, as we will see in Chapter 25, "Yorktown: 'A Most Glorious Day,'" the French fleet at long last realized its full promise in the American Revolution.

### Fightin' Words

In an age in which there was no easy way to communicate with commanders at sea, officers were often given **discretionary orders,** very general instructions to accomplish some particular objective or set of objectives by whatever means and to whatever extent they deemed possible.

## England Regains the Upper Hand—Too Late

The Royal Navy would suffer its most decisive defeat of the war against De Grasse at Yorktown; however, it recovered some of its lost luster when Adm. Rodney returned to command in the West Indies. Rodney had returned to England, broken in health. A British patriot, he rallied, recovering to rejoin Hood in the Indies on February 19, 1782. In a major battle off Saints Passage during April 9–12—after De Grasse triumphed at Yorktown—Rodney captured the French admiral aboard his sumptuous flagship, the *Ville de Paris*.

This triumph was somewhat diluted, however, by the aging British admiral's failure to press the chase of the French fleet. Hood, Rodney's ever-frustrated subordinate, believed that at least 20 French ships could have been taken, and the French fleet thereby utterly broken. Still, even following this disappointment and the earlier disaster at Yorktown, the British could console themselves with the action at Gibraltar, six months later, in which Adm. Howe, called out of retirement, had decisively ended Spain's three-year siege of Gibraltar. While this victory came too late to affect the outcome of the Revolution, it did mean that Britain could assume its place with dignity and honor at the peace conference in Paris, which would end the war.

# Reign of the Privateers

Naval power was important in the American Revolution, but it was never the decisive factor the British might have made it. In the end, perhaps the most effective use of seapower was not exercised by national navies, but by privateers.

Most of the states issued bundles of *letters of marque and reprisal*. In all, anywhere from 1,200 to 2,000 privateers went out to sea—a huge force motivated by the promise of prizes. Commissioned by the states to capture British merchant shipping, thereby cutting off British supplies while appropriating them for the patriot cause, the privateers were allotted substantial portions of whatever they took.

During the war, some 600 British ships fell prey to privateers—far more than the Continental navy did or could have done. Nevertheless, some historians have questioned how much of a boon this really was to the Revolution; for privateers also sapped resources that might have been even more effectively employed by a large national navy under central command. This issue may be debated endlessly. One thing is certain, however. British commerce was badly damaged by the privateers, and, as influential Britishers were repeatedly hit in the pocketbook, support for prosecuting the war against the rebels steadily eroded. Whether or not the privateers compromised the effectiveness of a national navy, they certainly helped bring the war to a successful close.

### Fightin' Words

**Letters of marque and reprisal** were documents in effect authorizing piracy on behalf of one belligerent nation against another. The captain in possession of such documents could not legally be prosecuted for piracy.

---

## The Least You Need to Know

➤ The Royal Navy, while large, was also in poor condition during most of the Revolution.

➤ The fledgling Continental navy had to compete for resources with 11 state navies and as many as 2,000 privateers.

➤ The single most spectacular sailor of the Revolution—on either side—was John Paul Jones, whose record of enemy prizes taken has never been equaled.

➤ The British were repeatedly frustrated by the French navy's strong defensive tactics and did not gain the upper hand at sea until 1781, by which time the Battle of Yorktown had been lost and the outcome of the Revolution almost certainly determined.

# Backcountry Battles

Early in the Revolution, during 1775–76, patriot forces either gained or maintained control in the South, and, for the most part, 1777 came and went as a quiet year in the Southern theater. The quiet was shattered in 1778, when Maj. Gen. Robert Howe (no relation to the British general and admiral) took command of patriot operations in the South. His plan to capture St. Augustine, Florida, disintegrated when militia commanders refused to cooperate. As we saw in Chapter 21, "Southern Exposure" the British were able to mount countermoves that resulted in the fall of Savannah. From this point on, the South became a very bitterly contested theater of combat.

## Seasons of Failure

In September 1778, the Americans replaced Howe in the South with Maj. Gen. Benjamin Lincoln. A courageous and energetic officer, Lincoln was not a brilliant tactician. His attempt to retake Georgia from the British failed in 1779. As described in Chapter 21, autumn of 1779 brought another patriot failure, when the Franco-American amphibious attempt to retake Savannah fizzled.

# Massacre at Waxhaws

The year 1780 brought yet more American defeats in the South. The British forces in America had few aggressive leaders, but one exception was Banastre Tarleton, who had participated in the capture of Gen. Charles Lee at Basking Ridge, New Jersey, in December 1776 (Chapter 20, "White War, Red War") and, from that point, was steadily promoted.

Tarleton came into greatest prominence during the Charleston Campaign of 1780. As covered in Chapter 21, the patriots lost Charleston, South Carolina, and Lincoln surrendered his army during this action. The fall of this great southern port city was devastating, but Tarleton understood that it hardly wiped out rebel resistance in the Carolinas. He was assigned to mop up patriot forces in the countryside. Monck's Corner (April 14, 1780) was Tarleton's first victory, resulting in a major defeat for Gen. Isaac Huger. Next came the Battle of Lenud's Ferry, South Carolina, on May 6, an action against survivors of Monck's Corner and fresh troops under Col. Anthony White. White had captured an officer and 17 men of Tarleton's command, but was in turn surprised by a sudden cavalry charge Tarleton led. Not only were the prisoners liberated, but five American officers and 36 men were killed or wounded, and seven officers and 60 dragoons were captured.

Abraham Buford's 3rd Virginia Continentals, about 300 men, were marching to reinforce Charleston during Clinton's siege against the city. The city fell before Buford reached it, and this American commander now found himself leading the only substantial body of organized American troops remaining in South Carolina. Gen. Charles Cornwallis, having taken Charleston, was determined to wipe out all insurrection in South Carolina, and he ordered Tarleton (and others) to pursue Buford's unit. Learning that Buford had halted at Waxhaw Creek to rest, Tarleton galloped to intercept with 40 men of the 17th Dragoons, 130 cavalry, and 100 infantry, mostly Tories of the Loyal Legion. For the sake of speed, many of the infantrymen rode double with the cavalry, and, in the Carolina heat of late May, this proved fatal to many of the horses. Tarleton stole replacement mounts and pressed on.

By the early afternoon of May 29, Tarleton reached the tail end of Buford's column, having ridden 105 steamy wilderness miles in 54 hours. Tarleton sent an emissary to Buford under a flag of truce. He exaggerated his numbers and demanded immediate surrender. "If you are rash enough to reject the terms," Tarleton wrote in his note, "the blood be upon your head." Buford replied: "I reject your proposals and shall defend myself to the last extremity."

Tarleton then attacked swiftly and savagely. Buford's forces were strung out in weak defensive positions. Officers ordered men to hold fire until the British and

**Sites and Sights**

Lenud's Ferry is located where U.S. 17 now crosses the Santee River. It may be difficult to identify because it is often spelled Lenew or Laneau. Of Huguenot origin, Lenud is pronounced *Le-noo*.

loyalist forces were within 10 paces—a disastrous tactic when the defensive line is thin, because a few men cannot deliver sufficient firepower to prevent being overrun. Overrun the Americans soon were, and Buford hoisted a white flag to ask for quarter.

After the battle, patriot propagandists spread the story that Tarleton had ordered the massacre of Buford's men after they surrendered. Although the fighting was fierce and Buford's losses severe, this tale is probably untrue. However, many South Carolinians believed it, and the phrase "Tarleton's quarter!" (meaning no quarter at all) became a battle cry of the patriots, on occasion inspiring atrocities against loyalists.

Meanwhile, the surrender of Charleston, and the submission of most of South Carolina's leaders to the British (many members of the former state government took oaths of loyalty to King George) temporarily put an end to patriot resistance in South Carolina.

### Voices of Liberty

"This bloody day only wanted the war dance and roasting fire to have placed it first in the records of torture and death in the West."

—"Lighthorse Harry" Lee, commenting on the Waxhaws Massacre, 1780

*Lighthorse Harry Lee.* (Image from the National Archives)

# Camden Disaster

After Gen. Lincoln's capture, George Washington nominated the capable Nathanael Greene as his replacement, but the Continental Congress overrode the commander in chief and put in overall command of the South the man who had been given credit for the victory at Saratoga, Gen. Horatio Gates.

Gates marched against Camden, South Carolina, held by 2,200 troops under Lord Cornwallis's personal command. Along the way, Gates acquired militia reinforcements to augment his Continentals, amassing a force of 4,100. Through wishful counting, Gates persuaded himself that he had not 4,100 men, but 7,000. Moreover, Gates dismissed his officers' warning that many of the men were sickly, so that only half were fit and ready to fight, with the remark that "there are enough for our purposes."

Then Gates made his men even sicker. Lacking the rum ration that eighteenth-century officers believed indispensable to the smooth functioning of an army, Gates ordered a distribution of molasses as a substitute. This, combined with generally bad food, created a sudden, urgent epidemic of dysentery among the ranks. By nightfall of August 15, 1780, Gates's men were "much debilitated." Nevertheless, the general ordered a nighttime march to Camden. By coincidence, Cornwallis had ordered his troops out of that town to search for the Americans. The two armies met at about 2:30 on the morning of August 16.

## We Hold These Truths

A Congressional inquiry in 1782 cleared Horatio Gates of wrongdoing, accepting his claim that his reason for departing the field had been to reach safety so that he could rebuild his army. Whether prudence or cowardice, the flight of the 52-year-old general from Camden to Hillsboro, 180 miles in three days, was truly remarkable. He made the first leg of the journey, 60 miles to Charlotte, on the fastest horse he could find. The rest of the trip was made on a relay of mounts.

The defeat at Camden effectively ended Gates's career, although he was permitted to rejoin the army at Newburgh, New York, for the final days of the war.

Despite the condition of Gates's men, he enjoyed an advantageous position, but taking no chances personally, he withdrew to the rear, leaving other officers, including Baron De Kalb, in charge. De Kalb's skill, however, had little effect on the sickly Virginia and

North Carolina militiamen of the left flank, who panicked and caved at the first British onslaught. The American right wing, manned by seasoned Maryland and Delaware troops, ignored the panic on the left and stood their ground. But after the two American officers, Ortho Williams and De Kalb were wounded—De Kalb fatally—the situation turned hopeless, becoming a terrible rout.

Of 4,100 American troops engaged, only 700 reached the safety of Hillsboro three days later. As many as 1,900 Americans died, and nearly 1,000 were taken prisoner. British losses, by comparison, were light: 68 killed, 350 wounded. Horatio Gates had fled the field after the collapse of his left wing.

# King's Mountain and Cowpens

Lord Cornwallis left Camden on September 8, 1780, having driven the American army from South Carolina. His objective now was North Carolina, and he moved northward in three columns. While he took the main force, Tarleton headed up the British Legion and the regular light infantry, and Maj. Patrick Ferguson led the Tories.

In North Carolina, the British met stiff resistance from diehard patriots. They took Charlotte, North Carolina, on September 26, 1780, but, in the process, suffered substantial losses inflicted by patriot militia under Col. William Davie. Having taken Charlotte, Cornwallis found it tough to maintain communication with his base in Camden. His supply lines were continually subject to patriot attack, as were *foraging parties*. The war in the Carolinas, like the war in New Jersey, New York, and other northern states, was dissolving into a series of local feuds between patriot and Tory neighbors.

**Fightin' Words**

**Foraging parties** were small groups of soldiers sent to find food and other supplies in the field. Even well-supplied armies tried as much as possible to live off the land.

In an effort to recruit into the regular British army some of the many Tories who were undertaking guerrilla activities against their patriot neighbors, Cornwallis assigned Ferguson to lead the Tories along the foothills. Observing this, a group of patriot militia leaders, colonels Charles McDowell, John Sevier, Isaac Shelby, William Campbell, and Benjamin Cleveland, attacked Ferguson, who retreated to the Catawba River and then up King's Mountain, on the border between North and South Carolina.

Here Ferguson took his stand on October 7—and was completely surrounded by the patriot forces. Ferguson was slain in the act of killing an American officer. The Tory force surrendered, having lost 400 killed and wounded. The patriots suffered 88 casualties. Seven hundred Tories became prisoners, 12 of them summarily hanged for British executions of Tory deserters who had taken up arms against their former comrades. For the Americans, King's Mountain was a gloriously welcome triumph on the heels of a string of disasters. Cornwallis's advance was not only stopped, the British general pulled his troops back into South Carolina. Even more important, the battle ended Tory influence in North Carolina once and for all.

There was more good news for the patriots in the South. After the failures of Lincoln and Gates, Washington at last succeeded in appointing Gen. Nathanael Greene to overall command of the region. If anyone could salvage the South, Washington believed, it was Greene, a commander at home with conventional military forces as well as guerillas.

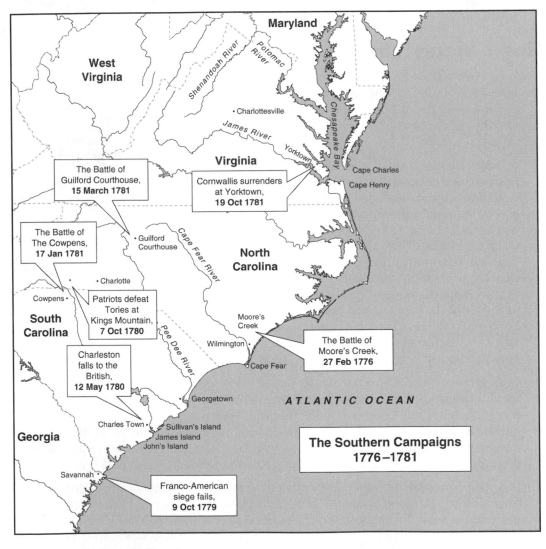

*Southern campaigns and battles.*
(Map by Kevin D. Smith)

Appointed to command in October, Greene did not reach the field until December 1780. In the interim, South Carolina *partisans* continually harried the British forces. Cornwallis relied on Tarleton to handle the guerrillas, even though he did so with ever-decreasing effectiveness.

Part of Greene's competence as a leader was knowing when *not* to make changes. Arriving in the theater of operations, he recognized that Cornwallis outnumbered him and that, therefore, it was best to pursue the guerrilla tactics that had proven effective so far. The best guerrilla leader Greene knew of was Daniel Morgan, a man some historians have deemed the only military genius to emerge from the Revolution. Greene assigned Morgan to harass British positions in the western wilderness of South Carolina while Greene himself supported the operation of partisans in the north-central portion of the state.

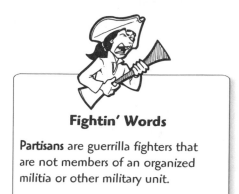

**Fightin' Words**

**Partisans** are guerrilla fighters that are not members of an organized militia or other military unit.

*Daniel Morgan, engraved from a painting by Alonzo Chappel.*
(Image from the National Archives)

But Morgan did more than merely harass. Recognizing that Greene had divided his forces, Cornwallis dispatched Tarleton to take care of Morgan while he personally led an attack on Greene. On January 16, 1781, Morgan, commanding 1,000 men, learned that Tarleton was nearby with 1,100 Tories and regulars. Retreat for Morgan was out of the question, because, for militiamen, retreat was an invitation to disband and go home. If there was to be a fight, it would have to be now. Morgan decided to make a stand at the Cowpens, little more than a backwoods South Carolina cattle pasturage, and proceeded to intentionally violate every tenet of military common sense. To begin with, he positioned his men so that the Broad River cut off any retreat. It would be do or die. Second, he put his rawest militiamen in the front line, backing them up with the Continentals and seasoned men from Virginia. Farthest to the rear, he held his cavalry—conventionally, front-line troops—in reserve.

Banastre Tarleton thought that Cowpens would be the perfect place for a bayonet charge, which had so terrified the provincial troops at Camden. Tarleton had not counted on the genius of Morgan, who had positioned his men perfectly and had coached them well. "Look for the epaulets!" he had commanded his riflemen, describing just when to fire on an advancing line. "Pick off the epaulets!" After firing in this manner, the American front line, the green recruits, sheared off to the left and around to the rear. Now the British moved against the second line, the seasoned men. Tarleton's troops were overconfident and attacked in very poor order. This was a blunder, and, in a brilliant action, Morgan ordered his green troops, who had returned to the American rear, to swing out and behind Tarleton's left while he put his cavalry into motion at last, around to rear of Tarleton's right.

It was a classic double envelopment. Deep in the southern wilderness, Morgan had emulated the tactics the great Carthaginian general Hannibal had used to defeat the Romans in 216 B.C. But it was, of course, more than a classical victory. Cowpens saved half of Greene's army and cost Cornwallis 100 killed, 229 wounded (and captured), and 600 captured (unwounded). Particularly hard hit were the British officers; of 66 engaged, 39 died. American losses, in contrast, were 12 killed and 60 wounded. Moreover, Morgan's victory had pulled the American forces from the brink of dissolution and despair. From this point, patriot fortunes in the South turned upward, and the myth of invincibility that had gathered around Banastre Tarleton was shattered.

# Exploits of the Swamp Fox

Daniel Morgan may or may not have been the only military genius the Revolution produced, but he was not the only effective guerilla leader among the southern patriots. Francis Marion, grandson of fiercely independent Huguenots who had settled in South Carolina as early as 1690, was "small enough at birth to be put into a quart mug." Indeed, he grew up sickly and frail, and was always short and slight—anything but the figure of a military man.

By 1761, he was active in the local militia fighting Indians, and in 1775 he was active in patriot politics, as a delegate to the South Carolina Provincial Congress. Named captain of the 2nd South Carolina Regiment in June 1775, he took part in the defense of Charleston the following year and was promoted to major and then lieutenant colonel.

Marion fought gallantly in two American disasters, the ill-fated defense of Savannah and the disastrous Battle of Camden. In the first, he led his regiment in a spectacular but unsuccessful assault. At Camden, he provided a ray of hope in a hopeless battle. On August 20, 1780, following the American defeat, a detachment of Tories and British regulars escorting a large number of American prisoners was hit fast and hard by men who suddenly materialized out of the swamp. The attack came so swiftly that the Tory and British soldiers released their prisoners and ran, assuming they were about to fall prey to a major force. In truth, it was diminutive Francis Marion at the head of no more than 17 men. By this time, Tories and patriots alike were calling him the Swamp Fox.

## Tearcoat Swamp

The action at Tearcoat Swamp (in South Carolina, near where present-day U.S. 301 crosses the Black River) is vintage Swamp Fox action. By this time, Marion had managed to recruit 150 men, which he deployed against a Tory militia on the night of October 25, 1780. Surprise, as usual, was total. Marion and his men simply appeared out of the swamp and routed the Tories, leaving three dead, 14 wounded, and taking 23 prisoners, together with 80 horses.

The action was sufficiently dramatic to put down a Tory uprising—and convert a good many Tories impressed by the Swamp Fox to the patriot cause.

## Halfway Swamp

In the "Battle" of Halfway Swamp, December 12–13, 1780, Marion and an uncharacteristically large force of 700 mounted men descended upon a British column escorting recruits from Charleston to Winnsboro.

The British lines began to cave when their commander, Maj. Robert McLeroth, sent a message under a flag of truce, protesting the manner in which Marion's snipers picked off *pickets*.

The Swamp Fox coolly replied that he would shoot pickets as long as the British burned houses. McLeroth had also dared Marion to come out and fight in the open. To this challenge, the Swamp Fox replied: "If Major McLeroth wishes to see mortal combat between teams of twenty men picked by each side, I will gratify him."

It was an incredible moment, and both sides chose their champions. The contest was called off by the British officers, however, who ordered their men off the field. In the end, Halfway Swamp was anticlimactic. American militia captain James Coffin had assumed a position with 140 men at a modest homestead called Singleton's Hill. His troops, who had the drop on McLeroth, fired but a single volley—then ran. To the British, this was inexplicable. What they didn't know is that the

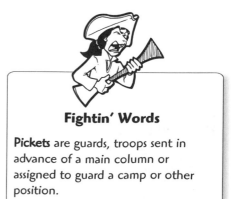

**Fightin' Words**

**Pickets** are guards, troops sent in advance of a main column or assigned to guard a camp or other position.

Americans had learned of the presence of another enemy. The Singleton family were all down with smallpox.

Neither King's Mountain nor Cowpens, nor the guerrilla skirmishes of the "Swamp Fox," were major battles in a military sense, but their combined effect on British public opinion made them crucial in deciding the outcome of the war. The British were growing weary of an expensive worldwide conflict that endangered valuable possessions outside the colonies. Only a quick victory in the Carolinas would convince British policy makers that the war in America was worth fighting.

# A Battle at Guilford Courthouse

Following Cowpens, Cornwallis was hardly idle. He stripped his remaining troops of the baggage that encumbered British armies in the American wilderness: wagons, tents, certain provisions. Supplies were restricted to what the men could carry on their backs. Thus streamlined, Cornwallis pursued Greene's army northward, all the way to the Dan River, near the Virginia border.

Once across, Greene took all the boats with him. Cornwallis found himself on the near shore of the river, desperately low on supplies. He returned to Hillsboro for resupply. In the meantime, Greene assumed the initiative. He recrossed the Dan into North Carolina and harassed Cornwallis's lines of communication. Yet Greene was careful to avoid an all-out action until he had assembled enough men. In the meantime, operations against local Tories—including a massacre of 400 of them by Gen. Andrew Pickens—largely deprived the British general of his base of loyalist support.

At last, on March 14, 1781, Greene picked his battle site: Guilford Courthouse, North Carolina. He aimed to duplicate the success of Daniel Morgan at the Cowpens, so he put his greenest troops up front, with the more seasoned veterans backing them up. The battle commenced the next day, with Greene ordering the frontline militia to fire two volleys before withdrawing to the rear.

Unfortunately, the militia, having discharged its volleys, did not retire in an orderly fashion, but rushed back chaotically. This prevented their getting into position for the envelopment Morgan had pulled off at the Cowpens. Nevertheless, had Greene now launched his cavalry, running it around the rear of the British positions, he might have still forced the surrender of Cornwallis' army. But it didn't happen that way. An able general, Greene lacked Morgan's willingness to gamble. He did not want to risk his cavalry in a single bold stroke. This provided Cornwallis the opportunity to retaliate. He raked the enemy with grapeshot, managing to kill not only American soldiers, but many of his own men as well. Guilford Courthouse ended in a technical victory for the British, in the sense that Cornwallis had not been driven from the field. Yet the battle cost him a fourth of his army, and he decided to vacate the interior of North Carolina.

Continuing patriot resistance, manifested in the battles of late 1780 and early 1781, made it doubtful that the Carolinas would be quickly subdued. In many ways, the political consequences of these battles were more important than their military importance. Given time, Cornwallis could have crushed patriot resistance. Yet the British public would not give him time. Greene knew that if the British commander ventured north into Virginia, he would meet Washington. Rather than pursue, Greene resolved to turn south and reclaim South Carolina and Georgia. Indeed, Cornwallis now marched to Virginia and to battle with the forces of George Washington.

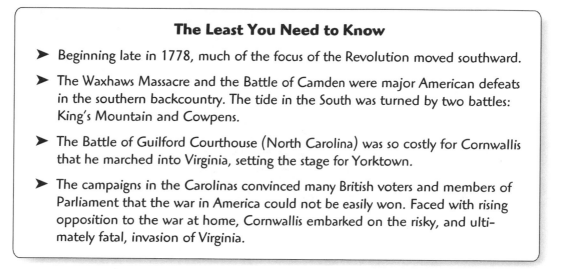

### The Least You Need to Know

➤ Beginning late in 1778, much of the focus of the Revolution moved southward.

➤ The Waxhaws Massacre and the Battle of Camden were major American defeats in the southern backcountry. The tide in the South was turned by two battles: King's Mountain and Cowpens.

➤ The Battle of Guilford Courthouse (North Carolina) was so costly for Cornwallis that he marched into Virginia, setting the stage for Yorktown.

➤ The campaigns in the Carolinas convinced many British voters and members of Parliament that the war in America could not be easily won. Faced with rising opposition to the war at home, Cornwallis embarked on the risky, and ultimately fatal, invasion of Virginia.

# Chapter 25

# Yorktown: "A Most Glorious Day"

## In This Chapter

➤ Benedict Arnold invades Virginia

➤ Lafayette as military leader in Virginia

➤ Cornwallis's plan to conquer Virginia

➤ The siege of Yorktown

➤ The British surrender

Virginia, in the upper South, the state that had given the Revolution so many of its leaders, including George Washington himself, was untouched by the war until 1779, when Lord Dunmore burned Norfolk (Chapter 21, "Southern Exposure"). Later that spring, Vice-Admiral Sir George Collier, of the Royal Navy, took the town of Portsmouth and a few other coastal Virginia settlements, engaged in the looting of some plantations, and appropriated or destroyed a significant number of ships.

Yet, even as late as 1780, the British commanders had a difficult time deciding just how Virginia should fit into their overall strategy for prosecuting the war. Cornwallis believed that gaining control of Virginia would bring the Revolution to an end, and he even asked Clinton to withdraw from New York and concentrate everything against Virginia. It was probably a sound strategy. But Henry Clinton declined to follow Cornwallis's suggestion, although, at the end of 1780, he did at last send a substantial detachment to Virginia.

Its commander was Benedict Arnold.

# Benedict Arnold as a Redcoat

Although he hadn't made good on his promise to deliver West Point, the British did not leave Benedict Arnold in the lurch. He was compensated for property losses and commissioned a brigadier general of the British Army. His overall mission was to raise a legion of Tories and deserters from the patriot forces, and his first assignment was a raid into Virginia.

Arnold set sail from New York on December 20, 1780, with 1,600 men, including John Graves Simcoe and his band of Tory Rangers. Rough weather on the journey down reduced Arnold's effective strength to 1,200 by the time the expedition reached Hampton Roads on December 30. Fortunately for Arnold, Thomas Jefferson, governor of Virginia, was curiously inept as a wartime leader. Despite Washington's repeated warnings that Virginia must urgently prepare to defend itself, Jefferson did little, and Arnold easily captured American ships, sailed up the James, took the *battery* at Hood's Point (January 3, 1781), and then entered Richmond on January 5. The militiamen who were supposed to defend the town fled without firing a shot.

Sending Simcoe and his Rangers to Westham to destroy a foundry and gunpowder factory—as well as public records stored for safekeeping—Arnold burned as much of Richmond as he could, then traveled downriver.

# Steuben and Lafayette in Virginia

Gen. von Steuben now commanded patriot forces in Virginia. Where his Teutonic sternness had been invaluable in holding together the frozen, ragtag army at Valley Forge, in Virginia it was seen as insufferable arrogance. He had a difficult time inspiring his troops. He attempted to ambush Arnold en route to Westover, but was deftly outmaneuvered. Arnold turned on Steuben's forces and neatly routed them. The turncoat then encamped at Portsmouth for the winter.

Yet, as his British superiors saw it, Arnold had not covered himself in glory. He had failed to recruit a credible force of Tories, and, in the spring of 1781, he was replaced by Maj. Gen. William Phillips. Steuben would soon be out of the picture, too, at least temporarily. In June 1781, he turned over his 450 Virginia Continentals to Lafayette and, exhausted and ill from his exertions in the South, took sick leave until he rejoined Washington's forces for the Yorktown siege.

Lafayette had been dispatched by Washington at the start of 1781 to fight Arnold. He took three light infantry regiments from the ranks of New England and New Jersey Continental troops to rendezvous with a French fleet. Because of a British blockade of Newport, Rhode Island, however, the French fleet was delayed and overtaken by a British fleet under Adm. Marriot Arbuthnot. The Battle of Chesapeake Bay, March 16, 1781, was a narrow French victory—but it prompted French admiral Charles-René-Dominique Destouches to abandon the plan to join the Virginia expedition. In the meantime, British commander in chief Clinton was able to ship 2,000 reinforcements to Benedict Arnold—along with Arnold's command replacement, William Phillips.

The failure of yet another Franco-American amphibious operation put the patriot cause in grave peril. Steuben had a handful of Continentals and a miscellany of militia troops, to defend Virginia against the onslaught of 3,000 British regulars and Tory auxiliaries under Phillips and Arnold. Lafayette was at Head of Elk, on the Chesapeake, a full 150 miles from Richmond. As for Washington, he was facing the very real prospect of watching his main army disband for want of food.

In the meantime, Phillips and Arnold conducted a series of destructive raids throughout the state. On April 30, Phillips and Arnold, with 2,500 men, were on the James River, poised to take Richmond. What stopped them was the arrival—just hours earlier—of Lafayette and 1,200 Continentals. With the failure of his countryman to meet him with the fleet, the young Frenchman had moved heaven and earth to reach Richmond by a series of breakneck forced marches.

Turning away from Richmond, then, Phillips and Arnold withdrew to Petersburg to join up with Cornwallis.

### We Hold These Truths

After he was replaced in the South by Gen. William Phillips, Arnold raided his home state of Connecticut, putting 143 buildings to the torch in New London on September 6, 1781. Arnold was never warmly embraced by the British, who simply distrusted a proven traitor. He wasn't very successful raising Loyalist forces, which didn't improve his standing, either. Assigned to recruit 800 men for a "loyal legion," he scraped together a mere 212. In December 1781, Arnold left America for England, settling in London until 1785, when he moved to St. John, New Brunswick, as a merchant shipper and then reentered the West Indies trade.

Ultimately, Benedict Arnold felt himself a man without a country. In his late 50s, he developed what was described as a "nervous disease," to which he succumbed in 1801, aged 60. His wife, Peggy Shippen Arnold, died three years later, at the age of 44.

# Cornwallis Arrives

In truth, Cornwallis wasn't supposed to be in Virginia. *He* believed in the central strategic importance of the state, but his superior, Henry Clinton, feared that Washington would mount an all-out attack against New York. Clinton requested that Cornwallis return most of his army to New York. Instead, Cornwallis set his sights on destroying Lafayette and his small army.

## Chasing Lafayette

In his memoirs, Lafayette quoted a remark Cornwallis is supposed to have made in a letter: *"The boy cannot escape me."* While many historians doubt that Cornwallis ever wrote those words, he had reason to be confident. The forces he gathered in Virginia amounted to 7,200 men by late spring of 1781. Even with various militia units added to his original contingent of Continentals, Lafayette could muster no more than 3,000.

At this time, in Petersburg, Gen. William Phillips suddenly succumbed to typhoid fever. Cornwallis now assumed direct command of all British and Tory forces in Virginia. Recognizing that he greatly outnumbered Lafayette, Cornwallis ordered an advance out of Petersburg and pursued Lafayette northward.

The Frenchman repeatedly eluded the British commander, who finally gave up the chase. He would just let John G. Simcoe and Banastre Tarleton loose on the Virginia countryside, to do to the rebels here what they had done to the rebels in the Carolinas. Why waste energy chasing Lafayette? Instead, he would continue to beat up on Virginia, making use of the British fleet to transport him, at will, to any theater in the state, where he could do even more damage.

Safe for the moment from Cornwallis, Lafayette at last received reinforcements, three Pennsylvania regiments under no less a commander than Mad Anthony Wayne. With 4,500 men—and officers of Wayne's caliber with them—the Frenchman felt ready to make a decisive move. He now turned upon Cornwallis's army, which was traveling down Virginia's York Peninsula. Lafayette sent his army southward by a variety of roads to give the illusion of greater numbers. On June 26, 1781, elements of Pennsylvania and Virginia regiments caught up with Simcoe's Tories—the highly disciplined Queen's Rangers—at a tavern called Spencer's Ordinary. A short, sharp fight developed, in which neither side could claim victory, and the Rangers broke free, leaving their wounded behind in the tavern.

## Ambush at Jamestown Ford

Cornwallis's main body of troops encamped around Williamsburg, where the British commander pondered his next move. Despite Lafayette's ruse, sending his troops down a number of roads, Cornwallis knew that the numbers were with him. But just how would he use this advantage? His hand was at last pushed by the caution of Henry Clinton. The British commander in chief, fearing an imminent American move against New York, ordered Cornwallis to send 3,000 troops to him there immediately. Three thousand troops! Precisely the numerical advantage Cornwallis enjoyed over Lafayette!

The general briefly stewed and fumed, but then he saw an opportunity to transform this order into a final triumph against Lafayette. He moved his entire army out of Williamsburg and to the north bank of the James River and the Jamestown Ford, the place at which the 3,000 troops demanded by his superior would have to cross in order to reach Portsmouth, from which ships would take them to New York. Cornwallis decided to make it appear as if he were, in fact, evacuating Virginia lock, stock, and barrel. He quite shrewdly believed that Lafayette and Wayne would attack when they figured Cornwallis was most vulnerable, with his army in the process of crossing the

James and therefore divided on either side of the river. Thus having used part of his contingent to lure his prey, Cornwallis would attack from ambush and destroy the smaller American force. This accomplished, Virginia would be firmly in British and Loyalist hands.

On July 6, 1781, it did appear that the 23-year-old Frenchman and the older, far more seasoned Wayne had swallowed the bait, as well as the hook, the line, and the sinker. Wayne's men advanced on what they took to be Cornwallis's rearguard, not realizing that the great bulk of the British force was still lying in wait on the north bank.

Had Cornwallis acted immediately, he could have swiftly crushed Wayne's 500-man attacking force. But he held back. He did not know where Lafayette and the rest of the American force were, and he decided to wait for them to show their faces before committing all of his troops. Not content with wiping out Wayne, Cornwallis was determined to destroy Lafayette as well—a blow that would surely end the Virginia campaign.

The Revolution hung in the balance. Watching the action at the ford, Lafayette was about to commit the rest of his troops to the action. But then he became suspicious. Was it only the British rearguard that remained on the north bank of the James? Or were there more troops? Instead of sending in the entire army, he committed only a detachment to reinforce Wayne. This was enough to persuade Cornwallis that

Lafayette was marching boldly into his trap. He ordered his massed troops to come out of hiding and move against what was now 900 Americans. Wayne could see how badly outnumbered he was, but instead of panicking and causing a rout, he boldly ordered a counterattack. This so unnerved the British that the onslaught was checked briefly. It soon resumed, but Wayne was able to effect an orderly retreat. He lost 28 killed, 99 wounded, and 12 missing in action.

Clearly, it was a defeat for the Americans, but hardly the decisive victory Cornwallis had hoped for. Lafayette had had the presence of mind to *preserve* his army, and Wayne the courage to *save* it.

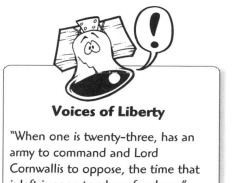

**Voices of Liberty**

"When one is twenty–three, has an army to command and Lord Cornwallis to oppose, the time that is left is none too long for sleep."

—Lafayette, 1781

## On to Yorktown

Cornwallis chose not to pursue the Americans. Instead, he pressed on to Portsmouth, apparently intending to follow Clinton's orders to send troops to New York. But, at this point, the situation became highly confusing as Clinton began to dither. Having ordered troops to New York, he now had second thoughts about abandoning Virginia. On July 8, he changed Cornwallis's orders from Manhattan to Philadelphia. Then, on the 12th, he changed them back to New York. On the 20th, brand-new orders were cut: Cornwallis was to occupy and hold a position in Virginia. His men were to stay where they were.

Clinton ordered Cornwallis to establish himself at Old Point Comfort, on the north shore of Hampton Roads, believing that it would make a good naval base for amphibious operations. Surveying the site, Cornwallis concluded differently and marched instead to Yorktown, a once-bustling, but now quite sleepy, tobacco port on the York River. To secure a means of supply and escape, Gloucester Point, on the opposite bank of the river, also had to be occupied, Cornwallis realized. He committed forces there as well. There was nothing very special about this moribund little tobacco town. Nor did it afford great advantage as a defensive point. There were fortifications, but they weren't very well laid out. The outer works were too close to the inner works to afford space for the most effective defense. Worse, there was no position high enough to provide a commanding field of fire against a siege.

On the plus side, however, Cornwallis had a large force of extremely good soldiers— some of the best in the British army, as well as Tarleton's legion of Tories, and four contingents of German troops. He had a strong artillery presence as well—and the support of the Royal Navy.

# Washington and Rochambeau Talk

Cornwallis was right about at least one thing: Coordination between the army and the navy was the key to victory. Young Lafayette had made the same observation in a letter to the Count de Vergennes, the French foreign minister, in January of 1781: "With a naval inferiority it is impossible to make war in America." Lafayette put the emphasis on the *need* for naval power, while Cornwallis trusted in the *presence* of naval power. He had faith in the invincibility of the Royal Navy, and in placing himself at Yorktown so as to have access to that navy, he also made himself vulnerable to being cut off by an enemy naval force.

*Comte de Rochambeau, French collaborator in Washington's victory at Yorktown.*
(Image from the National Archives)

Of course, the hitherto dismal record of the French fleet in the American Revolution strongly argued that getting cut off in this way was not very likely.

## A Plan Is Made—and Scrapped

George Washington met with Jean Baptiste Donatien de Vimeur, Comte de Rochambeau, at Wethersfield, Connecticut, on May 21, 1781, to plan how the French and American armies would coordinate with the French fleet, under Adm. François Joseph Paul, Comte de Grasse. Washington, like Lafayette, was convinced that sea power would bring success.

The plan arrived at—despite Rochambeau's doubts—was a joint attack against New York (as Henry Clinton had feared), supported by De Grasse. Never thoroughly committed to the plan, Rochambeau left De Grasse the option of operating against the British either at New York or Virginia. This flexibility, in part, caused Washington ultimately to scrap his own plan.

*Comte de Grasse, the French admiral instrumental in the victory at Yorktown.*
(Image from the National Archives)

Early in July, the French army joined the Americans above New York. Initial contact with the enemy, however, persuaded Washington that the British were prepared to defend the city fiercely. Worse, De Grasse decided that the Chesapeake Bay offered the best approach to the mainland from the West Indies. He would not come as far north as New York. It was now clear to Washington that a New York campaign was out of the question. He turned instead to Virginia. With Rochambeau, Washington would reinforce Lafayette and Wayne against Cornwallis while De Grasse would cut off the British commander's seaborne sources of reinforcement, communication, and supply. De Grasse would also land three West Indian regiments for use in the campaign against Cornwallis.

**321**

The plan had excellent prospects for success, provided that the troops could be moved south fast enough and that De Grasse could maintain control of the waters in the vicinity of Chesapeake Bay. Washington was pitted against the clock. For France, the American Revolution was part of a far-flung conflict with England, and De Grasse was under orders to remain in North America no longer than October 15, in part to reach safe haven in advance of the hurricane season. After this date, Washington would not have the support of the French navy. And if the British bottled up the French fleet in and around the Chesapeake, all would be lost. (As it turned out, De Grasse did not return to the West Indies until November.)

There was another big problem. The war had gone on far longer than anyone had expected. The American treasury was all but bone dry. Just as the situation looked bleakest, Rochambeau came to the rescue with an offer to his ally of half his own war chest. By August 21, then, the march to Virginia was on.

Wisely, the two commanders tempered the need for speed with the objective of deceiving Clinton into believing as long as possible that New York remained the allies' target. After crossing the Hudson, Washington and Rochambeau divided their commands into three columns and sent them in a somewhat roundabout path. It would be September before they would start a swift, direct march to Virginia. In the meantime, De Grasse was on his way to support the armies.

## De Grasse at the Battle of the Capes

On September 1, Henry Clinton finally concluded that Washington and Rochambeau were headed to Virginia. British admirals Samuel Graves and Samuel Hood set out from New York to intercept De Grasse's West Indian fleet and a French supporting fleet, under Adm. Jacques-Melchior Saint-Laurent, Comte de Barras, which had left Newport, Rhode Island.

For the first time in its North American campaigns, the French fleet operated with brilliant efficiency. De Grasse beat the British to the Chesapeake, and French cruisers assumed positions in the James River to block Cornwallis, preventing his escape to the south. More French vessels blockaded the mouth of the York River, while the rest of De Grasse's fleet waited for the approach of the Royal Navy at the mouth of the Chesapeake. For the present, Cornwallis was bottled up at Yorktown and could only await the onslaught of Washington and Rochambeau. However, if Adm. Graves acted boldly, he could still smash the French fleet and free Cornwallis.

The two navies made contact on September 5, 1781, in Chesapeake Bay, at the Battle of the Capes. Adm. De Grasse enjoyed the advantage of numbers and firepower. His flagship, *Ville de Paris*, bristled with 110 guns, making it the largest warship afloat at the time. With De Grasse were 24 more ships of the line, mounting anywhere from 64 to 80 guns each, and 6 frigates. To oppose this force, Admirals Graves and Hood had 19 ships of the line and 7 frigates.

Despite an advantage of wind and position, the British were clearly outgunned. To give De Grasse full credit due him, they were also outmaneuvered. The Battle of the Capes began at 4 P.M. and was over by 6 P.M. Graves and Hood withdrew from the Chesapeake and returned to New York, leaving Cornwallis to face his fate alone.

# Yorktown Investment

By September 9, De Barras's fleet arrived to join De Grasse in Chesapeake Bay. With complete control of the bay now secured, De Grasse was able to land additional troops, so that, when the allied forces were all assembled at Williamsburg, they numbered fully 16,000 men. In a war in which combat units were often only a few hundred men, this was indeed a formidable force. Against this onslaught, Cornwallis had some 6,000 men. Tarleton's Legion was posted at Gloucester, while the main force was bottled up within the fortifications of Yorktown.

In preparation for battle, Washington personally greeted all of the principal officers. Major commanders included Lafayette, Wayne, Benjamin Lincoln, and Steuben. Rochambeau led four regiments that had come south from Rhode Island and three De Grasse had brought up from the West Indies. French cavalry, artillery, and marines were also poised for battle. On September 17, Washington and Rochambeau met aboard the *Ville de Paris* to plan the investment—the siege—of Yorktown. The plan was simple: While De Grasse maintained control of the sea, the allies would encircle Yorktown and bombard it, using guns landed by De Grasse's ships. While this went on, allied *engineers* would dig trenches by which to approach the fortifications.

With such an advantage of numbers, it was almost certain that the siege of Yorktown would succeed, if the allies made no gross blunders. However, if Cornwallis could somehow hold out long enough, Washington would lose De Grasse's fleet, leaving the way open for Cornwallis to receive reinforcement by sea or to escape.

### Fightin' Words

**Engineers** in the eighteenth-century military dealt mainly with either building or breaching fortifications; the latter typically involved systematically digging trenches ever closer to the objective. From the cover of these, bombardment could proceed at closer and closer ranges.

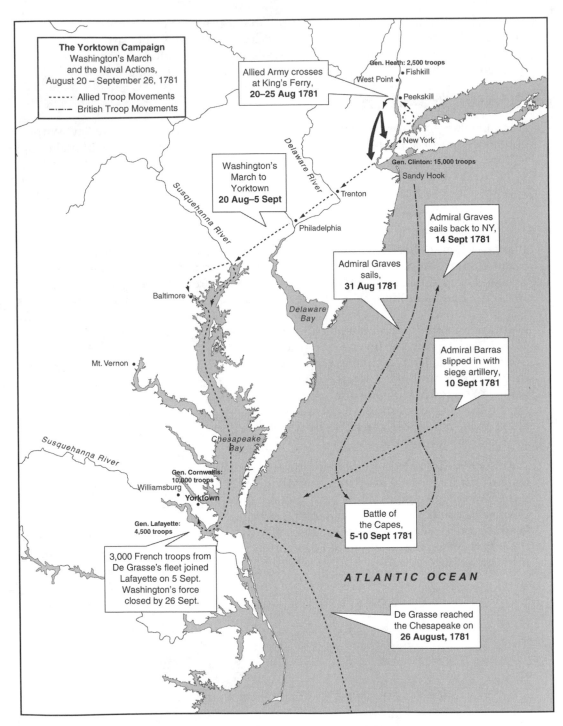

**The Yorktown Campaign**
Washington's March
and the Naval Actions,
August 20 – September 26, 1781

- - - - - Allied Troop Movements
—·—·— British Troop Movements

Allied Army crosses
at King's Ferry,
**20–25 Aug 1781**

Gen. Heath: 2,500 troops
West Point • Fishkill
• Peekskill

New York

Gen. Clinton: 15,000 troops
Sandy Hook

Washington's
March to
Yorktown
**20 Aug–5 Sept**

Delaware River

Trenton

Philadelphia

Admiral Graves
sails back to NY,
**14 Sept 1781**

Admiral Graves
sails,
**31 Aug 1781**

Delaware
Bay

Susquehanna River

Baltimore

Admiral Barras
slipped in with
siege artillery,
**10 Sept 1781**

Mt. Vernon •

Chesapeake
Bay

Susquehanna River

Gen. Cornwallis:
10,000 troops
Williamsburg
**Yorktown**

Gen. Lafayette:
4,500 troops

Battle of
the Capes,
**5-10 Sept 1781**

**ATLANTIC OCEAN**

3,000 French troops from
De Grasse's fleet joined
Lafayette on 5 Sept.
Washington's force
closed by 26 Sept.

De Grasse reached
the Chesapeake on
**26 August, 1781**

*The Yorktown Campaign: operations at sea.*
(Map by Kevin D. Smith)

**324**

# Cornwallis Bagged

On September 30, 1781, Cornwallis ordered the outer works of Yorktown to be abandoned. Determined to wait for relief from the sea, he wanted to conserve his resources. The Allies advanced to occupy the abandoned works, placing artillery on them. Beginning on October 1, 1781, American batteries started pounding Yorktown from these very fortifications.

On October 6, Washington, with an uncharacteristically ceremonial flourish, personally broke ground for the first *approach trench*. Within three days, more artillery was brought forward, and, again in the spirit of ritual, Washington fired the first shot. French and American artillery was so well positioned that it not only bombarded Yorktown proper, it could reach Gloucester Point, and it drove the last two remaining British frigates out of the river.

On October 14, Alexander Hamilton and a French officer led a furious nighttime bayonet attack against defenders of two redoubts near the York River. These objectives secured, the approach trenches were now extended all the way to the river, completely cutting Cornwallis off. In desperation, on October 16, Cornwallis sent out a sortie of 350 men against a line of allied trenches. The defenders of these positions fell back, but the attackers were soon repulsed by French grenadiers.

There was, perhaps, a final hope for Lord Cornwallis: a nighttime breakout across the York River, to Gloucester Point, and then a forced march northward, all the way to New York. The first troops, the Guards and units of light infantry, were sent out in boats. The plan was for them to reach the Gloucester Point side, then send the boats back for more troops. A sudden storm, however, stranded the boats at Gloucester. It was now clear: There would be no escape.

### Voices of Liberty

"If you cannot relieve me very soon, you must be prepared to hear the worst."

—Letter from Lord Cornwallis to Henry Clinton during the siege of Yorktown, September 23, 1781

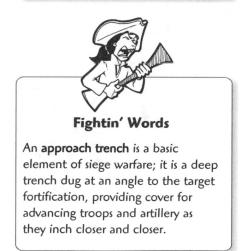

### Fightin' Words

An **approach trench** is a basic element of siege warfare; it is a deep trench dug at an angle to the target fortification, providing cover for advancing troops and artillery as they inch closer and closer.

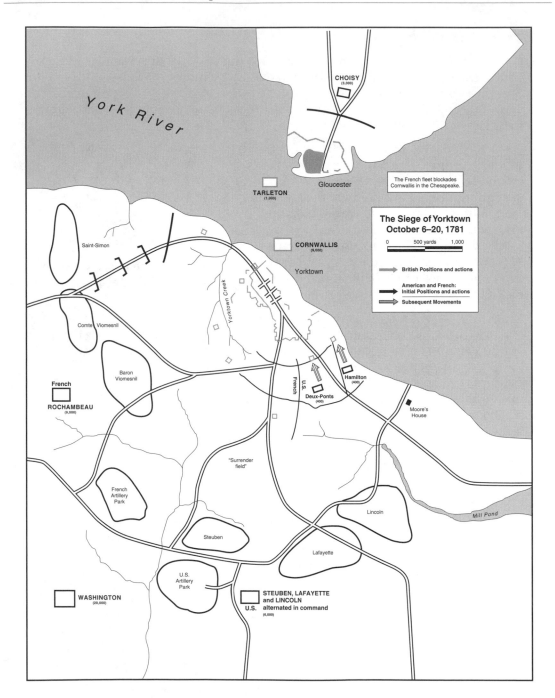

*The Siege of Yorktown.*
(Map by Kevin D. Smith)

## *"The World Turned Upside Down"*

On the morning of October 17, 1781, a Lt. Denny of the Pennsylvania Line surveyed Yorktown from one of the approach trenches. About 10:00, he reported, he had …

> *the pleasure of seeing a drummer mount the enemy's parapet and beat a parley [a signal requesting a truce], and immediately an officer, holding up a white handkerchief, made his appearance outside their works. The drummer accompanied him, beating. Our batteries ceased. An officer from our lines ran and met the other and tied the handkerchief over his eyes. The drummer was sent back, and the British officer conducted to a house in the rear of our lines. Firing ceased totally.*

Washington met the officer's request for an extended armistice to discuss terms of surrender with no more than a two-hour cease-fire, by the end of which he must have Cornwallis' proposal in writing. The British commander produced the proposal, asking for the parole of his troops and their safe conduct to England. Washington replied that nothing short of unconditional surrender would be acceptable. By day's end, Cornwallis had agreed.

On this very day, in New York, Henry Clinton at last prepared a rescue expedition. En route to Virginia, Clinton would receive news of the surrender and turn back.

The date was October 19, 1781. "This is to us a most glorious day," wrote Dr. James Thacher, a surgeon attached to the Continental army, "but to the English, one of bitter chagrin and disappointment." The allied troops were assembled in a double line one mile long, Americans on the right, the French on the left. At the head of the line, Washington was mounted on his horse. At its foot, Rochambeau was on his horse. After about an hour, the British began to troop out of the fort, their *colors cased*. They sullenly threw down their weapons, keeping their eyes fixed on the French and refusing even to look at the American soldiers.

Cornwallis, pleading that he was ill, did not personally surrender to Washington, but sent his sword in the hands of Gen. Charles O'Hara. The officer presented Washington with the blade, but the commander in chief allowed Benjamin Lincoln, who had been forced to relinquish Charleston, to accept instead. Ceremonies concluded, 7,000 British prisoners of war now marched off to prison camps. Cornwallis and his principal officers were spared the indignity of captivity and were paroled to New York.

**Fightin' Words**

To march with **colors cased** is to proceed with national and regimental flags tightly furled in a gesture of defeat and surrender.

# The Meaning of Yorktown

In 1828, a book by Alexander Garden, *Anecdotes of the Revolution*, reported that, throughout the surrender, the British regimental bands and pipers repeatedly played a tune called "The World Turned Upside Down." This may or may not have actually happened, but the notion of the British playing this tune seems so right that the anecdote has assumed the status of absolute historical fact.

*Gen. Charles Cornwallis: "I have the mortification to inform your Excellency that I have been forced to ... surrender."—Letter to Sir Henry Clinton, October 20, 1781.*
(Image from the National Archives)

When the news of the surrender of Yorktown reached London late in November, Lord North (according to Lord Germain) took it "as he would have taken a ball in the breast."

"Oh God!" Prime Minister North exclaimed. "It is all over."

The fact was that 30,000 British troops remained in North America, and the British held all the major American ports, except for Boston and Philadelphia. Yet, after six years of frustrating, costly combat in a war that hardly enjoyed universal public or political support, the British will to fight had been sapped. The ignominious defeat of Lord Cornwallis destroyed whatever little of that will remained. Facing possible action against the combined fleets of Spain and France—and still reeling from De Grasse's victory at the Battle of the Capes—the British Parliament, on December 20, concluded that it was no longer possible to continue to fight to hold America.

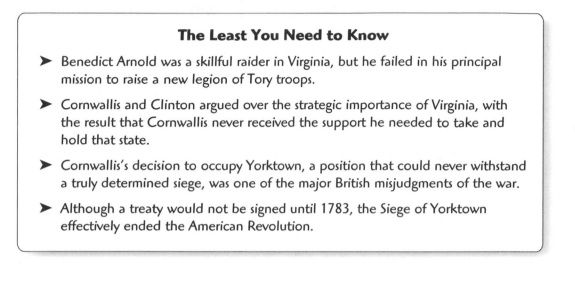

### The Least You Need to Know

➤ Benedict Arnold was a skillful raider in Virginia, but he failed in his principal mission to raise a new legion of Tory troops.

➤ Cornwallis and Clinton argued over the strategic importance of Virginia, with the result that Cornwallis never received the support he needed to take and hold that state.

➤ Cornwallis's decision to occupy Yorktown, a position that could never withstand a truly determined siege, was one of the major British misjudgments of the war.

➤ Although a treaty would not be signed until 1783, the Siege of Yorktown effectively ended the American Revolution.

# Winning the Peace

# Chapter 26

## In This Chapter

➤ The southern theater after Yorktown

➤ Warfare persists in the West

➤ Parliament pushes for peace

➤ American treaty negotiators break free of France

➤ The Treaty of Paris ends the war

It was one thing for Parliament to resolve to make peace in America, as it did on December 20, 1781. It was quite another to persuade the king to go along. George III angrily rejected Parliament's recommendation, insisting that to give up the American colonies would be to renounce England's place as a great world power. Lord George Germain, no longer willing to prosecute the war, attempted to resign as secretary of state for the American colonies, but the king brushed him off, telling Germain that he would simply find someone to replace him who was willing to continue the fight.

Surely the irony of the present situation could not have escaped George's more thoughtful subjects. Against the will of Parliament, the king was behaving in the very way the Declaration of Independence had accused him of behaving: like a tyrant. The people of England would not start a revolution over this, but they would end one.

Lacking support in Parliament—and in the army—the war would end, the will of King George III notwithstanding.

# Greene Wraps Up in the South

Cornwallis's surrender did not end the fighting in the Carolinas. Nathanael Greene had been campaigning in the South since December 1780, and while the Yorktown operation was underway in Virginia, he fought the very able Francis Rawdon-Hastings and, after Rawdon-Hastings fell ill, Alexander Stewart. While the British held on to Savannah and Charleston, Greene kept the backcountry in turmoil.

On September 8, 1781, Greene, reinforced to 2,000 men, decided to go on the offensive. Stewart was camped with an equal number at Eutaw Springs, South Carolina, on the Santee River. Greene's forces fell upon a British party gathering sweet potatoes and took captives. Next, a cavalry scouting party under Maj. John Coffin, a Tory from Boston, was ambushed—but Coffin escaped to alert Stewart to the approach of Greene's army. Losing the element of surprise was a severe blow. The British were able to form a line of battle in front of their camp, and although Greene's militiamen performed magnificently—it is said that they fired 17 volleys without so much as flinching—the British were able to break through the militia line.

Behind this force, however, Continentals from Maryland and Virginia were able to stand fast and, with bayonets, drive the British back into their camp. Then the American forces suffered a fatal lapse in discipline. Entering the British camp, they fell to plundering the soldiers' tents instead of pressing the attack just as Stewart's army was on the verge of collapse. This provided time and opportunity for a British contingent under Maj. John Majoribanks to come out from a thicket on the right, where they had been held in reserve, and attack.

After cutting down many American dragoons, Majoribanks led his men to a brick house, from the safety of which they poured deadly musket and *swivel-gun* fire upon the Americans. Many American soldiers now grabbed British stragglers who had been unable to get inside the house before the door slammed shut. They used these men as human shields as they backed away from the gunfire.

### Fightin' Words

A **swivel gun** was a large-caliber gun, smaller than an artillery piece but larger than a musket or rifle, which was mounted on a swivel for ready aiming.

Rallying his men again, Majoribanks sortied out against those American soldiers who were still busily looting the British camp. Although Majoribanks was himself cut down, he had turned an almost certain American triumph into a British victory—of sorts. Greene, with 500 casualties out of 2,000 men engaged, was forced to withdraw, but the British, who remained in possession of their camp, had suffered 693 killed, wounded, and missing, also out of a force of 2,000 or somewhat less. It was the highest rate of loss any army had suffered in the Revolutionary War, and Eutaw Springs was the last out-and-out, stand-up battle of that war.

Demoralized, Greene's army, reduced to 1,000 men through casualties, illness, and expiration of enlistments, camped in the Santee Hills. Mutiny was brewing—a threat Greene quelled by shooting a man, one Timothy Griffin, who mocked an officer's attempt to instill discipline.

Even after Cornwallis's surrender and the fierce contest at Eutaw Springs, there was a Tory uprising to put down and a British outpost at Dorchester to be cleared. But by December 9, 1781, the British had been confined exclusively to Savannah and Charleston. They evacuated from Savannah on July 11, 1782 and from Charleston on December 14, whereupon Greene moved into Charleston and remained there until August 1783, after news of the Treaty of Paris had reached him.

# The Uneasy West

If, following the defeat of Cornwallis, the spirit of battle had been extinguished among the Commons and Lords in London, it continued to flame fiercely in the West, especially in Ohio and Kentucky.

After militia colonel David Williamson massacred peaceful Indians at Gnaddenhutten, Ohio (Chapter 20, "White War, Red Blood"), Delaware Indians undertook massive vengeance raids throughout the region. In response, militia colonel William Crawford launched the so-called Second Moravian Campaign to destroy "hostile" Indian settlements. His army was a ragtag rabble of 450. A colorful officer with Crawford named John Rose—a Russian nobleman whose real name was Baron Rosenthal, self-exiled from his native land after a duel—described the force as one in which "regularity and precaution were looked upon as ... mere Moonshine."

On June 4–5, 1782, Crawford's disorderly command was caught unawares by a force of Shawnees and Delawares near Sandusky in present-day Ohio. The undisciplined militia panicked, broke, and fled. Forty or 50 were killed or captured, and 28 wounded. Among the prisoners was Crawford, whom the Indians slowly roasted to death. The defeat of Crawford inflamed the upper Ohio. The Tory Indian leader Joseph Brant and the infamous Tory scout Simon Girty now led the raids on Kentucky that are described in Chapter 20.

"The West"—in the eighteenth century, the country between the Appalachians and the Mississippi River—would remain at war for years after the Treaty of Paris, as British traders continued to support Indians in their resistance to American settlement. The Treaty of Greenville, negotiated in 1795 by Mad Anthony Wayne after he defeated the Shawnee and other hostiles at the Battle of Fallen Timbers, would bring some 15 years of stability and control to the region. However, claims that British interests were inciting Indian violence persisted and were among the chief causes of the War of 1812.

### We Hold These Truths

Simon Girty (1741–1818) and his brothers, James and George, were frontier boys captured by Indians during the French and Indian War, then released to the British at Fort Pitt (present-day Pittsburgh, Pennsylvania) in 1759, having lived with their captors for three years. During the rest of the French and Indian War and in Lord Dunmore's War (1774), Simon Girty served in the Ohio country militia and with British regulars as a scout and interpreter; he was fluent in the Iroquoian language.

At the start of the Revolution, Girty enlisted in the Virginia militia, but in 1778 defected to the Tory cause and served as a liaison with Great Britain's western Indian allies. Eagerly embracing Indian battle tactics and the warrior culture, Girty led Indian sorties against the Americans, ordering Col. William Crawford burned alive in 1782, and led Indian and Tory assaults on settlements in Kentucky.

Girty sided with the Indians in the various frontier wars that followed the Revolution. After the 1795 Treaty of Greenville brought American control to the Ohio country, however, Girty fled to Ontario. He died there in 1818.

## The Costs of War

### United States

**Population:** 2,148,100 (1770)

**Strength:** Over the course of eight years, 231,771 men served in the Continental army and 164,087 in the various state militias; however, rarely did any more than 20,000 men serve at any one time in the armed forces of the United States. The American armies reached their greatest strength in 1778, when 35,000 men were fielded.

**Casualties:** 4,435 died in battle; 6,188 wounded but survived.

### Great Britain

Figures for British strength and casualties are approximate only.

**Population:** 11,000,000

**Regular British army:** Standing army (worldwide): about 42,000 at the outset of the war. Recruiting drives added more troops.

**German mercenaries:** During eight years of combat, the British employed 29,875 German mercenaries (popularly called "Hessians").

**Loyalists:** In addition, Tories—American loyalists fighting for the British—numbered perhaps 50,000 during the entire course of the war.

**British-allied Indians:** Difficult to estimate; certainly in the low thousands over the course of eight years.

At any one time, total British strength in the colonies did not exceed 32,000 men.

Total British casualty figures are not readily available; however, it can be safely assumed that the losses were very similar to those of the Americans.

Battle casualties include only those injured or killed by wounds. In the 18th century, disease was far more destructive to the armies. On both sides, disease, including exposure, probably claimed about twice as many lives as did bullets and bayonets.

# Parley in Paris

On February 11, 1782, King George III finally accepted Lord Germain's resignation. Although the king continued to resist giving up the American colonies, his governmental majority in Parliament had evaporated. On March 4, the House of Commons resolved that anyone who attempted to continue the war in America was an enemy of king and country. On the 20th, Lord North, seeking to avoid a no-confidence vote in Parliament, resigned, leaving the king no choice but to form a new government with the opposition.

The new prime minister was the Marquis of Rockingham, the man responsible for repealing the Stamp Act back in 1766. Long a friend of America, he insisted that Great Britain recognize the independence of the United States. Under the new regime, Lord Shelburne, who had always favored reconciliation with the colonies, was named secretary of state in charge of American affairs, with the responsibility of negotiating a peace.

On April 12, Richard Oswald, the man Rockingham appointed to sit at the peace table with the Americans, arrived in Paris. Oswald liked America and Americans and was related to Eleazer Oswald, an American artillery officer. When he arrived, only Benjamin Franklin was present. John Adams was in Holland, desperately trying to negotiate a loan for the infant republic, and John Jay was in Madrid, wrangling with America's difficult Spanish allies. The fourth commissioner, Henry Laurens, had been a British prisoner of war since 1780, when he was captured en route to Europe aboard the American brig *Mercury*. Oswald would personally post the £50,000 bail required to gain Laurens's release from the Tower of London. Thomas Jefferson, offered a post as a treaty commissioner, had declined and remained in Virginia.

*John Jay, in a portrait by Gilbert Stuart.*
(Image from the National Archives)

## The French Squeeze

The "times that try men's souls" may have ended, but Benjamin Franklin's time of trial was just beginning. His instructions from Congress had been to secure from Great Britain recognition of independence. Beyond this, he was to follow, faithfully, the instructions of France.

Yet, with the fighting over, it immediately became clear that France had less interest in supporting the new United States than it had in promoting Spanish claims in the New World. As John Jay was discovering in Madrid, the Spanish, although allied with the French and the Americans against the English, had no desire to acknowledge American independence. Indeed, Spain wanted American territorial claims sharply limited. Spain, instead of directly helping the United States, had instead taken the opportunity to expand its territory. Spain had overrun much of British Florida by 1781, and was also launching raids from Spanish Texas across the Mississippi River. As it enjoyed a position of strength during the peace negotiations, the Spanish government was insistent on maintaining dominion over Florida and the entire Mississippi Valley, including control of Mississippi River navigation. Jay, when he arrived in Paris from Madrid on June 23, called Spain almost as great an enemy to the cause of American liberty and sovereignty as Britain.

Franklin—and the other commissioners, as they arrived—could not afford to alienate France, yet they could no longer slavishly follow the French lead in negotiations without sacrificing the independence so hard won.

## A New *Declaration of Independence*

For the commissioners, three objectives now assumed paramount importance: recognition of independence, of course, but also adequate continental territory and access to international waterways and to the rich fisheries of Newfoundland. It was appearing increasingly unlikely that France would favor the second two of these objectives.

Then, on September 9, 1782, John Jay learned that Vergennes, the French foreign minister, had sent his secretary to England to conduct separate peace talks with the British. What Vergennes was working toward was peace based on the map as it appeared at the end of the war. That is, Britain would retain Maine, New York City, a significant portion of the Old Northwest, and the cities of Charleston and Savannah.

Seeking now to cut the French off at the knees, Franklin, at Jay's urging, proposed that Great Britain authorize Oswald to treat with the "United States" rather than the 13 colonies. This would instantly resolve the question of the recognition of American independence, which would, effectively, free the United States from diplomatic dependency on France. On the face of it, it might seem to be to England's advantage to endorse the French position, which would give England more American territory and would generally limit American expansion. However, the British government was more interested in driving a wedge between the Franco-American alliance, and a *de facto* recognition of American independence seemed a small price to pay for this purpose.

On October 1, Franklin and Jay began formal negotiations with Oswald, excluding the French. By the 5th, an agreement had been hammered out, specifying United States boundaries, a program for the evacuation of British troops, access to the Newfoundland fisheries, and free trade and navigation of the Mississippi.

### Voices of Liberty

"I mean only to say that if we lean on her love of liberty, her affection for America, or her disinterested magnanimity, we shall lean on a broken reed, that will sooner or later pierce our hands ...."

—John Jay, on the dangers of trusting the French to negotiate in the interests of the United States, November 17, 1782

In the meantime, John Adams, having concluded a treaty of commerce and amity with the Netherlands (October 8), arrived in Paris (October 26) and concurred with Jay and Franklin that the treaty with the British should move ahead without the French. By November 5, all the commissioners—Laurens having just arrived—reached agreement on a final draft of the articles of peace. On November 30, 1782, Franklin, Jay, Adams, and Laurens signed a provisional treaty, pending ratification of the governments.

They had achieved all of their objectives, which went far beyond what the French had wanted to allow. And, in December, it fell to Franklin to tell Vergennes of the provisional treaty. "I am at a loss, sir, to explain your conduct and that of your colleagues on this occasion," Vergennes sputtered in a letter of December 15. But Franklin replied on the 17th that "nothing has been agreed in the preliminaries contrary to the interest of France."

Through tact and great personal charm, Franklin kept the breach between France and America from widening. The proof of this came in a new French loan to the United States of 6 million livres.

# "Never a Good War or a Bad Peace"

It was now up to England to make final peace settlements with France and with Spain. These were concluded through 1783. The stage was now set for the formal signings.

## *The Treaty of Paris Signed*

On September 3, 1783, the Treaty of Paris, having been duly ratified by the governments, was definitively signed. Great Britain recognized the independence of the United States and acknowledged its boundaries as excluding Canada, but extending westward through the Great Lakes to the Mississippi, southward to the 31st parallel, and east to the Atlantic Ocean. In addition:

➤ Americans would have the right to fish off the banks of Newfoundland and Nova Scotia.

➤ Legal debts would be honored by each country.

➤ No further penalties would be enacted against citizens of any country involved in the hostilities.

➤ All remaining British troops would evacuate.

➤ The Mississippi River would be open to navigation by the United States as well as Britain.

**Voices of Liberty**

"With an heart full of love and gratitude I now take leave of you. I most devoutly wish that your latter days may be as prosperous and happy as your former ones have been glorious and honorable."

—Washington's parting words to his officers at Fraunces Tavern, New York, December 13, 1783

## *Reception of the Treaty*

One of the thorniest issues between the American and British treaty commissioners was the "Loyalist question": the matter of restitution to or indemnification of the Tories. The British government wanted the rights of the loyalists protected and any confiscated property restored. The American commissioners, who looked on the Tories as traitors who had practiced a particularly ruthless form of warfare, would brook no such program. In the end, the British agreed that Congress would merely "recommend" to the states that they "correct, if necessary," any acts of confiscation of the estates of British subjects.

Lord North, no longer in power, spoke for the outrage of his more conservative countrymen: "What, are not the claims of those who—in conformity to their allegiance, their cheerful obedience to the voice of Parliament, their confidence in the proclamation of our generals, invited under every assurance of military, parliamentary, political and affectionate protection—espoused with the hazard to their lives and the forfeitures of their properties, the cause of Great Britain!"

If anything made the Treaty of Paris less than universally popular in England, it was a feeling of grave injustice having been done to the Loyalists. Yet war weariness prevailed, and the treaty was carried through.

## We Hold These Truths

On December 23, 1783, before the Congress assembled at Annapolis, Maryland, George Washington resigned his commission as commander in chief of the Continental army. "Having now finished the work assigned me," he tearfully declared, "I retire from the great theater of action, and bidding an affectionate farewell to this august body under whose orders I have so long acted, I here offer my commission, and take my leave of all the employments of public life."

With this, Washington withdrew the documents of his commission from his pocket and handed them to the president of the Congress, Thomas Mifflin. He then set off for Mount Vernon, his beloved plantation on the Potomac. For Washington, as for everyone else, the Revolution was over, but, contrary to his belief, he would not long be absent from "the employments of public life." In 1789, Washington would begin his first term as the first president of the United States.

At home, in the United States, the Treaty of Paris was greeted with almost unanimous jubilation. Franklin, ever the sage, observed simply that "there never was a good war or a bad peace."

*Washington bids farewell to his officers at New York's Fraunces Tavern. (Image from the National Archives)*

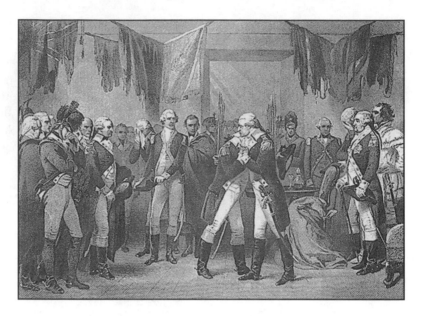

## The Least You Need to Know

➤ Victory at Yorktown ensured the successful end of the Revolution, but it did not bring an end to the fighting in the southern backcountry or in Ohio and Kentucky.

➤ The Battle of Eutaw Springs, South Carolina, was the last big battle of the war—and cost the British their highest casualty rate of any battle in the eight-year conflict.

➤ Against the will of George III, Parliament pushed for peace, making American independence inevitable.

➤ The American negotiators were lucky to be dealing with a British government that consisted of pro-American opponents of George III. As a result, the United States obtained extremely generous terms from the British, who were now pursuing a policy of conciliating their former colonists in order to reduce French influence in America.

# Chapter 27

# A New Order of the Ages

---

## In This Chapter

➤ The end of the Revolution brings economic crisis

➤ Government under the Articles of Confederation

➤ The fate of Tories and slaves

➤ The Constitution is born

➤ Why Washington was the "Father of His Country"

---

Take a dollar bill out of your wallet or purse, and look at the back. On the right and left, you'll find the obverse (front) and reverse (back) of the Great Seal of the United States. It was adopted by Congress on July 20, 1782, but committees had been working on it since 1776. On the obverse is an eagle with the arrows of war in one talon and the olive branch of peace in the other. In its beak it grasps a ribbon bearing the motto *E pluribus unum: Of many, one.* On the reverse are two more mottos, placed above and below a pyramid: *Annuit coeptis: He [God] favors our undertakings,* and *Novus ordo seculorum: A new order of the ages,* or *A new age now begins.*

The sad fact is that most "successful" revolutions either usher in disorder rather than a new order, or they introduce a new age more dreadful than the old. The American Revolution was different. It really did bring about a *novus ordo seculorum*—although the beginning of it all was rather uncertain, loose ends abounded, and pitfalls were plentiful.

# The Fruits of Liberty

The end of the war brought rejoicing, as the end of war always does. It brought hope as well. Even the most ordinary citizens were aware that something momentous in human history had been achieved.

Yet many of the fruits of liberty were bitter. The Continental army, chronically underfed, undersupplied, and unpaid, nearly rose in mutiny on March 10, 1783. Only the steady presence of Washington—who, on March 15, called for patience and obedience to civil authority—brought a measure of calm. However, on June 17, in the so-called Philadelphia Mutiny, disgruntled soldiers surrounded the Pennsylvania State House, where Congress sat. Although the soldiers were peacefully dispersed on the 24th, Congress prudently moved, first to Princeton, and then to Annapolis.

## We Hold These Truths

Robert Morris, who had earned a great personal fortune, possessed a magnificent financial mind. Although he declined the office of secretary of the Treasury in President George Washington's Cabinet, he was a staunch champion of a strong central government.

Ironically, Morris ended his own life in poverty. He overextended himself in speculation of western lands and partnership in a tract of East Coast wilderness that would become Washington, D.C. The Napoleonic Wars caused a worldwide financial panic, and Morris found himself land poor—possessed of much property that no one could afford to buy from him. Unable to pay his taxes or the interest on his loans, he was arrested in February 1798 and spent three and a half years in debtors' prison. After his release in 1801 under new federal bankruptcy laws, he lived out the last five years of his life in a tiny Philadelphia house—a far cry from the "palace" that Pierre L'Enfant, the man who would soon lay out the plan for the city of Washington, D.C., had been commissioned to build for him just before his financial empire collapsed.

Then there was the economy. Lacking the power to tax, Congress had had to figure out another way to finance the $170,000,000 it cost to fight the Revolution. The *Continental currency* it issued was no more than a series of bills of credit, backed by virtually nothing. The individual states also issued their own currency, which typically had some backing, but hardly enough. The result was massive inflation. In 1780, the worst year of the inflation, what had cost little more than a Continental dollar in 1776 now cost more than $1,000 in Continental currency.

The creaking economy, propped up by foreign loans, collapsed in 1781, whereupon Congress called on merchant and financier Robert Morris to act as financial czar, and it was largely through his direction that the later years of the Revolution were financed.

With the Revolution over, massive debt remained—some $27,000,000 demanded in gold—and the government, without the power of taxation, had no way to pay it off. In 1786, the low point of the new nation's economic crisis, the United States defaulted on interest payments to Spain, France, and the Netherlands.

### Fightin' Words

**Continental currency** was paper money printed by the Continental Congress during the Revolution; without backing by "hard money" (gold or silver), its value quickly depreciated, bringing on massive inflation.

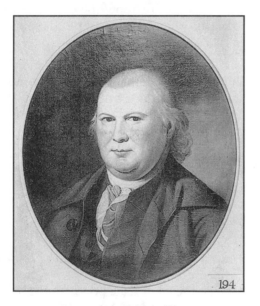

*Charles Willson Peale's portrait of Robert Morris, "financier of the American Revolution."* (Image from the National Archives)

## Government Under the Articles of Confederation

Understandably, the architects of American government during the Revolution were highly leery of giving much power to a central government. The war, after all, was being fought to overcome the tyranny of just such a government.

But, of course, some form of government was needed to administer the nation as it fought a desperate war. Drafted in 1777 and ratified in 1781, the Articles of Confederation became the first constitution of the United States.

The document originally conceived by Pennsylvania's John Dickinson in 1776 provided for a strong national government, but the states clamored for more rights—especially the exclusive power of taxation—so that Dickinson's document was drastically watered down by revision and amendment.

The Articles of Confederation created not a nation, but a "firm league of friendship" among 13 sovereign states. The Articles did provide for a permanent national Congress, consisting of two to seven delegates from each state—though each state was given one vote, regardless of its population—but the document did not create an executive or a judicial branch. Under the Articles, Congress was charged with conducting foreign policy, declaring war, making peace, maintaining an army and navy, and so on. Despite these responsibilities, however, Congress was left essentially powerless, wholly at the mercy of the states. Although Congress could issue directives and pass laws, it had no means of enforcing them. The states were free to comply and cooperate or ... not. Moreover, while Congress had considerable authority in pulling the purse strings, it had no means whatsoever of filling that purse.

That the Articles of Confederation held the states together during the Revolution is little short of miraculous. But once that compelling crisis had ended, the deficiencies of government under the Articles became increasingly apparent.

**Fightin' Words**

**The Articles of Confederation,** drafted in 1777 and ratified by the states in 1781, was the first constitution of the United States. It created a very weak central government, without the authority to levy taxes. It was replaced by the Constitution, ratified in 1789.

## Northwest Ordinance

Within the narrow constraints of the Articles of Confederation, Congress was able to take one momentous step toward asserting the authority of a central government. On July 13, 1787, it enacted the *Northwest Ordinance*, which specified how territories and states were to be formed from the western lands won in the Revolution.

The ordinance divided the Northwest, later called the "Old Northwest"—the vast region bounded by the Ohio and Mississippi rivers and by the Great Lakes—into three to five territories. Congress was empowered to appoint a governor, a secretary, and three judges to govern each of them. When the adult male population of a territory reached 5,000, elections would be held in the territory to form a territorial legislature and to send a nonvoting representative to Congress. When its adult male population reached 60,000, a territory could write a constitution and apply for statehood.

Whereas Britain had refused to make its American colonies full members of a national commonwealth, the Northwest ordinance ensured that the frontier regions would only temporarily be mere colonies of the established coastal states, then would become full partners. This principle of representation helped pave the way for a stronger central government—one with the power to tax—for it guaranteed that Americans would never be taxed without representation.

Another profound provision of the Northwest Ordinance was its prohibition of slavery in the territories. This was the first national stand against that institution. (Historians have noted, however, that the anti-slavery provision of the Northwest Ordinance was more concerned with the corrupting effects of slavery on whites rather than with the wrong it committed against African-Americans.)

Finally, the document also guaranteed that the territories would enjoy such basic rights as trial by jury and freedom of religion.

## What About the Loyalists?

The loyalists—the Tories—had been persecuted throughout the Revolution, and, when they fought back, they conducted a particularly savage form of warfare. Sooner or later, most revolutions degenerate into a most bitter kind of civil war. In many parts of the country, combat between loyalists and patriots had degenerated into precisely this kind of conflict, but an outright and enduring civil war never erupted. During the Revolution, most of the states confiscated Tory property. In 1783, as part of the peace agreement, the British established a commission to examine the claims of some 4,118 Tories; it ultimately disbursed £3,300,000 to compensate loyalists for their losses.

Although the Treaty of Paris specified that no one would suffer further penalties for actions during the war, the persecution of Tories continued for some years after the war had ended. In the treaty, Congress had agreed to "earnestly recommend" to the states that loyalists who had not borne arms for the British be allowed to reclaim their property. In most cases, such recommendations were ignored.

Faced with scorn and financial ruin, many loyalists simply gave up and left the United States, fleeing either to Canada or the West Indies in numbers between 60,000 and 80,000.

## What About the Slaves?

Another segment of the American population that was denied a taste of the fruits of liberty were the slaves. As evidenced by the Northwest Ordinance, slavery did not sit

### Fightin' Words

The **Northwest Ordinance,** the most important piece of legislation produced under the Articles of Confederation, spelled out how territories and states were to be formed from the western lands acquired as a result of the Revolution; it ensured democratic government in these regions, and it was the first federal legislation aimed against slavery.

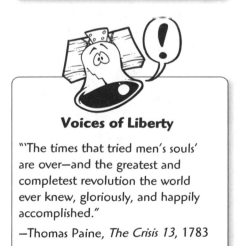

### Voices of Liberty

"'The times that tried men's souls' are over—and the greatest and completest revolution the world ever knew, gloriously, and happily accomplished."

—Thomas Paine, *The Crisis 13,* 1783

well with many white Americans. Yet the Revolution did not free a single slave. In 1790, the first U.S. census counted 697,897 slaves. In 1808, the nation banned the importation of slaves; yet the institution of slavery was so firmly established that the 1810 census counted 1,191,354 slaves, a 70 percent increase over two decades earlier.

The Constitution, which would replace the Articles of Confederation in 1789, acknowledged the institution of slavery, but treated the subject as nothing more or less than a problem of representation, not a moral issue of right versus wrong. The Constitution apportioned representation in the federal government, in part, according to population; the more representatives a state could claim, the more influential it would be in the federal government. With representation proportional to population, the South wanted its slaves counted as population. The North objected, of course, arguing that the slaves should be excluded entirely from the calculation. A peculiar-sounding solution was reached. Embodied in the Constitution as Article I, Section 2, the "Three-Fifths Compromise" managed delicately to avoid the word *slave* altogether:

> *Representation and direct taxes will be apportioned among the several states according to respective numbers determined by adding to the whole number of free persons including those bound to service for a set number of years and excluding Indians not taxed three-fifths of all other persons.*

For purposes of levying taxes and apportioning representatives, slaves were counted as three-fifths of a person, and the question of slavery itself was left to fester, a cruel irony in this revolutionary republic, and one that would ultimately tear the nation apart.

# Rope of Sand?

The Tories and the slaves were not the only Americans who had reason for discontent and despair. With each day that passed following the Revolution, the weakness of the central government under the Articles of Confederation became increasingly apparent. Some politicians began to refer to the bonds uniting the states as nothing more than a "rope of sand."

### Voices of Liberty

"Our citizenship in the United States is our national character. Our citizenship in any particular State is only our local distinction. By the latter we are known at home, by the former to the world. Our great title is AMERICANS."

—Thomas Paine

## Shays's Rebellion

A dramatic demonstration of just how ineffectual the government of the United States was came in 1786. During this time, the Massachusetts government, dominated by mercantile interests, enacted heavy taxes to retire state debts, but simultaneously rejected paper money and laws intended to provide debtor relief. This "double whammy" created a wave of foreclosures and imprisonment for debt.

The situation became intolerable, and, in August 1786, armed mobs of beleaguered farmers began forcing the closure of courts in Massachusetts's frontier counties. A charismatic Revolutionary War veteran, Daniel Shays (ca. 1747–1825), emerged as the leader of what came to be called Shays's Rebellion. Not until January 25, 1787, was a state militia force able to disperse rebels in Springfield, and another force, supported by private contributions from merchant interests, effectively crushed the Shaysites at Petersham on February 4.

Shays's Rebellion revealed just how powerless the federal government was in cases of insurrection. Lacking both the mandate and the means to intervene, Congress stood idly by during the Shays affair.

## The Constitutional Convention

At about the time of Shays's Rebellion, Congress was also confronted with a crisis when Rhode Island issued a mountain of absolutely worthless paper money. Confronted with the prospect of state after state compounding the chaos of an economy in disintegration, Congress could, in fact, do nothing beyond convening, in 1786, a convention at Annapolis, Maryland, to discuss problems of interstate commerce. The delegates soon recognized that these issues were part of a much larger issue that could only be addressed by a revision of the Articles of Confederation. The Annapolis delegates called for a constitutional convention, which met in Philadelphia in May 1787.

The task of revision almost immediately blossomed into a project of building anew. By the end of May, the delegates agreed that what was required was a genuine national government, not a mere hopeful confederation of states. Fifty-five delegates convened in Philadelphia and elected George Washington as president of the convention, wresting him from Mount Vernon and the retirement he craved. Much as Washington had held the Continental Army together during the ordeal of the Revolution, so now he managed the disputatious delegates with dignity and fairness.

The Virginia delegation, led by Edmund Randolph, proposed the boldest course for the convention. The so-called Virginia Plan, drafted by James Madison, called for the creation of a central federal government consisting of a *bicameral* legislature, an executive branch, and a judicial branch. The chief executive was to be elected by the members of the legislature, who, in turn, were elected by the citizens. The Virginia Plan further specified that representation in the bicameral legislature would be proportionate to state population—a provision that worried and angered representatives of the smaller states.

With debate raging over the Virginia Plan, William Paterson of New Jersey introduced an alternative scheme labeled with the name of his state. The New Jersey Plan retained most of the Articles

**Fightin' Words**

**Bicameral** means "two-chambered," and refers to a type of legislature consisting of two groups of representatives. In the case of the British Parliament, the two houses are the House of Lords and the House of Commons; in the case of the U.S. Congress, they are the Senate and the House of Representatives.

of Confederation, giving each state equal representation in the legislature, but it added a separate and independent Supreme Court.

### Fightin' Words

The framers wanted to avoid election of the president directly by the people. As provided in the Constitution, each state has as many electors as it has senators and representatives combined. Together, the electors constitute the **Electoral College.** Originally, the electors were voted in by the state legislatures. This evolved into election by the people. (Today, we may think of ourselves as voting for a president every fourth November, but we are actually voting for electors pledged to cast *their* votes for a particular candidate.)

Paterson's New Jersey Plan only served to intensify debate, and Roger Sherman, delegate from Connecticut, proposed a compromise between the two plans. This so-called Great Compromise called for a bicameral legislature; however, the "upper house" of this body, the Senate, would provide each state with equal representation, whereas representation in the "lower house," the House of Representatives, would provide representation proportionate to each state's population. The Senate and the House were also distinguished by the method of their election. The House was elected directly by the people, the Senate indirectly, by state legislatures. Indirect election, the Founding Fathers believed, would insulate senators from the common folk, and ensure that the Senate represented the interests of men who possessed considerable property. Likewise, the chief executive—the president—would not be elected by the representatives in the legislature, but by an *Electoral College.*

With the compromises in place, William Johnson (secretary of the Convention), Alexander Hamilton, James Madison, Rufus King, and Gouverneur Morris wrote the actual Constitution document, the product of three and a half months of debate. When 38 of the 55 Convention delegates approved the document, it was sent to Congress, which submitted it to the states for ratification.

Now a titanic struggle began. Those who supported the proposed Constitution were called Federalists; those opposed, Anti-Federalists. Although Delaware, Pennsylvania, and New Jersey instantly ratified the Constitution, a total of nine states were required for passage of the document into law. The process was hotly contested in many states and nowhere more so than in the key states of Virginia and New York. To convince New York voters to ratify, Alexander Hamilton, James Madison, and John Jay collaborated on a series of essays collectively called *The Federalist Papers* and published during 1787–88 in various New York newspapers under the collective pseudonym of "Publius."

*The Federalist* is a brilliant defense of the Constitution. The tenth essay penetrated to the very heart of the principal anti-Federalist argument that the nation was simply too big to be regulated by a central government. Madison argued that precisely *because* the nation was so large, it would be most effectively governed by a strong central government, which would prevent any single special interest from taking control. Essays 15 through 22 deftly analyzed the four major weaknesses of the Articles of Confederation:

➤ If Congress could legislate only for states and not for individuals, it could enforce no laws.

➤ If Congress had no power to tax, it could not dependably fund government or form relations with foreign powers. In effect, no nation would exist.

➤ If Congress lacked the power to regulate commerce, all foreign relations were meaningless, since most treaties (even those of peace) were concerned mainly with trade.

➤ The Articles of Confederation were almost impossible to amend, since amendments had to be ratified by all 13 states. The document was bound to be fatally inflexible.

In the end, rational argument probably had less impact on voters than various acts of electoral sleight-of-hand performed by supporters of the Federalists. This does not alter the fact that the Federalist position was, indeed, rational, and we may condone the political chicanery in this instance on the principle that a good end justifies any means. The state of Virginia ratified the Constitution by a close vote of 89 to 79, but only after the anti-Federalist argument that the Constitution failed to address the rights of individuals was satisfied by the promise that a "Bill of Rights" would be added. In New York, the pro-ratification vote was even more of a squeaker: 30 to 27.

## The Bill of Rights

James Madison spearheaded the effort to create the first 10 amendments to the Constitution, the Bill of Rights. He carefully examined and synthesized the enumeration of rights already included in several state constitutions and documents, especially the Virginia Declaration of Rights, which had been adopted in 1776.

As ultimately ratified on December 15, 1791, the Bill of Rights explicitly protects (in its first amendment) freedom of religion, freedom of speech, freedom of the press, and the right of popular assembly for the purpose of petition for redress of grievances.

The second amendment guarantees the right to bear arms, and the third severely limits the quartering of soldiers in private homes. The fourth amendment forbids unreasonable searches and seizures and requires warrants to be specific (not blanket documents) and to be issued only upon probable cause.

The fifth amendment mandates grand jury indictments in major criminal prosecutions, prohibits "double jeopardy" (being tried more than once on the same charge), and guarantees that no one need testify against himself or herself. The amendment also forbids taking private property for public use without just compensation and prohibits deprivation of life, liberty, or property without due process of law.

The sixth amendment guarantees a speedy public trial by jury. It specifies that the accused shall be fully informed of the accusation, shall be confronted with the witnesses against him or her, shall have the power to subpoena (summon) witnesses for his or her defense, and shall have access to legal counsel. The seventh amendment guarantees jury trials in civil cases, and the eighth prohibits excessive bail, unreasonable fines, and "cruel and unusual punishments."

The ninth and tenth amendments are special: The ninth explicitly provides that the enumeration of rights in the Constitution does not deny others retained by the people, and the tenth expresses the "doctrine of reserved powers": All powers not explicitly delegated to the United States are reserved to the states or the people.

# Father of His Country

Far from *perfect*, the newborn republic was nevertheless extraordinarily *good*, and much of what made it so was directly attributable to the wisdom and the character of those who built the government. Chief among these was George Washington.

The new Constitution was put into effect on March 4, 1789, and the next month, the U.S. Senate convened to count ballots cast by members of the Electoral College for the first president of the United States. The result surprised no one. George Washington had been unanimously elected, and John Adams became his vice president.

## Washington as Leader

In fact, the framers of the Constitution entrusted so much power to the chief executive with the understanding that Washington would be elected. For Washington had amply demonstrated not only a genius for leadership in commanding the Continental Army, but had shown his skill as a statesman in presiding over the Constitutional Convention. Equally important, he demonstrated the character of a true republican. Too often, revolutions are followed by new tyrants and tyrannies. Washington, it was clear to Congress and the people of the United States, was no tyrant.

The new president was inaugurated in New York City on April 30, 1789. Even with a Constitution in place, it was up to Washington to create much of the American government and in particular to shape the office of president. He quickly created key executive departments, naming Thomas Jefferson as secretary of state, Henry Knox as secretary of war, Alexander Hamilton as secretary of the treasury, Samuel Osgood as head of the post office, and Edmund Randolph as attorney general. Certain of these departments Washington organized into a close body of presidential advisers, the Cabinet.

## Washington as Example

Washington became the model for the presidency, and the chief quality he introduced into the office was restraint. He avoided conflict with Congress, believing it was not the chief executive's duty to propose legislation. He also opposed the formation of political parties—although, by the time of his second term, two opposing parties had, indeed, been formed: the conservative Federalists, headed by John Adams and Alexander Hamilton, and the more liberal Democratic-Republicans, headed by Thomas

Jefferson. But it is a measure of Washington's steadfast refusal to become a post-revolutionary tyrant that he declined to stand for a third term of office. The two-term presidency thereafter became an inviolate tradition until the twin crises of the Depression and World War II prompted the nation to elect Franklin Delano Roosevelt to a third and a fourth term. (While the nation was grateful to FDR, it also approved the 22nd Amendment to the Constitution on February 26, 1951, restricting future presidents to no more than two elected terms.)

Washington not only created the office of president, he signed key treaties with England and Spain, approved the creation of a national bank, proclaimed neutrality in what would become a long series of wars between England and France, and he successfully quelled a spasm of internal rebellion. He was an able executive, but it was his character more than anything else that helped establish the United States among the other nations of the world. The classical Romans reserved one title for their greatest leaders—*Pater Patriae*, Father of His Country—and almost immediately, a grateful nation accorded this epithet to George Washington.

**Fightin' Words**

**Pater Patriae** is Latin for Father of His Country; a title bestowed upon certain heroes of ancient Rome, it was likewise freely applied to George Washington by a grateful nation.

# A Revolution for the World

The American Revolution gave birth to a new nation. That much is beyond dispute. Did it also give birth to a new *idea* of government? Not really. The idea of a truly representative republic was at least as old as classical Greece and Rome. But not until the American Revolution produced the United States was this idea fully realized—in word and deed, in flesh and blood—in a living nation.

The seventeenth and eighteenth centuries were rich in political and moral philosophy, exemplified in the work of John Locke, Jean-Jacques Rousseau, and Voltaire. Of all the people of the world, the Americans had seized these new political and moral ideas, synthesized them with the best of ancient thought, and suddenly made them real. From the beginning, propagandists such as Thomas Paine understood the value of putting the Revolution before the world, of making it something more than a local rebellion. The idea that the issues of the Revolution belonged to all humankind was not a product of mere propaganda, however. It was the truth.

*Novus ordo seculorum*—depending how you translate it, *a new age now begins;* or, *a new order of the ages*. Both were—and remain—accurate descriptions of what the American Revolution had wrought in the world. It had introduced a new age and a new order for all ages to come.

Cynics might argue that the American Revolution began because a group of powerful merchants and farmers were tired of giving over their profits in taxes to the Crown. In part, this is true. But this alone would not have carried Washington and his men through the Valley Forge winter, nor through one defeat and heartbreak after another, nor to victory at Yorktown.

From the beginning, those who led the Revolution understood that it was a struggle not only bigger than mere profit, but bigger than the emerging nation itself. It was a battle not against a hidebound king or a corruptible Parliament. It was nothing less than a war to create a new age that would inform, enlighten, and give hope to every age yet to come.

---

### The Least You Need to Know

➤ The end of the Revolution brought severe economic crisis, which the federal government, powerless to levy taxes, was unable to alleviate.

➤ The Articles of Confederation was the first United States constitution, and the Northwest Ordinance was the first important piece of genuinely federal legislation.

➤ The economic crisis and a desire for national identity motivated the United States to scrap the Articles of Confederation, which formed a weak central government, for the Constitution, which created a stronger central government.

➤ The American Revolution was—and remains—an example to the world of the realization of the ideals of liberty and representative democracy.

---

# Who Was Who in the American Revolution

**Adams, John (1735–1826)**   A "Founding Father" instrumental in organizing and conducting the Revolution; a negotiator of the Treaty of Paris; first vice president and second president of the United States.

**Adams, Samuel (1722–1803)**   Revolutionary rabble rouser, master propagandist, and organizer; chief figure in the Massachusetts resistance on the eve of the Revolution; delegate to the Continental Congress.

**Alexander, William "Lord Stirling" (1726–83)**   Major general in the Continental army; key roles in New York, New Jersey, Branydwine, Germantown, and Monmouth.

**Allen, Ethan (1738–89)**   Controversial Connecticut leader of the Green Mountain Boys; instrumental in the capture of Fort Ticonderoga (1775), but captured in the failed invasion of Canada.

**André, John (1751–80)**   British officer and *Benedict Arnold*'s espionage contact; executed by the patriots as a spy.

**Arbuthnot, Marriot (1711–94)**   British admiral who repeatedly lost to the French in American waters.

**Arnold, Benedict (1741–1801)**   Brilliant and daring Continental general (instrumental in the capture of Fort Ticonderoga, savior of the army during the Canadian fiasco, instrumental in the victory at Saratoga); turned traitor with a plan to surrender West Point to the British; fought for the British as a brigadier general after the failure of the West Point scheme.

**Attucks, Crispus (ca. 1723–70)**   Runaway slave living in Boston, who became the first victim of the Boston Massacre (1770).

**Barras, Louis, Comte de (died ca. 1800)**   French admiral who served under the *Comte de Grasse* in the Yorktown Campaign.

**Barry, John (1745–1803)**   Often called the "Father of the American Navy"; served with distinction during the Revolution.

**Brant, Joseph (1742–1807)**   Mohawk political and military leader; Britain's most skillful and effective Indian ally.

**Burgoyne, John "Gentleman Johnny" (1722–92)**   British general whose grand plan to deal a decapitating blow to the Revolution by severing New England from the other colonies failed, resulting in his defeat at Bemis Heights in the Saratoga Campaign (1776).

**Carleton, Guy (1724–1808)**   British general and governor of Canada; effectively repelled the American invasion of Canada in 1775.

**Clark, George Rogers (1752–1818)**   Outstanding patriot commander of troops in the brutal western theater of the Revolution.

**Clinton, Henry (1738–95)**   Second in command to British commander in chief *William Howe,* he succeeded Howe in May 1778; like Howe, Clinton was competent but overly cautious.

**Cornwallis, Charles (1738–1805)**   British general who played key roles at Brandywine and the capture of Philadelphia, as well as in the South (scoring a great British victory at Camden, South Carolina); Cornwallis blundered by occupying Yorktown, Virginia, where he was besieged in the culminating battle of the Revolution. His defeat at Yorktown effectively ended the war.

**De Kalb, Johann (Baron de Kalb) (1721–80)**   German volunteer officer serving in the Continental army; mentor to *Lafayette;* mortally wounded at the Battle of Camden.

**De Grasse, François (Comte de Grasse) (1722–88)**   French admiral who commanded the French fleet in critical supporting action during the Yorktown Campaign.

**Deane, Silas (1737–89)**   Member of the Continental Congress; American representative in Europe, instrumental in securing the economic aid of France; a controversial figure, later suspected of embezzlement and disloyalty.

**D'Estaing, Charles Hector Theodat (1729–94)**   French admiral who repeatedly failed in the execution of early Franco-American amphibious operations.

**Dickinson, John (1732–1808)**   Revolutionary political theorist, whose *Letters from a Farmer in Pennsylvania* (1768) disputed the right of England to tax the colonies.

**Franklin, Benjamin (1706–90)**   Colonial printer, author, editor, inventor, scientist, philosopher, politician, statesman, diplomat, and revolutionary activist; instrumental in negotiating French aid and alliance, and one of the principal negotiators of the Treaty of Paris.

**Gage, Thomas (1721–87)**   Last royal governor of Massachusetts; Gage failed to put down rebellion in and about Boston and was recalled to England late in 1775; *William Howe* replaced him as commander in chief of British land forces in America.

**Gates, Horatio (1728–1806)**   Major general in the Continental army; overall commander at Saratoga; implicated in the "Conway Cabal" to discredit *George Washington.*

Given command of the Southern Department, Gates was replaced by *Nathanael Greene* after suffering disastrous defeat at the Battle of Camden.

**George III (1738–1820)**   King of England during the American Revolution.

**Germain, George Sackville, Lord (1716–85)**   British secretary of state for the American colonies; had overall responsibility for prosecuting the war.

**Greene, Nathanael (1742–86)**   Major general in the Continental army; Greene served in New York, New Jersey, at Brandywine, and at Germantown, but truly distinguished himself as commander of the Southern Department from October 1780.

**Hale, Nathan (1755–76)**   Connecticut schoolmaster turned patriot spy; apprehended by the British in Manhattan, he was hanged, having uttered his final words: "I only regret that I have but one life to lose for my country."

**Hamilton, Alexander (1757–1804)**   Dashing officer in the Continental army, Hamilton was instrumental after the war in organizing the Constitutional Convention and was a brilliantly effective advocate of a strong central government. He served President *George Washington* as the nation's first secretary of the Treasury, formulating policies that helped the fledgling republic achieve economic viability. Hamilton was killed in a duel with Aaron Burr.

**Hamilton, Henry (died 1796)**   British lieutenant governor of Canada and commandant of the British fort at Detroit; coordinated the action of Britain's Indian allies, who called him "Hair Buyer," because he paid a bounty on patriot scalps.

**Hancock, John (1737–93)**   Merchant activist in the revolutionary cause; president of the Continental Congress; author of the most conspicuous signature on the Declaration of Independence.

**Henry, Patrick (1736–99)**   Fiery orator of the Revolution, whose March 1775 speech advocating armed resistance to the Crown concluded with the stirring phrase, "give me liberty or give me death."

**Herkimer, Nicholas (1728–77)**   Tough American militia general; fought bravely at the Battle of Oriskany, in which he was mortally wounded.

**Hopkins, Esek (1718–1802)**   First commander in chief of the Continental Navy; successful in an early raid on Nassau, but his failure to capture HMS *Glasgow* resulted in his dismissal from command.

**Howe, Richard (1726–99)**   British admiral, commander in chief of Royal Navy forces in America, and brother of *William Howe;* tried with his brother to negotiate an early end to the war.

**Howe, Robert (1732–86)**   Continental major general; commanded troops who suppressed the mutinies of Pennsylvania and New Jersey troops in 1781; no relation to the British Howe brothers.

**Howe, William (1729–1814)**  Replaced *Thomas Gage* as commander in chief of British forces; brother of Adm. *Richard Howe*; his decision to capture Philadelphia instead of coordinating operations with *John Burgoyne* contributed to Burgoyne's disastrous defeat at Saratoga.

**Jefferson, Thomas (1743–1826)**  Statesman and revolutionary activist; principal author of the Declaration of Independence; revolutionary governor of Virginia; third president of the United States.

**Jones, John Paul (1747–92)**  Scottish-born American naval hero, whose record of naval victories during the Revolution was unmatched on either side.

**Knox, Henry (1750–1806)**  Continental general who commanded American artillery throughout the war; served President *George Washington* as secretary of war.

**Knyphausen, Wilhelm von (1716–1800)**  Commander in chief of German mercenary ("Hessian") forces in America.

**Kosciuszko, Tadeusz (1746–1817)**  Polish patriot who volunteered services to the Continental army; his engineering expertise was critical at Saratoga and West Point; served with distinction under *Nathanael Greene* in the South.

**Lafayette, Marie Joseph du Motier, Marquis de (1757–1834)**  Most famous of the foreign officers who volunteered to serve the patriot cause. Became an intimate of *George Washington* and was instrumental in the Yorktown Campaign.

**Laurens, Henry (1724–92)**  Patriot diplomat; one of the negotiators of the Treaty of Paris.

**Lee, Arthur (1740–92)**  A principal American representative in Europe during much of the Revolution.

**Lee, Charles (1731–82)**  Second in command to *George Washington*, Lee proved to be a disappointing and untrustworthy general; court-martialed and suspended after failure at the Battle of Monmouth.

**Lee, Henry "Lighthorse Harry" (1756–1818)**  The most dashing and skillful of American cavalry leaders; probably saved *Nathanael Green*'s army at the Battle of Eutaw Springs in 1781.

**Lincoln, Benjamin (1733–1810)**  Major general in the Continental army; served with distinction in the northern campaigns (especially at Bennington and Saratoga), but failed in the South and was taken prisoner when Charleston fell in 1780. Paroled later in the year, he was present at Yorktown and accepted Cornwallis's sword at the surrender ceremony.

**Marion, Francis "The Swamp Fox" (ca. 1732–95)**  Wily and brilliant leader of patriot partisans in the Carolinas; famed for his ability to materialize from and disappear in the swamps, he was highly effective in harassing, demoralizing, and generally exhausting British forces in the Carolina backcountry.

**Montgomery, Richard (1738–75)**   Valiantly led the American assault against Quebec in 1775 and fell in battle there.

**Morgan, Daniel (1736–1802)**   Considered by some historians to be the only military genius to emerge from the Revolution, Morgan led crack Virginia rifleman in key roles at Saratoga and was in command of light infantry at the Battle of Cowpens, in which he dealt *Banastre Tarleton* a decisive defeat.

**Morris, Robert (1734–1806)**   "The financier of the American Revolution"; appointed superintendent of the department of finance in 1781, he did much to prevent the total economic collapse of a revolutionary government that lacked the power to tax.

**Moultrie, William (1730–1805)**   Continental general who led the successful defense of Fort Sullivan against the British assault on Charleston in 1776.

**North, Frederick, Lord (1732–92)**   Prime minister under King George III.

**Paine, Thomas (1737–1809)**   Greatest of the patriot pamphleteers; his *Common Sense* and *The Crisis* helped shape the course of the American cause.

**Pulaski, Casimir (1747–79)**   Polish officer who volunteered for service in the American cause; helped to create a Continental cavalry force; mortally wounded at Savannah.

**Putnam, Israel (1718–90)**   Major general in the Continental army; one of two principal commanders at Bunker Hill. His poor planning on Long Island was partially responsible for defeat there.

**Revere, Paul (1735–1818)**   Prosperous silversmith; patriot activist and courier for the Massachusetts Committee of Correspondence; his Midnight Ride in 1775 roused the minutemen before the battles of Lexington and Concord.

**Riedesel, Baron Friedrich von (1738–1800)**   German mercenary officer.

**Rochambeau, Jean Baptiste Donatien de Vimeur, Comte de (1725–1807)**   French general who collaborated with *George Washington* in the Siege of Yorktown.

**Schuyler, Philip (1733–1804)**   Major general in the Continental army, who was replaced as commander of the Northern Department after the British recaptured Fort Ticonderoga.

**Stark, John (1728–1822)**   Nettlesome but skillful Continental army and militia general who served well at Bunker Hill, Trenton, Princeton, and especially Bennington.

**Steuben, Baron Friedrich Wilhelm von (1730–94)**   Prussian general in volunteer service to the Continental army; Steuben's greatest contribution to the American cause was his work in training the army to European standards.

**Sullivan, John (1740–95)**   Major general in the Continental army; served in New York and New Jersey and at Brandywine and Germantown. He was in command of the disastrous Franco-American assault on Newport, Rhode Island, in 1778; in 1779, he led a task force in the destruction of Iroquois villages in upper New York.

**Tarleton, Banastre (1754–1833)**   A dashing and inventive British officer, who became notorious for his ruthless use of Tory forces; finally defeated at the Battle of Cowpens.

**Ward, Artemas (1727–1800)**   Major general of the Continental army; the highest-ranking officer at the outbreak of the Revolution; one of the two commanders at Bunker Hill.

**Washington, George (1732–99)**   Commander in chief of the Continental army; first president of the United States. No military genius, Washington was nevertheless a leader of great skill, extraordinary nobility of character, and boundless courage.

**Wayne, "Mad Anthony" (1745–96)**   Perhaps the most skillful and successful of all American commanders, Wayne combined solid military sense and excellent skills as a strategist and tactician with bold impetuosity. His greatest triumphs came at Stony Point (1779) and at the Battle of Green Spring (1781). After the Revolution, his victory at the Battle of Fallen Timbers ended Little Turtle's War and brought relative peace and stability to the Old Northwest until the War of 1812.

# Fighting Words

**abatis**   An obstacle of sharpened wooden stakes (trees that have been felled and sharpened at one end), positioned to make it difficult to storm a fortress. A *berm* is a ledge between a fortification's parapet and moat.

**adjutant general**   In Washington's army, the adjutant general was the chief administrative officer of the army.

**Algonquian**   The name of a family of Indian languages. Tribes related through dialects of this linguistic family are collectively referred to as Algonquian—*not* Algonquin. The other major Indian linguistic family in eastern North America is the Iroquoian.

**Algonquin**   The name applied to certain of the various Native American peoples who live or lived in the Ottawa River Valley of Quebec and Ontario. Compare Algonquian.

**apprenticeship**   In eighteenth-century America, as in England at that time, *apprenticeship* was not only the chief method of earning a profession, it was the principal form of education in general. An apprentice was typically bound to a master for a certain period, working in return for room, board, and training.

**approach trench**   A basic element of siege warfare; it is a deep trench dug at an angle to the target fortification, providing cover for advancing troops and artillery as they inch closer and closer to the objective.

**Articles of Confederation**   Drafted in 1777 and ratified by the states in 1781, it was the first constitution of the United States. It created a very weak central government, without the authority to levy taxes. It was replaced by the Constitution, ratified in 1789.

*bateau* (plural, *bateaux*)   A long, flat-bottomed boat with sharply pointed bow and stern, used to navigate rivers in the north country.

**bateauman**   Navigated and managed a bateau, the typical wilderness lake and river boat of the era.

**bicameral**   Literally, "two-chambered"; refers to a type of legislature consisting of two groups of representatives. In the case of the British Parliament, the two houses are the House of Lords and the House of Commons; in the case of the U.S. Congress, they are the Senate and the House of Representatives.

**bivouac**   A temporary military encampment.

**breastwork**   A modest, temporary fortification, reaching no higher than a man's chest—hence the name.

**brevet**   A promotion in rank but not pay, usually of a temporary nature, and typically for bravery or other distinction in the field.

**brigadier general**   The junior-most general officer rank, equivalent of a modern one-star general. A brigadier commands a brigade, a military formation consisting of two or more regiments. (In the Continental army, a full-strength regiment consisted of 728 officers and men.)

**brigantine**   A two-masted, square-rigged sailing vessel.

**broadsiding**   The act of maneuvering so that a ship's main cannon can be fired effectively against a target.

**Brown Bess**   The standard-issue infantry firearm in the British army since the early eighteenth century. By the 1770s, it was 39 inches long, weighed 14 pounds, and fired a 0.75-inch, one-ounce bullet.

**carcass**   A hollow cannonball filled with pitch, ignited, and then fired. Shattering on impact, the *carcass* spread the burning pitch, igniting whatever it hit.

**charter**   A combination of royal permission to establish a colony, a definition of the boundaries of the colony, and a constitution for the colony.

*chevaux de frise*   A defense consisting of obstacles from which spikes or barbed stakes protrude. The name means "horses of Frieseland," and is named after the Dutch location where the defense was first used against cavalry in the sixteenth century.

**client tribe**   A modern term describing the relationship of certain lesser Indian tribes to greater ones, a relationship similar to that between the eastern European "satellite" nations and the former Soviet Union.

**colors cased**   To march with *colors cased* is to proceed with national and regimental flags tightly furled in a gesture of defeat and surrender.

**Continental currency**   Paper money printed by the Continental Congress during the Revolution; without backing by "hard money" (gold or silver), its value quickly depreciated, bringing on massive inflation.

**convoying**   The grouping together of merchant vessels and/or troop transports with warships in order to protect the unarmed ships.

**cornet**   The lowest-level officer in a regiment of cavalry or dragoons—roughly the equivalent of a modern 2nd lieutenant.

**council of war**   A meeting among the commander in chief and his field officers and immediate subordinates to establish tactics and strategy for a critical operation.

**crossing the T**   A basic naval battle maneuver in which a ship maneuvered so that its guns were directed against the fore or aft of the enemy ship—locations without guns—instead of against the enemy's broadside, from which the enemy could easily fire back.

**defeat in detail**   To attack the divided elements of a larger, even superior, force in order to defeat them individually.

**discretionary orders**   In an age when there was no easy way to communicate with commanders at sea, officers were often given *discretionary orders*, very general instructions to accomplish some particular objective or set of objectives by whatever means and to whatever extent they deemed possible.

**dragoons**   Mounted infantrymen. Like the cavalry, they ride to battle; unlike the cavalry, upon arrival, they dismount and fight as infantry.

**Durham boats**   Designed to carry iron ore, grain, whiskey, and similar bulk freight between Philadelphia and New Jersey, *Durham boats* were 40 to 60 feet long, but drew only 20 inches of water when fully loaded to their 15-ton capacity.

**dysentery**   A debilitating bacterial infection of the gastrointestinal tract, characterized by violent diarrhea and fever; was a plague in eighteenth-century military camps and was certainly responsible for more casualties—including fatalities—than were bullets and bayonets.

**East Indiaman**   A merchant sailing ship specifically built for the long-haul trade with India (called East India to distinguish it from the Caribbean islands of the West Indies).

**elector**   A German prince in the days when the disparate German states were part of the Holy Roman Empire. Electors were entitled to elect the Holy Roman emperor.

**Electoral College**   The framers of the Constitution wanted to avoid election of the president directly by the people. As ultimately provided in the Constitution, each state has as many electors as it has senators and representatives combined. Together, the electors constitute the *Electoral College*. Originally, the electors were voted into office by the state legislatures. This evolved into election by the people. (Today, we may think of ourselves as voting for a president every fourth November, but we are actually voting for electors pledged to cast *their* votes for a particular candidate.)

***Encomienda* system**   The early Spanish practice of granting colonists tracts of land together with the right to exploit as laborers the Indians living on that land.

**engineer**   In the eighteenth-century military, an *engineer* dealt mainly with either building or breaching fortifications; the latter operation typically involved systematically digging trenches ever closer to the objective. From the cover of these, bombardment could proceed at closer and closer ranges.

**enumerated articles**   The Navigation Acts included a list of *enumerated articles*, items that the colonies could export only to Great Britain or to other British colonies.

**Ethiopians**   In "polite" eighteenth-century white society, Africans and African Americans were frequently referred to generically as *Ethiopians,* even though the vast majority of African American slaves came from West Africa, not the northeast.

**firelock**   Also called a *flintlock* or *matchlock.* A musket or other firearm that uses a gunlock with a flint embedded in the hammer to produce a spark and ignite the gunpowder charge.

**flatboat**   A vessel of a type that varied greatly in dimensions, but all shared one characteristic in common: their flat bottoms. This enabled these vessels to navigate often shallow and vegetation-clogged rivers. Typically, a flatboat was propelled and maneuvered by a long pole thrust into the river bottom.

**flintlock**   See *firelock.*

**floating battery**   A large river raft or barge on which guns were placed. The craft could be towed into position or floated with the current.

**foraging parties**   Small groups of soldiers sent to find food and other supplies in the field. Even well-supplied armies tried as much as possible to live off the land.

**frigate**   A warship, typically three-masted, of medium size, and capable of high speeds.

**garrison**   A unit of troops stationed in a city, town, or fort for the purpose of defending that position.

**grapeshot**   A cluster of small iron balls fired from a cannon as an antipersonnel weapon.

**grenadier**   Originally, a soldier armed chiefly with grenades, explosives meant to be hurled. Because this required great physical strength, grenadiers were typically the tallest, strongest, and most able of soldiers. By the eighteenth century, the grenade was not their weapon of choice, but the name stuck as a description of elite troops chosen for their imposing physical presence.

**guerrilla**   In French, "little war" is *la petite guerre,* a phrase that has since transformed into the single word *guerrilla* to describe a limited, covert style of warfare as well as the combatants who fight such wars.

**gundalow**   A flat-bottomed, open boat with pointed prows on either end. The word is derived from *gondola.*

**Hessians**   Mercenary troops in the British employ. While some were from the German principality of Hesse, they came from various German states. Three of their principal commanders were, however, Hessian.

**House of Burgesses**   The colonial Assembly of Virginia.

**howitzer**   A light, relatively portable artillery piece, used to deliver high-trajectory projectiles.

**impressment**   The Royal Navy practice of kidnapping young men from merchant vessels (typically British or American ships) and from such sailor haunts as waterfront grog shops and pubs and "impressing" them into involuntary service as seamen on warships.

**impressment of goods**   A euphemism for the government seizure, without payment, of urgently needed supplies, food, or transportation.

**indenture**   Most of the colonists obtained passage to the New World by signing a contract called an *indenture*, thereby becoming *indentured servants*—in effect, slaves for the seven-year term of the agreement. This would prove a very popular method of bringing settlers to the fledgling English colonies. The curious word *indenture*, which comes from a Latin root signifying *tooth* or *bite marks*, originated from the toothlike notches (indentations) made in the edges of medieval official documents in order to match up multiple copies.

**inspector general**   A position outside of the normal chain of command, with responsibility of monitoring the efficiency of other units.

**invalids**   Disabled soldiers assigned light duty, such as garrisoning forts.

**invest**   In military parlance, to *invest* a place is to surround it and hold it under siege. The payoff of this "investment," if successful, is the fall of the besieged town or fortress.

**Iroquois**   A cultural and political confederation of Indian tribes, the Mohawks, Oneida, Onondaga, Cayuga, Seneca, and (after 1722) the Tuscaroras.

**Iroquois League**   A confederation among the Mohawk, Oneida, Onondaga, Cayuga, and Seneca tribes. In 1722, the Tuscaroras, refugees from North Carolina, migrated and became the sixth member of the League. At the height of their power in the mid seventeenth century, the Iroquois League occupied territory stretching from the Hudson Valley to Lake Ontario, and controlled much more territory and dominated tribes far to the west.

***jäger* corps**   An elite unit specializing in advance-guard and reconnaissance tactics, especially in the woods or wilderness. The term is German for hunter.

**letters of marque and reprisal**   Documents in effect authorizing piracy on behalf of one belligerent nation against another. The captain in possession of such documents could not legally be prosecuted for piracy.

**liberty pole**   A tall pole erected as a symbol of defiance and rebellion. British colonial authorities would often tear down these symbols, which townspeople would then re-erect. Liberty poles often served as the rallying points for anti-British protest and riots.

**light dragoons**   Lightly armed mounted troops who specialized in reaching their objective with maximum speed, then dismounting to fight not as cavalry but as infantry. Such units were often called "light horse."

**light infantry**   Elite advance guard or shock troops of eighteenth-century armies. Lightly equipped, they were expected to move quickly and aggressively.

**line of battle**   The standard eighteenth-century troop formation for most effective fire. Typically, it consisted of a line two or three men deep, so that one row could fire while the other reloaded.

**lobsterback**   A mocking name colonists applied to British soldiers, whose backs often bore the scars of numerous floggings—the chief tool of discipline in the British army.

**longhouse**   A ritual meeting house for Iroquois leaders; figuratively, the longhouse also represented the six Iroquois nations.

**loyalists**   Throughout the revolutionary period, Americans who supported the Crown were called *loyalists* or *Tories* (the Tory party was England's conservative political party). Compare *patriots*.

**major general**   Rank one step above brigadier general and one step below lieutenant general. In modern terms, it corresponds to a two-star general.

**matchlock**   See *firelock*.

**mercantile system**   A form of economic nationalism that called for strict governmental regulation of trade and commerce and held that the sole function of colonies was to enrich the mother country by furnishing raw materials, gold, and silver, as well as exclusive markets for goods produced by the mother country.

**Moravian Indians**   Members of the Delaware tribe in Pennsylvania who had been christianized by local Moravian missionaries.

**mortar**   A thick, squat artillery piece intended to fire projectiles into a high trajectory in order to assault forts and other stockaded or high-walled places.

**mutiny**   A term usually thought of in connection with the revolt of ship's crews; however, it applies to any mass revolt against the constituted authority of superior command in any military unit.

**Navigation Acts**   A series of British laws enacted during the seventeenth and eighteenth centuries regulating and restricting colonial commerce. See *enumerated articles*.

*Noche Triste*   Spanish for "sad night" or "night of sorrow"; the name the Spaniards gave to June 30, 1520, when they were (temporarily) driven out of the Aztec capital, Tenochtitlan.

**Non-Importation Agreement**   Concluded in 1764 and revived in 1767, the agreement was a colonial boycott of English goods in protest of high import duties.

**Northwest Ordinance**   The most important piece of legislation produced under the Articles of Confederation; spelled out how territories and states were to be formed from the western lands acquired as a result of the Revolution; it ensured democratic government in these regions, and it was the first federal legislation aimed against slavery.

**Old Northwest**   In the eighteenth and early nineteenth century, the "Northwest" was the frontier area lying north of the Ohio River and east of the Mississippi. Historians call this the *Old Northwest.*

**outflank**   To maneuver around and behind the flank (side) of an enemy force, attacking where the enemy is most vulnerable.

**palmetto**   A small tropical palm tree with broad, fan-shaped leaves. In company with a crescent moon, it graces the state flag of South Carolina, in commemoration of the defense of Charleston. (The flag that was flown over Fort Sullivan bore a crescent moon above the word LIBERTY.)

**parliamentary monarchy**   A form of government in which the power of the king is balanced against and limited by the power of an elective body representative of the will of the people.

**partisans**   Guerrilla fighters who are not members of an organized militia or other military unit.

***Pater Patriae***   Latin for "Father of His Country"; a title bestowed upon certain heroes of ancient Rome, it was likewise freely applied to George Washington by a grateful nation.

**patriots**   A modern name for supporters of independence during the Revolution; called *rebels* by the British, but are known to history as *patriots.* Compare *loyalists.*

**patroon system**   The Dutch form of colonial settlement, whereby tracts of land were granted to absentee landlords, in effect making Dutch New Amsterdam a colony of tenant farmers.

**peasantry**   The agricultural working class of a nation; compare *proletariat.*

***philosophes***   French for "philosophers"; the influential political philosophers of eighteenth-century France, including, among others, Descartes, Voltaire, Montesquieu, Diderot, and Rousseau.

**pickets**   Guards; troops sent in advance of a main column or assigned to guard a camp or other position.

**Pilgrims**   The Puritan Separatists who voyaged on the *Mayflower* to New England in 1620. The label was conferred on them by their most important contemporary historian, William Bradford.

**plantation**   As used in the seventeenth century, *plantation* referred to a newly established colony or settlement. Only later, by the end of the eighteenth century, did the word came to mean a large farming operation, especially in the South.

**primogeniture**   From the late Latin, meaning first ("primo") birth ("geniture"); *primogeniture* signifies the right of the firstborn child—almost always exclusively the *male* child—to inherit the whole of his family's wealth, titles, and privileges.

**privateer**   A merchant ship (and its commander) authorized by the government to attack and capture enemy vessels.

**prize ship**   A captured vessel put into service by the victors.

**proletariat**   The industrial working class; compare *peasantry*.

**Puritanism**   A movement within the Anglican Church, which advocated reforms in religious doctrine, discipline, and ceremony to distance Anglican practice as far as possible from that of the Roman Catholic church.

**quarter**   The military equivalent of mercy. Asking for quarter is the equivalent of surrender—in the hope of kind treatment.

**quartermaster corps**   The name applied to the supply service of the army.

**rangers**   Elite wilderness troops who often specialized in work behind enemy lines.

**reconnaissance**   The gathering of advance information about the strength and movement of an enemy. In the eighteenth century, *reconnaissance* was typically a job for highly mobile cavalry, which Washington's army was slow to develop.

**reconnaissance in force**   A relatively small advance unit sent to do reconnaissance work, but large enough and sufficiently prepared and equipped to engage whatever enemy their reconnaissance may turn up.

**redoubt**   A small, usually temporary defensive fortification.

**regency**   A *regency* is an institution, comprised of one or more individuals, called regents, that governs in place of a monarch who is absent, disabled, or too young to govern in his or her own right.

**Regulators**   Self-constituted, loosely organized frontier vigilantes and anti-government protesters active in North and South Carolina chiefly during the 1760s.

**Renaissance**   French for "rebirth"; a historical period that extended from the fourteenth through the sixteenth centuries, beginning in Italy and spreading throughout Europe. It was a general reawakening of humanistic learning.

**rout**   A chaotic retreat, characterized by panic and heavy losses.

**rowing galley**   A shallow-draft gunboat propelled not by sails but by oarsmen; well suited to river navigation.

**salutary neglect**   The longtime policy of the British mother country toward its colonies. For many years, until the reign of George III, import-export duties and restrictions on colonial commerce were not strictly enforced.

**scurvy**   An extremely debilitating, sometimes fatal, disease; is characterized by bleeding gums, hemorrhages under the skin, and great weakness. Caused by a deficiency of vitamin C, it was a common scourge of sailors, who received no fresh fruit on long voyages.

**Separatists**   Radical Puritans who, in the seventeenth century, believed the Church of England was too corrupt to be reformed. Unlike most Puritans, the Separatists advocated the setting up of new churches, independent of the Church of England's authority. A minority of Separatists, such as the Pilgrims, left England in order to practice their religion without persecution.

**ship of the line**   Any warship big enough to take a position in the line of battle. In practice, these were typically vessels with more than 74 guns.

**specie payment**   Payment in gold or silver as opposed to currency, payment in paper money, which has no intrinsic value.

**spiking a cannon**   Driving a spike through the barrel of a cannon to render it inoperative and beyond repair. Spiking was a quick way of disarming an enemy.

**spy**   As eighteenth-century military commanders saw it, a *spy* was anyone who served in a military capacity behind enemy lines and without a uniform. Captured, a spy was subject to execution by hanging.

***status quo ante bellum***   Many peace treaties specified a return to the *status quo ante bellum*—conditions as they were before the war. Wars thus ended cost lives but settled nothing.

**Suffolk Resolves**   Adopted by the First Continental Congress on September 17, 1774, declared the Intolerable Acts unconstitutional, urged withholding taxes from the Crown, and recommended economic sanctions against Britain.

**swivel gun**   A large-caliber gun, smaller than an artillery piece but larger than a musket or rifle, which was mounted on a swivel for ready aiming.

**Tories**   See *loyalists*.

**Townshend Acts**   Oppressive taxation and customs legislation sponsored by Britain's chancellor of the exchequer Charles Townshend in 1766. They provoked much colonial protest and resistance.

**triangular trade**   Describes a colonial trading pattern in which New England merchants transported simple manufactured goods to Africa in exchange for slaves. The slaves were transported to the West Indies, where they were traded for rum and molasses, which was sold back in New England.

**wampum**   The Anglicized version of the Algonquian word *wampompeag*. White settlers used the term to describe any kind of valuable item regarded as the equivalent of money, but, originally, the Indians applied it specifically to cylindrical seashells strung on strings or beaded into belts and used as money or as tokens of good faith; wampum belts were exchanged at treaty signings, for example.

**wilderness forts**   Typically not military structures, but private homes that had been reinforced so that they might be used by militia for purposes of defense.

**winter quarters**   Camps established to shelter armies during the winter; in the eighteenth century, armies typically avoided combat during the entire winter.

**works**   A general term for any defensive military fortification, including walls, trenches, barricades, and so on.

**writs of assistance**   Commands compelling provincial officers to cooperate with royal customs officials in curbing attempts to evade commerce regulations and import-export duties.

# Battles, Battlefields, and Historic Sites

This appendix lists the major battles of the Revolution, then provides a list of battlefields and historic sites you can visit today.

## Major Revolutionary Battles

**Lexington and Concord, Massachusetts, April 19, 1775**   Patriots harass the Redcoats who retreat to Boston.

**Capture of Ft. Ticonderoga, New York, May 10, 1775**   Triumph of Ethan Allen and Benedict Arnold.

**American Retreat from Canada, December 31, 1775**   Disastrous invasion attempt.

**Long Island, New York, August 27, 1776**   Washington is defeated and retreats to Manhattan.

**New York City falls to the British, September 15, 1776**   Washington retreats across New Jersey to Pennsylvania.

**Trenton, New Jersey, December 26, 1776**   Washington counterattacks and defeats Howe.

**Princeton, New Jersey, January 3, 1777**   Washington victorious at Princeton.

**Brandywine, Pennsylvania, September 11, 1777**   Washington's defense of Philadelphia defeated; Howe captures Philadelphia on September 22.

**Germantown, Pennsylvania, October 4, 1777**   Washington's counterattack against Howe is defeated.

**Saratoga, New York (Freeman's Farm, September 19, 1777; Bemis Heights, October 7, 1777)**   Burgoyne surrenders his army to American forces (October 17).

**Monmouth, New Jersey, June 28, 1778**   Hard-fought draw.

**Cherry Valley (New York) Massacre, November 11, 1778**   Major raid by British-allied Indians.

**Savannah, Georgia, falls to the British, December 29, 1778**  Major blow to the patriot cause in the South.

**Stony Point, New York, August 19, 1779**  Triumph for the Continental army's "Mad Anthony" Wayne.

***Bonhomme Richard* defeats *Serapis*, September 23, 1779**  John Paul ("I have not yet begun to fight") Jones's most famous victory.

**Charleston, South Carolina, falls to the British, May 12, 1780**  The British now control all major American ports, except for Boston.

**Camden, South Carolina, June 13, 1780**  Costly defeat at the hands of the British.

**King's Mountain, North Carolina, October 7, 1780**  American victory begins to turn the tide in the South.

**Cowpens, South Carolina, January 17, 1781**  American Daniel Morgan defeats the hated British leader of Tory forces, Banastre Tarleton.

**Guilford Court House, North Carolina, March 15, 1781**  A tactical draw that inflicts heavy losses on the British.

**Siege of Yorktown, Virginia, October 9–18, 1781**  Franco-American triumph forces Cornwallis to surrender his army and, for all practical purposes, ends the Revolution.

**Treaty of Paris ratified, September 23, 1783**  America wins independence.

# Revolutionary Sights and Sites

**Acoma Pueblo**  Site of the "first" American revolution, Acoma Pueblo, in Valencia county, west-central New Mexico, (64 miles west of Albuquerque), is known as the Sky City. It is currently occupied by about 50 Indians, who live in terraced dwellings made of stone and adobe atop a sandstone butte 357 feet high. Phone 505–252–1139 to arrange for a guided tour of the pueblo.

**Adirondack Park**  The most dramatic way to gain an appreciation of the difficulties of war in Hudson-area wilderness is to visit the 6-million-acre Adirondack Park, which encloses 1,000 miles of rivers and some 2,500 lakes. Hikers and river enthusiasts who think the American West has a corner on spectacular wilderness need to explore this region. Contact the Visitor Interpretive Center at 518–327–3000.

**Bennington Battle Monument**  Commemorates Gen. John Stark's victory. 15 Monument Avenue, Bennington, Vermont; also visit the Bennington Museum on West Main Street; 802–447–1571.

**Boston Tea Party Site**  Atlantic Avenue and Pearl Street; visit nearby *Beaver II*, a replica of one of the Tea Party ships; 617–338–1773.

**Bowery Street**  Stuyvesant's bucolic Bouwerie became, by the nineteenth century, a neighborhood of inexpensive dwellings and gaudy theaters, which became increasingly disreputable as the years passed. By the early twentieth century, the rural cow path traversing Stuyvesant's farm had become the Bowery, a dismal and dilapidated urban avenue of cheap bars frequented by derelicts. Today, though still gritty, the Bowery is a Lower East Side mecca for some of Manhattan's creative community, including a number of young artists.

**Bunker Hill Monument**   Marks the site on Breed's Hill where the Patriot militia stood, holding fire until they saw the whites of the enemy's eyes. Monument Street, Charlestown, MA; 617–242–5641.

**Cambridge, Massachusetts**   In 1636, the New World's first college, Harvard, was founded in Cambridge, across the Charles River from Boston. Today, Harvard University is the central presence of Cambridge, and is joined by Radcliffe College and the Massachusetts Institute of Technology. Cambridge also features a host of museums, including the Fogg Art Museum, the Arthur M. Sackler Museum (specializing in ancient Greek, Roman, Egyptian, Islamic, and Asian art), the Busch-Reisinger Museum (Central and Northern European art), and others. Little of Cambridge's revolutionary heritage remains in evidence.

**Charleston, South Carolina**   Charleston, South Carolina, is one of America's most beautiful cities, and a great many of its Revolutionary-era buildings still stand, especially below Broad Street. From the elegant Battery, at the southern tip of the city, it is easy to appreciate Charleston's strategic position at the confluence of two important rivers, the Ashley and the Cooper. Call the Charleston Area Visitor Information Center at 803–853–8000.

**Colonial Williamsburg**   The seat of much revolutionary thought is preserved in Colonial Williamsburg, the first American theme park (opened in 1934) that uses history for amusement. Among the meticulously restored buildings in this capital of colonial Virginia is the House of Burgesses, where Patrick Henry made the "if this be treason" speech as well as the even more famous "Give me liberty or give me death" speech on the eve of the revolution. Call 1–800–447–8679 for Colonial Williamsburg visitor information.

**Conference House, Staten Island**   The peace conference took place in the Billopp House, now also known as Conference House, at the west end of Hylan Boulevard in the Tottenville section of Staten Island. Built about 1680, the house is open to visitors.

**Cowpens National Battlefield**   Site of the Patriot victory in 1781. Route 11, Chesnee, South Carolina; 803–461–2828.

**Freedom Trail**   A 2.5-mile walking tour of Boston's most important Revolutionary sites.

**Germantown**   Like all great English-style houses, the Chew residence had a name, Cliveden. Built in 1763, it still stands at 6401 Germantown Avenue, now a part of Philadelphia, and may be visited; call 215–848–1777. During part of his presidency, George Washington lived in Germantown, in the Deshler-Morris House at

5442 Germantown Avenue (215–596–1748). Germantown, occupying higher ground than Philadelphia proper, was believed to offer some protection from the Yellow Fever epidemics that periodically plagued the city.

**Golden Hill**  Golden Hill is the site of present-day John Street, a few blocks north of Wall Street, in Lower Manhattan. The "Battle" of Golden Hill was fought approximately where John Street now crosses William Street. Farther north, in Greenwich Village, colorful Macdougal Street and Macdougal Alley are named for rabble rouser and, later, Patriot general Alexander McDougall (notwithstanding the variation in spelling).

**Independence National Historical Park**  A mile-square chunk of Philadelphia (Visitor Center is at 3rd and Chestnut) that includes the First Bank of the United States, Carpenter's Hall (where the First Continental Congress convened), Army-Navy Museum, Marine Corps National Memorial, Independence Square, and Independence Hall. The Liberty Bell is also enshrined here. At 239 Arch Street is the Betsy Ross House, home of the woman who is believed to have sewn the first American flag. Park phone: 215–597–8974.

**King's Mountain National Military Park**  Site of the Patriot victory of 1780. I-85 near Blacksburg, South Carolina; 803–936–7921.

**Lenud's Ferry**  Lenud's Ferry is located where U.S. 17 now crosses the Santee River. It may be difficult to identify because it is often spelled Lenew or Laneau. Of Huguenot origin, Lenud is pronounced *Le-noo*.

**Morristown National Historic Park**  Just outside of suburban Morristown, New Jersey; the site of Washington's winter quarters during 1777 and during 1779–1780. Visitors can explore the Ford Mansion, Washington's headquarters in 1779–80, and reconstructed soldiers' huts. Call 201–539–2085 for information.

**Old Barracks**  A museum now occupies the building in which the Hessians found a rude awakening when Washington attacked the night after Christmas 1776. Barrick Street, Trenton, New Jersey; 609–396–1776.

**Old North Church**  Oldest church building in Boston; site of the one-if-by-land, two-if-by-sea lantern signal arranged by Paul Revere. 193 Salem Street, Boston; 617–523–6676.

**Paul Revere House**  Oldest house in Boston, the home of the silversmith-courier who alerted the Minutemen before Lexington and Concord. 19 North Square, Boston; 617–523–1676.

**Plymouth Rock**  Plymouth Rock is enclosed within a Grecian-style temple by the sea at Plymouth, Massachusetts, about 40 miles south of Boston. There are no contemporary mentions of the rock, but tradition says that, upon it, the first Pilgrim foot stepped. The town of Plymouth also features (much more interestingly) a replica of the *Mayflower* and a reconstruction of "Plimoth Plantation." Call Plymouth's Visitor Center at 508–747–7525 or 1–800–USA–1620.

**Roanoke Island**    Roanoke Island, part of North Carolina's Outer Banks, features *Lost Colony*, an outdoor drama about the ill-fated Roanoke colonists, regularly staged *except* from September to mid June. Call 1–800–488–5012. On the island, you might also visit the Elizabethan Gardens (919–473–3234) and the Fort Raleigh National Historic Site (919–473–5772), a reconstruction of what is conjectured to be the original fort.

**San Salvador, Bahamas**    If you are fortunate enough to vacation in the Bahamas, why not visit the lovely island of San Salvador? The Columbus Monument, at Long Bay, a white cross, erected on December 25, 1956, commemorates the landfall of Christopher Columbus on October 12, 1492. In the little town of Palmetto Grove, nearby, you'll find the New World Museum, which houses local pottery and artifacts from an original Arawak Indian settlement—the kinds of artifacts Columbus saw.

**Valley Forge**    Located at the intersection of routes 23 and 363 in Bucks County, Pennsylvania (610–783–1077), the park offers a wealth of exhibits that serve as monuments to the endurance and sacrifice of American soldiers during the Revolution.

**Washington Crossing State Park**    Where Washington crossed the Delaware to attack Trenton. Route 546 and the Delaware River in New Jersey, and Routes 532 and 32 in Pennsylvania; 609–737–0623 or 215–493–4076.

**Yorktown Battlefield**    Site of the culminating engagement of the Revolution, includes a museum and observation deck. Colonial Parkway, Yorktown, Virginia; 804–898–2400; also visit the Yorktown Victory Center, Route 238 off Colonial Parkway; 804–887–1776.

# Revolutionary Reading

Axelrod, Alan. *Chronicle of the Indian Wars: From Colonial Times to Wounded Knee.* New York: Macmillan General Reference, 1993.

———. *The Complete Idiot's Guide to American History.* New York: Alpha Books, 1996.

Barnhill, Georgia, B. *American Broadsides: Sixty Facsimilies Dated 1680–1800.* Barre, MA: Imprint Society, 1971.

Bernstein, Richard B., with Rice, Kym S. *Are We to Be a Nation? The Making of the Constitution.* Cambridge, MA: Harvard University Press, 1987.

Boatner, Mark M. *Encyclopedia of the American Revolution.* New York: D. McKay Co., 1966, 1974.

Burnett, Edmund Cody. *The Continental Congress.* 1941; reprint ed., Westport, CT: Greenwood Press, 1975.

Commager, Henry Steele, and Morris, Richard B., eds. *The Spirit of 'Seventy-Six: The Story of the American Revolution as Told by Participants.* New York: Harper & Row, 1958, 1976.

Cresswell, Donald H., comp. *The American Revolution in Drawings and Prints: A Checklist of 1765–1790 Graphics in the Library of Congress.* Washington, D. C.: Library of Congress, 1975.

Farrand, Max, ed. *The Records of the Federal Convention of 1787.* New Haven, CT: Yale University Press, 1911, 1986. 4 vols.

Hutson, James, ed. *Supplement to Max Farrand's "The Records of the Federal Convention of 1787."* New Haven, CT: Yale University Press, 1987.

Gephart, Ronald M. *Revolutionary America, 1763–1789: A Bibliography.* Washington, D. C.: Library of Congress, 1984. 2 vols.

Gross, Robert. *The Minutemen and their World.* New York: Hill and Wang, 1976.

Jensen, Merrill. *The Articles of Confederation.* Madison, WI: University of Wisconsin Press, 1940, 1970.

———. *The New Nation: A History of the United States during the Confederation, 1781–1789.* 1950; Reprint ed., Boston, MA: Northeastern University Press, 1981.

Leckie, Robert. *George Washington's War: The Saga of the American Revolution.* New York: HarperPerenial, 1992.

Madison, James. *Notes of Debates in the Federal Convention of 1787.* Athens, OH: Ohio University Press, 1987.

Maier, Pauline. *From Resistance to Revolution.* New York: Vintage Books, 1972.

Morris, Richard B. *The Forging of the Union, 1781–1789.* New York: Harper & Row, 1987.

Paine, Thomas. *Common Sense.* New York: Penguin, 1986.

Prucha, Francis P. *The Great Father: The United States Government and the American Indians.* Lincoln, NE: University of Nebraska Press, 1984.

Purcell, L. Edward, and David F. Burg. *The World Almanac of the American Revolution.* New York: World Almanac, 1992.

Rakove, Jack N. *The Beginnings of National Politics: An Interpretive History of the Continental Congress.* Baltimore, MD: John Hopkins University Press, 1982.

Rossiter, Clinton L. 1787: *The Grand Convention.* New York: W. W. Norton, 1987.

Rossiter, Clinton L., ed. *The Federalist Papers: Alexander Hamilton, James Madison, John Jay.* New York: New American Library, 1961.

Royster, Charles. *A Revolutionary People At War.* New York: W.W. Norton, 1979.

Smith, Page. *A New Age Now Begins: A People's History of the American Revolution.* 2 vols. New York: Penguin, 1976.

Smith, Paul H., ed. *Letters of Delegates to Congress, 1774–1789.* Washington, D. C.: Library of Congress, 1976.

Stokesbury, James L. *A Short History of the American Revolution.* New York: William Morrow, 1991.

Szatmary, David P. *Shays' Rebellion.* Amherst: University of Massachusetts, 1980.

Wood, Gordon S. *The Creation of the American Republic, 1776–1787.* Chapel Hill, NC: University of North Carolina Press, 1969.

# Index

Bushnell, David, 235
water machine, 177
Bute, Lord, 64
Butler, John
Battle of Oriskany, 204
Cherry Valley Massacre,
259-260
Butler, Walter, 205
Butler, William, 76
Butler, Zebulon, Cherry
Valley Massacre, 260
Butterfield, Isaac, 141
Button, Thomas, 18
Bylot, Robert, 18

# C

cabal against Washington,
235-239
Cabeza de Vaca, Alvar
Nuñez, 16
Cabinet, creation of, 350
Cabot, John, 18
Cadwalader, John, 188
duel with Thomas
Conway, 238
Cajuns, 55
Caldwell, James, 254
Calvert, Cecil, 29
Calvert, George, 29
Cambridge, Massachusetts,
371
Camden, Battle of, 306-307
camp fevers, 137
Campbell, Archibald, Battle
of Savannah, 273-275
Campbell, Samuel, Cherry
Valley Massacre, 259
Campbell, William
Battle of Cowpens,
307-310
Battle of King's Moun-
tain, 307-310
Canada
Articles of Confedera-
tion
provisions for mem-
bership, 134

campaigns in, 133-144
invasion of, 134-144
Quebec Act, effect on,
134
Capture of Ft. Ticonderoga,
369
carcasses, 128
Carleton, Guy, 134, 172,
196, 354
Carlisle Commission,
254-255
Carolinas, establishment
of, 29
Cartier, Jacques, 18
casualties
America and Great
Britain, 334
official statistic requi-
sites, 335
Caswell, Richard, 272
Catherine of Aragon, 23
Cerda, Don Luis de la
(Count of Medina Celi),
14
Champlain, Samuel de,
33-34
chandeliers, 154
Charles (Bavarian Arch-
duke), 48
Charles I (King of England,
Scotland and Ireland), 26,
29
execution of, 26
Charles II (King of En-
gland, Scotland and
Ireland), 29
Charles II (King of Spain),
48
Charles VI (Holy Roman
Emperor), 51
Charleston, Battle of,
272-273, 275-277, 371
Charleston, South Caro-
lina, establishment of, 29
Charter of 1691, 160
Chase, Samuel, 167
Chatterton Hill, Battle of,
181

Cherry Valley Massacre,
259-262, 369
chevaux de frise, 232
Chew, Benjamin, 216
Church, Benjamin, 46, 49
Church of England, estab-
lishment of, 24
Clark, George Rogers,
262-263, 354
Indian Campaign,
265-266
Clark, Jonas, 106
Clark, Joseph, 214
Clark, William, 263
Claus, Daniel, 202
Clement VII (Pope), 24
Cleveland, Benjamin
Battle of Cowpens,
307-310
Battle of King's Moun-
tain, 307-310
client tribes, 42
Clifton, Richard, 24
Clinton, George, 174
Clinton, Sir Henry, 129,
175, 354
Battle of Bunker Hill,
124-128
Battle of Charleston,
272-273, 275
Battle at Monmouth
Court House, 249-250
Battle of Stoney Point,
251-253
Battle of Yorktown, 327
promotion of, 249
"Silver Bullet Message,"
224
temptation of Benedict
Arnold, 282
West Point plan,
283-284
Clinton, James, Cherry
Valley Massacre, 261
Coercive Acts, 93
Coffin, John, 332
Colonial Williamsburg
theme park, 371

**380**

Louis XVI (King of France)
  participation in American Revolution, 195
  recognition of American independence, 245
Louisiana Territory, claiming of, 34
Loyal Ethiopians, 271
Loyal Nine, 88
loyalists, 78
  expulsion of, 338-339
  southern colonies, 270-271
  treatment of after war, 345

# M

macaroni, 111
Madison, James
  Bill of Rights, 349-350
  Constitutional Convention, 348
  *Federalist Papers, The,* 348
  Virginia Plan, 347
Magna Carta, 7
Mahwood, Charles, Battle of Princeton, 191-192
major generals, 280
Majoribanks, John, 332
malaria, 137
Manhattan Island, purchase of, 35
Manhattan Retreat, 176-177
Mansfield, Margaret, 280
*Manual of Arms,* 109
*Margaretta,* capture of, 296
Marion, Francis, 356
Marquette, Jacques, 34
*Marriage of Figaro, The,* 243
Martin, Josiah, 77
Martin, Joseph P., 250
Maryland
  establishment of, 28-29
  St. Mary's City, establishment of, 29

Mason, John, 44
Massachusetts, 26
  Boston, 146-147
    British evacuation of, 154
    establishment of, 27
    insurrection in, 81-84
    siege of, 146-147
  Cambridge, 371
  Continental Congress, 94
  General Court, 27
  Port Act, response to, 95
  Provincetown, establishment of, 25
*Massachusetts Circular Letter,* 73
Massachusetts Indians, massacre of, 27
Massacre at Maxhaws, 304-305
Massasoit, 44
Maxwell, William, 142
*Mayflower,* 25
Mayflower Compact, 26
Mazarin, 34
McCrea, Jane
  description of, 201
  murder of, 200-201
McCurtin, Daniel, 173
McDougall, Alexander, 78, 181
McDowell, Charles
  Battle of Cowpens, 307-310
  Battle of King's Mountain, 307-310
McLane, Allen, Battle of Stoney Point, 251-253
McWilliams, William, 236
Mellon, Robert, 203
mercantilism, 38
Mercer, Hugh, 181
  Battle of Princeton, 191-192
Mexico, Cortés, Hernan, 15
*Midnight Ride of Paul Revere,* 103

Mifflin, Thomas, 174, 188, 236, 339
  discontent with Washington, 235
military engineers, 232
Minuit, Peter, 35-37
minutemen, 96
Mississippi river
  discovery of, 34
  Northwest Ordinance, 344
Mohawk Indians, 36
  British alliance, 258
  Cherry Valley Massacre, 259-260
  raids, 259-262
Mohegan Indians, 44
Molasses Act of 1733, 68
"Molly Pitcher," 250
Monckton, Robert, 55
money laundering, France and Spain, 243
Monmouth Court House, Battle at, 249-250
Monro, George, French and Indian War, 58
Montcalm, 58
Montesquieu, 4
Montezuma II (Aztec Chief), 15
Montgomery, Hugh, 83
Montgomery, Richard, 357
  invasion of Canada, 135-144
Montreal, Quebec, Invasion of, 138
Moore, James, 48, 50
Moore's Creek Bridge, Battle of, 272
Moravian Indians, 267
Morgan, Daniel, 140, 222, 309-312, 357
  Battle of Cowpens, 309
  Battle of Freeman's Farm, 221
  Battle of Halfway Swamp, 311-312
  Battle of King's Mountain, 309

# S

## Y-Z